AN EMPATH

"The art of Cate Farrand"
https://www.facebook.com/CateFarrand/

An Empath

The Highly Sensitive Person's Guide To Energy, Emotions & Relationships

Alex Myles

Copyright © 2016 by Alex Myles.

Library of Congress Control Number: 2016910387
ISBN: Hardcover   978-1-5144-6551-6
                 Softcover   978-1-5144-6549-3
                 eBook   978-1-5144-6550-9

All rights reserved. No part of this book may be reproduced or transmitted in any form or by any means, electronic or mechanical, including photocopying, recording, or by any information storage and retrieval system, without permission in writing from the copyright owner.

Any people depicted in stock imagery provided by Thinkstock are models, and such images are being used for illustrative purposes only.
Certain stock imagery © Thinkstock.

Print information available on the last page.

Rev. date: 07/15/2016

To order additional copies of this book, contact:
Xlibris
800-056-3182
www.Xlibrispublishing.co.uk
Orders@Xlibrispublishing.co.uk
516175

CONTENTS

DEDICATION

This book is dedicated to Carl G. Jung. I will be eternally grateful for his teachings and for the inspiration and the empowering energetic influence of his words.

We are all connected to each other, biologically. To the earth, chemically. To the rest of the universe, anatomically. ~ Neil DeGrasse Tyson

The universe is within you.

You are the universe.

You didn't recently arrive.

There are no beginnings or ends.

You have existed for approximately 4.5 billion years when a giant nebula erupted and fractals were cast out to the vast distance.

You are a whirlwind, a spinning vortex of universal energy.

Your celestial body is a collation of scattered remains formed from the remnants of ancient stars, asteroids and comets.

You consist of an almost unthinkable and unimaginable amount and variety of gases, minerals and metals, such as calcium, copper, hydrogen, nitrogen, iron and more.

The universe delivered everything needed for evolution.

Your consciousness created your visible existence.

You rotated in motion. Determined to express yourself . . . pouring energy into every cell until eventually your unique tangible being was born to planet Earth.

Stardust gifted your extraordinary physical structure, but it is your awareness that miraculously allowed it to form and gravity's gentle force magically holds it in place.

Everything you need is internally vibrating, building momentum as your existence unfolds.

And in this rare "life" form you can create whatever inspirations your imagination conjures up.

Your magnetic field attracts an infinite number of possibilities.

Whatever you wish for can manifest . . . if you *believe*.

You see, you are connected to all that exists through invisible powerful threads of eternal energy that entwine and weave us all as one.

You are not alone. Not now and you never will be.

Your energy just spins on a different frequency to all that surrounds you so you can perceive how incredible, significant, perfect, and exquisitely essential and individual you are.

You are both electric and you are magnetic. You radiate, attract and repel.

You pull towards you experiences that you need and push ones away that you are not yet ready to receive or that you do not need during this lifetime.

Your energy is constantly communicating, entangling, and interlocking with other energy.

There is no separation.

There is fluid and continuous transformation.

"Energy cannot be created or destroyed, it can only be changed from one form to another." ———Albert Einstein

So without your existence, nothing would make sense.

You are a vital component whose presence adds to the collective.

You may brush things off as coincidences, but they are not. They are all synchronicities. Little signs and signals that can guide and light your way.

If only you place your trust in them.

You matter more than your mind currently allows you to comprehend.

You are not here to wither. You are here to unravel. You are here to expand.

Your quest is to channel and challenge every exquisite thought in that ingenious mind of yours until your awareness grows and allows you to finally understand . . .

Look up to the sky. Do you see the stars? Fascinating and beautiful, aren't they? Now look at yourself. Similar stars are in every one of the trillions of cells in your body.

You are not just a constellation—you consist of galaxies that swim through a mass of intergalactic space.

You are limitless. A cosmos. A collection of asteroids, planets, comets, and clusters of stars and nebulae.

You exist now and you will continue to exist.

A universe within a universe.

This is the universe's greatest mind trick. It recreated itself over and over so that it can explore every angle of every truth of itself.

You are necessary for this eventual mass understanding.

Without you, the universe just would not make sense.

The universe delivered a miracle.

It delivered itself.

So you could see it, explore it, and find that you already hold all of the answers within...

You always have.

PREFACE

"The most beautiful thing we can experience is the mystical. It is the source of all true art and science." ——Albert Einstein

I am an empath, an infinite amount of spinning and vibrating vortices of interactive energy.

I feel everything intensely and I am affected by everything. Deeply.

My existence is enveloped by energetic waves from the universe. I am entangled with the world and its avalanching universal energy.

I have always known I was a little different. I wish I could say that my journey has only been filled with adventure, magnificence, and wonderment, though unfortunately it has often been quite the opposite. It has also been bewildering, chaotic, overwhelming, confusing, lonely, and even at times quite devastating.

Gianfranco Guerra on LinkedIn

While navigating turbulent times, I felt there was no one I could turn to. I didn't know anyone who could help me understand the rocky road I was on. So I searched back avenues and looked for answers in books, philosophy, spiritual traditions, healing practices, holistic therapies, and even sought herbal and prescribed medication to guide me through. I still didn't find the answer.

Distraction and escapism allowed me to avoid the chaos I felt around me. Now I know that those things were just a temporary, misguided form of self-preservation.

The answer was here. Rooted deep within myself. I am an empath. I feel . . . everything. I just needed to recognize, acknowledge, and fully understand it.

I feel the pain of all humans and animals alike, and the slightest emotional or physical wound that is inflicted upon others can embed within my body and mind. Remedies I previously tried only provided mild, if any, relief.

For years I felt like an alien on this planet. I believed "I am not of this world." I didn't know many people who were like me, who felt emotions so intensely, who saw the world alternatively, or who voiced their inquisitive, extraordinary concerns about the invisible threads that weave and bind us as one seamless matrix. Neither did I come into contact with anyone who could relate to or resonate with the subtle sensations that are felt when energetic vibrations suddenly disrupt the peace.

I often thought other people's behavior was strange, or they thought mine was. There seemed to be no strong correlation between myself and the outer world, even though I felt the electric charge of an invisible connection. I didn't have many close friends and I couldn't understand how everyone else seemed to relate and make sense of one another, yet no one could easily make sense of, or relate, to me.

Discovering that there was a name for what I was experiencing felt as though I had been thrown a lifeline. Although I am not one for labels, I frantically clung to every piece of information available that could help me learn more about my existence.

I embraced the word "empath." While many people may not relate to this, it is likely that they will not have existed in a world that they found entirely complex to navigate and understand, or a world that seemingly did not understand them.

Those who are empaths have usually been acutely aware of their incredibly high sensitivities to all living things from a very young age. We are also aware of what we can only describe as magical and mysterious happenings and inexplicable experiences. As children we didn't need to make sense of it all, although as we reached adulthood and our world became more logical and rational we may have begun to feel out of place. We find it difficult to share our inner world as we do not come into contact with many others who can grasp it.

It was never easy to turn to friends or family to discuss the inner trembling that regularly shook me. Whenever I did, they would look to me blankly and question if I was losing my mind. They would probe, "What has got into you?" They never quite realized that it was exactly that. The earth and everything upon it had crawled underneath my skin and was affecting every cell and altering its structure.

A child of the universe. No different from anyone else, except I feel the universe's laughter in me as powerfully as I feel the wrath of its scorn. Nothing escapes me. From Earth's core to the outer layers, I feel it all.

If I ever tried to talk about the "unusual" experiences from my younger years, it usually resulted in me being laughed at, mocked, or told I must have dreamed too much fantasy or read too many tales. I know that my encounters were real. The reason? I didn't need to see, hear, or touch any of my experiences, or prove to any of my five senses that they existed. Instead, I *felt* them.

From childhood I was aware that I was highly sensitive and that my heart bled profusely. I also quickly realized that being emotional could lead to being perceived as vulnerable and at the time, as I did not stand in my vulnerability and honor it, it became a weaknesses instead of a strength. Society seemed to condemn me for freely showing my feelings. And when I was told to "Stop being so hypersensitive," the words were delivered with strong disapproval rather than with care. This caused me to bottle up many of my emotions as I quickly discovered that pain, fear, or frustration was not openly accepted and should not be expressed in public. Wearing my inside on the outside and freely sending out love were condemned as "too much" or seen as neediness, instability or desperation. Therefore, rather than being able to release my feelings outward so that they could be put into context and connect to their source, I turned everything inward and felt every biting sensation eating away at my sense of self. I self-blamed, shamed and grew frustrated with myself.

I was misunderstood and I could not clearly understand anything externally. The world did not make sense to me. It taught how to energetically disconnect and separate rather than how to integrate and process our feelings and experiences. This means that mostly, we do not receive the opportunity to channel how we feel so that the positive can thrive, grow, and gain momentum, and the negative can be acknowledged, validated and understood so it does not have the ability to harmfully affect us.

Every subtle external entity has the power to dramatically affect and alter us all internally. It is my belief that it is vital that we surrender to universal life force energy so that we can respect it, attune to it, and be at one with it. Not fight against it and try to live in conditions that feel unnatural for living creatures to exist in.

Before I understood this, anxieties, nerve, or digestive problems invaded me whenever I was exposed to any form of violence or trauma. If I was unable to resolve emotional issues, they manifested in my underactive solar plexus and resulted in excruciating stomachaches and pains. I would have unbearable headaches or earaches, though there was never any medically explainable physiological cause. Of course there wasn't. The causes were external vibrations. Any uncomfortable sensations I absorbed would not dissipate. They stayed with me and showed up in the form of tremors, flashbacks, and nightmares.

When I saw or felt someone else suffering physically or emotionally, tears would often spill out. I would avoid or be unable to talk to people whose energy made me uneasy. When I was younger, without knowing how to safeguard and protect my energy and often unable to sleep, I purposefully "lost" myself in ethereal worlds, where I explored the enchanted realms of fairies, magic, unicorns, mermaids, aliens, and invisible, imaginary friends.

Previously, the most striking thing for me about being an empath was how other people's physical, mental, and emotional pain hit me as though it was my own. If someone was suffering, rather than feeling "for" them and imagining their pain, I felt "with" them, and my body and mind suffered simultaneously. I have since learned how to alter this, although it is not always easy and often I am left temporarily energetically paralyzed due to the weight of stimuli I absorb.

When I am not consciously aware and fully present, energy triggers my emotions and feelings and I experience other people's situations similarly as though they are happening to me. The line between other people's reality and my own reality is not always easily seen or felt. I often absorb the tension in other people's energy and my senses instinctively react.

Empaths naturally absorb the intensity in energy, so we are aware of how other people are feeling and possibly even thinking. However, we are not always able to read every aspect of other people's minds. Therefore, we might not know the intentions or the agendas that are taking place or what may trigger people to act or respond in certain ways as we don't always immediately access their previous or future occurrences to know exactly what they may say or do next. While we can feel how they feel in that moment, unless we have fully developed our ability to read energy, we won't always know what they are capable of.

This is why it is essential to learn how to protect ourselves, as when we are highly sensitive to energy we can very easily leave ourselves open and vulnerable to energetic harm. I have now learned a variety of ways to protect myself while I process and effectively transmute energy. I have also discovered how to avoid confusing other people's emotions and feelings with my own.

I used to find it very difficult to shake off negativity, and I still do at times. Aggressive, volatile, or traumatic conflicts can linger in my energy field for hours or days following an event. This can be, and has been, emotionally and physically crippling, and it has caused me to suffer tremendously. Empaths are often described as being porous, similar to a sponge. We may ingest every emotion and every particle of energy until it has such an impact on us that it can alter our own emotional and energetic state. We can eventually become congested with debris that does not belong to us and it can consume us at times.

For me, finding out that there was a reason for how I felt was one of the most overwhelming and life-changing things that have happened. Not only did I discover that what I was experiencing was simply just "being an empath," I also found there is a whole tribe of empaths. I'm sure the majority of empaths will agree that identifying with the empath concept and discovering that we actually do "belong" to this world feels like a miracle.

For years, many of us feel ostracized and secluded, then out of the blue, like magic, we find out that we aren't actually alone at all. We are interconnected to everything and everyone through energy. And not only that, there is a community of empaths. Even if the connection we make is with someone on the opposite side of the Earth, we instantly know that we have made a soul-deep connection. Probably for the first time in our lives we will have met someone who understands us, and importantly, shares our alternative perceptions and language. Empaths know how incredible that feeling is. To exist in a world where we feel we don't belong, and then to suddenly find out we have been home all along.

The word *empath* propels us on to a new, though sometimes arduous path of self-realization and self-discovery. A journey that is exploding with triumphs, traumas, and tribulations, and one that unravels a million colorful threads that were once knotted and deeply embedded and hidden within us.

We are a paradox. We are at peace, yet our entire being continuously rattles and vibrates. We are complex creatures. We have gotten used to people failing to comprehend us.

I was not fortunate enough to meet many other empaths until recent years. Empaths are kindred spirits, a soul family.

"Your Soul Family are those that are tuned in to your frequency. You sense a strong connection beyond blood or race; you're connected by energy and vibration. Through quantum communication, they intuitively answer your silent call and show up bringing unconditional love and support at the perfect times. You share an unspoken level of understanding . . . they just get you and what you're about. For those people, be thankful . . . they are your reminders from the Universe that on the deepest level of our existence we are one." ——Kianu Starr

Being an empath is not for the fainthearted. We test ourselves, push ourselves to the limit, and refuse to settle. We battle relentlessly through some of life's fiercest and most turbulent storms. Although we are tender, we are also tough and resilient souls, so we eventually conquer whatever comes our way, even when we have wandered the shadowy paths or the ones less trodden.

We don't need scientific proof to know we are empaths. We have faith in our sensations, our heart and our mind. We have an immensely strong inner knowing, and as soon as the word "empath" appears we relate and identify with it immediately. Being highly affected by the energy not just from other people but from the whole universe and then having the ability to read and decode it is an unmistakable and almost indescribable way of being. Unless someone else encounters life this way, they could find it difficult to resonate, understand, or intimately relate to our experiences. Some people think we identify as empaths purely because we are highly sensitive or because we can be highly emotional. And although that is part of it, it doesn't even come close to explaining our existence and eclectic possibility.

Those who are not empaths often struggle to figure out the intricate wiring of our minds and we may regularly be misinterpreted or misunderstood. Often people cannot see what compels us to stand with one foot placed on the edge of the proverbial cliff. Empaths don't just need to see a better view. We also need to know exactly how the view *feels*.

"She always had that about her, that look of otherness and eyes that see too much and of thoughts that wonder off the edge of the world." —Joanne Harris

Learning more about being an empath has helped me tremendously, as not only do I now understand myself better, I also know how to guard myself so that my energy does not spill out from every orifice, and especially, so that harmful external entities do not seep in and negatively affect me. It has also given me the insight I needed to understand how to lift my vibration. Therefore, I am now far less likely to attract situations similar to the toxic and dangerous ones I previously encountered. It also means that many of the connections I now have are with those who vibrate on a similar frequency. If someone hits the C chord on a piano, the C chord on the guitar resonates and vibrates. Humans are the same. Our electromagnetic vibrations resonate and cause a reaction with other similar vibrations.

Now, I observe, define, process, and channel universal energy rather than absorbing and owning everything and anything that comes my way. This prevents me from becoming overwhelmed, ungrounded, exhausted, suffering mentally or physically, and also from becoming overly sensitive and uncontrollably emotional.

Storms run through me and over me. And yes, much of what has happened to me during my life has been extraordinary and at times quite difficult to deal with or explain. The life I have led does not reflect the "norm," which is why I am grateful for learning so much about being an empath. As soon as I grasped the meaning of it and discovered others who sensed the world similarly I instantly knew I'd found kindred spirits, a tribe, a road home. For the first time, I was able to hold conversations without the need to censor myself or feel unnerved or self-conscious about my thoughts and feelings. Many empaths know exactly how it feels to be misunderstood and labeled as weird, crazy, or strange for far too many years and then to suddenly find out they are actually magical, mystical, miraculous beings.

It is something we truly never envisaged. We often feel as though we are a different species of human, as dramatic as that sounds, and we slot our puzzle pieces together and then find we are entirely whole and complete.

I am forever hearing people say that we should become more consciously aware of how we are living. I agree in part. However, I also think that before we get to the stage of living consciously we first need to explore everything that exists in our subconscious and unconscious minds. They are treasure chests spilling over with data, although not all of what is held there is trustworthy and much of it does not even belong to us. A lot of what has been stored has been picked up along the way through a variety of conspicuous sources. We need to figure out what is rusty and harmful, and what is valuable so that we can identify and lovingly discard whatever no longer serves us. We will then be able to trust the messages our subconscious and unconscious send to our conscious mind and also understand how they are responsible for much of our instinctual and impulsive thoughts, emotions, and feelings.

We have lifetimes inside us and we have somehow forgotten we have avenues with lights and signposts that can lead the way. Cables and wires have been wrongly fused together and our inner compasses have lost their magnets.

"**Your vision will become clear only when you** can look into your own heart. Who looks outside, dreams; who looks inside, awakes." ——Carl Jung

We don't just have our own lifetimes to dissect and decode. We have hundreds, thousands, maybe even millions of years of history that first need to be unraveled. So yes, I want to be conscious, though I'll also be willfully embroiled within my subconscious and unconscious. Communicating with the dreams of my ancestors and sifting through their imaginations and reality. I will be connecting the limitless dots together to figure out how I arrived here and what accumulation of sensations and vast amounts of debris are hidden internally that have been hindering rather than assisting me.

Empaths naturally communicate with people soul to soul when they are vibrating on the same frequency and with those who are an alternative frequency the communication is generally subconscious to subconscious, which is why we are easily able to determine what energetic data has been masked and stored within. We pay little attention to conscious dialect or when people try to override their true feelings. We delve straight into the midst of past, present, and future thoughts, emotions, feelings, and intentions, and we are rarely afraid of whatever is unveiled.

I'm proud to call myself an empath. I'm proud of the challenges that I, and others similar to me, have gone through and still go through to this day to make sense of who we and other people are.

An "Empath" may sound like an impossible or even ridiculous notion to some, though maybe that is because they have not experienced anything similar or they do not know any empaths well.

If someone is used to having others around them with whom they can easily resonate with and relate to, they may not understand why empaths struggle to secure their footing at times. Empaths are generally the misfits, the unusual, octagonal pegs, and the lonesome ones. We don't find connections so easily, so we tend to take shade in the background of society and we don't always open and expose our inner blueprint as it has been rejected and harshly judged so often.

For those who read this and don't really get what the fuss is all about, imagine living in a world where no one, not one person, seems to understand you. Then, suddenly you come across one small word and your whole life crystallizes, catapults, and begins to make sense. It is a feeling that is euphoric and everyone out there who eventually discovers they are an empath and makes sense of it would likely say the same.

We are empaths and whether the rest of the world likes or accepts us or not is entirely out of our control. We do not have the option to desensitize. Nor would many of us choose it if we could, at least not when it finally clicks that our sensitivities are a gift that have been bestowed unto us so that we can attune to energy and sense, *feel* and heal.

Unfortunately, all too often empaths are led to believe that our capabilities are not possible in today's world and our ways are criticized, disbelieved, or we are told they are wrong. Downplaying an empath's intuition and our sensitivity to energy will benefit someone who may be trying to manipulate, use trickery, or someone who has very little faith that our skills and abilities exist.

We cannot change our empath state. It isn't possible. Even though we are traveling a road that many would choose to avoid. However, when all the pieces click into place, everything, absolutely every aspect of our life, begins to make sense. We are altered forever.

Unfortunately, I cannot make false promises that when empaths read this book they will be free from experiencing intense emotions or that they will no longer soak up and absorb everything that surrounds them. These things will always happen, though possibly to a far lesser extent. However, I do hope that other empaths will gain an insight into how I handle, process, and control energetic forces rather than energy controlling and negatively affecting me and then through perceiving my experiences they may relate and connect my theories in some way to their own.

The one thing that keeps empaths locked in pain is when we are only functioning as receptors and we are not processing and transmuting energy. As soon as we see ourselves as transmitters and we recognize that we have the capability to transform any energy we receive and then send it back out, we will alleviate the majority, if not all, of the disturbances.

Empaths are here on earth for a divine reason. To *feel*. And through feeling we are able to create what may seem like small changes, although accumulatively the alterations merge to create fundamental social change and they help to develop a world that is a more equal and harmonious place to exist in.

Our feelings are necessary. They cause us to cry out when there is injustice, to stand up and represent those who have fallen, to radiate healing to those who have fallen or feel broken, to show love and compassion where there is hatred and resentment. Our feelings cause us to courageously shine rays of light where there is immense darkness. However, whenever we feel compassion we also feel responsibility, and this is what can cause us to feel as though we are holding the emotional weight of the world.

"We live in a time when science is validating what humans have known throughout the ages. That compassion is not a luxury; it is a necessity for our well-being, resilience, and survival." ———Roshi Joan Halifax

We are empaths and we will always feel everything deeply, however we can discover the location of the key that unlocks and releases a lifetime of pain. We can find understanding through the knowledge that is available and learn how to exist in a world that feels raw and harsh to our sensitive, paper-thin skin, and one that tests our fragile but warriorlike hearts.

We cannot dig up and replant our roots or un-become empaths. However, when we tend to and nurture the soil, our inner and outer worlds are no longer torn apart and fragmented due to the explosions from numerous hidden minefields. Everything unveils and we finally recognize that nothing and no one will ever be able to break us. We are energy. We cannot be broken. There are no halves; every cell of our existence is a whole and there are billions of them. We are already enough, complete.

". . . and then the day came when the risk to remain tight in a bud was more painful than the risk it took to blossom." ——Anaïs Nin

Instead of being in conflict and feeling inner discord, we breathe through our emotions and accept them as part of who we are knowing they are essential for our soul's mission and our higher potential and purpose.

As painful as our existence is, empaths are here to make a difference. We absolutely *must* feel and channel the energy that we are presented with. Through feeling we create change. The difference gaining understanding makes is that we learn not to be afraid of our feelings and instead we can identify, embrace, process, transmute, and then breathe through them so they continue their energized journey.

We never need to hold on to emotion. Emotions energetically visit us for a reason. Empaths are emotionally and energetically intelligent, and we have been given this role and responsibility to understand what the reason for this way of being is. We can try to deny the overwhelming number of emotions we are sent, though if we do we will experience a painful existence, as energy does not dissipate until it has been acknowledged and redirected. We can change the structure of energy and recharge it with positivity so that it does not cause us or anyone else energetic harm.

As hard as we try, we will never be able to completely avoid absorbing energy. It isn't possible. We have been created this way for a divine role. Our only option is to open up our empath hearts and *feel*. We can then connect to our feelings, raise our vibration, and shine brilliantly so that our energy radiates outward and entangles with every living thing that exists on Earth.

First, though, we must believe that we are no different from a butterfly that is able to create avalanches through the smallest of change. On one corner of the world, the tiniest fluttering of a butterfly's wings can cause a rippling effect that results in a tornado on the other side.

INTRODUCTION

There are many empaths who have worked tirelessly at developing their abilities and may already know and resonate with some of what I have written. I am not a medical professional or a psychologist. I am an empath, a reiki master, a qualified yoga and meditation teacher, and an avid student of the effects of universal energy. This book has been written from my personal experience and other than where I have quoted someone or described a widely held theory, it is an explanation of how I have perceived my life living as an empath. Much of what I have wrote is based on my own beliefs, therefore, I would recommend that it is all taken with consideration that anything I have described is just an insight into how I have observed and then understood the subjects detailed. This book isn't meant to teach anyone or influence anyone or to change any already upheld beliefs. Although it has been presented with an inclusive style, as in "we/empaths" it is for all. This is just how I found it easier to fluidly explain all of my thoughts, beliefs and theories. There is not one "right" way or one wrong way to perceive, all perceptions are valid ~ this book is an insight into how I perceive at the current time of writing and I hope that it offers the reader an alternative perception to take into consideration.

I hope that developed (functioning empaths, those who are able to balance and transmute energy well), as well as undeveloped (impaired empaths, those who easily become overwhelmed by energy and have not yet mastered it)—energy is something that we will always be mastering—will, in some way relate to the chapters included here. I have set up a group on Facebook for empaths and anyone who wishes to connect. It is called "An Empath," so please feel free to connect and discuss theories or beliefs in more detail and from alternative perspectives.

The terms "developed" and "undeveloped" empaths may sound as though we are all at different levels, although that is not the case at all. There are simply stages of awareness and each one alerts and awakens us a little bit more so that we are able to enhance and integrate our abilities into our energetic expressions, and exchanges. The stages change from moment to moment as we ignite our inherent traits and finely attune to our core self as well as to the varying frequencies of those around us and the universe.

Even when we have developed our abilities there is always more to open up to and explore, and we may still lower our guard from time to time and be susceptible to unexpected entities, situations, or experiences whereby unwelcome or unpleasant energy can invade. It can feel like a full-time endeavor to keep ourselves shielded from negativity and we will all go through times when we are more vulnerable than others and when we are more easily influenced by internal or external forces.

Like with all things, there are numerous variations. Some people may identify strongly, while others may recognize their selves in a small percentage of the traits or encounters explained in this book. Although we are empaths, we are all unique expressions and we each have individual strengths, weaknesses, and levels of capabilities that allow us to navigate and work with the set of skills and gifts we possess. We can try not to judge or compare our progress to anyone else's as some people find it natural to process and transmute energy while others will be drastically affected by it on a daily basis. One minute we may be feeling protected and have high energy levels, and the next our vibration can come crashing down.

This book describes my personal take on being an empath and how I have come to understand and make sense of the energetic realms. Everyone will have their own perception and experience, so if anything in the book doesn't relate, that's understandable, as although I have put it all together it doesn't mean that everyone will engage with the same feelings, situations, and people that I have dealt with. There may be things I have missed out, there's always the possibility I will write again in the future, as even though I have explained many aspects in depth there will always be more I could clarify on by going into far greater detail.

There are numerous types of empaths, some may be stronger at psychic abilities, others may resonate more with animals, and there will be those who relate strongly to the planets and outer world activity. Although there are differences, the majority of empaths will generally share a lot of the same traits or constellations of characteristics that have been outlined in this book. The reason for this is that all empaths, regardless of their awareness, are exceptionally sensitive to energy. We read and understand energy far better than we could ever read a book.

Alex Myles - Writer Page
https://www.facebook.com/Alex-Myles-Writer-Page-
1608329939496791/?skip_nax_wizard=true

Chapter 1

AN EMPATH

Empaths are highly sensitive to the energy that emanates from everything that exists in the universe. We both voluntarily and involuntarily tap into other people's experiences and objectively perceive and interact with them as though they are our own. When we acknowledge and accept that we are conduits of energy, we can then channel all energies so that they fluidly flow through us. We are then able to intuitively and intelligently decode the information within the energy, which allows us to identify, process, transmute, and ultimately transform harmful entities. This also enables us to naturally and effectively heal ourselves and others, regardless of proximity.

When we enhance our abilities and easily understand how energy works, we naturally pick up on past, present, and future intentions, motivations, thoughts, emotions, and feelings.

Empaths have exceptionally high sensory levels and we are always on energy alert, so we are acutely aware of the energy that vibrates within and around us. Humans, along with everything that exists, are constantly vibrating, and our vibrations each have their own unique signature. Our intuition and inner *knowing*, also known as a sixth sense, allow us to easily recognize and decode these energetic signatures.

Jad Alexander, who coined the term "empath" in 1997, believed that empaths have a highly developed nervous system and a heightened sensitivity to external stimuli. Alexander's research found that with empaths the interaction between the stimuli and the brain is different from what is considered as the "norm."

"Empath" is a relatively new way of describing someone who is hypersensitive to energy. Since Alexander's discovery, many people from across the world have identified with the word, as it defines and groups together various characteristics that up until this point were difficult, if not impossible, to explain.

Alexander describes the concept as, "An Empath is a type of 'psychic,' but instead of reading the 'future' or viewing remote objects, the Empath specializes in reading people . . . I suggest using the word Empath as a hybrid form of psychic, more of a realistic/grounded version of our potential for extra-sensory perception. An Empath is sensitive to the visible as well as the invisible. An Empath reads body language, tone of voice, body movements, the words people choose when they speak, the words they avoid, the logic they use, and the hidden things that only an Empath can sense inside another person. A fully developed Empath reads on what could be considered a 360-degree scope."

If we are not aware of our abilities or do not understand how to utilize them, we may lose sight of who we are and the connection to our inner self and suffer incredibly for it. We feel the world around us at such high intensity that we can become immersed in the chaos, not knowing which energy belongs to us and what belongs to other people.

When we are highly in tune with our self and skilled at reading others, we will often be able to pick up on someone else's emotional energy and thought processes even if they are thousands of miles away. Empaths can quite accurately determine other people's emotional, psychological, and physiological states simply by tuning in and exploring existing energy. If we are not aware that this is possible, or if we are suddenly caught unaware, we will unconsciously absorb other people's energy and internalize it. This can cause us high levels of confusion, anxiety, stress, bewilderment, chaos, and suffering not only during but also long after the particular transfer has taken place.

Distinguishing between our own energy and the energy that has been transferred from someone else can be a struggle. Therefore, there is a risk that we may accept incoming emotions, psychological, and physiological traumas and feel and identify them as though they are our own. This is one of the reasons we can easily become perplexed with our identity and why we often feel as though we are a contradiction, possibly even believing we might be bi-polar. Not only are we dealing with all of our own emotions and experiences, we are also battling to comprehend and deal with everyone else's too.

A lot of empaths do not attribute the qualities of an empath to themselves until later on in life. Part of the reason for this can be due to our natural abilities being unexplored. We may have been considered as strange, delusional, or even impossible to understand by our peers, family, or close friends, so we ignored our inherent traits.

From early childhood, many of us were wrongly conditioned to believe that the invisible world does not exist. Instead, we were taught to place high value on the logical mind and on what is tangible. Due to the majority of an empath's world being invisible to the untrained or doubtful naked eye, others can struggle to understand how our experiences and abilities are a possibility.

We may have been told that only what takes places in the physical world is a reality. Fortunately, science can now prove that is not the case. Therefore, more people are finding the confidence and courage to come forward and speak out about the innate abilities they have known of from a very young age. These advances have resulted in what are often classed as "supernatural capabilities" becoming more widely accepted by society.

Many people believe that physical presence and material matters are highly valued entities and that the invisible, energetic world is not to be trusted or invested in. Ironically, it is the attachment to material goods that prevents us from achieving inner peace and significant self-growth, even though plenty of people spend the majority of their lives focused on accumulating possessions. What truly matters and nourishes the soul is internal, not external.

We may have previously feared our gifts or been wary of the judgment of them, causing many of us to deny or suppress our individual self. We might then create a defense mechanism that protectively tells us not to express the aspects of our being that are at risk of being condemned. Therefore, by the time we reach adulthood we have not always developed our abilities due to the fear of the unknown or the fear of being isolated further.

Before we can have absolute faith in how we feel, we first have to rewind through the years to unlearn many of the things we have wrongly been conditioned to believe. We can reteach ourselves that it is entirely possible to have faith in what others may believe to be "impossible" simply by trusting what exists within without casting or allowing shadows of doubt to creep in.

Empaths are magical and magic is real. Fortunately, today scientific evidence can back almost all of it up. And for whatever science cannot yet confirm, it likely won't be long before it can. Besides, it is my belief that not everything can be proved or has to be proved using science, and it is limiting to rely on it as the ultimate decider of possibility.

When we open our mind and awaken our inner abilities we realize we are here for a specific reason, and this leads us to uncovering our soul's higher purpose. We are visionaries and our sole focus is to create a harmonious world for everyone and everything that exists. Our intention is to leave Earth in a healthier condition than it was in when we arrived here.

Being an empath is a challenge and one that requires daily work to remain grounded, harmonized, and mindful as we feel our way through life with one foot on the planet and the other in the ethereal world. It is essential that we develop ourselves so that we are aware of how energy works and also so we can keep ourselves protected and safe to avoid being drawn into anything that may be harmful.

Empaths are learning. We try to be honest with ourselves, and though it isn't always easy, we accept we are a work in progress and our work will never be complete.

We face the light. We face the shadows. We face the dark. We are often petrified, flooded with emotion and even riddled with anxiety, though whenever we find the courage we face the entirety of our internal selves.

Empaths are born empaths. Although I personally don't believe it is something someone can "become," it is absolutely possible to develop empathy and become more in tune and strengthen the abilities inherent in an empath. Some people are natural empaths and every fiber of their being interacts with the energetic world intrinsically. Other people tune in and adapt to the energy as it is not instinctual for them to sense, feel and perceive the invisible world at the same level as they sense, feel and perceive the physical world.

An empath's traits can lie dormant for years. Not everyone knows that they are an empath. Therefore, until they awaken to it and become more aware they will not be enhancing, maximizing, or exploring their full potential and their highest individual possibilities and purpose.

We are quite mystical beings, and although being an empath is not something that can be learned, those of us who are empaths can magnify our abilities so that we can possess and develop abilities and skills akin to having superpowers. These rare abilities help us to successfully navigate both our own and other people's inner and outer worlds far more effectively.

Empaths are not "gifted," although yes, we definitely have gifts, though so too does everyone else in the world. Our gifts are just different. It does not mean we are higher or lower than anyone else, or any other ridiculous notion along those lines.

Being an empath does not equate to being a "good person," neither does it mean that we are further along a "spiritual path," or pure, virtuous, and enlightened in our thoughts and intentions. Nor does it make our existence one of limitless joy, love, peace, and light. It is unnatural to be constantly in a "happy" place as life constantly delivers a myriad of contrasting positive and negative encounters so that we are able to learn that the universe requires an energetic balance to exist. We often put so much pressure on ourselves to maintain happiness that the high expectation of it causes us unhappiness.

In the Universe, positive energy from light and matter balances the negative energy from gravity. For humanity to thrive,and be in sync, we need to achieve acceptance of ourselves as a whole so that we are harmonious.

Empaths are here to work with energy so that internal and external stability can be mastered and maintained through channeling energy. We do this through transmuting its properties so that negativity is neutralized and positivity is enhanced. Universal energy cannot ever be destroyed, it can only change form and move from one place to another; therefore, we can change negative energy to positive and positive energy to negative at any time. Energy is constantly moving through and around us, and when we work with it we can achieve universal balance.

As empaths are sensitive to energy, we generally, have a high level of awareness , which gives us a greater insight into reality. Within this reality we find it easier to accept that we have positivity and negativity running through our veins and we will constantly be challenged in our attempts to grasp a full understanding of the elements of both.

Our earthly existence requires us to live in unity in these physical vessels we have been gifted with. Unfortunately, there is unrest here on earth. Empaths are natural healers and as we seek harmony, we can work towards enabling peace. This may seem as though we are faced with an arduous task too great for a few, although, everything has a beginning and an end. We are at the beginning of this mission, and as more empaths awaken on a daily basis, eventually, even if it is many generations ahead, our messages of love, peace, equality, and harmony will roll out. We may feel as though one small act of transforming negativity to positivity will go unnoticed—although, it will not. Positivity and negativity are both contagious. Eventually the status quo will refuse to accept the destructive behaviors displayed toward humans, other living creatures or to the earth.

Every miniscule alteration to energy has a far-reaching, long-lasting consequence. Energy entangles with other energies in the atmosphere, so everything we do holds a memory in the universe. Even though we have a long way to go, we are each a part of something quite incredible. The hardest thing to deal with is the effect this has on our energetic body. Because we feel everything intensely, we are going to experience sensations that sometimes may seem too overwhelming to bear.

Sensing and feeling is not a bad thing. It lets us know that we are alive and that we have been alerted for a divine reason - to process our own and other people's negative feelings, change their properties to positive loving ones, redirect them, and then let go of them so they can flow from us and float freely around the universe, causing no further harm.

Empaths don't always have the required coping techniques or tools to navigate difficulties effectively. We feel everything deeply; therefore, we may also react at this level, so our responses can be quite dramatic and extreme. We may have mood swings, become frustrated, project and blame other people for our pain, feel angry toward ourselves or other people, carry around with us huge amounts of guilt due to the amount of hardship that exists, and we often feel helpless when we are unable to resolve or eradicate suffering.

When we receive pain, we then have the opportunity to heal it. Experiencing pain is a blessing, as without it we would not be able to acknowledge what triggers are hidden within ourselves or other people that are responsible for the majority of destructive behavior.

Empaths often have what are known as "outer body experiences." This can happen if we have not grounded ourselves sufficiently and we are wandering into the ethereal (invisible/energy) world without being aware of it, or we can intentionally travel there as we let go of the limits within the conscious mind and move to a higher realm/consciousness. We may also have similar experiences due to being caught up in very high or very low vibrational energy. This can make us feel unbalanced, ungrounded, and spaced out due to being pulled into a frequency very different from the one we usually vibrate on. This often happens when we are drifting into other people's energy fields unknowingly or if we are not in tune with our own energy.

The external world can seem harsh, abrasive, and may even feel toxic to an empath. The majority of the negativity arises from emotions, actions, abuse of either humans or animals, the desire for money or materialistic items, stressful workplaces, traumatic events, pollution in the atmosphere, family dynamics, or even from friends and unhealthy and unproductive relationships. All of these things can cause someone who is highly sensitive to feel anxious, tense, nervous, or in emotional, psychological, or physiological pain. Due to this, it is beneficial to routinely protect and cleanse our personal energy field (aura) to avoid becoming overloaded and overwhelmed with what can feel like the weight of the world.

Empaths can also identify with and experience other people's intelligence and interpersonal abilities. This enables us to adapt to other people's mindsets and lifestyles so we can resonate and relate with people from all walks of life. Generally, we do not base our opinions of others on external appearance, behavior, social status, or material wealth. Instead, we firstly allow the information within energy and then our intuition or inner *knowing* to assess, though we try to keep our mind open to all possibilities.

Empaths do not tend to make judgments based on what we hear from others or from what we visually witness. We observe all aspects of human nature and the surrounding conditions, so our assessment derives from our instincts or once we have access to the bigger picture. We try not to listen to idle gossip or rumors and we also don't believe everything we see or hear. We live and let live and see everyone as equals, regardless of past or present stories. We are all on our own personal journey and we have all had different opportunities, experiences, and backgrounds, and we are all altering, growing, and evolving on a momentary basis.

Rather than condemning anyone, we look at the root cause to understand why someone is behaving in a specific way. Compassion and understanding is offered, and even if we have been treated badly or hurt during the process, we try to look past our own wounds to heal the suffering of those who have caused us pain so that we gain clarity and peace.

We are born survivors, and with each test that is sent our way we somehow manage to turn things around and create something positive. If all else fails, a tough lesson will have been taken onboard and learned—at least, temporarily. Empaths don't always have great energetic boundaries. We are quick to forgive, and while we also consciously forget very easily, the after-effects burn and aggravate our subconscious mind and we will be triggered by that information until we fully acknowledge and resolve the root cause of the issues. To block out negative entities, we may carry weight on our physical bodies as a barrier between ourselves and the outer world. We may also turn to comfort eating as a way to fill the voids that have been caused by emotional trauma.

Empaths may find it very difficult to be around people who are egotistical or those who enjoy putting others down to make themselves appear "better." Instead, we are more likely to rise to the defense of the people who have been rejected, oppressed, ostracized, or bullied in any way. Empaths struggle to gain harmony with people who are diagnosed with narcissist personality disorder. This is because empaths extend their focus and attention outward toward other people, whereas narcissists attention is focused inward toward them selves. Interactions with narcissists are challenging for empaths, as they are motivated to solely benefit themselves, whereby, empaths seek to be a benefit to others. We often find ourselves in relationships with narcissists and these dynamics force us to confront some of our oldest wounds, weaknesses and beliefs, while maintaining compassion, understanding and loving unconditionally.

The reason we find this difficult is because we are generally compassionate and spend countless hours thinking about or feeling the emotions of other people and trying to figure out ways to reduce the pain and suffering across the world. Narcissists are quite the opposite. Instead of thinking of or feeling for others, they are egotistical and will step on others to elevate themselves and use other people as a way of getting their egos' needs met. Narcissists' tendencies are selfish and empaths' tendencies are selfless. The two are at polar ends of the spectrum and there will almost always be a level of friction and conflict between the two.

When we raise our vibration high enough so that we transmute negativity and turn it to positivity, we will not only be less affected by any harmful energy, but we will also be less likely to karmically keep attracting relationships that are emotionally unbalanced, unhealthy and overall extremely difficult to sustain.

Empaths prefer to connect with people at heart level, though not everyone is willing to reciprocate the connection. We look for similarities so we can find others with whom we can closely resonate. It isn't often this happens, so when it does we sometimes forget to slow down, protect ourselves, and see with clarity who or what we are getting intrinsically involved in.

Love, trust, and friendship are usually offered instantly by empaths, which sometimes leads to us getting our fingers burned due to being impatient, blindsided and eager. Often we don't want someone to let us down or we hope they won't; therefore, we close our eyes and imagine it won't happen or that it hasn't happened, even when it has.

Although we are sharp, have strong instincts, and an incredible insight, we don't always put our faith in any of these things. We have a very thin layer of skin. Our boundaries aren't always great. And despite our strong inner *knowing*, we ultimately want to trust people, and this can be our downfall. This leaves us open and exposed to being used for materialistic, financial, sexual, or egotistical gains, and these things are usually what result in us gradually withdrawing from society.

Empaths are observers. We study the presence of those around us and we watch closely for changes in body language, aura, tone of voice, and behaviors. This enables us to detect subtle differences that allow us to determine what is going on beneath the surface. We have a profound and natural ability to see through the superficial exterior that others sometimes portray. However, we may allow emotions (other people's or our own) to cloud our sight when we are in the thick of a relationship, and our vision can then become drastically distorted. When we step away from the center and clear any residue of emotional energy, we are able to see things with clarity once again.

We are able to sense primal emotions and pick up on feelings that run far deeper than what is being projected outwardly. We are then able to relate to other people on an inner, deeper, more intimate level. This allows other people to feel safe to unravel and reveal their inner selves without feeling emotionally exposed or vulnerable.

As empaths are compassionate and often show empathy, people may trust us easily and this encourages them to communicate without the fear of being judged, condemned, or rejected for expressing how they think or feel. Some empaths are capable of becoming almost chameleonlike when in other people's company, as it enables us to blend the two energies and characteristics so that a close connection forms and bonds. We may also find ourselves mimicking body language or even accents as a way to acutely understand how other people and also how they might perceive the world. Entangling energy this way allows us to interrelate and communicate at a far deeper level. We could find we can be quite agreeable in the company of certain people as our energies interact and blend, so we are able to see and feel the world almost exactly as the other person would see and feel it. This enables us to empathize and finely understand the other person's experience purely through absorbing, sensing and then reading the energy."

If we are not aware of our sensory abilities or we do not keep ourselves grounded and our emotions organized, all the accumulated energy that is soaked up from our environment will lodge within our energy field. We can become overwhelmed and suffocated as the stagnant energy manifests in emotional, mental, or physiological ailments, aches, and illnesses. This means that being an empath can either be an incredibly tormenting or exquisitely beautiful way to experience life. It is simply a double-edged sword. It can help; although, it can also hinder us. That is, until we figure out how to manage our gifts so that they elevate and construct us rather than causing devastation and deconstruction.

If energy is not channeled and we push against it or absorb it all, not only can this be emotionally debilitating, it can also result in energetic trauma with depression, stress, and anxiety taking a toll on our body and mind. There is also a very high chance of suffering from the effects of emotional, mental, or physical burn out.

We generally avoid conflict and turbulent situations as we find them overwhelming, immobilizing, and fraught with emotion.

Dramatic outbursts can cause empaths to freeze, withdraw socially, and in certain situations it can leave us so anxious that we are unable to express ourselves and communicate effectively.

Empaths tend to be great listeners and extremely compassionate, and some people find themselves naturally drawn to us. People generally feel safe around us and confide in us easily because we have a genuine concern for their wellbeing. Certain people will use this to their advantage. If we have not first taken precaution to protect ourselves, we can be left exhausted and overloaded. This means, we will take on and absorb other people's problems, and unfortunately, we can sometimes be used as a sounding board so that others can offload their emotional baggage and leave it for us to deal with.

Communication is one of the tools that help us to release our emotional energy and gain an in-depth understanding of it. When we express our feelings, we are also able to put them into context and we then gain a greater insight into ourselves and others.

An empath's mind is an inquisitive one, constantly searching for answers and theorizing, scrutinizing, and philosophizing. We look for solutions to difficulties and we are avid students of life, seeking out deep, hidden knowledge and wisdom. Our mind will not rest until we have made sense of a situation, though first we look down each avenue and view it through multifaceted lenses. Empaths are on a mission to clear the cobwebs from illusions, and although it is often painfully blinding to view reality, our perception adjusts continuously until we have a transparent image.

We take responsibility for our lives, and our instincts and inner knowledge help us to merge onto our intended path. Desperate to discover the meaning of the life mapped out for us, we sift through the subliminal messages and synchronicities that everyday life delivers. Empaths regularly experience moments of déjà vu and many things happen to us that cannot be explained as mere coincidences.

Empaths have a strong "inner knowing" and psychic ability and many are clairvoyants even if they are not yet fully aware of their ability. We are able to pick up on energy regardless of proximity, as our capabilities are not determined by time, space, or distance.

It doesn't matter where, when, or how something happened, highly developed and natural empaths will be able to tap into the experience and decode the energy so that the meaning it holds can be translated.

Empaths are imaginative, creative, adventurous, and with varied interests, rarely aligning with just one practice or belief. Our minds are accepting and remain open to all cultures, ideologies, and religions so that we gain a broad and diverse perspective along with an alternative view of reality. Empaths do not have the need to gain formal or educational qualifications to prove intellect, abilities, or skills. Instead we find the route to our own version of success. Success to an empath will begin and end with soul nourishment, and that comes when we are aligned to our authentic thoughts, feelings, beliefs, and values, and through being of service to others. Anything else that results from success is simply a by-product and holds little value in comparison.

"The plain fact is that the planet does not need more successful people. But it does desperately need more peacemakers, healers, restorers, storytellers, and lovers of every kind. It needs people who live well in their places. It needs people of moral courage willing to join the fight to make the world habitable and humane. And these qualities have little to do with success as we have defined it." —— David W. Orr

Many empaths feel like the "black sheep" of the family and the "lone wolves" of society. Other people might find it difficult to understand our behavior or the way we feel and experience the world. They may not get us and think that we are dramatizing how sensitive we are, when ironically, most of the time, we are trying desperately hard to mask how excruciatingly vivid and unbearably intense our emotions and feelings can be. Oftentimes, empaths are perceived as weak and fragile, however, that is usually by people who do not know how heavy the emotional load we are carrying weighs. They are not aware that we are feeling every subtle and severe sensation that is around us, in every moment of every day. If they looked inside us, truly looked, they would very quickly realize the greatness of our strength.

We can come across as shy, nervous, or awkward in front of people. While these things can be true, they are usually more noticeable in front of large groups of people or those whose energy feel particularly harsh to us. We can feel vulnerable and exposed when the surrounding energy is particularly raw or heavy; therefore, it can numb our minds so that communicating freely is difficult.

We are also, generally, very aware of everything that is taking place moment to moment, so we can finely tune in to how people are thinking or feeling about us when we are in their company. This can push us even closer to the edge of social groups as we think people are insincere if what they are feeling is very different from what they are saying or displaying.

We may sometimes struggle, feeling alienlike while in the company of others who cannot or will not try to relate or resonate with our experiences. Empaths are otherworldly and can feel out of sync, often believing as though we exist in an alternative dimension entirely separate from everything around us. This is because we do not always bond well with others, especially if our energy is vibrating on a very different frequency.

Communicating and connecting with others can become an issue, as we can appear aloof, rude, or even hostile at times. Some people may even consider us to by shy, which, although some empaths may be, this is still not the sole reason for our withdrawal. Regardless of how hard we might try, we will struggle to remain present and engage, however hard we try to force ourselves, whenever we feel increased and elevated levels of friction and tension.

Although it would be ideal to be able to freely converse with anyone, when we talk, the tone of our voice and our expressions will sound and feel fake and insincere. Therefore, backing away from social situations is often the chosen option, and this is one of the reasons we can become introverted and may even opt to live in solitude.

We often recreate our families by forming a bond of friendship with those who are similar in some way. It is common for empaths to refer to the deeply resonating connections we encounter as "soul families," "tribes," or similar.

We may not understand why certain words have to be spoken as in our minds energy speaks far clearer and stronger. Empaths do not enjoy saying things just because we feel pressurized or forced to say them. Instead, emotions or any other subjects are discussed only when it feels natural to do so. If we have told someone we loved them once, we may not feel there is a need to continually repeat it, instead thinking that, of course, the other person must know. Surely they can feel it? Besides, we would tell them if something had changed—and trust us, we would.

Empaths have very tender hearts and can take everything literally, which can mean that we are hurt easily over jokey behavior or seemingly innocent comments. Issues around breaking trust or loyalty can be deal breakers. We may be offended and also get upset or irritated very quickly about things that may seem trivial or not as upsetting to other people. We might be viewed as overly emotional or highly dramatic as we are ultrasensitive and we pick up on even the subtlest of insults or passive-aggressive behaviors.

Empaths are caring and compassionate, and struggle when there is injustice, so we rise to defend the underdog. This is mainly because we experience similar sensations to the person who is being mistreated and feel bouts of the suffering and pain they are experiencing, so we instantly try to alleviate it to regain peace. We have an innate desire to serve humanity, and our ideal world is nonviolent, equal, and harmonious for all.

". . . for there is nothing heavier than compassion. Not even one's own pain weighs so heavy as the pain one feels with someone, for someone, a pain intensified by the imagination and prolonged by a hundred echoes." ——Milan Kundera, *The Unbearable Lightness of Being*

Empaths are the ones those whose hearts bleed on a daily basis and the ones who lie awake helplessly praying things were different. We don't turn a blind eye however much it pains our soul. We care enough to create change, regardless of how insignificant it may at first appear. We are the voices for the innocent, vulnerable, and defenseless. We often feel helpless in a world that appears too big to fix.

We want to feel at one with the earth and long for humans, animals, and all living organisms to unite and be treated respectfully. Empaths find it difficult to rest and relax while there is instability and disharmony on earth.

To reduce the simultaneous pain empaths experience with other people, great lengths are traveled so that we find a solution to problems. This can cause us to neglect or sacrifice ourselves in order to soothe the aches and pains we bear that do not belong to us. Once absorbed in someone else's pain, we may then find it challenging to work out what is our own and what belongs to other people. Empaths are often activists and advocates for environmental and humanitarian issues, usually spending long nights thinking up ways to reduce the suffering in the world due to being highly empathetic toward humans, animals, and nature.

We find calm and feel at ease when spending time roaming around the outdoors. Somewhere close to nature is where we head to unwind and release all the built-up tension that we carry around. Even when we are not outdoors our soul is constantly calling out to be next to the sea, deep in the forest, sat by a lake, or just lying out in the middle of a fresh grassy field under the sun, stars, or moonlit sky.

Listening to or watching tragic regional or worldwide news can be traumatic as news programs use shocking headlines and images to engage and entice reactions. The pain or violence that we are shown transfer onto us and we may feel similar symptoms as though the distress and suffering are our own.

Environments where the energy is low are exhausting, draining, and debilitating for an empath. This includes hospitals, clinics, or any place where there is suffering, pain, or illness. Many empaths are drawn to heal, and choose to study and take on roles that assist people with emotional, mental, or physical health. It often isn't until they are actually working in these environments that they find out how difficult it is to keep their own energy levels stable while also being of service to others whose energy levels are extremely low. It is possible though, by remaining grounded, centered, and aware, to protect our energy field so that other people's energy is not overwhelming.

Violence, aggression, spite, wars, and deliberate acts of callous behavior can all have a direct effect on our emotional and physical state. An empath senses everything at all times, so whatever it is we are subjected to, whether real or a drama on the television, it can enter our energy field and remain lodged until we consciously make the effort to shift it.

Supermarkets, stadiums, bars/clubs, family gatherings, and any crowded event can be energetically overbearing. Frequent downtime or escapism to a garden, bathroom, or kitchen will take place so that we can temporarily break away from the intensely high energy that occurs when many people are together in close proximity.

Empaths are highly sensitive to sounds, strong smells, bright lights, and the texture of certain fabrics. The most highly irritating forms of stimuli come from artificial sources, so UV lamps, spotlights, sound from speakers/telephones, and manmade fabrics are all likely to cause a reaction. Headaches, irritable behavior, fatigue, anxiety, and stress are all symptoms that signal we are overwhelmed through external factors. Natural lighting or candlelit rooms will soothe us instantly, so will background music being kept to a minimum unless it is a harmonizing melody. Volatile external stimuli can heighten an empath's senses and leave us vulnerable to anxiety, crippling fear, and bursts of anger or frustration. Negativity can build up in our energy field until it becomes unbearable and brings on unexpected mood swings or emotional explosions. This is why it is essential that we effectively process the energy we absorb.

We need to feel intrigued by our surrounding environment and we struggle to maintain our focus or attention on things we do not find interesting or challenging. Whether it is a movie, a lecture, or a conversation, we will zone out and daydream to escape anything that our brain perceives as unstimulating or mundane.

Many empaths choose their music, movies and environments very carefully to avoid taking on any negativity that is generated and radiating from those things. We may repeatedly play the same tune, watch the same films, or read the same book as we resonate on such a deep level that our soul is calmed.

We prefer our living space to be clutter free and minimalistic. Chaotic surroundings make for chaotic minds and we have enough inner sensations without bombarding our psyche further. However, we do tend to treasure anything that has a good vibration or a sentimental memory attached. We will not keep hold of anything that has negative energy connected to it.

After we have ended a relationship or if something has gone terribly wrong, we may no longer be able to be around certain items without the associated vivid memories returning. We find that when we look back on our experiences we remember the feelings connected to that period rather than individual memories. All of these feelings are generated by energy and the energy that lingers on items from the past can evoke those sensations in us, causing traumatic memories to resurface and repeat as though they are happening in current time.

There will be many reading this who think being an empath is a painful way to exist. While many people may recognize themselves in all the above traits, there will be some who see a lot of these things as how they used to be before discovering how to protect and transmute their energy. Within this book there are a variety of ways to work toward understanding various aspects of daily life and relationships so that being an empath becomes a pleasurable rather than tormenting experience.

The key to thriving as an empath is to step into our personal power by fully understanding how our energy field works. Then we can acknowledge each of the traits individually and spend time pondering them so we can look at how they may negatively impact or hinder certain aspects of our daily lives. When we have a good understanding of how a specific thing adversely affects us, we can figure out ways to turn any negatives into positives. The key to resolving things that cause us difficulties is knowledge and a good understanding of what lies at the root of it. We just have to take a step or two back before we can go forward.

It can seem overwhelming discovering we are an empath and coping with living with a heightened state of awareness and also understanding all the intense internal and external sensations. Fear is one thing that really holds us back, and when we conquer it we can open ourselves up to a whole new world of wonders that are waiting patiently for our exploration.

Empaths can be deeply misunderstood. It can take a little time to get to know us before we fully unravel and our magnificent spirit receives the opportunity to shine. We have lived with judgment all our lives, and now that we are connecting with other empaths and learning about ourselves it can be an exciting time, though it may also bring on bursts of anxiety as we awaken our inherent nature and unique abilities. Excitement and anxiety are similar in some ways; however, the former is fuelled by love and hope and the latter is fuelled by fear. All we have to do is find the courage to eliminate the fear and also enhance hope so that we embark on an exhilarating and extraordinary journey toward a new way of living.

I thrive when I am connected to those who vibrate on a high frequency, as the energy around me circulates with sincerity, authenticity and genuine intention. This isn't suggesting I only interact with people who are constantly positive - quite the opposite. Those with a high vibration accept all aspects of humanity with kindness and an open, non-judgmental, forgiving and accepting mind. When surrounded by those whose motivations are sincere and those who are hearted-centered with their expression, a high vibration is maintained, regardless of the situation or circumstances.

The people around us are mirrors reflecting our soul. Whatever we send out to the universe, we attract. The more positive energy we absorb, the greater amount of renewable abundant positive energy we will have to radiate outwards. When we radiate positivity, positivity will radiate back toward us. Positivity generates an expansive, limitless, fascinating cycle.

Physically, empaths look no different from anyone else. Human beings on the outside but with inner workings wired in ways that can be frustratingly difficult to explain or completely comprehend. We are even regularly internally bewildered and shook by our capabilities, so it is expected that not everyone externally will accept them.

Empaths are the free spirits, the adventurers, game changers, artists, writers, singers, creators, charismatic old souls, curious beings, philosophers, truth seekers, daydreamers, unconventional ones, peacekeepers, the mystical and magical ones, the warriors, and feisty creatures with tender hearts, wild imaginations, and tough, unbreakable spirits. The quirky types who live outside society's safely sealed box. Although it can seem to others as though our lifestyles are unconventional or unorthodox, our lifestyle suits us perfectly and feels to us as the most natural way to live. And when we discover and connect with other empaths, we no longer have to navigate this mysterious spellbound road alone.

Empath Checklist

- Feels "different" but can't always explain exactly why
- The ability to sense other people's true emotional states
- Significantly affected by other people's energy
- Struggles to shake off negative energy
- Finds it difficult to be in the company of people who are very negative and have very low vibrations
- Feels like an emotional sponge at times, soaking up everything in the atmosphere
- Avoids confrontations
- Affected by the weather and planetary activity
- Intrigued by sacred teachings and hidden knowledge
- Naturally senses what other people are thinking or feeling
- Finds it difficult to understand how people intentionally emotionally or physically hurt one another
- Needs alone time, possibly in the dark and in a room with no stimulation to recover from social events or to balance and reenergize
- Finds it difficult to say no
- Excessively open, heart-centered, honest and vulnerable and can easily be burned by those wishing to take advantage of these traits
- Easily overwhelmed and experiences anxiety when external stimuli is high
- Hypersensitive to emotional, physiological, and physical pain
- Sensitive to bright light, loud noise, strong smells, sharp taste

- Intolerant of certain food
- Becomes exhausted quickly when around people
- Not always easily able to communicate thoughts or feelings effectively
- Suffers from chronic fatigue
- Suffers from stomachaches and digestive disorders such as IBS
- Regularly feels an inner intense aching sensation
- Possibly introverted
- Startled easily
- Needs plenty of time alone and space; enjoys their own company although can often feel lonely and isolated
- Strong inner knowing feeling
- Knows when people are masking the truth
- Feels excessively anxious when exposed to aggression, confrontation, and conflict
- Very low energy or irritable when hungry, stressed, or fatigued
- Strongly dislikes being watched or observed
- Constantly aware of the people around and the impact of their energy field
- Able to read body language and facial expressions and knows when they are inauthentic
- Ability to sense when something significant is about to take place
- Takes care of other people before themselves
- Naturally drawn to healing
- Rich vibrant inner life
- Strong creative streak
- Taking on other people's emotions and feeling them as though they are your own
- Deep understanding of animals and a strong connection to nature
- Avoids news channels, violent TV shows/movies, and aggressive music
- Seems as though they see things very differently than how most other people perceive them

- Inquisitive
- Easily distracted if environment is not stimulating
- Absorbs other people's ailments
- Can temporarily lose their sense of self
- Struggles with fixed routine, unwritten rules, and limiting codes of behavior
- An unpleasant weighted feeling that lingers after being exposed to any type of conflict

This checklist is just a guide. Empaths are constantly altering and evolving as they awaken and become more attuned and aligned with universal energy, which provides a direct link from their core self to everything that exists, whether visible or invisible.

Chapter 2

EMPATHY

Empathy is a translation of the German word *einfühlung,* which means "feeling into." It can be a little tricky to fully describe as it has two components.

The first part to empathy is the capacity to sense and intuitively understand another person's subtle or more obvious emotional, psychological, or physical sensations and symptoms of distress or pleasure while being aware that their set of historic experiences and opportunities have in some way influenced their current, or past, general state of being. It is the art of seeing the world through the eyes of someone else by recreating in our own imagination the other person's set of circumstances. It encompasses consideration for their motivations, attitudes, beliefs, values, feelings, and emotions. And when we have a heightened sense of perception and tap into their energy, we could even access their thought processes. Therefore, we are able to view other people's conditions and situations similarly to how they might be feeling or perceiving them, rather than viewing them purely from our own perspective.

We feel empathy so that we gain an idea of how it might feel to exist as someone else, and this makes us more likely to refrain from impulsively and negatively judging, condemning, or ostracizing people based on differences. However, empathy does not automatically preclude that we will have a definitive understanding of someone. It just gives us an in-depth insight, and this depends on our ability to translate and make sense of the sensory information we receive with compassion, caution and consideration.

The second part to empathy is once we have objectively identified and perceived how they might feel, we can instinctively and compassionately respond to their state by communicating in a nonbiased, mindful, and heartfelt manner. When we are empathetic and able to view someone else's situation clearly, we are then more likely to be compassionate. We may even sacrifice our own comfort and potentially risk emotional, psychological, or physical pain in order to express unity, care, and support, and ultimately show acceptance and oneness.

Empathy encourages us to actively engage with others rather than being apathetic, disinterested, and indifferent. It is steeped in humanity, seeing everyone as interconnected and not as separate individual entities. When we understand that we are all as one with a unique set of experiences and social conditioning, we can create equality, peace, and harmony rather than excluding, rejecting, or denying people just because we do not understand them. Separation always derives from an element of fear, and that fear derives from the inability or unwillingness to understand people through being open-minded and empathetic.

"Compassion is not a relationship between the healer and the wounded. It's a relationship between equals. Only when we know our own darkness well can we be present with the darkness of others. Compassion becomes real when we recognize our shared humanity." ———Pema Chödrön

When we look outward, past our own thoughts and feelings, we can tune in to other people's experiences and gain a sense of understanding of how they might be thinking or feeling. Empaths naturally empathize with those who are suffering emotionally, psychologically, or physically, and we freely radiate tenderness and compassion. The greatest challenge is empathizing with people if we don't believe they are suffering, and we may also find it more difficult to show empathy to people we disagree with or dislike. Our empathy will always contain an element of judgment, as part of assessing someone else's situation requires us to judge. Judging someone is only harmful if the person doing it is biased in any way.

We can work on judging fairly by understanding that we all have unique journeys that have defined and shaped how we think and feel and what we believe in and value and it is the comparison between our own and other people's journeys that creates judgment. Therefore, our overall judgment of someone will never be accurate however strong our ability is to empathize, as we do not know exactly what has taken place in anyone else's life or what their entire experiences have been like or felt like. All of our experiences, thoughts, feelings, and beliefs, much of which have been conditioned, result in us being the current version of who we are in each moment. No one else can possibly tap into such a vast amount of data in order to wholly and effectively assess anyone else, regardless of their empathetic capability.

When other people insult, criticize, shame, or judge us through pessimistic eyes, they are projecting their own internal unacceptable or unpleasant thoughts, feelings, emotions, or beliefs onto us. Their condemnation derives from the collation of every experience they have ever had, every person they have met, every situation they have encountered so far, and their own desires, opinions, emotions, feelings, intentions, motivations, beliefs, morals, and values.

If we are open and compassionate, we will not judge other people with contempt and instead we will judge with the intention of expressing understanding, consideration, and care. We will then have the ability to observe and accept without scrutinizing and evaluating everything we see based on our own perceptions. However, we can still try to base our assessment on realism and not look through illusions or see the situation as we want or hope to see it. Being compassionate does not mean only looking for the best, it is about accepting things as they are and being sensitive, considerate, open and understanding.

At some level almost everyone judges and assesses, whether positively, neutrally, or negatively. It often happens instinctively and is hardwired in us for survival purposes. However, we can try to remember that just because someone judges, it doesn't mean they intricately know us or that their conclusion in any way reflects who we are. They cannot possibly accurately see who we are when they are looking through their own eyes, through their own perception, and especially if their judgment happens without any empathy. The way to question judging is to inquire if it is happening through compassion or fear. Is it through love and understanding, or is it because they are afraid and feel threatened?

Judging exists, and very often it is unfair. We can try to see that regardless how hard people try to deny that they judge, it usually happens subconscious and subtly and they may not be fully aware that they are doing it.

Judging alone is not the issue, it is how we are judged and for what reasons we are being judged that can make it so damaging. If someone is not empathetic, their judgment is not going to be delivered with any understanding whatsoever, so whatever conclusion they come to can be dismissed as irrelevant.

Before anyone judges, they first need to have a sound understanding of themselves and also have a firm grasp on the entire concept of empathy and be able to express it without any obstructive thoughts, emotions or feelings on their own part that could cause distortion. If empathy is not in place and expressed, all judgment, in whatever form, can immediately be discarded. Judgment is deemed worthless if the person judging has no idea of exactly what they are judging. Therefore, when it is exerted it does not need to be taken seriously. How can anyone possibly judge without first having a clear insight into someone else's mind, including all of their accumulated experiences? Basically, we never need to allow other people's judgments to define us. Neither do we automatically have to accept them as the "truth."

When we see that we all have totally different experiences and we are all individuals who think and feel very differently due to a variety of reasons, it then becomes more natural to be empathetic and potentially resolve any problems. If there is any conflict, we can try to imagine how it may feel from the other person's perspective, as they may be struggling to understand our point of view, or maybe tension has arisen due to a series of misunderstandings.

Recent research has shown how mirror neurons in the brain can cause humans to feel empathetically toward other people through watching their behavior. It is believed that humans and other sentient creatures simultaneously feel emotions depending on what they are witnessing. The studies explain how when we watch someone's actions, our own body corresponds by producing sensations as though we are experiencing what the person we are viewing is experiencing, so in effect we are mirroring them. My personal belief is that these theories do not directly relate to empaths. This is because empaths feel empathy due to the energetic vibrations emanating from another person and what we sense, not from what we witness or are told.

We automatically react to other people's feelings, emotions, or physical states through our ability to detect and make sense of the data stored in the stimuli radiating from their energetic vibration (energy field). Our ability to empathize with and understand someone on a deeper level does not come from what we are observing, as we would still experience empathetic feelings with our eyes closed. We experience empathy regardless of whether we are in the same room as someone or five thousand miles away. We *sense* the energy that is generated from emotions and feelings.

Those who are not sensitive to energy may experience and express empathy by "feeling" similar sensations to the ones the other person is feeling, the difference being they "feel" when they have received visual or spoken clues rather than tuning in to naturally absorb and decode the vibrating energy. They imagine themselves in the other person's shoes based on the information they see or hear, rather than how they instinctively sense and feel without external explanations or physical signs. Rather than sensing and feeling how the other person is feeling, they feel how they themselves would be feeling if they were in that situation.

** Unless someone is a psychopath, as empathy for other people is a characteristic they lack, it is thought that most humans have the ability to be empathetic.

One interesting finding from research carried out on psychopaths revealed that they have the ability to feel empathy for themselves, though they do not feel it for other people. Empaths are the opposite. We often struggle to feel empathy for ourselves, yet we feel excruciatingly high levels of empathy when other people are going through difficulties.

When we aren't showing ourselves empathy we aren't fully listening to ourselves, understanding our emotions or feelings, and ultimately we aren't expressing self-compassion either. The more advanced we become at showing ourselves empathy, the more natural it will be to feel and show empathy for others. If we are not paying attention to our own needs, we will not clearly identify and separate our emotions from other people's emotions. We will then sense when someone is struggling and take on the full force of their emotional energy as though it is ours, and our energy will absorb the dense and heavy weight and we will feel as though the crisis belongs to us. When we absorb other people's emotions we often feel them more intensely than we do our own and the reason for this is usually because we don't fully understand them and so we experience fear and anxiety along with whatever else the other person is going through. The strength of the emotional pain we feel is often the quickest indication that we are not fully present and that we have absorbed someone else's energy.

When we have high levels of empathy and we feel "with" other people, and we are sharing their emotions and feelings with them, in part, we are taking some ownership of them and can mistake them for our own. This is most likely to happen when we are already going through a difficult period and we are overwhelmed with emotion and not identifying it effectively. When our energy field is crystal clear, we are able to process our emotions effectively, we listen to ourselves, and have a good understanding of our emotions and feelings, and we will naturally be able to separate the energy and show empathy and compassion toward others.

Many people think that empaths must automatically be highly advanced at expressing empathy, due to the term "empath," however, that is not the case. We are only advanced when we first identify the emotions and also when we have a profound awareness and understanding of the energy that we are already in receipt of. Empaths don't pay as much attention to verbal clues as we rely heavily on energy; however, if our energy field is blocked and distorted due to a build up of repressed or unresolved emotions, we will not so easily be able to pick up on signals coming in from other people's energy fields. We need to ensure there are no energetic obstacles in the way before we can closely relate to and resonate with anyone else's experience.

Although there is much confusion due to the words *empathy* and *empath* being similar, there are variations between the two. One difference between empathy and empath is that empaths automatically and very naturally tune in to other people's experiences without the need to express compassion, sympathy, or empathy (although we often do). Whereas empathy is when compassion, empathy, and care are expressed. The two exist in their own rights and they don't always correlate. Just because an empath senses energy, it doesn't mean we are then going to be empathetic.

An empaths ability to sense energy means we gain a profound understanding of someone else's condition without immediately experiencing a strong emotional reaction. When we are tuned in to another person and our awareness is heightened, we are able to sense, without feeling overloaded with emotions. This means our mind will be clear and without emotions interrupting and triggering our behavior and we can then respond in ways that are mindful, well thought out, rational, reasonable and beneficial to the situation, rather than reacting in ways that are a byproduct of physiological chemical and hormonal impulses. It is an amazing thing to be able to feel, however, our emotions can leave us overwhelmed, irrational and powerless at times when what we really need is to be calm, collected and consciously aware and in control so that we can respond compassionately instead of irrationally. When we do this we then have a much clearer perception of the other person's experience and this enables us to connect deeply without our vibration being altered during the experience. We will then be in a position to lift the other person's vibration by radiating high frequency emotions while intimately resonating with them without actually feeling exactly what they are feeling and being adversely affected. At first this may sound strange as we are used to feeling other people's emotions, though when we try to sense rather than feel we will discover that we have the option to be deeply compassionate and clear headed so that we have the clearest understanding of their emotions and feelings. However, when we are strongly attached to someone we will find it much more difficult to sense their energy without feeling similar to how they are feeling and we will likely then emotionally react to their circumstances in response. This is one of the reasons why we often find we can't figure out what is going on in our own emotional connections and dynamics easily, whereas we can see other people's dynamics very clearly.

We are able to sense energy without feeling any emotional reaction and without feeling the need to outwardly express what we are sensing in response. When we are highly aware, we are able to sense, without feeling, we are then in a position to keep our mind clear and without emotions interrupting and triggering our behavior and we can respond in ways that are mindful, well thought out, rational, reasonable and beneficial to the situation, rather than reacting in ways that are a byproduct of physiological chemical and hormonal disruptions. It is an amazing thing to be able to feel, however, overwhelming emotions can leave us powerless at times when what we really need is to be calm, collected and consciously in control.

If we have closed off emotionally due to overwhelming emotions, or if we have safeguarded our energy field to block out stimuli, we will still feel the undercurrents of sensations radiating from the people around us. However, we may not have the excess energy required to reach out and offer support, so we might choose other options.

Many empaths naturally transmute energy, even if we are not consciously aware that we are doing so. We do this by sending high vibrational energetic waves of love, compassion, acceptance, forgiveness, and understanding, which neutralize the negative vibrations and transform them to positive ones without needing to express the usual empathetic response. However, we only naturally radiate positive vibrations when we are optimistic, processing our emotions effectively, and we are vibrating on a high frequency. When we are vibrating on a low frequency, feeling pessimistic, and our energy is overloaded, we will not be as able to automatically transmute negative energy.

The most significant thing that differentiates empaths from others is how we are able to resonate so intensely and intimately with other people's experiences solely through the energy we receive. When our energy field is healthy, we then empathize and feel compassion to such an extent that we can experience physical ailments or emotions such as pain, suffering, and joy at almost the same level as other people are feeling them. If our energy is low, we will still take on all of these emotions and feel them as though they are our own; however, we will also likely mistake them as our own, causing ourselves unnecessary and prolonged suffering, and we will also find it challenging to express empathy and show compassion to others. This is mainly due to not clearly seeing the line between our own and other people's emotions, so we deal with them as though they are our own.

We have to be extremely careful, as external emotions and feelings can imprint on us and we can absorb and filter them into our memory bank, where they become a part of our own internal belief system. We may then lose our sense of identity and begin to believe that other people's reality is our reality. This prevents us from being empathetic as we believe we are the ones highly suffering, not the other person.

If someone else has experienced violence, we may absorb the emotions and physical pain they are feeling and feel as though we too have been attacked emotionally or physically. We may find ourselves triggered to react as though we were the ones violated, rather than the other person. This is one of the reasons we instinctively jump in to defend and fight other people's battles for them, rather than allowing them to process and deal with any issues themselves. It is vital that we differentiate between the energy that belongs to us and that which belongs to other people.

We usually empathize with other people much more intensely when we have experienced a similar situation ourselves. For example, if someone is in emotional pain due to an altercation with a family member and we have experienced a similar situation with one of our family members, we will empathize more deeply and the emotions they are feeling resonate with us far stronger. Or it may be that someone has broken a particular bone and we feel excruciating pain if we have previously broken the same bone, or damaged a similar area, in our body.

The degree to which we empathize is often a signal to alert us to deep-rooted trauma or wounds of our own that we haven't yet healed, resolved, or properly understood. However, empathizing with someone else so that we feel exactly how they are feeling is not always healthy or beneficial for us or the other person.

The reason for this is that when we empathize to the extent that we feel exactly as someone else feels, our vibration drops lower so that it matches the frequency of the person suffering and we then vibrate in harmony with them. We will then feel similar sensations to the ones they are feeling. If they are experiencing anxiety, we feel anxiety. If they are raging with anger, we also feel their anger. If they are in physical pain, we feel that pain which can then affect us emotionally and mentally. All emotional, mental and physical injuries are interconnected and when we feel any trauma, whether or own or other peoples, it will ricochet through our energetic and physical body. Our vibration lowers every time we resonate simultaneously and feel into someone else's experience.

Unfortunately, when our vibration has lowered we are then adding our own low, dense vibrations to the overall energy of the situation. We are unable to support anyone else when we become part of the same situation. We are of far more benefit when we are vibrating on a high frequency with a clear mind, positive intentions, hopefulness and an excess of energy to take action if necessary. We will find it very difficult to transmute negative energy to positive energy when we are immersed in low vibrational energy, therefore, it is essential that we keep our energy levels high and healthy in order to assist and support other people.

"There will always be suffering. But we must not suffer over the suffering." ——Alan Watts

When we "put ourselves in someone else's shoes," it is vital that we do so without also absorbing and taking on the intense emotions associated with their experience. We can try to empathize without becoming too emotionally entwined and without living out other people's stories and feeling them as if they are our own. If we abandon our own sense of identity and become immersed in someone else's, we will likely find ourselves caught up in the same perpetual cycle and the low vibrational energy will pull us down. We will then be trying to alleviate the other person's emotional burden, psychological trauma or physical pain while also having to work hard to alleviate our own.

Until we are clearly able to discern the difference between other people's energy and our own, we can show compassion instead of empathy so that we can understand their situations without allowing sensations and emotions to cloud our judgment and alter our vibration. We can also try not to look at someone's situation and then express sympathy or pity through believing that they need our help. This can be condescending and patronizing and can make it appear as though we believe we are better than the other person just because we are not the ones injured in any way and because our vibration is temporarily on a different frequency. The best thing we can do in this situation is to disconnect emotionally while still remaining present with them and aware of their circumstances. We can then try to understand the position they are in from a rational mindset without feeling tempted to step into it ourselves. We can still tune in to their energy and sense what they are going through. However, we do not need to also absorb and take on the energy ourselves. We can then offer support by keeping our vibration high and relating to the situation with positivity, clarity, good intention, and genuine care.

This can take a little time to learn, as it feels very natural for us to wade in and try to lift and carry any low energy. It is entirely possible to understand someone else's situation by discerning what is in their energy field and without experiencing every fine detail of their suffering ourselves. Also, some forms of empathy can be altruistic, egotistic, and detrimental to our own or other people's health and wellbeing. For example, some people show empathy to boost their own self-worth or ego even if it means they suffer during the process. This may be because when they show care they feel as though they are a "good" or virtuous person for helping other people, rather than expressing genuine care purely for the other person's benefit.

Empaths can be altruistic and we can experience difficulties when we help other people, however we aren't usually empathetic with egotistical gains in mind. Gaining a good feeling from helping other people is wonderful if our intention for offering help and support is for their higher good and not so that we look or feel better in ourselves. When we have a high vibration and we know how to effectively transmute energy, we can serve others while also maintaining a healthy balance for ourselves and we then also transform the way we express empathy.

Often people who have suffered from abuse have learned to become highly empathetic so they are able to easily resonate with the person who is abusing them. This allows them to be able to read their abuser well enough to grasp an understanding of how and why they operate so they can safeguard themselves from them as much as possible. It enables the person being abused to be somewhat prepared emotionally, mentally, or physically for the abuse.

When we experience emotions and feelings in the same way as other people experience them, it gives us an in-depth insight into their emotional, psychological or physical state. Because we relate on such an intimate level, we discover profound insights into the reasoning for their state of being. If appropriate, we are then able to pass on our findings and explain in detail the root cause of their emotions.

Sometimes we take on other people's pain as though it is our own due to the fear that we may someday be in the same position ourselves. Even though our emotions are stimulated due to being empathetic, it is also due to the realization that we may potentially suffer similarly. It could also be that we have already been through an identical situation, so we have a firm grasp of how they are feeling.

When we are fully aware of our abilities and our capacity to sense and read energy is attuned, we can tap into the energy emanating from other people without absorbing it. We can sense energy without actually feeling it. This allows us to recognize that the sensations we experience are directly linked to the energy the other person is radiating, rather than feeling as though what we are sensing is part of our own personal experience.

When we sense other people's emotions intensely, it means that we are able to resonate on a very deep level and with clarity. We can then radiate compassionate, loving healing energy and ultimately transform their negative emotions into positive ones. We can do this without expectation for the outcome of their situation, realizing each person is on their own unique journey and this will also prevent us from becoming unhealthily emotional attached to their experience.

Attuning to someone's energy to be empathetic is just one of an empath's abilities. Empaths also have a myriad of other gifts and skills that have little relation to the general definition of empathy.

Chapter 3

ENERGY

"Everything in life is vibration." ——Albert Einstein

The Universal Law of Vibration states that everything in the Universe consists of energy or light in motion that vibrates at a certain speed and the resonation of it determines its frequency.

Although we may perceive our world and everything within it to be physical, quantum physics states that everything that exists in the whole universe is made up of energy that constantly flows and changes form. This has been proven many times by Nobel Prize award winning scientists, however because many of us are used to thinking about our selves, and everything in the universe as tangible, it can be quite difficult to accept that everything is simply energy.

Quantum physics discovered that our physical "reality" consists of physical atoms, which are numerous vortexes of spinning and vibrating energy, similar to a tornado. Whether we perceive this energy as a solid, liquid, or gas depends upon the speed of the atom. If we look at the atom under a microscope, all we would see is an invisible tornado of vibrating energy. When we focus on the structure of the atom closer, it becomes apparent that all that exists is a physical void. The atom does not have any structure therefore everything that is physical does not have structure to it either. All atoms are made from invisible energy.

"Concerning matter, we have been all wrong. What we have called matter is energy, whose vibration has been so lowered as to be perceptible to the senses. There is no matter." ——Albert Einstein

Albert Einstein's scientific calculation for his world-changing discovery explaining the relationship between energy and mass is:

$E = MC^2$

This calculation translates to:

energy (E) = equals mass (M) times celeritas/the speed of light (C) squared.

Energy and mass are a different form of the same thing and are interchangeable. Therefore, mass can turn into energy, energy can turn into mass. Energy is the basis for everything.

Even though everything in the universe appears to look different, it all comes from the same energy. It just vibrates at a different speed, therefore, it exists on a different frequency. Energy vibrates in continuous repetitive cycles, and the faster these cycles spin, the higher the vibration is. Energy that spins slowly has a low vibration. Very high vibrational energy is light and invisible, whereas low vibrational energy is heavy, visible and dense.

I often refer to energy throughout this book as positive and negative. I would like to point out that meanings can be attached to words. Often people perceive the word negative, as a "bad" word as it is can be associated with darker forces or unpleasant experiences. For the sake of understanding energy clearly, I choose the words *negative* and *positive* as all living things have protons and neutrons, and therefore a positive and negative charge, and the negative aspects (darker forces) are within us all. So the word is frequently used, but without "negative" judgment.

If we remove "negative" attachments or preconceived thoughts or beliefs about the word, we can view the term "negative energy" as meaning a low vibration, that describes the lower frequency energies and emotions and feelings on the lower part of the energy scale that are part of every aspect of all existence. It is simply our individual perception of the word that can change its meaning.

We are all electrical beings and we all have negative, neutral, and positive energetic charges. Positive energy vibrates on a high frequency and negative energy vibrates on a low frequency. When we look at energy as being on a hierarchy with various speeds and densities, and we can shift from the higher vibrational end to the lower end instantly depending on the speed of our vibration, we can see how we can accept all parts of ourselves and understand each aspect on a far more intricate level.

All of our senses, organs, flesh, bones, and everything else in our physical body is made out of the same energy as other human bodies, the only difference is that our energy vibrates at different speeds. Therefore, as we all share the same energy just at different speeds, we are all one. We are all part of the same energy, and all energy interconnects.

Energy is the building block for anything tangible that we perceive as a solid. Everything in the universe is an entity. An entity can be visible or invisible to the human eye. Human beings are entities. We are seen as physical beings due to the speed of our vibrating energy and its interaction with light, which results in us seeing "physical" energy in color. However, there are parts of humans that are invisible to an untrained eye, such as our electromagnetic field (aura). We exist in the visible (physical) form, though we also exist in the invisible (energy field) form.

Human beings, according to quantum physics, have no actual physical structure. We are vibrational repeated patterns of spinning vortices of interactive energy, with each having its own unique signature. This spiritual signature is what makes us all entirely different from one another.

We feel separate due to our energy vibrating on a different frequency from everything else that exists. However, we are intrinsically connected to everything and everyone as our energy interacts, connects, absorbs, interlocks, and communicates with other energy here on Earth as well as the incoming energies from the outer universe. We only perceive ourselves to be separate to all other entities due to the speed of the vortices of energy. If our energy speed altered dramatically, so too would the structure of our physical body.

Energy is not always seen. An entity that is invisible to the naked human eye still exists. Just because one of our five senses cannot detect an entity does not mean that it is not part of our reality. Many things that exist are not "actual" (visible) although they are still "real."

All humans consist of energy. In fact, everything in the universe is made up purely of energy. We often hear that humans are made up of cells. This is also true. We have over 75 trillion cells. However, our cells are made of molecules, molecules are made of atoms, and atoms are made of energy. So everything directly relates back to energy.

Atoms are also made up of protons, electrons, and neutrons. Protons have a positive charge, electrons have a negative charge and neutrons have a neutral charge. The protons and electrons magnetize to hold the atom together. Therefore, there is both electric and magnetic energy in each cell.

Our protons and neutrons are respectively positive and negative, and the dynamic works similar to yin and yang energy, which represent movement and change. The two opposing but complimentary forces need one another to create a harmonious and stable equilibrium. The positivity/light and negativity/dark that exists within each of our cells is also expressed through our thoughts, emotions, and feelings. This is why it is essential to achieve balance in the same way as yin and yang energies balance one another.

Although many people are naturally sensitive to universal energy, others become more attuned to it the more open they are and the higher their conscious awareness is. When our conscious awareness is high we are able to tap into incoming energy wavelengths and read the information that is stored within it. When harnessed and utilized, the influx of energy can guide us in our life and ultimately lead us to reach our full potential and our higher purpose on Earth.

One of the easiest ways to tell if we are sensitive to energy is how we feel when we are in the company of other people. We may pick up on the "vibe" and feel immediately overwhelmed or as though our energy has shifted depending on the stimuli from the energy of the people around us. We may notice that we regularly feel highly sensitive to energy, or as though we feel "too much" and it is possible that other people will pick up on this too. This can cause us to withdraw or lock down our emotions due to the fear of being viewed as irrational or overly emotional, when all that is happening is that we are aware of everything that is taking place in our immediate—or distant—environment and we are soaking it all up.

If we find that we easily and clearly sense and read the energy that radiates from others, we will also be able to sense the incoming energy from the universe, even if we are not fully aware of it. We might often feel as though we are telepathic, or we may just "know" things without any logical or reasonable explanation and then find it difficult to explain to others the source of our information.

We may also notice that we often feel as though we are on an emotional rollercoaster, as we are taking on everyone else's emotions as well as trying to process our own. This may cause us to become moody, irritable, experience headaches or avoid going to specific places or spending time with certain people. It is essential to remain alert when we feel any sudden changes to our emotional or mental state so that we can very quickly separate and identify which emotions belong to us and which ones belong to other people. We can carry out a similar process when receiving incoming energies from the outer realms, so that we do not absorb any energies that may lower our personal vibration and cause us harm in any way.

We are able to vividly sense other people's energy as thoughts, feelings, emotions and motivations all emit electromagnetic waves, which we are then able to feel in our own electromagnetic field. This is partly why we are able to be empathetic towards other people as when we attune to the frequency of these waves we can clearly and easily understand and feel how other people are feeling.

Our sensitivities can cause us difficulties, however, they are imperative for our individual growth and wellbeing. Although it may be tempting to close off our senses, it is not the recommended solution, as we will suffer with anguish and anxiety until we understand what is arousing the uncomfortable energetic feelings, channel them and use them to our advantage and also for the higher good of those around us and the planet as a whole. The reason it is not possible to just ignore energy is that it will not disappear until it has been acknowledged, understood and redirected.

Absorbing energy can be over-stimulating which can make us feel emotional, drained and debilitated very quickly, especially if we are passively taking the energy in without first protecting our own energy field (aura). Practicing meditation and mindfulness, spending time with nature, or taking time to be in undistracted silence, as well as keeping our mind positive, can all help combat this.

Everything is connected through fractals of energy. Therefore, we have access to anything and everything in the universe without having to seek for the meaning or find answers outside ourselves. All we need to do is keep our awareness high and allow our intuition to make sense of all existing energy that we have immediate access to.

Energy that vibrates slowly is on the lower end of the spectrum and is dense and tangible and energy that vibrates very quickly is on the higher end of the spectrum and is light and intangible. Our human form has slower wavelengths, in the whole scheme of the universe, so we are on a lower frequency, which is why we perceive ourselves as physical, tangible beings, although, we are still a mass of energy. These electromagnetic waves are sometimes known as "frozen" light.

"You are not a drop in the ocean. You are the entire ocean in a drop." ——Rumi

To perceive ourselves as collective, we can imagine a collection of humans existing as water exists in a glass. The water seems as though it is one complete thing. Though, as soon as we remove one droplet, the removed droplet becomes individual from the rest of the water. We may view the water as separate. And if the droplet was aware (some people believe that all energy has awareness), it might also think it is separate. However, it is connected to the rest of the water as its unique signature is almost identical and it is vibrating on a similar frequency.

To see how humans affect one another's energy, we can again perceive humans as water. If the droplet of water that was removed from the glass had poison added to it and was then added back into the glass, the poison would then infuse and alter the water around it. Everything that surrounded that one poisonous drop would be adversely affected, even if only very slightly, by the change in the structure of the added poison.

Even though each droplet is separate and can exist on its own, they are also part of something far greater, and when the droplets change they also affect everything around them by altering and influencing the speed of the energetic vibrations.

If we add the glass of water to the ocean, the water would blend in with the ocean's water. Although, every miniscule part could still exist on its own, water is far more powerful and effective when it is in a large group. The added glass of water is capable of altering the structure of the water that is immediately around it in the ocean, even though the changes would be minimal.

The frequency of the added water would change to vibrate in harmony with the surrounding water and the existing water would change its frequency slightly too.

Within every drop of water, there is energy that vibrates and that is what gives it its form. If water is cooled to an extremely low temperature its form is then perceived as ice. If it warms up, it turns back to what we perceive as water. We can also see how energy interchanges when we look at the difference between ice, water and vapor. They all transform from one to the other, the only change is the speed of the vibration.

Energy is constantly changing. We are able to see energy as a physical or invisible entity due to the speed of its vibration.

Another way we see water in a different form is through a rainbow. Usually, when we see light we perceive it as one color: white. However, through certain things, like water or glass, we are able to see the full spectrum of color. When we see a rainbow, the light is reflecting off the moisture in the air, which causes the light to refract from each droplet at an angle so that it is viewed as color.

Just as alterations with water affect everything around it, when our own energy alters, we also inflict similar ripples of changes on the people surrounding us. When we raise or lower our vibration due to our predominant thoughts, feelings, and beliefs, we automatically emit energy that interacts and is capable of altering other people's energy.

"One individual who lives and vibrates to the energy of pure love and reverence for all of life will counterbalance the negativity of 750,000 individuals who calibrate at the lower weakening levels."
——Dr. Wayne Dyer

Everything in the universe, even solid objects, has an energetic vibration that vibrates on different frequencies. This is known as *universal life energy*, a sustainable, renewable natural transformational energy that is within us all. Long before Einstein's discovery, many ancient spiritual practices and indigenous cultures lived by these beliefs.

Although the term *empath* is a recent one, the Incas, dating back to the thirteenth century, have viewed the world in a similar way, and they call this concept *kawsay pacha* meaning "living energy." The word *empath* is translated in Quecha, the Incan language, to *qawaq*, which means "one who sees," or *qaway*, meaning "to see living energy."

Thousands of years ago, the Incas also believed that the physical body has an energy field (aura) surrounding it. By using illumination, through means of light such as starlight, the sun, planets, or constellations, the Incas repaired damage to their energy field by transmitting the energy from natural sources when carrying out cleansing, strengthening, and healing practices.

We all have an electromagnetic (electric and magnetic) energy field (aura) that radiates outward. This energy field changes constantly depending upon internal and external influences such as emotions, feelings, and physical, emotional, and psychological health. We emanate a charge of energy that acts like a magnet pulling similar energy in and repelling energy that is not harmonious.

Our thoughts are electric and our emotions and feelings are magnetic. For our thoughts to magnetically attract and repel, they need to be infused with feeling. This is why we cannot attract something or someone purely by thought alone, there has to be *feeling* in our thoughts. As we have tens of thousands thoughts a day, we also need to ensure we keep thinking and feeling about what it is we want to attract to ensure those thoughts do not get lost in amongst the others. Similarly, if we are predominantly thinking and feeling negative thoughts, we can retrain our mind through meditation and remaining consciously aware and paying attention to our thought processes so that we do not attract unpleasant or dysfunctional circumstances or connections.

All energy starts out neutral. We alter energy to either positive or negative through our dominant thoughts, emotions, intentions, and feelings. We can also alter energy's vibration by transmuting it. If someone emits negative low vibrational energy, we can radiate loving, compassionate, high vibrational energy to change its form so that it transforms to positive.

Energy immediately alters when our conscious thoughts, feelings, emotions or intentions change. We have total control over our conscious mind, so we can control all of our thoughts and therefore control our energy. If we send out a positive charge, we are far more likely to attract positive energy. We are also able to absorb the incoming flow of positive energy easier when we are feeling positive. If we send out a negative charge, we are far more likely to attract the same energy in return. We also absorb negative energy easily when we are feeling negative. Therefore, if someone says something negative that reaffirms what we are thinking or believing, there is a higher chance that we will align with it and accept it into our subconscious mind as the truth. Regardless of whether it is or isn't the truth, it harmonizes and blends well with our own energy. The energy that we receive ultimately becomes a self-fulfilling prophecy. If the majority of what we currently or have previously known is negative we can very easily become addicted to low energy, as it feels familiar, and this same concept is applied to positive energy.

Positive energy repels negative energy and negative energy repels positive energy. We are far less likely to accept and absorb negative energy when we are radiating positive energy, and likewise, when we are negative it is not so easy to absorb positivity. When we are radiating a mixture of positive and negative energy, maybe because we are consciously thinking positive thoughts but our belief system is largely negative and not in line with our thoughts, we will feel a conflict. This may happen when we try to think positively but on an inner level we don't believe we deserve positivity, so we are not feeling positive. As positive and negative energy is incompatible, they repel one another, causing friction within our energy field - this friction can be sensed by others who also feel a conflict with their selves. We are then far more likely to attract push and pull relationships or situations that go around in endless circles, not going anywhere and thus making no sense. We will feel in that "one step forward, one step back" scenario where we want to create peace and happiness but our negative beliefs intervene and prevent us from achieving it every time we seem to make progress.

The connections we make with people are all due to the energy we are emitting. If we are feeling anxious and afraid, we will attract people who are also vibrating on a low frequency, and this is why it is often the case that empaths who have high anxiety levels, or are radiating other low vibrational emotions, enter relationships with narcissists. If we are sending out a vibration that lets other people know we are in an emotionally vulnerable or anxious mindset, those who desire power and control will cease the opportunity to enforce power and control. The instant we meet someone our energy is communicating far more clearly than we are speaking. We send out signs and signals constantly and those who read energy well are then in a position whereby they can easily take advantage, if they chose to.

Research at the Institute of Heartmath found that the heart's electrical component has approximately 60 times more amplitude than the brain, and the heart's magnetic field is approximately 5000 times more powerful than the brain's and can be detected from several feet away. The energy generated from the heart permeates every cell in our body. Therefore, whatever we are feeling has a far greater impact on us as well as those around us than whatever we are thinking about.

Findings from the research also showed that depending on what emotions we are feeling, our heart's rhythmic beat changes. Negative emotions such as anger and resentment send out an erratic, incoherent pattern, whereas positive emotions such as love and gratitude send out a smooth, ordered, coherent pattern.

Our electromagnetic pulses pull people towards us whose energy feels harmonious with our own. This doesn't mean that we are experiencing the exact same emotions, feelings, thoughts or intentions as the other person. It simply means our emotions are on a similar low frequency. For example, resentment, anger or bitterness, are low on the frequency scale and so are fear, despair and grief, which means two people may connect but have entirely different thoughts, feelings and intentions.

Low frequency emotions can become toxins at a cellular level and result in emotional, mental or physiological disease or trauma. This is why we often refer to relationships as toxic, as they are a poisonous insidious drip that leaks into to our body and mind.

Negative energy neutralizes positive energy, so when we experience these emotions we become stuck, and moving forward becomes strenuous, draining us of any of the positivity we try to instill. Negative emotions are a byproduct of fear and use up a ridiculous amount of energy, which eventually exhausts us. Whenever we feel afraid, the fear manifests itself in negativity. We may fear that we are not worthy or that we are in danger, or we may feel threatened by something or someone. All of our fear-based emotions cause us to be irrational as they close down our mind to put us in fight or flight mode so that our attention is focused solely on survival. Whenever we feel ourselves in a negative state, we have to focus on remaining consciously aware so that we are able to frequently combine positive thoughts and feelings, such as love and gratitude, together to achieve a harmonic heartbeat so that we are emanating powerful positive energy to counteract and consume the negativity.

Positive emotions such as hope and joy open us up to infinite possibilities. They allow us to feel calmer and lighter and we have greater clarity and can see everything with an open mind. We have access to more information, so we are able to see how everything connects and relates, giving us the opportunity to explore more options.

Each cell in our body has thousands of receptors and each one is connected to a peptide or protein. Our emotions release neuropeptides, which directly interact with our receptors and alter the structure of each cell. When our cells divide, they are more dominant in whichever peptides they have been exposed to. Therefore, if we are fuelling our cells with negative peptides resulting from our emotions, our cells will divide and create more cells that seek out similar negative peptides. This is why when we are feeling low we can very quickly spiral lower. If we are feeling high, we attract more peptides that propel our vibration higher. Unfortunately, we sometimes wallow more in low vibrational energy than we do in high vibrational. If someone says something that hurts us, we may think about it so often that eventually we end up believing the words. We find it far more complex to imprint positive experiences onto our cells than we do negative ones.

We can control what we think about and determine a healthy percentage of what is deposited. As soon as we consciously change our thinking, we can change our emotions and ultimately change how we feel. Just by changing our mindset to one where our intentions are genuine, sincere, loving, and joyful allows us to instantly manifest positive energy so that we radiate, attract, and absorb positivity all in one go.

Whatever we send out will be returned to us in abundance. If we give out one thread of happiness, that thread will not just reach one person, it reaches everyone and everything in the universe, and similar loving threads will radiate back toward us. When we set the intention to surround ourselves with positive energy, negativity may still seep in or out unexpectedly. We are all capable of feeling and expressing negative emotions and energy, so we have to go easy on ourselves and remedy it quickly by becoming consciously aware so that we can flood the negativity with positivity and rebalance. We simply have to be willing to define and take ownership for our emotions and feelings and the energy they carry so that we quickly recognize negative ones and halt them in their track.

The energy we radiate is mostly determined by our internal belief system. If we feel optimistic about life, we will easily accept positive affirmations. If we feel pessimistic, we will attract whatever confirms those beliefs and we will easily absorb negativity. Positive energy holds a different charge to negative energy. Positivity has a high vibration, whereas negativity has a low vibration. Everything we feel revolves around energy.

When our energy recognizes other energy with a similar frequency, the energies blend and entangle and we may feel magnetized toward the other person. We must be careful, though, as energy is contagious and it can quickly become intoxicating and addictive, even if the connection is a healthy, balanced one. We may bounce off other people's energy as it ricochets or dances in tune with our own and we may find the dynamic particularly desirable if we have not previously met someone with whom we "vibe" with so well. If we do not remain aware, before we know it we can fall into a "habit" of communicating with other energy and it may feel like we are falling in love. Although it very likely could be a deeply loving, heart-centered connection, desire might get in the way and we can lose ourselves temporarily, which means we won't notice if and when our energy field is experiencing friction and is actually repelling the other person's energy. Rather than being aware of the sensations this causes and acting on them, we sometimes ignore those subtle signs and continue regardless. This is what causes us some of the most difficult challenges in life. Although this won't always be the case, it is most certainly beneficial to be open to the possibility.

When we absorb energy without paying attention to it, we are rendering ourselves open to taking on not just the highs that the energy holds but the devastating lows too. Even though energy can be high vibrational one moment, it can dramatically change the next. Vibrations change moment to moment depending on how we are thinking, feeling, and also on our internal belief system. We may deliberately block people out or avoid them if the energy that they radiate carries an array of powerful emotions. If we are very sensitive to energy and read it well, we will realize the dramatic effect this energy is having on us. However, it may just be that the energy they radiate is positive and it conflicts with our own energy if we are radiating negativity, although it could be that their energy is negative and ours is positive.

If someone is radiating strong loving and compassionate emotions and we do not believe we deserve these emotions, our electromagnetic field will detect the friction and put barriers up against it. Or if someone is radiating negativity our self-protection mode may click into play to warn us of the possibility of perceived impending danger. Conflicting energy can serve us well, though only if we are willing to pay attention to it. Not only can it alert us to what is currently being upheld by our internal belief system, but it can also highlight what exists within other people's belief systems too. If we tune in to the energy, we can easily gain an insight into what is being radiated.

Friction alerts us when we are absorbing negative or positive energy that opposes our own, as friction is a protection mode (although it sometimes works against us). It will try using a variety of tactics to prevent us from accepting something that causes conflict with our own belief system. This friction may trigger us to erupt and have a temper tantrum, or we may project by blaming and shaming other people or rejecting teachings that do not align with what we believe in.

If we place awareness on the friction, it can show us areas that we need to work on so that we can explore any false beliefs that we have been conditioned to believe are true. If our core belief system is healthy and radiating with positivity, we will feel friction whenever negativity presents itself. Again, the friction will prevent us from automatically accepting information that does not affirm our stored beliefs. Being mindful will keep us remaining aware and alert at all times so that we can pay full attention to the subtle sensations within our energy field.

We may go certain places and feel the need to leave immediately as the historic collective energy is too intense. We sense past memories, emotions, or trauma that has taken place there and feel this energy in real time regardless of when it took place. Energy lingers everywhere and we may find that we sometimes instantly become overwhelmed by an occurrence that has previously taken place there. We might notice forceful physical sensations as we pick up on the energetic debris that consists of the charged emotions that have been left behind. We will experience these sensations as chills, shivers, goose bumps, or internal unrest, possibly disturbing our solar plexus in the upper abdomen area.

If our vibration is high, we can easily transmute the energy by sending out positive healing waves so that any negative charge held is dispelled.

Our energy fields interlock with other people's energy fields and the entanglement that occurs is capable of lifting or lowering vibrations. This can be as dangerous as it can be exhilarating. We are capable or intentionally or unintentionally altering other people's thoughts, moods, and belief systems. If we are not operating on a pure and high vibrational level, other people can be heavily influenced by our energy and their lives may be severely affected. A classic example is when someone is aggressive and their mood dramatically impacts the people surrounding them. They then carry the mood onward and it can influence various events during their day or even in the days following. This is why it is crucial that we are mindfully aware of ourselves and ensure we are vibrating positive energy as we can ultimately alter other people's routes without realizing we are doing it. This can be harmful to the person affected by our energy, as the road that has differed may not work out to be a stable one. People have their own maps and compasses and we need to be careful not to redirect or disorientate them by altering their energy field.

We can try to remain aware of how powerful energy is as one person's mood can sit in our energy field for days, festering away, affecting us emotionally, psychologically and physiologically, until it eventually explodes. When we think negative thoughts our energy is immediately adversely affected. It contracts and tenses as thoughts transfer to emotions, emotions turn to feelings, and then possibly on to actions. For example, when we talk about words that relate to hate, anger or violence, these words hold a vibration as they are an expression of how we are thinking or feeling. Words are fuelled by energy and the vibration is stronger and more powerful depending on how emotional the person who is voicing them feels.

Empaths are able to understand the meaning of energy far better than they are able to understand the meaning behind words. So much so that many empaths could listen to someone speaking in a foreign language and have a clear insight into what they are expressing. Empaths don't just listen to words or observe body language, we absorb the whole communication package, and we are able to translate the energetic vibrations and decode the meaning behind everything that is being voiced or expressed.

We are particularly susceptible to negativity as it depletes our energy, whereas when we are surrounded by positivity our energy relaxes, radiates, and our energy field (aura) expands outwards as our emotions and feelings flow freely and naturally without tension. The vibrations that emanate from negativity diminish and deplete our energy, and the vibrations that emanate from positivity recharge and replenish our energy. This is why empaths try to avoid all types of conflict and often shut down when we are confronted by it. This is our system going into self-protection and self-preservation mode so that it safeguards our vital energy and we do not become fatigued and emaciated.

Although it may be tempting to marinate our vibrations in someone, somewhere, or something else, we must protect and conserve our energy in order to prevent potential toxicity from causing us energetic harm.

"Take responsibility for the energy you bring to me." ——Jill Bolte Taylor

We can consciously choose who and what we allow the privilege of accessing, interfering with or influencing our immediate energy field. We also choose the type of energy we send out and to where and to whom. Our thoughts are so powerful that as soon as they radiate outward anyone else who tunes in to our frequency will instantly pick up on them and translate whatever is spinning through our mind, particularly if we are also emotional. When we know how to protect ourselves and remain fully aware and in the moment, vibrating highly, no one will be able to enter our energy field without our prior permission. When we have a good understanding of how energy works, it is equally vital that we are respectful and responsible for what we are radiating and who it might be affecting.

Energy can be like a drug. The more we delve into it, the more we are at risk of becoming addicted to it. Our energy, if not protected, will very quickly forget its own identity and we can lose our sense of self and spin madly and chaotically out of control as our energy gets caught up and entangled with other energy twirling in the air.

Empaths are able to decode the information vibrating in energy fields and we absorb it through our skin cell receptors that draw in energy. We are naturally able to sense the data stored within the "unique signature" held in the energy. When we are alert and aware, we will recognize the subtle changes that take place without needing to use any of our five senses: touch, taste, sight, smell, or sound.

Energy vibrates outwardly and it does not die out; it lingers in the air, attaches to objects or people, and other energies connect with it or absorb it. Our energy leaves an imprint everywhere we go. This is why we say some places have a certain "vibe" to them. The "vibe" of a place is dependent on the people or events that have been there.

When we realize our energy and other people's energy are constantly interacting regardless of time, space, or distance, we can become overwhelmed and feel as though we need to "pull ourselves back together." However, this is only because we have been conditioned to believe that we all are physical entities and entirely separate in body and mind.

Empaths have a deep soul longing to discover who we are and what our inner calling is. As we awaken, it can be an incredibly traumatic internal journey as we feel as though we have literally been fragmented into billions of pieces that need to be glued back together one by one to discover our truth. This is due to us realizing that we are not separate or individual; we are part of one whole thing, one energy: the universe.

There are many aspects to being an empath that we might sometimes find not easy to explain or reason, though that is mainly because we live in a world that mostly relies on logic, mathematics, and scientific studies. For anyone who is an empath, they instantly and strongly relate to and resonate with the traits and characteristics that are defined by the term. That is because we are fully aware that although it is sometimes complex to scientifically make sense of our energetic journey and how our energy interacts and connects with the universe, we *sense* and *feel* our way through life and we do not need scientists or any other professional to explain our inherently natural existence.

Those who live in fear of the unknown or those who do not want their thought processes to be challenged may downplay that a person such as an "empath" exists. People are often afraid when someone appears to be outside the box as it challenges the status quo and they might think it weakens their own or mass collective thoughts and beliefs. It is likely too that people who diminish or ridicule the term *empath* will not believe in the "magic" that energy is capable of creating, though that is merely because they have either not fully studied it or have not yet experienced it. To experience things that seem impossible or magical, one must first have an open mind and also be willing to seek out knowledge and ultimately believe in possibility. People often fear things they do not understand and this then limits the mind's ability to accept that there is far more to everything than we are currently able to see.

When we have a sound understanding of how energy works, we instantly uncover endless mind-blowing possibilities. For example, we will discover how limiting it is to keep a track on time, yet, time plays an intrinsic part in most societies. Our energetic self does not die out. It was not created; it will always exist in one form or another. When we determine our life by time, we are focusing on how much time we have left to live in this physical body. We are either in a hurry to make the most of the time we have here and fill it with experiences or superficial goods, or we may be lonesome and watching our life's clock tick by, wondering why it feels as though time passes so slowly.

We may have sold our time to work in jobs we dislike just so that we can pay for the numerous material possessions that are in our homes that many people barely get to spend any time in. Time is nonexistent in the universe. We create time and we have built our lives around it. If time were suddenly discarded, most people would probably not know how to cope! Placing importance on time often makes us uphold the false belief that this is our only opportunity to connect with the people around us or spend time on earth. When we reach the age of sixty or seventy, many people start to panic a little, believing they are running out of time to complete all the things they want to achieve in this lifetime. However, we are all energy that can never be destroyed. Our energy can travel throughout the universe. There are no beginnings, neither are there endingss. Our energy continues long after our physical body dies out.

Many people try to deny that human beings have an energy field and reject that this energy field is what keeps us alive. Due to our physical bodies being the only part of a human being they can see and touch, they think that the physical side is the only part that exists. However, this belief does not explain how we are able to think, feel, or sense.

Our thoughts and all of our sensations are not physical. We cannot touch them, yet we know they exist and are part of our reality. They exist due to energy. Everything in the universe exists because of energy, whether it is invisible or visible. Energy is what charges our emotions and feelings so that they can then be expressed.

Life force energy is visible, although we usually only see it if we focus. Our main source of energy is the sun, so on a clear sunny day if we look up to the sky—not directly at the sun—we will see tiny glowing particles in the air. These shiny particles are visible forms of energy.

We can raise our awareness of electromagnetic energy by placing our hands in prayer position and briskly rubbing them together. If we focus on our hands and hold the intention to channel life force energy toward them, we will feel our hands start to tingle. As we rub them together, focusing on the palm area, we are consciously stimulating our *prana* (life force energy). The palms are particularly sensitive and will begin to feel as though they are two magnets repelling one another. As we pull the hands slightly apart, we will feel a more intense magnetic force between them. We can then concentrate on our breathing and very slowly move the hands slightly apart and then back together again to increase the intensity of the sensation. This is a great simple exercise to instantly boost energy levels.

Some people have become accustomed to the term "to see is to believe," which makes them mistrust anything that is not clearly visible to the eyes. They mistakenly think that if something is not picked up by one of their five senses then it cannot possibly exist. However, things that might have been impossible to believe in only thirty years ago, such as the Internet, smart phones, and laptops, are now essential tools for many of us in our daily lives. Every detail that makes these things possible is entirely thanks to energy. So it is easy to see how many of the things people think are impossible now, will someday be proved to be true.

As Carl Jung explains, "I shall not commit the fashionable stupidity of regarding everything I cannot explain as a fraud." For some people, a clear explanation will never suffice. They require scientific evidence. To naysayers, an empath's ability to sense and "read energy" may seem preposterous. However, we haven't even discovered all of the possibilities that human beings are capable of. If we were to time travel 500 years ahead, we would likely find it impossible to believe that we didn't think reading energy was possible! We may also struggle to believe some of the other things we would see and discover.

We live in a day and age where it is not widely acceptable to believe that there are other entities out there that cannot clearly be seen with the eyes. Empaths don't need to see anything—we sense and feel it.

Finely tuning our frequency so that we keep our energetic vibration high to prevent from absorbing anything that will harm our energy field is ultimately the most harmonic, healthy, productive, and ultimately high vibrational way for us to exist.

Chapter 4

THE HUMAN ENERGY FIELD

The law of nature states that everything has its own vibration. Every atom that moves radiates and creates an energetic vibration. Every atom, cell, and particle in our body generates energy that creates a glow. The glow is our energy field/aura and surrounds every living thing. It is essential to understand that energy isn't just outside the human body. The human body *is* energy and the aura is the vibration of the energy that emanates from it.

Our electromagnetic field pulses, connects, and interacts with everyone and everything that exists. Everything we think or do—basically anything we put energy into—sends out an electrical charge and this charge magnetizes with other energies, absorbs them, and either repels the energy or draws it toward us. Whatever we send out, we attract similar back in. Our thoughts, emotions, and feelings all emit a charge that carries particular information. This information is our belief system. Whatever we believe and send out, we attract and receive.

Therefore, our conscious, subconscious, and unconscious beliefs are returned to us through the people, emotions, and situations we magnetically pull toward us. Similar energy attracts similar energy.

We are all fueled by energy from the universe and this energy sustains every aspect of our existence. All of our thoughts, emotions, feelings, and actions take place due to an electrical current known as universal life force energy (or *prana/chi*). Our thoughts, emotions, and feelings send out energy that creates our own unique electromagnetic field (aura). When we are positive, we continuously recharge our universal life energy. We then vibrate on a high frequency, feeling full of vitality, and we are radiant. When we are negative, we are vibrating on a low frequency. Our energy is zapped, and we will feel exhausted and fatigued as our life energy becomes depleted.

One of the main reasons we vibrate on a very low level is due to being unable to process and express thoughts, emotions, and feelings. As all three of these things are energetically charged, they must flow continuously so that they do not cause obstructions within our system. Whenever we vibrate on a low frequency we are susceptible to poor emotional, mental, or physical health as the energy becomes blocked and causes tension. This tension can be felt as aches or pains through the body or irritable draining sensations in the mind.

Energy is constantly in motion and it will not just dissipate if it is forced to slow down due to blockages. Our inner system is similar to a highway, with our emotions being the cars. If one car (emotion) gets stuck, all the other cars (emotions) will begin to get caught behind them, eventually causing a traffic jam. The cars will remain, as they cannot just disappear. They will move very slowly, nudging along the road little by little. Horns will sound and people may become aggressive, frustrated, and impatient. Unless the car (or cars by this stage) receives attention so that the issue can be fixed, it will stay there, causing a further build-up of problems.

This is a similar process to what happens when energy becomes blocked in our system. We cannot ignore it, as it requires us to pay attention and focus on it to make alterations to clear the road. The obstacles are emotions that we have left to the side to deal with some other time—they won't just go away. They ferment and grow rusty, like a car broken down, with others swerving out of the way to avoid it. Everything slows down just because of this one car (emotion.) The more cars that slow down or break down and get ignored, the bigger the problem is and the worse the traffic becomes.

It is crucial that we acknowledge any emotions that are clogging up our system. When we release each emotion one by one, we can understand, heal and repair them simply by focusing a little attention on them by showing understanding, tenderness, care, and compassion so that our emotions are recharged and able to start moving again. They can then continue their journey lighter, with the problem solved, replenished, and resulting in our life force energy recirculating fully. It is vital that our energy is fluid as it is the driving force behind all of our expressions. When we are freely expressing and communicating ourselves fully, our energy is also able to flow.

Every cell in our body requires oxygen. Oxygen is vital for our existence, so it is essential that we absorb oxygen effectively to keep our lungs and physical bodies healthy, our minds invigorated, and our energy circulating. One of the five principles of yoga is *pranayama*. The practice includes using our full breathing capacity. *Pranayama* regulates the breath through inhaling and exhaling in a rhythmic manner so that we keep *prana* energy (life force energy) flowing freely.

The physical body makes up one half and the subtle bodies (auric field) make up the other half of human beings. The two need to merge together so that we are able to function wholly and completely. Often we feel separation within ourselves and as though "something is missing." This is because there is a disconnection between our physical body and our subtle bodies. If our physical body and our energetic layers are not aligned, we can easily lose our way in life and feel as though we are not functioning effectively or moving toward our highest potential.

We all have a network of nerves and sensory organs that assist us in understanding and navigating our inner and outer worlds. Although many of us understand our physical body quite well, we are not all as familiar with how our energetic body operates. Our human energy field (electromagnetic field/aura) is the blueprint and matrix for our physical body and it is intricately connected to our existence on earth. Our aura is like a body double. It reflects everything that is happening within our physical body. It has various layers of energy that vibrate, and each of these layers has its own function and purpose. Our energy field stores information and is a template for our physical body.

We can tap into different layers of our aura when we focus and direct our consciousness. When we do this, we gain a far greater insight into who we actually are and not who we perceive ourselves to be. We will also be able to look at our outer world with clarity and break down all the illusions that are in place.

Chapter 5

AURAS

"This little light of mine, I'm going to let it shine!"
——Unknown

The light that glows all around us is known as our aura. Although not everyone can see auras, it doesn't mean they don't exist. We can all feel auras and are all influenced by them to some degree even if we are not consciously aware of it. Everything in the universe has a vibration and auras are quite simply the electrophotonic vibrations that emanate from all objects, living or otherwise. Our eyes are able to view auras as luminous colorful shades.

Empaths have a very high sensitivity to energy. Therefore we can easily gain an innate understanding of auric fields. It is essential that we take good care of our aura and keep it energetically clean as it absorbs and radiates thoughts, beliefs, intentions, perceptions, emotions, and feelings, as well as overall physical and mental health. If we do not look after our aura, then low vibrational energy will become lodged in it. This will block and prevent us from carrying out pure and high vibrational healing work, as well as weigh us down and make us feel exhausted and irritable.

61

Blockages in our aura make it difficult to clearly identify what is our own energy and what energy has been picked up from elsewhere, as when it sits in our aura for long periods of time we may automatically believe the energy originated from us, not from other people, and that we own it.

Auras are a flow of ever-changing energy that is constantly in motion and external energies can slow down and interfere with our vital energy supply. Understanding how auras operate allows us to read our own as well as other people's auras so we can instantly be alerted if we are in the vicinity of or absorbing anything that can do us energetic harm.

The easiest way to "feel" someone's aura is by becoming aware of how our senses and intuition react when we are close to someone. The subtle sensations we feel when we stand next to someone is their energy radiating (aura). Our aura and their aura connect and the energies interact and communicate. Within that energy is a multitude of information that tells us an incredible amount of detail about the other person. It holds a myriad of emotional, mental, and physiological information. Auras hold valuable knowledge that is very rarely tapped into. The more we are aware of how energy works and how it affects our aura, the more enhanced our ability becomes to instinctively sense and easily read them.

Even if we aren't able to see auras, we have an inherent natural ability to sense and feel them. This is why some people make us feel uncomfortable while we can naturally relax with others. When we receive a "vibe" about someone, this is a sign we have sensed their aura. The only reason we aren't all easily able to see auras is because we have not tuned in to them. We generally focus the majority of our attention toward the physical body by observing facial expressions and body language. Many people turn a blind eye to the energetic body as they either do not understand it or they might not believe that there is such a thing. Children can often easily sense and see auras and they may depict them in drawings by choosing colors for people that match the data they have picked up on. As children get older, they can lose this ability, especially if they are told or start to believe that the world and everything in it is solid rather than being made up of energy. When we work with the body's energy, we have the opportunity to gain access to all aspects of human beings, including deep wisdom and truths.

As our emotions and moods change, so too does our physical body. The changes in our body also cause our aura to change due to the chemical and electrical reactions taking place. These reactions are vibrations that make up the electromagnetic field (aura) that surrounds us. When we are able to read energy, we can figure out the true state of emotions and our own overall psyche, as well as those we connect with, regardless of how hard we or someone else may try to mask inner feelings.

When we think of auras as energy, we can see how we are affected by auric energy. Our mind contributes strongly to what is happening within our energy field. Energy is very powerful, and when we understand how it works and how our auras are formed, we will be able to identify the state of our own or someone else's overall physical health along with observing the conscious, subconscious, unconscious, and higher conscious mind.

When we stand next to someone, we are able to physically feel how infused with love, anger, or how much fear they have. This is where the phrase "you could cut the atmosphere with a knife" originates as we literally feel how their mood feels as it is flows through their outer energy. In times like these, we may need to distance ourselves or leave an area where the energy is high so that we receive the opportunity and space needed to recalibrate our own energy levels.

Auras can change moment to moment as our thoughts, emotions, feelings, beliefs, and intentions change. Our auras are a mirror reflection of what we are experiencing. We can view our own or someone else's inherent nature or current feelings by observing and reading an aura. Many people have learned to masquerade their intentions by using words and actions that are not a true reflection of how they are thinking or feeling. However, auras are not manipulated easily. Empaths generally feel quite uncomfortable when someone unexpectedly gets too close. It can feel as though our personal space has been invaded. If someone steps into our energy field, their energy immediately begins to actively communicate, and maybe cause friction, with ours. This is one of the main reasons we feel compelled to stand back from certain people so that we can keep them at a safe distance and protect our energy.

It is vital that as empaths we protect our aura as our first instinct is to heal and show compassion. Therefore, when we come into contact with someone who is emotionally or physically distressed our aura will instantly extend to reach out and wrap itself around the other person. The reason for this is that we instinctively radiate soothing and healing energy to lift out harmful or toxic energy. We just have to remember that during this process we can be picking up a whole host of low vibrational entities. Unfortunately, the negative vibrations in other people's auric fields or the surrounding environment can cause conflict in our own aura and the energy can be murky, heavy, and difficult to process. That is why we often become fatigued and debilitated when in the company of certain people or specific places. If our vibration is very high, we will not need to protect ourselves as much, though we still can remain aware of potential negativity, to prevent the energy from consciously or unconsciously seeping in and causing us energetic harm.

If other people's vibrations are on a low frequency, they will react with our frequency and if we are not grounded they may leave us with a dense, irritable feeling. We might feel the need to remove ourselves from a room if the vibrating energy begins to deplete us. Being in the company of people whose energy has an unhealthy vibration can leave us emotionally and physically drained. We may feel as though an energy vampire has sucked the vital life force energy from us.

We can cleanse our aura by smudging, using crystals, natural salt baths, essential oils, spending time with nature, or simply by being aware of our thoughts and the vibrations our emotions and feelings generate. Our aura instantly and dramatically changes as soon as we change the way we think or feel about something.

Chapter 45 will explain how to read an aura.

Chapter 6

TRANSMUTING ENERGY

Transmuting energy is an alchemical process that changes the form, character, or substance of energy. Some people transmute consciously and others do it subconsciously. If we are not aware that we are able to transmute energy, we will likely do it subconsciously and we may be transmuting energy constantly which could lower our vibration if we are not vibrating highly already, or if we are not aware that we are doing it. This is one thing that contributes to overload and what causes us to suffer with extreme fatigue and eventual burn out.

To transmute energy, we must ensure our vibration is on a high frequency. If something or someone is depleting our energy, our vibration will lower, so we must remain in a constant state of energy awareness. As we are sensitive to energy and are able to tune in to other people's emotions, we immediately pick up on how other people are feeling. This magnetically draws people toward us or us to them, as it feels natural for us to receive and process their emotions.

We are all alchemists and we all have the power to transmute energy, therefore, we can also transmute and alter emotions.

"Alchemy is the art that separates what is useful from what is not by transforming it into its ultimate matter and essence." —— Philippus Aureolus Paracelsus

When we are around emotional energy, we generally absorb it unless we have specifically blocked or guarded ourselves against receiving it. When we absorb emotions, we have to be cautious when we are identifying them so that we do not take them on as our own. Once we recognize where negative emotions come from and also the reason behind them, we can empathize with whoever radiated them and show compassion and understanding. Sometimes we may not be sure where the emotion has come from even though we can feel it affecting us. If we remain still and spend a few moments raising our awareness and going through names or images of people we know, we will feel a sense of recognition when the energy we are sensing resonates with the identity of whoever has sent it.

The reason we are able to empathize at such a deep and intense level is because temporarily we have taken on and felt the emotions as though they are our own. This is the cursed part of the "blessing and curse" gift of being an empath. Empaths have the natural ability to receive, process, transmute, and relay energy so that negative low vibrations turn to positive high vibrations.

Anyone is capable of transmuting energy. However, as empaths are emotionally intelligent, natural healers, and ultrasensitive to energy, we can identify negative entities quickly so that we can then express love, compassion, acceptance, forgiveness, and understanding, and we instantly alter energy's vibration, form, and direction.

Transmuting energy is part of an empath's soul's purpose here on Earth, and it can take us some time to accept and understand this and also to transmute energy effectively. This is why it is essential that we learn about energy and pay attention to it so we can discern and process every subtle sensation we receive. Even though it is a very natural process, it is not something many people are aware of and it is not a subject we will likely be taught in schools or learn from our peers.

The period we live in is one that is slowly waking up to human possibilities and we are beginning to accept that our capacity is limitless. As more information becomes widely available, empaths will naturally master these gifts, though for now we are in a period of mass learning and that includes trial and error. We have to go easy on ourselves as our abilities also come with responsibility. They are not just here to be used for our own benefit. We are able to positively change how humans, animals, and also how our environment vibrates. The main reason empaths have these unique abilities and why we are pushed toward learning more about them is due to us being born healers who are naturally highly compassionate. We empathize deeply and we offer acceptance, forgiveness, and understanding, which enable us to fluidly transmute harmful energy.

Negative energy can come from anywhere. It can be due to planetary activity, crisis on Earth. It can come from small gatherings or it can be directed from an individual through their thoughts, feelings, or emotions. Emotions are powerful conduits of energy, especially if someone is feeling particularly angry, envious, resentful, or aggressive. We can pick up on negative influences without any verbal clues and it can disturb our energy field until we recognize it and then consciously and mindfully deal with it. If we are picking up on the sensations from planets or from small groups that we have no connection to, generally the energy will dissipate quickly as it is not being directed solely toward us. We can still transmute this energy to clear it from our energy field and send peaceful vibrations outward to counteract any negative entities; however, if we don't it will eventually pass. However, emotional energy that is being sent out either consciously or unconsciously from someone else needs to be processed. This is so that we uncover the reason for the negativity arising so we can be aware if it is due to something we have done, and also so that we can radiate positive, loving vibrations to cancel out the incoming potentially harmful energetic vibrations.

Emotions carry a very strong vibration. The easiest way to describe an emotion is that it is energy in motion: E-motion. Positive emotions carry a high vibration and negative emotions carry a low vibration. High vibrations such as unconditional love, kindness, patience, compassion, generosity, understanding, forgiveness, and humility are capable of consuming and transforming low vibrations such as fear, bitterness, resentment, rage, anger, jealousy, spite, and hatred. Low vibrations can also consume and cancel out high vibrational emotions.

When we express emotion we are expressing an energetic vibration. Energy energizes emotions and puts them into action or motion. Every time there is an emotional response there is an expression of life force energy (*prana*). The stronger the emotional response, the greater amount of energy it carries with it and the more forcefully it will vibrate.

Transmuting emotional energy happens when we change the character of emotion. For example, if someone is venting anger we can pick up on the negative energy that is radiating and transmute the energy by emanating high vibrational loving and compassionate thoughts, emotions, and feelings so that the low vibrations are lifted and transformed to higher, more positive ones. Transmuting is easier and occurs more naturally when our vibration is high and we are aware of how to emanate positive energy so that any negativity is neutralized and transformed.

Setting the intention to transmute energy begins when we remain nonjudgmental regardless of how toxic the surrounding energy feels. If someone is directing low vibrational thoughts, emotions, feelings, or intentions toward us, we can radiate loving, light energy so that the energy does not affect us; however, we can try not to expect miracles or believe the other person will then change their thoughts, feelings, or intentions. This will only happen when the person who is radiating negativity is open to our response and willing to communicate energetically so that their vibration alters. Although our vibration can influence theirs, it will only have a mild effect if they have blocked emotions and they are not sensitive to energy.

The reason we experience other people's emotional, mental, and physical anguish is ultimately so that we are provoked to do something about it. Because we feel the pain, we are compelled to alleviate it—not just for the other person, but also for ourselves.

Empathizing in this way can be troublesome as our vibration will lower due to the influx of low vibrational energy. It is essential that we remain aware that the emotions we are absorbing are not our own. We can then consciously keep the incoming emotional energy separate so that it does not remain in our energy field for longer than the few moments it takes to transmute the energy. We can intentionally bombard the energy with high vibrational emotions so that it quickly dispels and leaves our energy field to return to the person who radiated it. The energy will no longer have a harmful impact as the vibration has lifted and it will heighten the other person's frequency as soon as we send it back to them, even if this is only minimally.

Part of the reason people feel negative is because they are afraid, and whenever they feel fear it is because they do not fully understand something.

If we do not understand where emotions are coming from, we will instantly attach fear to them. Whenever we are fearful, we add strength and negativity to emotions. When we have understanding of how emotions and fear work, we ultimately gain optimum control over emotional energy.

Showing someone understanding for the situation they are in also removes part of their fear. Fear is often the underlying reason behind whatever negative emotion is being felt or expressed. When we are emotional, everything appears very different from how it actually is. Fear is one of the emotions that obscures reality and causes the greatest delusions. Whenever fear is present, everything that we are going through is magnified and minute problems can feel like overwhelmingly powerful avalanches. Fear is a necessary tool as it alerts us to danger. However, much of what we are fearful of has nothing to do with real danger, it has to do with perception and paranoia. Therefore, a lot of the fear we feel is pointless and serves to hinder rather than benefit us.

When we work on our dysfunctional relationship with fear we will start to see that fear rises constantly where it is not needed. We can even get into a bad habit with fear and allow it to linger around everything we do as we become more familiar with its presence. Removing unnecessary fear allows us to see that that our difficulties are nowhere near as bad as we are imagining them to be. We will also start to see things with clarity and work around problems rather than denying, hiding or running away from them.

Fear is one of the most debilitating emotions and is the root cause of many of our other negative emotions. When we disable fear and are able to rationalize if whether what is in front of us is a genuine or an imagined threat, we immediately raise our frequency. Therefore, we are able to transmute energy more effectively. Fear is the biggest contributor to negativity, and as it feels like a primal and instinctive emotion, we place our trust in it far more than we should. It is vital to befriend fear and fully understand it so that we can easily transmute our own or other people's dark, dense energy. This whole process can be extremely exhausting for empaths.

Negative external stimuli can be detrimental to our wellbeing, so it is crucial that we take care of ourselves by remaining grounded and protecting our energy. We must look after ourselves first and foremost before we can try to take care of anyone else. This allows us a sacred space to transmute our energy so that it transforms to positive, and also so we can fully reenergize and replenish our reserves. If we are constantly recharging ourselves with abundant universal energy, we can make full use of this special gift we all possess and do what we do best: radiate healing energy.

When we are vibrating on a high frequency and we are expressing unconditional love, compassion, and healing energy, we automatically transmute energy without being consciously aware of it. Whenever we express any heartfelt emotions, our vibration is high and powerful enough to naturally transmute any negative energy into positive. How we react to emotions and how capable we are of transmuting them ultimately depend on our belief system and how we are feeling at the time. If we are overwhelmed by emotions or if we are not processing our emotions effectively, we may find it extremely difficult to then take on external emotions so that we can transmute them.

Whenever we are triggered by other people's emotions we can use the opportunity to look at the similarities and connections to our own emotions and feelings and why certain ones are felt more intensely. By becoming aware of any inner negativity we have been harboring, we can release our suppressed emotions and clear the way so that our energy flows freely and is then able to reenergize and heal others. When someone is projecting emotional energy toward us, it is essential to remember that the emotions do not belong to us and we do not need to absorb them or hold on to them as though they are our own. We also need to be aware of the emotional energy that is already lingering so we know exactly what is swirling around in our aura. We can then separate and work through what belongs to us and what other people are responsible for.

If there is negativity surrounding us, our unconscious initial response might be one of fear because we may not understand where it has come from or who has sent it. For this reason we can try to always be aware of what energy we are adding to the mix as it can make the incoming negative energy feel extra toxic and far more powerful than it actually is. We can spend a few moments clearing our own energy and breathing deeply while calming our energy field before setting to work on any external energy. Even though we can transmute all the energy from negative to positive, it is essential that we take ownership for our own emotions first so that we can acknowledge them and find the reason for their existence. Mindful awareness is all that is needed. When we have a sound understanding of our emotions, we can find their root cause and prevent old patterns from repeating.

We may also find that when we try to reroute our old ways of behaving we will come up against inner resistance. As long as we are aware that this is our natural defense mechanism kicking in as it is fearful of the unknown, we can override it and continue carving out new neural pathways. Otherwise, the resistance we feel may tempt us to step back and be afraid of change and continue going around in circles, responding and reacting in ways that feel familiar. The resistance we feel can be a positive occurrence, and when we overcome it we are making great leaps toward moving past old routines and making significant internal transformation. Whenever someone is trying to pull us into an argument and we feel an impulse to respond, we can practice transmuting the energy instead. Although this technique isn't always easy when we are not used to transmuting, it soon becomes a natural way to avoid reacting and responding. Transmuting will help to keep us feeling calm and pacified, ensuring the surrounding energy does not feel as tense. Even if our raised vibration doesn't visibly alter and positively affect the other person, it will still have neutralized some of the toxic entities in the energy and will have soothed and rebalanced our own energy levels.

When we clearly differentiate between our own emotions and other people's we gain a higher awareness so that we are prepared for the emotions that radiate from external sources. Regardless of whether emotions belong to us or not, we can still transmute them in exactly the same way. Although we can choose to deflect low vibrational emotions that do not belong to us, especially if our aura is well protected, when we transmute energy instead we effectively prevent dark forces from floating around and affecting other people. This is an important and essential reason for our higher purpose here on earth.

Keeping our energy field clear and free from negative emotions means we will be far less likely to attract and absorb more of the same. Like attracts like, and if we are experiencing negative emotions, we are far more likely to attract negativity. When we initially clear our energy field it is often an arduous task, although once it is done we will then easily be able to detect when we are responsible for generating negative emotions or when the emotions have come from an external source. If we are surrounded by people who are radiating negative energy and we are not vibrating on a high frequency we can quickly become exhausted. This can make it more difficult to transmute negative energy to a positive vibration.

Certain people's company can cause us to feel exhausted and overwhelmed, and it can feel as though we are endlessly transmuting. This is particularly debilitating for peacekeepers, as their aim is to neutralize, calm, and alter the energy around them so that the surrounding atmosphere is vibrating with positivity. Often, caregivers naturally and instinctively consume and absorb the emotional energy of a distressed baby. We see this clearly when we see how a mother or father might react when their baby screams or cries. When they pick the baby up to rock and soothe it in their arms, the baby calms down and becomes peaceful and contented. The parents have transmuted emotional energy and at the same time altered the behavior of the baby. If someone is not able to transmute energy easily, instead of being at ease while soothing the baby, they may engage with the vibration of the baby's emotion and grow tense and upset themselves. It then becomes far more challenging to regain harmony and peace.

Sometimes it takes a moment for the parent to calm down after the initial screaming has been heard. Then, as the parent expresses pure, loving emotions void of any tension, the energy begins to transmute. It is then clear to see both the parent and the baby calmer and more settled as the transmuted energy affects and transforms them both.

Transmuting will not always work as sometimes babies cry for reasons other than emotional ones, though it is a good example to ponder to see how we can instantly affect the emotions of those around us. Many animals transmute energy as they radiate unconditional love and are nonjudgmental, so their vibrations are able to positively affect our own. This is why empaths spend a lot of time around animals or why many of us have pets, as their energy is on a high frequency as it encompasses high vibrational emotions.

Recent research carried out at the Institute of HeartMath supports this theory, with findings showing that a mother's brainwaves can synchronize to her baby's heartbeat when they are in close contact. A mother can become more sensitive to the subtle information that is radiated from the electromagnetic vibrations of her child, which scientifically proves there is an exchange of energy from one human to the other. One of the aims that have risen from the findings of the study is to observe how this works on a mass-scale, to help shift global consciousness and create a more peaceful, harmonious heart-centered world.

When we constantly transmute energy, especially if we are in a relationship or around a friend, family member, or colleague whose energy is negative and very low, we need to be careful that we do not take on their emotions during the interaction. If our vibration is also on a low level, we will likely automatically absorb their emotions and experience them as though they are our own. Many people choose to block or guard themselves from emotional energy as it can be a full-time job keeping on top of vibrations, especially low ones, as they can quickly overwhelm and consume us. When we are surrounded with people who radiate positivity, not only will we feel less exhausted and not feel the need to protect ourselves so vigilantly, but we also have someone on hand to transmute our energy in times when negativity radiates from us. We are all triggered at times; therefore, we will all release a certain amount of negative emotional energy. This is why unconditional love and understanding are vital to ensure that we accept one another and lift each other's vibrations whenever they fall.

We are ultimately responsible for our own emotions and for keeping ourselves balanced so that our energy is harmonious. However, due to past conditioning, learned behavior, painful memories and experiences, negative emotions will emanate from us all at times. Even though we may be aware that we are expressing a negative emotion, having people around us to channel our energy when our emotions catch us off guard is a safety net for the times we that support.

Many empaths choose art as their vessel for transmuting energy. We find that we can unearth repressed or painful emotions and find a new place for them through creativity, where we can alter their vibration by attaching understanding and meaning. Music is also a way of transmuting energy, and this is why particular melodies are chosen to accompany meditation, reiki, and other healing practices. We can do visualizations and repeat mantras to assist with transmuting, although overall all it takes is for us to open up our minds so that we understand and accept one another and our consciousness will instantly shine a light on the energy and transform it.

Unconditional love generates from a profound understanding of ourselves and other people without fear or any other negative emotions being attached. If we all loved and accepted one another unconditionally and also knew how to transmute energy, the world would quickly become a very different place.

When we exist in our heart center and consciously transmute energy, we will not only notice an immediate difference in how we feel, we will also notice a vibrational change in those around us. The energy will radiate to create a peaceful and uplifting environment.

We are transmitters with invisible antennae and we are not just able to process emotions for those around us. We can process and transmute energy on any scale and at any distance. Our energy radiates powerfully, and along with anyone else who transmutes, we can collectively send out vibrations that create far-reaching transformational energetic changes. If we all transmuted, with time, the whole world could achieve harmony and be healed.

Chapter 7

RAISING OUR VIBRATION

"If you want to find the *secrets of the Universe*, think in terms of energy, frequency and vibration." ——scientist Dr. Nikola Tesla, 1942

The main contributors to our personal vibration are our thoughts, feelings, attitudes, emotions, intentions, motivations and overall beliefs. When any of these things change, our vibration instantly changes. All we need to do is consciously alter our intentions and our vibration adjusts to match the frequency. We have total control over how high or how low our vibration is.

Low vibrations disempower us. High vibrations empower us. When our vibration is low, there is a reason for it. If we are caught up in negativity, feeling anxious, resentful, bitter, envious, frustrated, angry, or stressed, our bodies and minds are exhausting themselves as they are storing up so much tension through blocked energy that it begins to slow us down. When we are slower, we are lower. Our body responds as our shoulders slump, we feel tense and heavy like a lead weight and as though we are trapped and our speech and movements are sluggish. We have limited energy flowing around us as a lot of it is dense and is congested so the burden weighs us down. Therefore, our vibration is slower and also lower.

Lower vibrations starting from the lowest moving up to the middle of the scale; fear, unworthiness, powerlessness, grief, despair, stagnation, self-hatred, insecurity, depression, shame, craving, guilt, rage, jealousy, resentment, hate, anger revenge, discouraged, greed, doubt, boredom, frustration, overwhelmed, irritation, impatience, pessimistic, boredom, apathy.

Higher vibrations starting from the middle of the scale and moving to the top to the highest vibration; peace, calm, contentment, motivated, dedication, hopeful, confident, happy, enthusiastic, fun, empowered, generous, contentment, eagerness, belief, optimism, engaged, abundance, passion, freedom, joy, love, appreciation, gratitude.

When our vibration is high, we are optimistic, healthy, aware, positive, inspired, compassionate, appreciative, loving, and understanding. Our body and mind are relaxed and light, as we are not holding tension due to a built-up of energy. The energy we absorb flows freely, so our body and mind also feel fine, light and free. Our breathing is full, so we are reenergized and revitalized. Our vibration is fast as there is nothing slowing or blocking its speed, so it is able to vibrate on a high frequency. Jad Alexander explains this theory as being relative to gravity. External and internal gravity equally affect us. External gravity influences the external body by aging it and keeping it grounded to earth, and internal gravity impacts the internal body by pulling down our thoughts and feelings to lower levels. If we are not aware of how inner gravity works, it can dominate us, making us feel less motivated, disinterested, and even pessimistic.

Alexander believes that as empaths we are intrigued by how inner gravity affects other people's thoughts, emotions, and feelings. As Alexander explains, our physical strength represents our relationship to external gravity. Our inner strength represents our relationship to internal gravity. When we are aware that gravity is powerful, we can ensure that it does not dominate us and instead we can master it simply by practicing self-control, will power and determination. Alexander describes this as putting EFFORT into our level of consciousness, and by doing so we can then maximize and have control over all of our empath capabilities.

Alexander also explains how "Absence of EFFORT is at the root of almost every problem, challenge or difficulty." The reason the word *effort* was capitalized by Alexander was to put emphasis on the meaning of it as it refers to the psychological energy we deal with when mastering gravity.

Throughout this human existence we will be forced to engage in battles between low/negative and high/positive vibrations. These battles are not the enemy, they are an internal personal war and they fight on such a shaded, shallow level that we may not know how to handle them or we may not even be aware that they exist. They arrive unexpectedly to test, challenge, and to ultimately make us aware of our hidden, denied, and rejected emotions and feelings, and also so that we can see how far we have traveled and how far we have yet to go. In every new round that we enter, fuelled with negative energy, our low vibrations will be watching carefully to see how much we can take and if we are going to give up and give in. Believe it or not, these low vibrations aren't there to break us. They are there to strengthen us, even though at the time we may not see it that way. They are alerting us to all of the ancient or even recent wounds we have stored and every small energetic cut or tear that needs our attention. Yes, we will regularly feel temporarily weakened by their attack, but if we keep ourselves nourished by relentlessly giving ourselves understanding, forgiveness, compassion, and unconditional love, the pain and injuries won't remain. Instead, we will shake them off, heal and bounce firmly back, emerging strengthened, sturdier, and more empowered than ever before.

All vibrations can be controlled by our mind, and even though the battles are vivid and real, they are not to be feared. Instead they can be welcomed and embraced. If we open our arms to the low vibrations we will see that they can become a loyal ally and one of the most significant teachers we will ever communicate with. Even if we eventually give in to the lowest and hardest hitting vibrations and allow them to win a round, they still won't let us rest. They won't see it as "winning," as our unique personal evolution will never be complete and they are an integral part of it. They will constantly reemerge, but in a slightly different form, to make us aware that we still have work to do. They will cause so much inner noise and unrest within that we will eventually have no option but to take notice.

As hard as it may be to accept, at times our low, negative, murky, dense, and heavy vibrations might pull us down low but they do not want to defeat us and they are not more powerful than our mind. Our mind has absolute control, and with positive, loving high vibrations on its side it can smooth the turbulence at any moment. Our darkness just wants to be unearthed and acknowledged. It wants freedom to pass and it wants peace. It doesn't want to be locked down and hidden or to be called hideous and made to feel unwelcome. It is searching for balance and harmony. When it shows up we have to love it and accept it as an inherent part of who we are. It is the only way.

Until we make the decision to hold hands with every part of ourselves, we will always be looking over our shoulder. We will always be in fear of every emotion and feeling we have hidden so very well within. It isn't difficult, although, it is painful. But once we see that pain is also a part of our experience, we will find the courage to stand beneath the glaring sun and rip our skin wide open so that everything that we once tried to deny will feel the brilliant rays from the sun. We are not vaults that are meant to hold the weight of years of emotional debris. We are energetic beings and everything needs to be free to flow through us and out. This is the only way to a higher vibration. To cut loose everything that has been holding us down.

We can get so caught up in daily life that we fail to notice when our vibration is significantly freefalling out of our control. Part of the reason is that we sometimes live through other people's eyes and choose paths that they prefer us to walk along. We make decisions that aren't true to who we inherently are and ultimately we become someone we barely recognize. This isn't always noticeable, and it isn't until we are forced to slow down due to our bodies and minds being overwhelmed that we are compelled to take notice.

"For what it's worth: it's never too late or, in my case, too early to be whoever you want to be. There's no time limit, stop whenever you want. You can change or stay the same—there are no rules to this thing. We can make the best or the worst of it. I hope you make the best of it. And I hope you see things that startle you. I hope you feel things you never felt before. I hope you meet people with a different point of view. I hope you live a life you're proud of. If you find that you're not, I hope you have the courage to start all over again." ——Eric Roth, *The Curious Case of Benjamin Button* screenplay

Instead of being true to ourselves, we may form codependent attachments and lose ourselves in relationships, in our family, our friends, and in our work. Rather than living a life that suits us we become a chameleon, constantly changing direction to suit each environment and desperately trying to sit on each high pedestal that others set out for us. We compare ourselves, compromise ourselves, and blend in time and again. We frantically search for answers to unlock the secret to our deep-seated unhappiness, and in doing so we can accuse, blame, demand, and find responses in all the wrong places. We have to stop and turn things back on ourselves. We have choices. Everything that is in front of us is there because we have chosen at some level to put it there. Until we take control of our own life and own it so that we are accountable for all of our thoughts, emotions, feelings, beliefs, decisions, and ultimately, lifestyle, we will be unable to find peace, as we will constantly reflect everything outward. We then wrongly believe that other people are responsible for our happiness or unhappiness as we align so much of our lives with other people's desires instead of existing in beat with our own natural rhythm.

How can we expect anyone else to value us when we are confused and conflicted and a mixture of everyone we allow to influence us, along with all the negative self-beliefs we have somehow inflicted upon ourselves? Our insides will ache with under-nourishment, and the reason is because we are not living the life that is destined solely for us. We will not be aware of our soul's purpose as we have focused our attention on everyone else. We will then feel disappointed and disillusioned when other people do not provide us with the key to optimum joy and happiness. The only route to inner harmony is through ourselves, not through other people or even other things.

Although we can change our vibration in a moment, when we change our consciousness we also have to deal with the reasons our vibration was low in the first place. We may find we have a lot of life changes to make so that our unique vibration is radiating on a high frequency. To implement permanent change, we need to figure out what is important to us and what gains us inner peace and contentment. We can try not to expect miracles overnight. It has taken us a long time to build everything that is around us and become who we are, so restructuring will be a process.

We can begin by asking ourselves if the place we are at now is the same place we want to be in five, ten, or twenty years' time. If it isn't, we need to look at the direction we are heading in and why. We can look at our lifestyle, relationships, friendships, hobbies, career, the area we live in, our diet, health, and our education. We can also think about the places we want to visit and all the things we want to experience. Although some of the changes we make will not be possible to put into place immediately, there are many things we can work on one small step at a time. We can enroll in courses, change our eating habits, find new hobbies, read the books we have been meaning to read, and focus more on cultivating meaningful, soul-nourishing relationships. Rather than setting a destination for an outcome, we can instead set a feeling. How do we want to feel on the *inside*? How do we want to feel emotionally, physically, and mentally? We can set the intention and keep it in our mind at all times.

Nothing is out of reach, and it is up to us to take control of our lives and realize that, within rational reason, anything is possible. If we don't add too much pressure by expecting instant gratification for the changes, we can allow everything to take a natural pace so it all absorbs and sinks in.

We can make a list of all the bad habits or patterns of behavior we want to eliminate, and instead of expecting overnight success we can work on them one by one. Instead of excusing, blaming, or shaming ourselves for our behavior or the mistakes we make, we can take full responsibility for them and accept that at each moment we were doing our best with whatever internal or external resources we have at this time. We can keep our mind optimistic so that we turn every negative into a positive.

Every time we mess up, we can confront it face on. Why, what and how have these things happened? We are likely stumbling over the same problems over and over again and we will keep coming face to face with them until we recognize where we are going wrong. Whenever we make errors, bad judgments, or we are careless with our emotions, we can think about what part we play in allowing these things to happen. When we live in the present moment, we are far less likely to keep tripping up. We will always, always make mistakes, regardless of how much we learn or how hard we try, so we can forgive ourselves each time and vow to do things differently in the future. We can also look at what stories we have been telling ourselves. So much of our belief system is based on poor conditioning or absorbing disempowering information because it feels familiar. We end up believing or convincing ourselves that we are not worthy of the things we want or that we are not capable of achieving the things we dream of. When we have little faith in ourselves, we attract all kinds of wrong relationships and dysfunctional situations to our lives.

We have to immediately make a conscious decision to stop filling our heads with negativity about our self. We are unique, magnificent, different, significant, enough, and absolutely worthy of the very best life has to offer. We just need to keep repeating these things and ultimately believe in them until they finally sink in. Practicing heartfelt gratitude allows us to put things into perspective so that we can see what we already have and take time to fully and genuinely appreciate it all so that instead of seeing what we don't have we can see how fortunate we are. Gratitude is not just about saying thank you and showing it through expression in exchange for something we receive. It is about living and breathing it in every waking minute, with a heart that is cracked wide open over spilling with love.

We have so much to be grateful for. What we receive from nature, our physical bodies, other people, the world, and beyond.

We have water, air, our senses, food, shelter, everything we need to survive and more. We are receiving every moment without realizing that something or someone has provided and given us more than we need. That is why it is essential that we pay attention to the fine details around us and show appreciation as it all ensures it is possible for us to exist and thrive.

When we are infinitely grateful we are happier, we express loving kindness, we have more vital life energy, we appreciate everything on a deeper level, and overall, the way we see, think, and feel about everything is transformed. We can then shift from the limitations of fear and embrace and open to infinite love. When we show gratitude for our lives we immediately lift our vibration. We are alive and we exist on a planet spinning through the universe alongside over 7 billion other people . It is a unique, miraculous existence. Each moment that we are alive is a blessing and every moment is one that we will never get back.

When we notice that there is an immeasurable amount that we can show gratitude for, we not only pay attention to how much we already have, but we put faith in the universe that it will deliver and take care of us now and in the future. Although it isn't always easy, this mindset is especially beneficial if we go through turbulent or difficult times. As soon as we unlearn all of the limiting nonsense we have absorbed and relearn how exquisite and magical we are, we can attract more than we could possibly dream of. Our souls are a mirror to the Universe, and whatever is going on in the inside radiates out and attracts similar reflections. The more love and acceptance we give ourselves, the more love we will receive back—like attracts like.

When we think about our lives in general and of those around us, we can focus on what want to create rather than waste energy thinking about what we don't want in our lives. We can also try to view our experiences without negative emotions attached to them as they distort our thinking and accumulate more tension that then resides in our energetic body. When we think negatively, we inadvertently magnetize negativity, and then unfortunately we end up drawing it toward us. It is imperative to keep the focus on positive energy and generate and radiate as much as we can muster, rather than wallowing in negativity that is heavy, murky, and that weighs us down.

We can begin to think long and hard about those who we love and those who love us. Do we regularly let them know how much they mean to us? Are we making them a priority in our lives? How can we spend more quality time with them to show them how valued and significant they are? We can make a conscious decision to appreciate each person more and let them know with actions rather than just words.

Possibly one of the most powerful questions we can ask ourselves is "If no one judged me, who would I be?" It can make us think about whether we are living our truth or living according to other people's expectations. So much of what we say and do on a daily basis is to fit in line with high standards placed on us, often by people we don't even know. Our lives are limitless. We can be whoever we want to be and do whatever we choose to. Those that truly love us will accept us all the same. To live free from being affected by judgment, we also have to stop negatively judging ourselves. We need to stop caring about what other people think about us and start caring about what we think about ourselves. We must think long and hard about what we need to do so that we are fulfilled, truly happy and at peace on the inside.

When we visit places, we can stop caring if people like how we dress, what we say, or about whether they value our opinions. All of these things bring an element of fear as we worry far too much about what other people think, and we will likely feel anxious about going places and meeting new people. We are all different and we are never going to be accepted by everyone. There will always be someone somewhere who will disapprove regardless how hard we try. We can stop trying to please the masses and instead work on pleasing the person that matters—ourselves.

When we begin to let go of all that we think we are, we have taken the first major step toward a higher vibration. We also need to remember to leave behind all the old emotional weight we have been unnecessarily carrying on our shoulders. When we do this, we open ourselves up to being authentically who we are. We cannot be who we are meant to be in this very moment if we are allowing ourselves to be consumed by the past or by other people's hopes and intentions for us. Learning to be our inherent selves and loving who we are is not always easy. However, it is the only way we can be fully energized, healthy, nourished, productive, and thriving on a high frequency.

When we meditate or remain fully present, our mind slows down and we are able to reduce repetitive and critical thinking. We can then take control of our thoughts and let go of ones that are unnecessary, causing us harm, or driving us crazy. We can pay attention to the loving background thoughts that are trying to make themselves heard. We can acknowledge these thoughts to see where they are coming from so we can understand them, show them compassion, and then let them go. We can stop judging ourselves so harshly or thinking badly about ourselves and instead replace those thoughts with positive, loving, and nourishing ones.

If we cease to judge not only ourselves but others too, we also take control of our actions and reactions. Living in the moment shatters illusions, and we can begin to get to know ourselves and other people through new eyes for the very first time. When we stop allowing our ego to influence us and instead just allow ourselves to be, we soon discover a much more realistic vision of who we are. This allows us to naturally see ourselves as well as everyone and everything else, exactly how they are rather than whatever image we are projecting .

It is not easy to remain in the present moment, and it is tempting to flip from past to present to future and back again. At times of stress or difficulties, it becomes even harder. However, these are the times we most need to remain present. By giving our mind a gentle jolt, we can very easily snap back to the current moment, where we will instantly find a release in anxiety or tension and an increase in calm and clarity.

One thing that we cannot change is the mindset of those around us. It can be frustrating and upsetting to see how others negatively judge us, especially those closest to us. This is something that we have no control over and we must remember that they too have their individual life experiences, conditioning, and unique thinking. All we can do is try to be the truest version of ourselves possible. By staying present and mindful, our inner selves will glow and radiate outward. As soon as we master this and see ourselves through a new, clear, and accepting light, other people's opinions and judgments will fade. As long as we believe in ourselves and trust that we are living with integrity and as morally and ethically as we can, other people can have the freedom to think whatever they want. To let go of the fear of being judged is liberating, refreshing, and one of the most loving things we can do for ourselves. We won't just feel different, we become different. We become ourselves. Our vibration will lift, as all that is needed for a high vibration is unconditional love, understanding, forgiveness, compassion, acceptance, and gratitude. And when we do all of these things for ourselves we automatically offer these things to other people. We will naturally vibrate with ease on a far higher frequency.

Focusing on our breathing is a simple way to raise our vibration. *Pra* translates to *first*, *na* translates to *vibration*, and *yama* translates to *breath*. We can do a simple *pranayama* exercise by inhaling deeply and slowly through the nostrils and then exhaling quickly through the nostrils. When we repeat this we are able to reenergize and replenish our inner system, flushing it through with *prana*, which is vital life force energy.

The most amazing thing about each moment is that we can change everything, as we know it, in an instant. We can do this simply by changing our mindset and altering the way we think. Everything is perception, and when we perceive ourselves to be floating through space, grounded to a planet that offers us everything we need to be nourished and function well, we can open our eyes, minds, and hearts wide so that we can clearly see how much we have to be grateful for. Even if we think life is not going well right now, we must remember that we only ever limit ourselves when we have limited our mind. As soon as we change how we see our circumstances, we free ourselves from all the pessimistic thoughts that are binding us. When we become aware of everything that is around us and everything that we are absorbing, we can reduce our negative intake and output and increase our positive intake and output.

Social media, television, newspapers, images, people, places, and the type of communication we involve ourselves in can all have an instant impact on our vibration. Everything has a frequency, and if the frequency has a low vibration we are at risk of it penetrating us and interfering with our vibration. When we change our scenery, change what we read, who we are interacting with, and how we act and react, we immediately change the possibility of being influenced and altered by any of these things and more.

Spending time outdoors with nature; eating high vibrational, healthy, nutritious, nourishing fresh food (food carries its own vibration); and drinking plenty of water, all dramatically affect how highly we vibrate. It really is true that we are what we eat. We need to ruel and energize our body by peacefully, respectfully and mindfully eating and drinking. There is a circle of energy and everything is interconnected. So when we feel hungry our vibration will automatically lower. Therefore, we can try to keep our bodies energized with healthy, clean, organic, locally sourced, ethical produce. The further our food has to travel, the lower its vibration is. We can also prepare and consume food slowly and peacefully. Whenever we honor and express gratitude for our food, we raise its vibration, as our thoughts are a powerful force for transmuting energetic vibrations. When we eat low vibrational food—for example, processed, factory farmed, canned, frozen or pesticide laced food and most meats and milk—we will feel sluggish, heavy, and our vibration will be dense and on a lower frequency. High vibrational food—for example, fresh fruits and vegetables, organic produce, raw nuts and seeds, raw honey, legumes, probiotic-rich fermented foods—and drinking plenty of filtered water, will keep us feeling highly energetic, our minds clear, in sync with the rest of the world, and overall we will feel lighter and with an abundance of positive energy.

Being kind, generous, grateful and considerate also raises our vibration. Whenever we show heartfelt loving kindness to ourselves or anyone else, our brain releases dopamine, which is a feel-good hormone that can lift us to a higher frequency.

"Make a gift of your life and lift all mankind by being kind, considerate, forgiving, and compassionate at all times, in all places, and under all conditions, with everyone as well as yourself. This is the greatest gift anyone can give." ——Dr. David R. Hawkins, author of *Power Vs Force*

To raise our vibration we can do a simple exercise at any time of the day or night. Spending between five to ten minutes with our eyes closed and our body relaxed, we can imagine a violet light flowing through and around us. Focusing on the light while deeply inhaling and exhaling, we can visualize the violet rays powerfully radiating from our physical body and out into the universe. We can do this practice at any time of the day or night, whether standing, sitting, or lying down. Any time our energy is low, we can take a few minutes out to relax and reenergize our body and mind.

Visualizing the color violet in the form of a violet flame, which is associated with Saint Germain, significantly pulls our vibration up to a much higher frequency. The color violet has the highest frequency of all seven colors on the visual spectrum and it cleanses the system of our toxic emotional, mental, spiritual, and physical blockages. We vibrate on different frequencies depending on our current mental, emotional, spiritual, and physical states. Our vibrations send out colors, which are seen in the form of an aura.

By infusing the violet light that emanates from the flame into all our thoughts, feelings, actions, and belief system, we can transmute any negativity into vital, abundant, positive energy that vibrates highly, while also removing blockages so that it flows freely. A violet flame is a visual fire that radiates a brilliant, warm, harmonious, loving, light, high vibrational healing energy that radiates out into the universe transmuting dense, dull, unresolved dark low vibrational energy. The violet glow is an accepting, compassionate, forgiving, and highly intelligent hue that is transformational as it provides us with a powerful and unique spiritual energy that enhances all aspects of our lives.

In every moment we have the opportunity to awaken and reclaim our personal power. There is nothing the world needs more than for people to discover how to reconnect to themselves and to live and breathe the life they were meant for. When we attune internally and externally to the subtle sensations within energy, we will awaken our inherent self so that we can tap into our soul's purpose and create the life we have, up until now, only been dreaming of.

Visualizing the flame helps us to heal old wounds, clear karmic energy of past mistakes, erase tormenting memories, and frees us from the heavy emotional load we are carrying. When we vibrate aligned with this glowing light, there are no judgments cast out to others and no resentments for any ways of life that do not align with our own. Our minds are fully open so that we see beyond what lies immediately in front of us. This enables us to view all sides of the sphere rather than having a limited, partially blocked view. Within ourselves and also our relationships we are able to find a balance between darkness and light as we are not afraid to explore and accept what may exist on either side. We also become very aware that as human beings we are often afraid to expose to one another the truth of who we really are.

When we connect with others who are also vibrating highly we can open up to them and connect mind to mind and heart core to heart core, and this dynamic will be one with no condemnation or judgment from either part. This means we are privy to the blessing of divine unconditional love, which opens us to the truest form of love, as we embrace the reality, instead of the illusions when we have interacted with only certain aspects of people..

A violet light emanates the purest, highest form of love we can experience. The reason for this is that we all make errors and we all have flaws, and when we vibrate on a high frequency everyone is loved and accepted equally. Love will be given and received in abundance as a free-flowing energy. It is not a limited force—it is limitless, endless. The more love that is produced, the higher our vibration will be as the momentum of love vibrates very quickly, and is expansive and grows stronger.

When two people radiate a violet flame and they meet, they will engage in an intense, magnetizing, and indestructible relationship. They will likely share a similar cosmic or energetic blueprint as one another. They are vibrating on the same frequency and their unique energetic spiritual signatures are spinning at a similar speed so their energy fields are magnetized towards one another.

Although the violet flame may feel natural, familiar and comfortable at times, it can also cause friction as we are constantly pushed to become the highest version of ourselves possible so that we reach our soul's true purpose. The light glows so brightly it will feel like we are looking through a vividly clear mirror and we may not always like what is being reflected back—however we will still be compelled to look. The reflection may show us parts of ourselves we may not be ready to embrace. We may question if we are able to deal with existing on a high vibration, as it causes us internal conflict and unrest as we deconstruct all of our old beliefs and prior ways of critical thinking. This is where the violet light comes into play. We can visualize turning up the flame of the violet light so that it glows brilliantly and helps us reach a place of self-love, self-acceptance, and achieve a higher sense of self-worth.

Whenever we begin to feel discord within the relationship and as though our energies are repelling one another we can reconnect to one another's heart centre and open our heart chakra wide so the energy can once again flow freely. When we have a profound understanding for the significant differences in one another we will celebrate them and appreciate that we can maintain a strong connection without having to always be in agreeance. When we are able to accept ourselves and our partner exactly as they are we will find total acceptance for those around us too. We will work through our flaws while having high levels of integrity, being accountable for our errors, encouraging and supporting one another regardless of whether we think and feel the same way about particular matters, and through it all radiating pure divine love.

The love that will be radiated is for the whole of humanity, the world we live in, for one another and ultimately for ourselves. The violet flame that is emanating a strong light pulsates and transforms our energy levels so that we vibrate highly. If one person's vibration level falls, the other's vibration will lift it and vice versa.

Igniting our violet flame is the greatest opportunity we will be given to develop personal growth. This being said, the flame does not glow purely for a personal benefit. Our high vibration will lift us to work towards our divine purpose, a selfless one, to be of service to others and transmute negative energies. We will beam a pure and radiant light out to the world. We can show those around us unconditional love as we selflessly let go of resentments through learning to understand, acceptance, and forgiveness.

Whether the mission is to help to create a more sustainable world to live in, to reduce suffering of living creatures, or to live as an example of soul growth, the message will be one that is necessary for the evolution of human beings on a mass scale. Even if it seems that individually we cannot make a huge difference, we can remind ourselves of the butterfly effect. Individually we can make a difference and collectively we can change the world. All that it takes is for our energetic vibrations to heighten. Once our flame is glowing we can carve a unique path by burning through all negativity. By setting aside a small amount of time each day, even if it is just for five minutes, we can change our frequency to connect with the violet flame.

Our voice helps to alter the frequency we are on, so we can choose a mantra to assist with manifesting the changes we seek. To invoke a violet flame, we can use a simple mantra such as "I welcome the violet light into my life." When we ask for a violet light, we must be willing to offer it all of our pent-up emotions such as frustration, anger, resentment, or anything else that is unresolved or has become blocked. By opening up our hearts and accepting the light, we can also surrender to it and flush away all impurities and toxins that have seeped into us.

We can repeat mantras as many times as we feel we need to and as often throughout the day as we choose. It is effective if mantras are spoken out loud (through the throat *chakra*) as our voices are powerful vibrational tools that are capable of changing our frequency and when we are chanting we are in a relaxed but alert state to absorb the high frequency transformational energy that is evoked.

Visualizations can help when repeating the mantra. If we close our eyes, we can imagine the pure violet ray of light burning from within and emanating from our body. We can visualize the flame burning through negativity so that we neutralize all remnants of anger or fear and replace them with ones of love and peace.

Initially it can be painful to uncover and revisit certain past memories, though if we imagine that we have sealed our aura with a healing white and blue protective shield we can prevent darkness from penetrating and influencing us and negatively affecting our light. We can use a mantra anytime we are feeling stressed or angry, or just allow it to become a ritual that takes place each morning before we begin the day. The more often a mantra is repeated, the more powerful and effective it will become.

It is our choice as to whether we spiral upward toward a high vibration or downward toward a lower one. As soon as we change our mindset, we instantly change the frequency we vibrate on.

Chapter 8

THOUGHTS

"What you think you become. What you feel you attract. What you imagine you create." ——Buddha

Although our thoughts are invisible, they are extremely powerful and radiate strong and far-reaching vibrations. It is believed that on average we have approximately 50,000 thoughts every day. Therefore, we have an incredible number of opportunities to make our thoughts count so that we can create seriously significant transformations in our lives. Although thoughts matter, we are never going to make the most of that many of them, so it becomes clear why it is necessary to slow the mind down with meditation and mindfulness so that we have quality thoughts rather than quantity.

Our thoughts are the vibrations responsible for creating every single thing that has been made in the world. Anything that is not in its natural form originated from a single thought. When we dwell on thoughts they can easily turn into emotions, which also vibrate strongly with energy. This energy expresses itself in words or actions. These words or actions can be repeated over and again until they eventually become a feeling, habit, or a belief. Our habitual patterns, feelings, and our belief system create our personality. So we are who we are and we behave how we do mostly due to the thoughts we think.

Thoughts, emotions, and feelings are extremely powerful forces. They vibrate in our electromagnetic field and connect with, attract, and repel other electromagnetic fields. We are similar to magnets and our energy pulls people or situations toward us or it pushes them away, depending on our vibration. As powerful as our thoughts, emotions, and feelings are, it is our belief system that ultimately reigns. We may think our thoughts, emotions, and feelings alone are powerful enough to attract similar energy toward us; however, unless our belief system is aligned to our thoughts, we will send out distorted and conflicting messages. It is not enough to simply voice or show through our actions what we want or what we *think* we feel—we have to fully *believe* in our words and actions in order to attract whatever we are thinking about or feeling.

We can think whatever thoughts we want to and our imagination can join in to help make our thoughts realistic and powerful enough so that we truly believe them, and also so we can feel them. When we believe we deserve what our thoughts, emotions, or feelings are requesting, we attract and receive a more accurate reflection of what we want, think, feel *and* believe. If our beliefs contradict our thoughts, emotions, or feelings, what we attract and repel will be very different from what we *think* we should be receiving.

We are able to create our own reality simply by changing our thoughts and then feeling and believing them. Our thoughts and feelings are powerful transmitters. We can want something with all of our heart, but if we don't put feeling and belief into what we want, it is unlikely that we will receive it. However, when we focus on our thoughts, believe in them, and then add meaning, they will naturally turn to feelings. When we focus on those feelings, believe in them, and then add meaning, they will ignite, be magnetic, and this charge will cause them to spin like a tornado and vibrate around us. We will radiate powerful signals that soar out to the universe with a message that says we are ready to receive. Our signal will then magnetize and interact with similar signals that are vibrating on the same frequency.

Our thoughts carry an electrical charge and our feelings carry a magnetic charge. We are attracting and repelling constantly without even realizing it. To alter what we attract and repel, we only have to alter our thoughts and become consciously aware of how we are feeling. At any moment we can choose to create an abundance of feelings that reflect the exact life we want and allow them to gain momentum so that they set a precedent for our future.

As our vibration lifts, we will be amazed by what we can achieve simply by retuning our internal signal. Not only will we be receiving what it is that we want, our thoughts and feelings will attract more of the same thoughts and feelings and we will be thinking and feeling more optimistically without having to try too hard—just simply by believing in ourselves!

To ensure we reach whatever it is we are aiming for, we must keep our vibration aligned to the vibration of whatever it is that we want. If we are seeking heightened levels of love, we must love ourselves and others enough so that our vibration is spinning accordingly. We can set the bar however high we want to and then simply attune our vibration so that it reaches a higher frequency. If we want to live in a peaceful, harmonious environment, we must maintain inner peace so that our vibration is sending out a signal on a similar frequency.

Energy is contagious. The more peace and happiness we radiate, the more it rebounds and provides us with limitless amounts of the same. Our vibration can lower at any moment, so it is our responsibility to keep our awareness on it and work hard to keep it from being forcefully gravitationally pulled down if we encounter negativity.

Energy can create a beautiful or disastrous cycle, and we can alter that cycle simply by remaining focused and regularly altering and attuning our thoughts so that we do not get entangled in patterns that could be harmful. If we have always been aware of how powerful our thought processes are, then we will have very likely learned how to master them. Therefore, our life will reflect how we have consciously chosen to live rather than our subconscious mind (autopilot) deciding for us. Although our subconscious can work in our favor, it will only do this if whatever exists there is an authentic reflection of how we feel currently. This means we need to keep our awareness on it and ensure it is healthy, clear, and not clouded with wounded historic remnants of our most painful experiences.

If we have not mastered our thoughts and we are not aware of what is contained in our subconscious, and we are relying on our subconscious to make our decisions and to attract our circumstances, we may be trapped in a circle of fear, pain, and frustration as the outside world can seem overwhelming and fraught with difficulties and disaster. The negativity from our surrounding environment can sneakily seep into our mind without us even realizing it. If we then think about any negativity, it grows in strength and our thoughts can solidly confirm to our mind that there is a requirement for concern. If the thoughts are repeated and absorbed into our subconscious mind, we may believe that we need to live in a constant state of fear and worry.

Even if we don't think about harmful external entities, we could still take in this information subliminally from our environment and it may then exist in our mind as irrational fears as we have not consciously assessed, rationalized and organized them. Underlying fear can manifest in our daily lives and can alter our feelings and decisions without us being consciously aware of it. If our subconscious or unconscious fears lead us to doubt that we can achieve what our conscious mind wants us to, we are more likely to fail at whatever we are aiming for. We must have absolute faith both consciously and subconsciously in order to manifest the things we wish for in our lives.

If we manifest with the right intention, the high vibrational positive energy involved will naturally provide synchronicities that make our wishes more fluid, and we will be rewarded with internal fulfillment and satisfaction. If our intention is negative, even when we want something that is positive, the negative and positive discordance will result in confusion and cause difficulties by placing obstacles in our way to prevent us from obtain whatever we desire, or from succeeding. For example, if we want wealth but we want it primarily for egotistical gains so that we can show off to those around us rather than wanting it for security and comfort, we may feel unsettled within and we will likely not fully appreciate the wealth or feel fulfilled or internally satisfied. The feelings we are radiating will be distorted by the negative vibrations that come into force when our ego is leading the way. Therefore, when we receive wealth we may also receive entities that are negative in nature and which prevent us from achieving inner peace and happiness.

Like attracts like. Frequencies are magnetic. Positive energy attracts positive energy and negative energy attracts negative energy. We attract and we repel. When we mix the two, friction occurs. If we think or feel in pessimistic low vibrational ways, our vibration will be pulled down. This is why we feel so low when our mind is flooded with critical, irrational, or unpleasant commentaries. The moment we switch to sincere, positive thoughts, our vibration lifts and we instantly feel better, more productive, and energetic.

Unfortunately, if we have been conditioned to believe that the world is a scary, dangerous place and we have been brought up feeling fearful, anxious, and nervous, the energy radiated by our thoughts, emotions, feelings, and beliefs will contain negative stimuli. Even if we try to tell ourselves on a conscious level that everything is okay, we need to totally believe that all is well and that we are capable of handling whatever comes our way, before we are able to vibrate energy that carries the same message.

If our conscious and subconscious minds are in conflict, with one part radiating positivity while the other radiates negativity, we will send out conflicting and confusing messages. It is impossible to reach the destination we *think* we have set our sights on when our energy is leading us in the opposite direction. It is vital that we pay attention to what we are attracting and what is currently in our lives so that we understand the direct correlation between our thoughts and our reality.

We often believe in our mind that our thoughts are pure and we have a clear vision of what it is we want. However, our thoughts are often infiltrated not just with what we want, but also with what other people want for us. Among this pool of thoughts are also the fears and desires of others that disturb and cloud the energy. As with the Law of Attraction, quite often, when we focus intently on something we then manifest it. If we focus on negative thoughts and terrible outcomes, it is likely that these things will materialize. However, if we focus on loving, abundant, nourishing thoughts, we are more likely to attract great things to our lives, quite simply by thinking, feeling, and then believing in the power of possibility.

When we are in a relationship and there are difficulties, we are often focusing too much on the past or the future and forgetting about the present moment. Now, the present moment, is the only time that we are ever able to experience authentic emotion. Looking forward or back in time will either conjure up false illusions or our selective memories will create delusional images instead of seeing or feeling a realistic vision that truly reflects what we once had or what we one day want. It is impossible to truly feel how things once were or to gain an accurate representation of how things will be, we will always be adding outdated or preconceived thoughts and intentions, so our conjured up thoughts can never be relied upon.

When we obsessively think too much about the future, we subconsciously plant seeds that grow into our future. Our future will then be based on what we wanted in a previous moment and not on what is right for us when the future finally arrives. Our future will arrive naturally and organically and not when it is forced to develop in ways that suited an out-of-date longing. While we can lightly project our minds toward what we hope to achieve, without adding unrealistic expectation, our thoughts will carry the energy of how we want to *feel* in the future rather than generating an abundance of tormenting worrying thoughts or ones that are infused with materialistic or superficial desires.

When we think too much about the past, we become trapped in it and we inadvertently miss out on the present. This causes us to procrastinate, which then delays or prevents us from reaching our future goals.

The most vital way we can assure our future is one that will be rewarding: is to emanate loving, warm, and optimistic vibrations that are free from attachment and then bask in them. We can get to know that feeling and set it as the precedent for how we want to continuously feel, however, we can just leave it open to be altered constantly as our thoughts, feelings and beliefs change. Of course, our vibration will regularly lower when occurrences test our resilience. Fortunately, though, our feelings are similar to memory foam. Cell patterns repeat continuously based on how we feel in each current moment. The higher number of cells we have vibrating on a high frequency, the easier they will bound straight back onto that frequency whenever an entity that has lowered it has passed. Every moment we are changing and to advance and grow we can allow our mind to freely evolve and accustom to the changes too.

It is extremely important that we do not allow our thoughts to threaten our present or our future, or distort our past. We can focus on surrendering wholly and marinate within each moment we are given. When our thoughts are in the here and now and we engage in the present moment, we achieve so much more and the benefits for our own wellbeing and also for our relationships are endless. We fully connect with the reality of life rather than perceiving an unrealistic version of how things were, should, or could be.

Living in the present moment takes a little practice and there will be many times when our mind skips forward or back. When this happens, we just need to remind ourselves to let go of the thoughts that aimlessly spin so we can fully relax in the feeling of now. We miss out on so much by not being aware of what is happening currently. Often we are so busy multitasking and juggling life's many demands that we fail to notice the really important things that are happening within and in around us. Our mind can become so full of nonsense that we find it hard to process our simplest and most significant thoughts and feelings, and this can cause life to pass us by without having a great deal of meaning to it.

The only thing that is accessible is what is happening now and it is the only thing that we have control over. The past has gone, the future is not yet here, so we can make the most of what we have here in this very moment. We can't live in the past or the future, so it is pointless allowing our thoughts to live there.

Simply by becoming consciously aware of the thoughts that are running through our mind is the easiest way to achieve being present. As we take notice of our thoughts, we can begin to discard any negative ones that aren't connected to the present so we can focus on how it feels to be fully present.

When we continuously press repeat on negative thoughts or feelings from the past or the future, we recreate fearful, tormenting, and destructive scenarios, when instead we can concentrate on what is happening now, as this is the period that is important. We can lose so much of life's experiences simply by not keeping our minds focused on the present moment. When we recognize our thoughts jumping back to the past or out into the future, we can slowly and gently nudge them back toward the present moment. We can learn to calm what is known as the "monkey mind"—the constant chatter in the back of our mind.

Just by concentrating on our breathing and letting go of any thoughts that are not connected to the moment is the easiest way to bring ourselves back into the here and now.

When our lives are in a routine, it can be very easy to switch to autopilot and go through the day without paying full attention to everything that is going on around us, including our loved ones, which can cause us to take everything for granted and fail to appreciate what we have. Being in the present moment is beneficial for emotional awareness. When we are focused on what is happening now, we feel the reality of the emotions that are connected to it. Sometimes this can be uncomfortable if we are going through a particularly painful or stressful period. However, it is much better to be fully present and aware so that we can deal with things with a clear, rational and focused mind.

From time to time, it is healthy to reflect on the past so that we can avoid making repeated mistakes and also enjoy reliving precious moments. If we don't pay attention, we can allow the momentum of the past to run free so that it determines the future, rather than taking charge of where our lives are heading.

We can also take some time out to think about and make plans to ensure we are constantly adjusting in order to reach our goals and ambitions for the future. Whenever we project to the future, we can try to retain a connection with how we currently feel to ensure that where we want to be heading is based on an accurate reflection of how we feel in the here and now.

When we are not fully present in the given moment, our ego can take over, which will try to tell us that we are not good enough, too good, or basically anything other than who we actually are. The ego creates a false persona, and the only way to have any control over it is to be in the present moment, aware of who we are and of how we are feeling. By doing this, we gain a clearer sense of all that is going on around us. We will have greater clarity about the true state of our relationships and a better insight into any problems that may need focusing on.

To prevent the ego from controlling our thoughts, all we need to do is keep ourselves aware and gently bring ourselves back into the moment every time we feel our mind drifting. We will instantly have a clearer perspective of what is surrounding us, and we will feel lighter as we will no longer be carrying the weight from the past or the future. We just need to take a breath, let go of any attachments to our thoughts, bring the mind to the moment, and experience how we feel right now without anything clouding our thoughts. The more often we practice this, the easier and more natural it will become. One day, without even realizing it, we will suddenly find ourselves living in the present moment without having to touch and remind our mind.

Chapter 9

THE MIND

We sometimes think our bodies are the ultimate be all and end all of our human existence. We put so much pressure on them to look good, to perform, and to keep us alive that we forget that there is something far more powerful that affects every function of our body and every cell on the inside and the outside. We forget about the mind.

The mind regulates the vast amount of information and energy that is contained within the brain. The mind gives us the ability to extract whatever the brain has stored and use the data for our daily survival. However, our mind needs help. It needs us to remain consciously aware, as left to its own devices it may either exist on autopilot to keep us "safe" in the world and stuck in our comfort zone, or it may spiral out of control if the majority of our hidden or rejected experiences dominate and create a false sense of self, an ego. Our mind is what keeps everything about our human experience operating, whether positively, neutrally, or negatively. In reality, our physical body is just a puppet that is controlled by the mind.

Yet we give our mind very little credit. We often pay far more attention to physical ailments than we do to mental or emotional ones and we focus on the body by showcasing it as though it is a reflection of who we are.

Our mind, and our heart, both influence us greatly and reflect who we are. Our mind, can be the cause for some of the physical pains our body experiences. Just as we experience physical injuries in our physical body, emotional injuries also manifest and are felt in our physical body. Our physical body has a matrix in place that alerts us via the brain with either thoughts or feelings whenever our emotional health is adversely affected or in danger. Our thoughts, feelings, or sensations let us know when our emotions need attention by directing us toward the part of our body where there are blockages of dense, low vibrational energy. We experience this emotional energetic build up through physical pain or discomfort.

If we remain still the next time we feel emotional pain, we will be able to clearly sense it slowly moving around within our body. When we have identified which area of the body it is associated with, we can then correlate it with the associated chakra so we can understand it on a more intricate level.

Our mind needs to be taken care of so that if anything is not functioning well it can receive attention and treatment with the same urgency as we take care of our physical self. It is vital that we know what is being fed to our mind; how, why, and when we are feeding it; and if what we are feeding it is nourishing or poisoning it.

We can appreciate our mind and prioritize it as, along with our heart, it coordinates much of our behavior, so it has a huge influence over the life we are creating. It is responsible for so many things, including our impulses, motivations, intentions, actions, and also what we attract and repel.

We also have to realize that our mind is capable of far more than we give it credit for. We have infinite possibilities, yet depending on how open and accepting our mindset is, we may believe we are incapable or that we are limited. The incredible thing is we can change our whole mindset the very moment we decide to take control of what we are feeding our mind and what we believe in that exists there.

"The beginning of freedom is the realization that you are not the "thinker." The moment you start *watching* the thinker, a higher level of consciousness becomes activated. You then begin to realize that there is a vast realm of intelligence beyond thought, that thought is only a tiny aspect of that intelligence. You also realize that all the things that truly matter – beauty, love, creativity, joy, inner peace – arise from beyond the mind. You begin to awaken."——Eckhart Tolle

Our mind is a little complex, but when we get to know it a little better we will be amazed at the possibilities it opens up for us and how it can entirely and dramatically transform our life. We can learn to distinguish between our conscious, subconscious, and unconscious mind so that we know which part is responsible for how sections of our life are playing out. Each part of the mind processes uniquely and has various functions and capabilities, and these are known as the conscious, subconscious, unconscious, and higher conscious. Our unconscious mind uses approximately 20 percent, our subconscious uses around 70 percent, and our conscious mind uses around ten percent of our brain capacity. Our higher conscious is used the least, if at all, by many people.

Only a small amount of stimuli that we come into contact with is readily available for our conscious mind to absorb, therefore, it becomes clear to see why we need to focus our attention more by remaining alert and aware at all times. If we intentionally focus on something, it has a higher chance of being deposited into our subconscious mind where it can then be stored and become part of our overall belief system. To restructure what is in our subconscious, we need to continuously focus our attention on anything that we feel is important and we need to repeatedly think and feel strongly about those same things over and over until those things replace whatever currently exists in our subconscious mind. It is a process or elimination. Identifying what we see as valuable and then using our focused attention to allow that information to sink in so that it can support our belief system and replace any conditioned data that we have subliminally, subconsciously absorbed.

Our unconscious mind stores information that is not easily accessible. It contains the distant memories and occurrences that we have suppressed, forgotten, or blanked out. This is also where we hold the attachments to our body, desires, and also to the physical world. The data stored in our unconscious mind is also responsible for a lot of our instinctive behavior and is the root cause of many of our thoughts. Our conscious mind cannot directly gain easy access to our unconscious mind; however, our unconscious mind is constantly feeding our conscious and subconscious with snippets of the memories, experiences, beliefs, and associated sensations, feelings, and emotions that are stored there. Whenever our conscious mind is triggered, the cause for the trigger stems from either our subconscious or our unconscious mind.

Our subconscious mind runs in the background and controls most of our bodily movements, involuntary actions, and is also responsible for our belief system, memories, and feelings. We can access our memories and what is stored in our subconscious when we focus our conscious awareness on it. It is believed that the majority of our feelings, emotions, and behaviors derive from our subconscious. Our subconscious mind generates and stores feelings, beliefs, and sensations and communicates through them. It is a subtle force that is brought to our attention when the conscious mind is calm and we go within ourselves and heighten our awareness.

Our conscious mind is our awareness of whatever is taking place in the current moment. It is capable or reasoning, logical thinking, and having a rational insight into the past and possible future. Our conscious mind is capable of filtering information. It also generates emotion when we wallow in our thoughts or consciously repeat them until they gain momentum. Our conscious mind communicates with words, pictures, and thoughts and its messages are loud and clear.

The conscious and unconscious minds communicate via the subconscious mind. Our higher conscious is an awareness of our soul's purpose and the overall meaning of our life. It is a high vibration that elevates with spiritual growth. It offers a profound understanding of the universe and the ability to see how we all exist as one with no separation. It allows us to view the world and our self from an alternative dimension and without the involvement of the ego.

We are born with the ability to connect with our higher conscious and this connection allows us direct access to our conscious, subconscious and also our unconscious mind. Not all empaths are aware of how they can connect to their higher conscious however most do it without even realizing it.

Our higher conscious allows us to easily interact with the other three layers of our mind so that we can delve into the inner knowledge that is stored there and extract the relevant information required to navigate life. We can then question what is held in our conscious, subconscious, and unconscious minds to find out how much of it is authentic and how much exists due to negative thinking, conditioning, and also due to the interference of our ego.

Although it may seem as though our conscious mind is the most dominant, our subconscious and unconscious minds subtly rule. Even though our conscious mind can easily regain control of our actions and words, it cannot regain control of our internalized hidden, denied, or forgotten emotions and feelings quite so easily. For example, if we are feeling angry or resentful about something, we can consciously tell ourselves over and over to relax and calm down but our subconscious and unconscious minds are not so easy to retrain or guide. Our instinctive reactions quite often come from our subconscious and these deeply felt responses have usually been triggered by patterns that we have learned and repeated over time. Our conscious mind can also be responsible for creating emotions. For example, if we linger on a thought for long enough our emotions are alerted, and they respond by producing a chemical reaction, which then causes a physiological reaction that provides us with a feeling. Therefore, both our subconscious and our conscious minds are capable of creating emotion and also feelings.

Although our conscious mind is capable of being logical, rational, and analytical, whereby when our subconscious mind has been left to its own devices it is reactive, irrational, and full of illusions, many of us function on autopilot, allowing our subconscious to be the one in control. When we think about it consciously, it makes no sense. Functioning on autopilot from what is held in our subconscious is only advisable when we are confident that the data that is stored there can be trusted to guide us.

Our subconscious is a huge memory bank that stores our belief system, feelings, and emotions. And when we can trust that those things are authentic, rational, and true reflections of our experiences, we can then trust our subconscious to be responsible for our reactions. When our subconscious is filled with illusionary feelings and beliefs and we exist on autopilot, we will replicate the same patterns of behavior, keep attracting similar circumstances, we will be triggered due to past occurrences, and we will make judgments and decisions based on this stored data, when a lot of the data has no correlation with the truth. It is only beneficial to allow our subconscious mind to be in control when we are aware of the data it holds and we are able to understand and rationalize it. Our subconscious mind must also constantly be able to flow and change continuously, as we are altered in every moment through encountering new experiences.

Empaths have a very strong connection to their subconscious and we are able to connect with it and understand and translate the messages it sends out and receives. We also have the ability to directly connect with other people's subconscious mind and this is what gives us an in-depth insight into how other people are feeling, how they are processing and experiencing their emotions, and also what historic data is causing them to think, feel, or act the way they do.

Although many people function by allowing their subconscious to lead the way, they often do not have a close connection with it, so they do not understand how it operates. They may not know what exists within it, so therefore it would not be advisable to blindly allow it to take pole position.

It is not as likely that those who are not highly sensitive to energy and are able to read it well finely tuned to other people's subconscious. Empaths, are highly tuned to both their own and other people's subconscious minds. We are able to communicate with the subconscious without words or thoughts. We pay attention to the sensations that arise within us and can detect these similar sensations within other people too. Empaths don't feel the need to communicate by talking. We communicate through energy and are able to read people on a very deep level and make sense of information that many people don't realize they are radiating through subtle vibrations. These messages are not always easy to decode, and sometimes it can take us a little time to find out the meaning within them. If we are trying too hard to consciously figure out a message it will very likely elude us. We just need to be still, trust in our inner sensations, and have faith in our ability to translate the energy we are connecting with so that we can translate what the message we have received means.

Many people try to use their conscious mind to overrule what they are subconsciously feeling. However, when this happens empaths are not easily fooled. We are able to understand the information that people radiate subconsciously. This is why some people feel very vulnerable in the company of empaths as they realize that we are able to read their energy and see through the facade and masks they may wear to hide their inherent nature.

The subconscious mind stores the majority of that has happened throughout our lives, including memories and experiences we think may have been forgotten. When we align ourselves with other people's energy and tune in to what is in their subconscious mind, we are naturally able to empathize with and intricately understand other people.

Negative emotions are stored as energy and the energy becomes hardwired in our cells. This energy can get blocked when it has been suppressed, which is why it is sometimes difficult to talk about past experiences without becoming tearful, frustrated, or angry. Empaths have a way of understanding people, showing compassion, and encouraging them to release the contained or pent-up emotions.

When we release energy by acknowledging it, understanding it, and then letting it flow, we can move past the pain that it causes and break free from the energetic cords that bind us to it. Therefore, we are able to transcend past our experiences rather than suffering and being held back by them.

All of our memories, experiences, and conversations have been logged and our subconscious mind uses all the data so that it can be retrieved as and when it needs to in order to help us to navigate life. However, there is a lot of backlog and deep-seated emotions stored there that we no longer require. They prevent us from moving forward and they also constantly trigger us to behave in ways that we do not understand and that do not serve us.

When we free our emotions, our body feels lighter and more energized as it releases the aches and pains that are caused by holding on to things that have hurt us. We are similar to computers. Our subconscious is our software, and whatever we add to it reprograms and updates the software constantly. We are able to function on autopilot as our subconscious runs in the background. It is always switched on to survival mode and its function is to ensure that it makes quick decisions based on all the knowledge it has collated, continuously working with the conscious mind to pull out pieces of stored data.

We have to ensure that it is able to process without disconnections, obstructions, and badly fused wires. Our subconscious mind stores easy-to-recall memories and experiences, and our unconscious mind stores those that we are unable to consciously remember regardless of how hard we focus. Although the impression of the event has already imprinted on us, our conscious mind does not have open access to our unconscious mind so that it can recollect it. Our subconscious mind can access our unconscious mind but not with ease.

Our conscious mind is in the present moment and works in real time, commanding and controlling with complete awareness. Our conscious mind works with thoughts and language and our subconscious mind works with sensations, emotions, and our basic senses; for example touch, sound, and smell. Our subconscious is not capable of distinguishing between the past, present, and future. It experiences everything as though it is in the current moment.

Our conscious mind is similar to a human using a computer. It can overrule the subconscious mind (the software) at any time or even reprogram or change the software completely. Humans are capable of ensuring their internal database is running well or they can get in its way, creating obstacles and making it complex to process all the information.

We have to monitor what our conscious mind and our surroundings are feeding our subconscious mind as it is quite vulnerable and has faith in the information it is gathering. All the information it absorbs eventually becomes our reality. It is essential that it is nourished and provided with as much authentic information as possible so that the feelings and sensations that it receives and sends out are based on true balanced data.

"Bring the mind into sharp focus and make it alert so that it can immediately intuit truth, which is everywhere. The mind must be emancipated from old habits, prejudices, restrictive thought processes and even ordinary thought itself." ———Bruce Lee,

Therefore, we have to be as rational and reasonable as possible when thinking things through and repeating information in our conscious minds so that we can be sure that our thoughts are rational. Otherwise, these thoughts will very quickly turn to emotions, and then result in feelings that turn to our beliefs. When repeated, these beliefs eventually lead to the activation of our react and response system that is operated by our subconscious.

Our subconscious minds can pick up bugs and faults and will regularly need to be serviced and recalibrated. Without realizing it we subliminally pick up negativity from our environment and from those around us, and all of this data is backed up in our subconscious. Along with soaking up everything from our outer world, our subconscious mind also absorbs our thoughts. Our thoughts can become bad habits, and even though they take place in our conscious mind and we have control over them, they often replicate negative beliefs over and over again, thus adding more junk into our subconscious database.

Our subconscious mind is constantly listening out for any new information that is being sent by the conscious mind. As our subconscious cannot think, it cannot rationalize either, so it takes on and believes whatever it is being given. This then creates a vicious circle. We are basically caught up in a cycle and we will repeat the patterns over and over again until we choose to rewire and reprogram them.

Before we can change our internal belief system we need the conscious mind to filter the messages to our subconscious that align with the changes we want to create. We need to stop allowing negativity to seep through and flood our subconscious mind and instead replace it with thoughts that reflect how we want to feel. If we are just thinking thoughts but attach no feeling to them, it will be very difficult for our thoughts to be strong enough to affect our overall belief system, unless they are repeated continuously and wallowed on.

Thinking a single thought is not enough to attract whatever it is we want. When we make affirmations we can't just say the words, we have to really feel the words as emotions, repeat and internalize them until they are believable enough that they create change.

When we repeatedly think negatively, these thoughts may transfer and become emotions. Our subconscious mind picks up on this and absorbs the emotions and turns them to feelings that then become ingrained in our subconscious and become part of our overall belief system.

Our thoughts very soon become how we feel. How we feel subconsciously is then picked up by our conscious mind and affects how we think and causes our reactions. It seems as though there is no ending and no beginning. However, we can override and reprogram our subconscious at any time by changing our conscious thinking. Once a thought becomes conscious it enters our subconscious and becomes a memory. The stronger the thought is, the more emotion that attaches to it and the more influence it then has within our subconscious.

We can connect with our subconscious mind when we meditate and are fully present and aware of ourselves in every moment. When our mind is peaceful, still and calm, our subconscious is what exists when nothing else is creating any noise. Our subconscious can tell us everything we need to know about what causes us to feel triggered to respond and also what causes us to replicate patterns of behavior.

The difficulty in trusting what exists within our subconscious is that much of what is there is a result of repeated thought patterns, some of which are unhealthy, that have been continuously relayed from our conscious mind. That is why it can be confusing to know what is our true identity and what false identity we have created for ourselves. We literally have to pick away at all the negativity, or anything that feels unaligned, that exists in our subconscious mind so that we can dissect each particle, understand it and then let it go. The negativity is what keeps us remaining stuck in situations and what causes us to attract more of the same. Holding on to negativity does not serve us, it only hinders and debilitates.

There is often confusion about whether the conscious mind rules or if it is the subconscious taking control. It is a constant circle, with one feeding the other. The conscious mind assists with the outside world to feed the subconscious and then the subconscious responds with the information and creates reactions based on what it has been fed. It also feeds the conscious mind.

Ultimately, though, the conscious mind can regain control by remaining aware of what it is mixing into the subconscious pot so that whatever is being added is vitally nourishing and not an insidious, dripping poison. The subconscious mind can then react with healthier and more balanced responses rather than being triggered and erupting due to the toxic data that has previously been entered.

As we look at the negative data we have stored, we can address it and figure out what caused its presence in the first place. Even if we cannot figure out the cause of the negativity, we can at least diffuse it by acknowledging it, taking responsibility for it, and then letting it go so that it is not controlling how we perceive ourselves. Whenever we divert our focused attention on to something and then we raise our vibration to one on a higher frequency, whichever thoughts, emotions or feelings currently exist will immediately be transmuted. We may have to practice this many times over and reason so that we recondition our mind to fully believe that we no longer need to carry this negativity around with us. Although we may soothe, balm and think we have healed a wound because we have focused on it once, our thoughts become a habit and they may keep throwing irrational suggestions our way to remind us of any pain that we have previously experienced. We may have to calm and rationalize the mind many times over before all traces of negativity associated with a particular emotional injury have been transmuted. There is no time scale with healing. It takes as quick or as long as it takes. Patience and understanding are essential ingredients to ensure the healing absorbs and is long term and not a quick fix.

The more we can release negativity and put positive thoughts in place, the healthier our subconscious will become as we nourish ourselves rather than continue a process that leads us to self-fulfilling prophecies and onward to self-destruction.

We have spent our whole lifetime gathering information that has conditioned us to feel a certain way. Therefore, if we feel unworthy on the inside, whenever we are treated as though we are unworthy we make excuses for it so that we can accept it as it matches how we feel and also aligns with the identity we have given ourselves. It becomes clear to see why we allow people to treat us in certain ways and also why we respond the way we do to their treatment.

If we feel like we are victims, we will naturally fall into the role of being a victim. We only remain as a victim while we are blaming someone or something else for our circumstances. When we take responsibility for how we feel and refrain from placing the blame for our emotional state externally, regardless of what may have happened, we are no longer a victim.

When we try to blame someone else for how we feel, we not only lose our personal power, we also forsake the ability to change how we feel. We will then be less able to alter what we are attracting and we will also find it hard work to change our current situation. When we feel powerless, we will attract situations that affirm that we are powerless, and this false belief is sustained until we forcibly choose to change.

We are constantly validating our belief system by matching what is imprinted on the inside to whatever is available on the outside. If our stored data tells us we are not good enough, we will attract people and situations that reaffirm this false belief. If our conscious mind continuosly confirms negativity by unquestioningly believing what it perceives or what it is told, this information will keep being added to our subconscious mind. Once we start reprogramming, we must not only work to eliminate old negativity but we must also remain consciously aware so that we add nourishing data instead of adding negativity.

We can view this similar to a computer game that detonates all bombs that have the same color-coding. When we blast away one negative thought pattern that is stored in our subconscious, all similar thought patterns will line up and disintegrate at the same time. If we have one train of thought that repeatedly narrates to us that we are insignificant, all similar ones that talk of low self-worth will form a matrix and be neutralized simultaneously. We can destroy a lifetime of unnecessary negativity with just a single moment of faith in ourselves as well as in the power and capability of our mind.

We can let go of any false self-beliefs that we have simply by focusing in on them, reassessing them, rationalizing them, and then sending them love, kindness, and understanding. This affirms to our feelings that we are learning, evolving, and constantly growing. We are not in the same place we once were when we accepted those beliefs. We have a choice. We can look at it all from a different angle so that we can significantly alter our perception and ultimately what we believe, or we can remain stagnant. Condemning ourselves is limiting and keeps us feeling as though we are not "enough" or unworthy. We can remember to speak to ourselves in the same way we would speak to someone we care deeply about. If we wouldn't say destructive words to someone else, what reason can there be for saying them to ourselves? They don't help us, they hinder. Wallowing in negativity always slows us down.

Self-berating and harmful thoughts shake our insides and cause us to experience rocky and turbulent emotional and physiological terrain. So why would we choose that when at any given moment we can instead choose to make ourselves feel stable, cherished, loved, and valuable? We can still be aware of our flaws and areas that we need to focus more on, but we can do that with care and compassion rather than cruelty and cutting, careless criticism.

This process may sound complicated but it is actually very simple, and all it takes is for us to become consciously aware and then we can immediately begin to transform from the inside out. We cannot allow our subconscious to take the reins and have responsibility for the way we operate. We can only trust our subconscious when it is has been focused on and tended to so that we are sure that what exists there is authentic, entirely nourished and healthy.

"I never believe my stressful thoughts. I have questioned them and found them all to be untrue." ———Byron Katie

Beliefs change our lives and they have a tremendously powerful effect over us. Beliefs create our most powerful emotions and they are also what cause our emotions to linger and repeat continuously. Beliefs are magnetic so they are also responsible for what we attract and repel. When we believe in something, it can easily become our reality, whether good or bad. Therefore, we have to believe in ourselves so that we attract to our lives the reality that aligns with what we want, but to do this we have to first believe in the positive, loving thoughts that we filter into our subconscious mind.

We can validate our persistent thoughts, even if it is just to hold them for a fraction of a second before letting them go. As soon as we acknowledge, soothe or understand them, they will feel free to float calmly on their way. We do not need to believe all of our thoughts so they are accepted as "truth." All kinds of thoughts will swirl in our minds that are in no way a representation of the truth. We have the ability to discern all of our thoughts, and by doing this we avoid suppressing them so that they linger. If we ignore, deny and reject our unpleasant thoughts, feelings, or emotions, they then sink deeply into our unconscious mind, where they will remain until they resonate when something within our subconscious triggers them. Our subconscious mind will communicate with our unconscious and hook up anything that confirms what is currently occurring. The subconscious pulls out pieces of information that aligns with our belief system. It basically searches for back up and will sift through all kinds of hidden, forgotten memories and feelings until it finds something, anything, to associate with our present lingering thoughts, emotions, or feelings.

We have vast amounts of data stored within our unconscious mind that we have no idea exists. Our subconscious mind is triggered by this data constantly. All of our dark, negative emotions and feelings or anything that we deny will be repressed and held there until something happens that resonates with a particular piece of energy. As soon as the resonation strikes, the old energy will spark back to life and instantly jump from our unconscious mind and into the subconscious and align so that it is consistent with whatever our subconscious feels or believes, giving it far more power and a more forceful response. It prefers to keep us in our comfort zone and will fire all kinds of thoughts, feelings, and beliefs at us to keep us rooted in whatever way we have become accustomed to living. Just because our old ways feel familiar, it does not mean they are serving us well.

We absolutely have to awaken to this potential minefield and become fully aware of the damage our subconscious and unconscious minds can cause us if they have been subjected to too much negativity over a lifetime. When we start becoming consciously aware of the information we are processing, we can ensure our inner processing is rational, compassionate and loving so that we have complete control over our lives, including who and what we allow into them.

"Until you make the unconscious conscious, it will direct your life and you will call it fate." ——Carl Jung

We don't need to wait for the next person to take advantage of us or until things go terribly wrong before finally turning our lives in the right direction. We can make alterations at any moment and the effects of those changes will be internally felt immediately. The more determination and courage we have in facing up to ourselves and admitting that we need to change, the more significant the changes will be. Change begins when we recognize what is taking place within, and by consciously altering and reprogramming how we think and feel about ourselves.

Unresolved or unhealed painful memories radiate powerful magnetic negative energy. It is crucial that these inflictions are acknowledged and worked on. To heal, we need to focus awareness on whatever is causing emotional irritation. When we are consciously aware of where the dense sensations are being generated from, we can then look deeper and see what outdated belief or unacknowledged emotion or feeling is vying for our attention. All of our wounds just want to be seen, validated, and understood.

When we locate exactly where this conflict has originated from, we can then show tenderness, kindness, forgiveness, and express love, so that our irritable vibrations are recognized, heard, and feel empowered to shift. The wounded energy immediately speeds up and takes on a higher vibration so that it can break free and continue its journey. We will then be relieved of whatever limiting emotion, feeling, or belief we had unknowingly been wallowing in and holding hostage.

When the work is done, rather than attracting the same types of energy and relationships that encourage the onslaught of old traumatic patterns, new energy and love will radiate, which will then attract a similar vibration to that which we are sending out.

"There is no coming to consciousness without pain. People will do anything, no matter how absurd, in order to avoid facing their own soul. One does not become enlightened by imagining figures of light, but by making the darkness conscious." ——Carl Jung

Chapter 10

EMOTIONS

Emotions are a vital and essential part of our human experience. They alert us when situations need our attention and they can gracefully lift us higher or violently pull us down lower. When we are emotionally intelligent we are able to clearly identify and separate our own emotions from everyone else's and we can then work on transmuting the energy that is associated with them. It can be incredibly difficult to discern whether the emotions we are feeling belong to us, or whether they are emanating from other people. This is mainly because we feel emotions as powerful vibrations regardless of their origination. Often they feel far more powerful when they belong to other people, which is usually the reason we mistakenly think they are our own.

We are often told that our emotions can cause us complexities or that it is inappropriate to express them freely when communicating and interacting with others. This can cause us to feel ashamed of our emotions so that we deny them and become separated and disconnected from them. Our emotions will then become suppressed rather than being a mechanism that allows us to scrutinize exactly how we are feeling and why. The only time we need to keep emotions at a safe distance and refuse to allow them to negatively affect us is when we are unexpectedly absorbing other people's emotions, as otherwise, we may react toward them as though they are our own.

It is essential that we remain alert and aware so that we are in touch with how we are feeling before we are in any one else's. When we are able to clearly identify our own emotions, feelings, and behavior, we can easily notice when we suddenly feel something wash over us that is associated with someone else. For example, if we come into contact with someone who is very aggressive and raging with anger, instantly we will feel a discord and tense up, as the energy vibrates in our aura. If we aren't fully aware of what is happening, pretty soon we will begin to believe the emotional energy belongs to us and we may react and respond as though we are the ones who are angry.

We may try to contain the emotional charge; however, it will build inside us and want to explode like a ball of fire. It can become overwhelming as the anger seems as though it came from nowhere, so our rational mind will struggle to work through it and place where it has come from and what course of action to take to resolve it.

When we are skilled at identifying and transmuting energy we will easily be able to process the anger, neutralize, then transform it so that we turn the emotion into positive energy and let it go. Holding on to charged fiery emotions will cause an internal burn, and if we don't pay attention to the heat it will cause emotional or physiological damage either to us or to someone else when either we react to it uncontrollably or we pass it on as it is too hot to contain.

Although we absorb other people's emotions we also have to take responsible for the ones we create on our own. Every thought we linger on causes a chemical reaction and that reaction causes a physical response. How severe this response is, is down to our perception of the situation. When we carelessly repeat emotionally charged words or memories in our minds it can set off a running dialogue of thoughts. When we add visuals to the mix, we create our own unique illustrated storybook complete with emotions and feelings that make it believable. If we read this storybook over and over, it can cause the smallest spark in our minds to burn out of control until it significantly affects our emotional well-being and as well as our physical body.

There are particular emotional wounds that can affect us strongly and can tremendously influence our lives if we do not process and heal the energetic injuries caused by the occurrence. These wounds are particularly; abandonment, betrayal, fear, guilt, humiliation/shame, injustice, and rejection. These inflictions stay open and grow bigger and more painful if they are not acknowledged. If we have been hurt deeply and we have not processed the pain, we may eventually form a belief system that tells us that we must have somehow deserved whatever happened to us. We might have picked up on vibrations from arguments around us, or we may have read, seen, or heard something that for some reason causes us to resonate with the message. Even if we only consider this belief for a fraction of a second, it can deposit in our belief system and become part of our overall opinion of ourselves. Our belief system is irrational, so it will absorb everything and take ownership of it. If we feel something and resonate with it, we will quickly start to believe it too. This can cause us to experience incredible amounts of unpleasant emotions that are unrelated to our present encounters.

Although the emotions we are holding on to belong to us, they only exists for as long as we choose to hold on to them. When we dissect them and look at where they came from and why they exist, we will see that they erupt from past circumstances, often nothing to do with our current moments, yet they are causing us discomfort in the present. We can free them at any moment. To do this all we need to do is relax and breathe deeply so that our conscious mind calms down and we have a heightened awareness of our inner sensations. If something particularly triggers us or is demanding our attention, we can focus on why that emotion or feeling exists and we will likely find that it is connected to an earlier memory or a time that we felt in a similar way.

Whenever we shine a light on any of our hidden, shadow emotions, feelings, or beliefs, we will bring then into our conscious mind where they can be rationalized and processed. Many of our emotions are stored unnecessarily and we can free this energy at any moment very simply just by understanding them and prioritizing their place in the current moment. Often we see that many of our emotions and feelings have no place in our current life and they are just reoccurring remnants of past occurrences. This is why it is essential to keep letting go of past emotions, beliefs, memories, feelings, and experiences as otherwise they will keep imprinting their pain over and over until we fully grasp how much emotional harm we are doing to ourselves. Not only that we have already felt the pain previously and it has become part of our identity, we don't need to keep reaffirming what we have already been through. We now have responsibility for the pain, even though often it was actually someone else's behavior that resulted in us absorbing the energy and feeling this way. When we identify our painful memories, we can reorganize them and gain inner peace, which allows us to recreate an identity based on our current experiences so that we are not carrying with us vast amounts of accumulated pain.

Although people may have behaved in ways that have hurt us, it is our choice whether we accept the pain or work through the feelings and free them. Just because we hold on to pain, it does not mean that we deserved it or that it belongs to us or is in any way relevant to our past, or our life today. Even if it was our pain, it had served its purpose long ago, so we do not need to keep punishing ourselves daily for it. We are only emotionally injured if we allow ourselves to be. We have the option to let it all go in every new moment.

Often we cling on to past pain as it feels familiar, although all it does is hurt us over and over again when we are reminded of it. Then, the pain gets worse when we attract situations to our lives that are similar. This also leaves us vulnerable to other people noticing the pain. And if they are not compassionate or their intentions are not wholesome, they may regard us as emotionally fragile or weak. They then may dig up our old pain and deliberately prod and poke around in it to garner an emotional response.

Some people are masters at detecting past wounds and they may intentionally try to trigger us by mirroring back at us some of our worst fears or painful memories that are associated with the wound. They may say or do things consciously or subconsciously that affirms to our irrational belief system that we deserved the pain and it is all we are worthy of. We will then not only relive the old pain, but we will also be taking on new emotional pain. This is why it is imperative that we let go of all that has taken place in the past so that we, or others, are not able to consistently use our past emotional trauma to hurt us.

When we keep our past pain with us, we will likely attract more people who will show us more of the same. Even if it is not someone else who keeps on showing us our pain, we may keep it alive by constantly reminding ourselves of it. When we keep reliving pain through our emotions as though it is still part of us, other people may innocently or intentionally do or say things that trigger i and our reactions to it may be unpredictable and irrational. Whenever we are shown a situation that reminds us of our unhealed past our self-dense mechanism and survival instincts jump in the way to "help" us respond by fighting the situation as though it is fighting the pain from the past, even though the encounter is in the present moment. It feels as though it knows the situation it is dealing with as we have been in a similar position before, so it reacts impulsively.

Old unresolved feelings are drawn to the surface and they can become the basis of how we think and feel today. This may happen even if there is no direct correlation between the two situations other than we have received a memory of what happened to us in the past that recognizes something in the present moment. For example, we may have been hurt when someone we loved went on a work night out and cheated on us. When our current partner goes on a work night out, our fears rise to the surface and our survival instinct clicks into place. This brings in feelings related to our previous pain and fear and we start to believe we may be cheated on again. Therefore, our self-defense mechanism restores the old associated feelings, believing it is protecting us. We may then feel we are threatened in the present moment, maybe even accusing our partner of cheating, when the threat is from the past and has no rational link to the new event. All of this can be happening at an unconscious or subconscious level and we may behave automatically on autopilot rather than remaining consciously aware that it is possibly due to an old connection.

When we hold on to our old emotions, we are constantly going to drag everything associated with them into our new experiences. This is why it is essential that we let go of them so that we can rationally deal with the current moment without the past coming to irrational conclusions. While it is good to have learned lessons along the way, we can try to remember the lessons without attaching old, outdated, and often highly irrational emotion to them.

Our emotions cause a release of chemicals and these chemicals make our thinking cloudy and hazy. We never respond in a calm and rational way when our old emotions are out of control and directing our reactions. Emotions are valuable tools that help us to discern what we feel is right and wrong in our life, although wallowing in them or rejecting and repressing them can cause us to become so overwhelmed that we react impulsively, irrationally, and out of character. When we consistently think about unhappy memories or repeat our old tormenting stories, we are causing ourselves to repeatedly suffer as we experience regret, fear, anger, frustration, grief, longing, or sadness. We will remain caught in a cycle, and it will become difficult to see our emotions clearly or to put them into context so we can disconnect from them. Many of our past emotions are shrouded in illusions, as we never think rationally when emotions are powerfully fuelling our thoughts and feelings. While we are trapped in an unrealistic version of our past, our present moment and our future will be delusional as we are carrying all the emotional baggage along into it.

We sometimes cling on to our emotions, especially if they are repeats and almost identical to ones we have encountered previously. This causes them to become stronger and gain momentum, and within moments they can change how we feel physiologically. Pema Chödrön explains that if we allow an emotion to exist for ninety seconds without paying excess attention to it or passing any judgment on it, it will quickly dissipate. Chödrön describes the feeling as "the hook," as thoughts hook, line, and then sink us. Chödrön's explanation led me to discover brain researcher *****Jill Bolte Taylor's book, *A Brain Scientist's Personal Journey.*

Taylor describes the ninety-second rule as "Once triggered, the chemical released by my brain surges through my body and I have a physiological experience. Within 90 seconds from the initial trigger, the chemical component of my anger has completely dissipated from my blood and my automatic response is over. If, however, I remain angry after those 90 seconds have passed, then it is because I have chosen to let that circuit continue to run."

Taylor explains in her book that all emotions initially last for less than ninety seconds. Whatever continues after that is because we have added our own story to them and allowed old emotions to surface and held on to our newly associated emotions. When we do this, we cause our emotions to escalate further and we also ensure they last much longer. According to Taylor, if we are aware that emotions take ninety seconds to surge through our system, we can allow them to naturally pass through and then freely flush out. When we choose to engage with the emotion and interact with it, adding more memories, feelings, and emotions without being conscious and rational, we emphasize it further. We will then need to fight the emotion again and again as it gains momentum and the power to control us.

To override irrational or outdated emotions, we need to pay attention to the physical changes that are taking place as soon as we notice an emotion engaging. We will feel the sensation of our muscles tensing, an increased pulse, shortness of breath, our face flushing and our vocal cords tightening. During this process we can stay alert so we are consciously aware that our emotions are at risk of escalating. We can then remain in control and pay attention to what happens next.

If we are calm, grounded, fully present, balanced, and try to remove or avoid any irrational thoughts that occur, we can inhale and exhale deeply for around ninety seconds to give the chemical surge an opportunity to pass while keeping our mind calm and focused. We can master and assert self-control and patiently wait ninety seconds while the emotion intensifies, dissolves, and then passes. As our emotions heighten, we can notice how we are feeling and what other emotions are trying to surface. By gently naming our emotions as they arise, we can look at how they are strong enough to ignite a physical reaction. Once we have lightly acknowledged them, we can then take the lead by letting them pass rather than allowing them to become more intense and take over.

Although we needn't pay much attention to them at this point or else they will grow stronger, we can analyze the reason for those particular emotions existing so that we can see why they are lingering around unhealed or unacknowledged. Emotions only gain control of us when we do not fully understand them. When we are emotionally intelligent and aware of how our emotions work, they serve us and we are in control, which means we will not be acting irrationally or hotheadedly.

We can look at emotions with clarity and rewire our thinking so that rather than fuelling an emotion we can soothe it with healing, loving words. If we normally berate ourselves or feel frustrated when we feel a particular emotion, we can decide to show self-compassion by repeating caring expressions such as "I am learning and I forgive myself" while breathing deeply.

The moments soon pass. Any emotional responses that occur following the ninety seconds are ones that we are choosing to hold on to. By paying attention and incorporating into our lives the ninety-second rule, we can take accountability for how we are behaving, practice letting go of our thoughts, and alter our patterns of behavior. We can avoid being triggered by irritations that sneak up on us momentarily and take hold of us not just for a moment or two, but ones that recite themselves repeatedly so they control us for years.

When we have awareness that all emotions initially last for ninety seconds, we can allow emotions to ripple through us, causing a wave without any resistance. Then we can let them go so they do not cause further reaction. If we do engage and interact with our emotions, we will allow them to cause an inferno in our minds and they will become more powerful and eventually rage inside us until they explode. When this happens, we can then look at what narratives we have attached to our emotions that have caused them to heighten and trigger a response. We will begin to see why we are replicating similar patterns of behavior and what is causing our emotions to escalate and remain.

When we become aware of any self-harming behavior we express, we will discover that all of our impulses are basically a fear-led strategy to gain something our subconscious or unconscious mind thinks we need. When we recognize what unmet needs we have, we are then able to identify which emotions are associated to them. We will then be able to focus our attention on acknowledging whatever we feel we are lacking, whether that is security, fulfillment, love, validation, or even freedom. We can then make a conscious decision to work on providing ourselves with these essential elements for survival so that our behavior is not a reflection of something we currently feel is missing.

When we have understood our behavior and the associated emotions, we will feel empowered to override any irrational or outdated emotions when they arise. This means that rather than reacting subconsciously, due to the red mist or rose tints that haze our perception, we will be consciously aware of the reasons our emotions are making themselves felt.

Recycling old pain is known in the Buddhist tradition as *Samsara*. With a very simple concept, we can choose whether we escape pain or whether we suffer with it for a lifetime. When we understand what lies at the roots of each of our emotions, we can trust our emotional responses entirely so they can enter to alert us momentarily and then quickly pass.

"Pay attention to what you are thinking, and then decide if those are thoughts that are creating the kind of life you want created. And if it's not, then change your thoughts. It's really that easy." ——Jill Bolte Taylor

Chapter 11

PROJECTION

We all have unpleasant negative emotions, feelings, and beliefs stored in our unconscious mind. They exist because we have either denied, rejected, unclaimed, repressed, hidden, or forgotten them, and until they are acknowledged we run the risk of externalizing these emotions so that we attribute our unaccepted qualities to other people by means of projection.

Psychological projection usually happens unconsciously and innocently, although it can also be carried out consciously and deliberately. Either way, the effects of it can be quite devastating. Mostly those who project onto others are not even aware that they are doing it. That is why it is imperative that we learn exactly why we project and what we can do to prevent it.

Projection happens when we do not take responsibility for our unorganized emotions, feelings, or beliefs. It is associated with vulnerable emotions that arise when we feel incapable, insecure, inadequate, unworthy, undervalued, rejected, unloved, or unimportant. Instead of understanding why we are feeling a certain way, we may project our underlying feelings onto other people. It is a self-defense mechanism triggered by a weakened ego that involves rejecting and shifting unwanted, uncomfortable, embarrassing, or undesirable thoughts, feelings, and emotions so that they are transferred and assigned to someone else.

When we automatically expel what we are experiencing, it means we do not need to take on any guilt, blame, or shame, and instead associate and pin our thoughts, emotions, and feelings on the people around us as we assume, or prefer, they belong with them.

Emotions and feelings are fueled by energy, and when we try to suppress them they will seep out of us and can then be directed toward other people. We sometimes assume that others are thinking, feeling, or acting in the same way as we are, or would, so we identify this energy with other people instead of identifying it with ourselves.

If projection is subconscious (innocent), it is usually due to deep-rooted emotional wounds that have not been taken care of. We disassociate with the emotions as we find them too painful to deal with. If projection is conscious (deliberate), it is usually to make the other person appear to look guilty or so that they take the blame for our behavior. This means we internally lie to ourselves and appear innocent and try to make other people take responsibility for our negative thoughts, emotions, feelings, or beliefs.

When we project how we are feeling, we paste the image onto other people to make it seem as though they are at fault and that the way we feel is authentic and justified. We basically blame and judge other people instead of compassionately judging ourselves, although essentially when we project we are actually judging ourselves as the negative energy initially belonged to us. Therefore, what we see in the projected image is actually our own behavior.

Basically, we accuse others or believe other people to be the ones responsible for disorganized and unacknowledged thoughts, emotions, or feelings that occur within ourselves. We might believe that someone is cheating on us because we don't trust ourselves, are thinking about being unfaithful or because we are paranoid that they may cheat on us. We may think someone doesn't like us because we don't like them, or maybe because we don't like ourselves. We may think someone is a threat to us because we are fearful of them. We may say things to other people that we don't want them to say to us, which are ultimately the things we need to gently say to ourselves. We also project our expectations onto other people. If we have a strong desire for an outcome, we may focus our hopes onto someone else so that they then have the responsibility for living up to our expectation. We may then become frustrated if they do not achieve what we hoped they would, instead of realizing we are projecting our own desires and then placing high and unreasonable demands on other people that possibly cannot be reached.

Another type of expectation we can project is when we are in a relationship. We may project onto our partner our ideal image of a relationship. This is especially evident when we first meet someone. We can project onto them who we think they are and also how we expect them to behave. When someone does not match our idealized image, we can feel hurt, disappointed, and let down and as though they were being false in the beginning. What has really happened is that we were not being realistic and did not accept them for who they actually are. We fell "in love" with the perceived image that we projected onto them. When this image falls apart as their true selves shine through, we can then feel as though we were tricked or deceived by them pretending to be someone they were not, when the truth was we were projecting a false image onto them all along.

Insecurities are often passed onto other people. If we aren't feeling good about ourselves, we may then imagine that other people are having the same thoughts or feelings and we may think that they also do not believe we are "good" enough. We can very easily become paranoid by perceiving other people to be thinking or talking about us negatively, when realistically we are just in denial and not willing to accept that we are the ones thinking these thoughts and then projecting them outward and toward others.

When we are emotionally intelligent and are able to separate our own emotions and behavior from other people's, we can absorb their energy and how they are acting and intentionally project and present it back to them simply by radiating the information out through our energy field. By doing this, other people are able to sense in our energy a reflection of their selves, without us having to speak a word or express any physical reaction. We can mirror this energy regardless of whether someone is behaving positively or negatively. This may also be one of the reasons why people who are constantly negative and pessimistic shy away from empaths as we have the ability to see through people and organize and reflect their emotions. They then may feel weakened or vulnerable as their underlying feelings are unmasked and revealed. Projecting in this way is not recommended, as it is not our responsibility to show other people how they behave, especially if it is done in a covert manner.

We may also project our energy onto objects or places. For example, if we have previously been somewhere that holds a bad memory it can pull a negative trigger, especially if we are also absorbing into our energy field residual debris from the place. We may then project the associated fearful feelings onto the place, making us wary and afraid to go there again. When we are aware we are doing this, instead of projecting we can transmute the energy we are feeling and turn it to positivity so that we deposit loving light energy to neutralize and transform any negativity.

Because empaths are highly aware of energy, we can also manipulate it very easily. While empaths are capable of projecting our own disorganized energy, we also soak up the emotional energy from other people and we may then project what we have absorbed all around us. Instead of projecting our own thoughts and feelings, we have taken on other people's thoughts and feelings and we then try to assign them to those we are associated with. As we have not clearly identified what energy belongs to us and what is other people's energy, we may become bewildered and can then throw all the energy back outward, projecting it onto anyone in our vicinity that we feel it matches with. We may then also become confused when we try to read people's energy, as we won't know whose energy aligns accurately with them and whose energy has been bombarded with what we have projected.

Although we can easily read energy, we can also become mistaken as to whose energy belongs to whom. For example, if we unconsciously project energy onto someone else and then we tap into that person's energy field, all we are doing is reading back whatever energy we have sent out. However, we will believe the energy we are reading confirms how they are thinking or feeling, not realizing that we projected the energy onto them in the first place.

All we are doing is reading back our own projected energy and wrongly identifying it with another person. I call this *mirrored projection*, as we are not only projecting onto someone, we are also reading its reflection and believing that it is theirs and we also presume the thoughts or feelings belong to them instead of to ourselves. This is deceiving as we fully believe the energy we are reading came from the other person when it didn't, it came directly from us.

We can visualize this concept as if it has been written as a note rather than invisible energy. For example, if we imagine we have written our feelings on a piece of paper describing deep-rooted feelings of anger and resentment. We then tape the note to the next person we interact with that even slightly behaves in a way that we believe is associated to the feelings in the note. Whenever we see this person, we read the note back and believe that they wrote it and think it confirms that we must have been right about how they felt. Instead of seeing that we chose to assign the note and the feelings to them, regardless of how they actually felt. We may mistakenly have picked up something in their behavior that wasn't there, purely because we were consumed with emotions and wanted rid of them. We wrote the note based on how *we* felt, nothing to do with the other person therefore, in giving to them we have successfully avoided dealing with the feelings ourselves and instead, we have transferred them to someone else to deal with and nothing gets resolved. In fact, it could ignite a fire. We haven't dealt with our emotions, and the other person now feels responsible for something that isn't theirs – it is no wonder there are so many misunderstandings and misinterpretations in human communication.

The more we do this, the more it can end up becoming a self-fulfilling prophecy. We end up defensive, deluded, paranoid, and believing our insecurities and that other people are thinking or feeling certain ways, all because we are reading energy completely wrong.

If, rather than adding negativity, we had added caring words to the note and turned it into a considerate, loving, compassionate letter, we would then transmute the energy. Therefore, it wouldn't matter whether it was ours, or if we passed it on to anyone else, as all we, or anyone else would be receiving would be genuine, heartfelt, positive energy.

It is essential that we clearly identify our emotions and feelings from other peoples' so that we can see what is our own, what we are absorbing, what we are denying, and what we are projecting. When we understand what projection means, we will become very aware of how easily and how often we do it and also when other people are doing it. We will then see that we have control over what we are receiving, absorbing, and projecting. At any moment we can stop and take responsibility for our own thoughts, feelings, and emotions. When we work through how we think and feel, we have to ensure that we are also understanding and processing what we are experiencing so that we do not deny or suppress the energy, as it will build up in our system or be projected out wrongly.

When we are aware of the thoughts, feelings, and emotions that belong to us, we can then clearly see when we are absorbing energy from others. Then, when we are around people and we absorb their energy, we will know whom it belongs to rather than accusing anyone in the vicinity of owning particular emotions or feelings. For example, if someone is feeling resentful toward us, we will pick up on that energy, know it is not our own, even though we may not know exactly where it has come from. If we choose we can focus on what has been happening lately and pay attention to the energy so that we can assign it to whoever originally delivered it.

If we spend a few moments in silence or meditating, we can sift through the subtle vibrations that we are feeling, think of all the people we have had associations with, and we will start to feel a resonance when the person that has expressed the emotion comes to our mind. The energy will just "sit" right. We will instinctively know where the energy is from, so we are better prepared to deal with the overall circumstances. We can then transmute the energy, rather than project it outward, then we also know we are not going to project and assign it to the wrong person. It can also be beneficial to figure out where it has come from, as if we choose, we can then contact the person to resolve any issues, or we can make try to gain peace or clear any tension in other ways that are relevant to the situation.

If we have been involved in a heated altercation with someone, we may be feeling our own anger or frustration as well as the negative energy the other person is radiating in our direction. Often we don't realize that part of why we feel so agitated long after the conflict has passed is due to absorbing the toxic energy they are still radiating towards us. As empaths, we soak up other people's emotions and we rarely deliberately send out negatively charged emotions in other people's direction. However, some people, particularly energy vampires, will continue to project their low vibrational energy with the intention that we feel it, until their boiling emotions eventually die down. Subconsciously we accept the energy, although some of us take in the energy consciously without actually realizing why.

The main reason we do this is because we do not want to anger the other person further by deflecting their energy and leaving them to deal with it alone. Part of this is because we do not want them to remain angry and the confrontation alive and ongoing. We may feel that by taking hold of it we are also diffusing it by allowing them to freely vent. It could also be that because we feel so low after the conflict, we accept it due to feeling partly responsible for the altercation, even if we were just caught up in it and did nothing at all wrong. When we accept the channeled energy in this way, we are allowing the other person to continue to affect us. At any moment we can transmute that energy, send love, forgiveness, and compassion, both for ourselves and the other person. As soon as we do this we will begin to feel the negativity dissipate, and also the other person will subtly notice that their energy is no longer affecting us. Depending on how the other person feels and on their intentions, they may express this change in various ways. It is likely that as soon as we stop allowing their energy to flow into us they will alter their own feelings. It may be that they lose interest in the energetic tie, or they may try an alternative route to gain a reaction. Mostly, how they react will depend upon whatever dynamic we have developed with them. If it is a one-off encounter with someone and there is no historic residual energy that is compounding the situation, then their desire to make us suffer energetically may drop off. If there is an accumulation of conflicted history between us and the other person, a pattern will have built up whereby they become familiar with our reactions and believe that we will keep absorbing the toxicity, so if we suddenly change how we respond, it can leave them confused and bewildered.

When we have been caught in a vicious cycle of receiving energy from someone due to their anger or resentment, it can take some time for them to realize that we are no longer willing to be a vessel for any negative energy they want to offload. They send us their unpleasant emotions, as they know we are sensitive and will be anxious due to the conflict and for a long time following it. That may conclude with us contacting them to make amends and gain peace, as we cannot bear to have the heavy uncomfortable friction bubbling in our cells.

When we consistently act in a specific way, not only will our behavior feel natural to us, it will also feel natural to the other person. However, that doesn't mean our responses are serving us or them. Whenever we feel any type of anguish, we have to raise our vibration and transmute the energy immediately, rather than being tempted to just block it. When we return negativity with positive, loving, and compassionate vibrations, even though the other person may still want to cause us energetic harm and make us suffer, the energy they are experiencing will dissipate far quicker. It may take some time for the other person to become accustomed to our new way of responding. So even though it may be extremely difficult to break through and alter our energy, we have to persevere for the long-term benefits for all involved. When we are empathetic we will find it far easier to understand and forgive the other person for the part they play, and we will also find it easier to soothe ourselves. Eventually we will naturally learn to return hate with love and we will no longer see our expression as forgiveness but as an acceptance that we all have darkness and we all struggle at times, and copious amounts of anger diminishes the light. We can try not to continuously absorb darkness through thinking we are helping someone to process it. If we do, we are not only hindering them, we are also hindering and hurting ourselves.

We have to take ownership for both the energy we are receiving and the energy we are casting out, and keep our thoughts, feelings, and emotions entirely separate from other people's so that we can identify why the energy keeps circulating and what we can do to alter it. Otherwise, we are ensuring a flow of conflict in our friendships, relationships, and also with strangers as we open the floodgates to allow them to project the imprints of their feelings directly onto us. The main difficulty in this dynamic is the person is not understanding and processing why they are feeling a certain way, so it is likely the behavior will continue and not only affect us, but also affect them severely too.

When we feel hurt, it is often because we have read and received someone's energy and tapped into their insecurity, fear, frustration, anger, jealousy, resentment, and overall personal pain. The person we are reading is a mirror and we are looking into it and seeing, feeling, and experiencing whatever they are feeling. If we find the reflection difficult to look at it may be because it reminds us of our own unique painful encounters and memories and the times when we felt those same emotions without knowing how or where to channel and alleviate them.

Hurt people pass on their hurt to other people purely because they do not know how to process it themselves. Their ego is working damn hard to avoid taking responsibility for it. And as difficult as this is for us to accept, if they do not recognize they are responsible for harmful behavior, they are going to find it almost impossible to fully own it and take accountability for it.

We have to get over the pain we are feeling so that we can acknowledge that however someone is acting is the version of a behavior that they may have spent a lifetime getting to know and feel familiar with. They aren't liklely to change overnight just because we gently touch them with an accepting, compassionate and unconditional loving vibration. They may feel petrified of this unknown energy we are sending them, and instead of embracing their own fear and misunderstanding, they may be far more likely to venomously spit out vitriol as soon as we get close enough to touch their ego-laced buttons. We may then end up feeling as though for no clear reason they are intentionally trying to hurt us by lashing out when all we were doing was trying to offer compassion and send healing. It can be bewildering, when realistically, all that has happened is our empathy has triggered their self-protection to prepare for an impending threat, even though, the only real danger is that they have been confronted by someone who has recognized and scratched the surface of an unhealed wound. They do not realize that their injuries need to be unearthed and healed, and even if they do they may be afraid of the pain they would go through when digging into those wounds.

Sometimes people find it easier to masquerade layer upon layer of pain by lashing out and projecting more pain. The majority of what hurts within is going to come out one way or another, and unfortunately for many people the easiest way to ease the built-up pressure is to project that pain onto those around them. When this happens, in their mind, they no longer have responsibility for it, and when we are absorbers of pain, we receive it and allow this toxic influx of energy to penetrate us and influence how we feel.

We can try to remember than no one else is capable of hurting us, we are hurting ourselves when we transfer other people's pain and make it our own. If we project that pain back out it is usually because, ideally, we are looking to find answers, clues, and an understanding of what has taken place, and we are hoping that the other person will resolve the riddle by taking ownership of this projected energy. However, we will never find the answers within anyone else as they are all found within ourselves. We have to remove both flows of projection so that we work within ourselves and not seek to prejudge or condemn anyone else's behavior. All they have done is remind us or made us aware of our own deep-rooted issues. Even if the only awareness is that we are allowing them to energetically vent while affecting our psyche as they do so.

Hurt people sometimes hurt other people, although it doesn't have to be that way. It can take a lot of unraveling before it happens but hurt people can choose to change how they express themselves so that they do not project their hurt onto others. Someone may try to pass their hurt to us however, it is ultimately our choice whether we absorb it and own it so it becomes our pain too or whether we recognize that it is just the other person's pain and refuse to allow it to affect us. Instead of feeling the result of their actions, we can radiate love and compassion for ourselves and the other person and refuse to interact with the emotions that are directed towards us. Although we may not dramatically alter other people's energy when we transform their emotional energy and transmute it, we will have made a subtle difference.

If we do not know how to transmute energy, we often just pass pain around, and every time it is transferred from one person to another its momentum grows, similar to a snowball. Each pass contains a little of someone's unique experience and holds the memories and pain they themselves have encountered and so the snowball grows. It isn't until one person holds the ball of pain and looks at it closely and distinguishes where it from, who it might belong to, and how it ended up in their hands that it stops.

This pain, whether it is anger, fear, resentment, frustration, or any other negative emotion, delivers a sensation that feels like friction in our energy field. Friction happens when we are unclear of exactly what emotions we are storing, so they ricochet around trying to get our attention and often it is easier and feels more natural to be defensive and reject it. Sometimes it is difficult to tell exactly where the friction came from. It is usually a dirty mixture of all the mud, grime and grit of a thousand or more experiences. To mess with it without knowing what to do usually causes nothing but more mess, confusion, and ultimately friction. So we can imagine what happens if we allow it to penetrate us when we take ownership of it and allow it to settle within our aura.

What regularly happens is when we are angry, resentful, frustrated, or in pain we try to offload some of the heaviness of those emotions onto other people. Unfortunately, we don't know quite where the load has come from, so we throw it back at either whoever we thought passed it to us or the nearest person to us. We just want to get rid of it as it feels heavy and ugly and we prefer to believe we can't possible claim it as our own. Therefore, our defense mechanism causes us to feel impulsed to project it. Whoever is in the vicinity and catches the projected load will feel and see that they are now holding the uncomfortable ball of friction. They won't have time to question or scrutinize it, they just want it gone. And so it continues. On and on, people reject and project huge amounts of unwanted, confusing friction made up of an accumulation of feelings.

Empaths have high levels of empathy and compassion, so we are capable of neutralizing and transmuting friction. We can end the vicious cycle that allows the friction to grow stronger continuing forcefully on its journey. However, unless we remain aware and alert, we are also not always able to hold on to the root of it to get a grip on the friction and see what exactly is happening. Even though empaths are able to transmute negativity, it doesn't mean we always find it natural and easy to do so. It is the tough, challenging, more difficult part of being an empath, especially if we are temporarily caught up in the density of the emotions. However, we can remain consciously aware that we, and others will instantly feel better when the energy is transmuted. We just have to break it down, cleanse, and bring in light and loving healing energy so that the friction transforms into something quite beautiful.

Even if no one else sees a tangible transformation, we will feel it internally and when we feel it, we naturally radiate it, and project it outward, and the energy change will be sensed and felt all around us.

"Be the change you want to see in the world." ——Mahatma Gandhi

When we change ourselves, we also change how other people perceive us, and that creates a butterfly effect of ripples of change that vibrate across the world. This is when we see that there is no separation in the world. Who we are is who other people are. We collectively create the world that we live in and we are each responsible for our own part in it. It doesn't matter whose friction we might have ended up with in our hands. We don't need to label, blame, or condemn someone for it, and we certainly don't need to throw it back at them.

One common way this is played out is when someone experiences road rage. They may feel angry because someone cut in front of them or didn't let them out at a junction, so they then beep their horn or shout expletives. Essentially, they are just trying to pass their contempt and anger onto someone else. The person they shouted at or alerted with their blaring horn now feels fearful, threatened, and a sense of indignation at how they have been treated and they have also been caught unaware. They won't see that maybe their driving was rude or inconsiderate, or even that the reaction by the other person was a response to their driving. They also won't see that there may be an unseen reason for the other person's behavior as they might have been trying to get to a hospital to see a loved one or in a hurry as they were late to collect their child from school. The person who may have been initially at fault would rather not open their mind in this way, as this means they don't have to take any responsibility for the reaction.

Road rage happens very suddenly, so it means people will feel momentarily vulnerable, as they would not have been expecting such an aggressive response seemingly arriving from out of nowhere. This means they are susceptible to taking on the friction without taking a minute to acknowledge it, recognize it for what it is, and then pass on the energy with forgiveness and understanding (transmuting the energy) for how they were treated, and they won't be willing to be accountable or take partial responsibility.

This is not excusing how the person who was expressing the rage treated them. Regardless of the other person's reasons for the volatile behavior, the one on the receiving end could still choose to transmute the energy so that it emanates compassion and a positive vibration. Instead, what usually happens is when they then feel the tension within the friction, they want to get rid of it quickly rather than deal with it themselves. Therefore, they pass it on to someone else by expressing it through anger at the next person they see that does something they perceive to be "wrong." Rather than each person dealing with the emotions they are faced with, they throw them on for other people to catch and process. It prevents the individual from feeling as though they are to "blame" and ultimately having to confront their emotions.

The person who has released the friction feels lighter as they have swiftly deflected it and project it onto someone else. They carry on their day without the full weight of the friction, although they still feel the remnants of the debris within them. These vibrations are waiting to reverberate if someone else triggers them. Meanwhile, the passed around friction bounces from person to person, each time gaining momentum, speed, and strength until it eventually explodes and someone receives not just friction but an avalanche of abuse and anger. Or the other option is that someone takes hold of it to soothes, calms, breaks it down, and transmutes it so that it vibrates on a totally different frequency, one that is filled with love, understanding, acceptance, compassion, forgiveness, and oneness.

When we are fully aware of our own emotions and feelings and have protected ourselves well, we will clearly see when someone else is projecting their pain or anger and ultimately that they are afraid of their emotions and are quickly triggered to react defensively. Even though we may have guarded ourselves so that the energy does not dissolve in our energy field, we can still receive it in a safe space that offers us the opportunity to acknowledge it and transmute it so that it will not harmfully affect us or anyone else.

However much we may protect ourselves, we cannot think we are invincible, and it is still possible that we may be triggered when someone deflects a ball of toxic energy in our direction. We have to take precautions and ensure we have raised our vibration high enough so that any negativity that surrounds us does not resonate with us in any way. Identifying our own emotions so we understand ourselves first and foremost and then transmuting any energy that we absorb immediately counteracts projection effectively every time.

www.VonGArt.com and the name is
Megan Guenthner Clark

Chapter 12

GROUNDING

Just as we "earth" our electrical appliances to ensure the currents are safe and the energy is correctly routed and stable, we can also connect ourselves to Earth so that we can ground and safely stabilize our own electromagnetic fields. When we ground ourselves, we solidly root our energetic selves to Earth so that our energetic bodies are stable and we don't get carried away with whatever is going on around us. This is often spoken of as "being down-to-earth." We are firmly living in our physical body as well as being stable in our mind. We are fully aware of everything that is going on, including our thoughts, emotions, feelings, and intentions, as our minds are not floating off and "detaching" from our physical bodies.

It is essential that empaths remain grounded so that we can maintain a healthy mind, body, and spirit, as we are constantly at risk of becoming overwhelmed due to the vast amounts of external stimuli we absorb. One of the reasons empaths sense and feel everything so intensely is because we have not effectively grounded or centered ourselves. When we remain grounded we also remain present. Simple meditations and mindfulness help to keep us grounded. They prevent our our mind from shifting from the past to the future and back making us feel dizzy and causing us to easily lose sight of whatever is happening in the here and now. We may then be vulnerable to toxic external energy seeping in and settling within our energy field.

When we are present and grounded, it is almost impossible for outer energy to negatively influence and affect us. We can also prevent the risk of our energy drifting outward and invading other people's emotional spaces, resulting in us absorbing and collecting loaded negative energy. If we have grounded ourselves and this still happens, we will find that we notice it faster, so we are able to react quicker and realign once again within our core selves.

To ensure we are creating a stable foundation, we must first achieve harmony between the spiritual and physical worlds and our conscious and unconscious minds. When we have faith in who we are and our beliefs are aligned, we can create a solid base layer as a safe foundation to keep us securely grounded.

We need to fully connect the mind to the body and acknowledge all parts of ourselves before we can become fully balanced. When we deny parts of who we are or what we are capable of achieving, we are effectively suppressing ourselves. If we reject our emotions, reject our natural capabilities, and deny the connection we have to everything that is out there in the universe, we will find it difficult to remain calm and stable, and we will struggle to reach our soul's purpose and our highest potential.

Our emotions and feelings are indications of what is taking place in our subconscious and conscious minds. Often we lose the link to our inner selves as we become so caught up with life's daily demands. When we are fully present and listen to the signs and signals that are delivered to us through our sensations, we can understand the inner workings of our mind with greater insight. By paying attention so that we are aware of what is triggering us to react, we can take charge of our lives rather than living on auto pilot and allowing repetitive patterns to occur.

We can try to keep our minds open to all possibilities so that we can explore who we are, why we are here, and where we are heading. It is essential that we are aware of all of our thought patterns and actions so that we take responsibility for them, and in doing so we have the opportunity to change them should we need to. As soon as we become consciously aware, we are able to see or perceive everything with far more clarity.

As we practice being fully present and grounded to Earth, we will notice how we deal with situations with a calmer, clearer, and more rational mind. Being grounded also helps us to connect to our inner and outer worlds so that we can naturally work out which emotions belong to us and the ones which belong to other people.

We can ground ourselves by working with the Schumann Resonance. The Schumann Resonances (SR) are a set of spectrum peaks in the extremely low frequency (ELF) section of Earth's electromagnetic field. It is named after the German physicist W. O. Schumann, who confirmed the spectrum peaks. Nikola Tesla was the first to discover Earth's resonance frequency but unfortunately he was ahead of his time and his studies were not taken seriously.

Research carried out by Schumann and Herbert König determined that the frequency between the Earth's surface and the inner edge of the ionosphere resonates at a main frequency of 7.83 Hz. During further research, König discovered that the brain frequencies of the most advanced organisms on earth also resonate at approximately 7.83 Hz, falling into the same rhythm as the Earth's beat. This is known as Harmonic Resonance. When we tune in to Earth's frequency, it is believed that we can ground, balance, heal, regenerate, replenish, repair, and rebuild ourselves, as the Schumann Resonance acts like a natural tuning fork.

******* Dr. Wolfgang Ludwig's studies found that electrosmog from technology drowns out Earth's natural signal. Being in resonance with Earth's signal contributes to a calmer and overall healthier wellbeing and this comes from being in natural environments, rather than being in condensed city centers. NASA found that when astronauts were in outer space and cut off from the Schumann Resonance their health deteriorated, so they introduced a Schumann stimulator device to modern space shuttles, which is a magnetic pulse that imitates Earth's frequency.

Ludwig also came across ancient teachings that explain that mankind needs two subtle environmental signals: the *yang*, positive masculine signal from above (the ionosphere), and the *yin*, negative feminine signal from below the Earth's crust to achieve and maintain optimum health. If either of these are denied or out of harmony, our health deteriorates rapidly.

Earth provides a natural source of energy, so simply walking barefoot on it recharges and stabilizes the electrical charge of our physical and subtle bodies. Our immune system requires a healthy amount of electrons and Earth's surface provides these vital electrons in abundance. Our feet are transmitters that absorb and discharge electrons through our skin. When we walk barefoot we harmonize our electromagnetic energy so that it is vibrating at the same frequency as the earth's surface. We also remove the electrosmog from energetic body that has been absorbed from being in close contact with electronic devices. Walking barefoot is the ultimate way to ground ourselves.

The majority of footwear is manufactured from materials that disconnect us from Earth. For those times that we are unable to walk barefoot, we can purchase conductive sandals that connect us to Earth's energy so that we receive a limitless and balancing supply. We can then rejuvenate, harmonize, and ground ourselves every time we are outdoors. These shoes are particularly beneficial while hiking or walking in natural environments.

A simple way to ground ourselves is through visualizing being rooted to Earth. If we are able to stand outside with bare feet on fresh grass or earth, the overall effect will be far more rewarding. We can visualize that there are roots or cords coming out from both of our feet and also from our root *chakra*.

These energetic cords dig into the ground and reach toward the center of the planet until they reach the heart of Mother Earth. As the cords burrow down into the ground, they become highly charged with energy. And when they reach the heart center, they reenergize and work their way back up and through us, infusing us with powerful waves of natural energy.

As we root ourselves to the ground, we can also imagine that we are flushing out any negative energy we may have stored. The Earth neutralizes this energy, so we can release any toxic debris that has collated and that is causing energetic obstruction. We can flush out all the negativity through our root *chakra*.

So that there is a continual flow running through us, we can visualize a fresh supply of vital energy entering through our crown *chakra*. As we imagine the flushing system proceeding, we will be energized from the roots, the sun, planets, and stars, and we can also gain a supply of energy direct from the Earth's center. In one process we can flush out negative energy and recharge and replenish our systems with positive energy from universal sources.

The perfect time to let go of negative charges is during a grounding practice as we are in a stable and harmonic energy state to safely channel energy. It is then able to flow through us without causing any emotional or mental harm or disturbance.

While we are grounding we can visualize a circle of light that exists all around us, with the outer layer a silver color to repel negative influences. The circle or bubble around us will keep us safe from harm and will safeguard our energy so that it does not become infused with any toxic debris floating around in the atmosphere. As we close our eyes, we can focus attention on our breathing. When we breathe deeply, we inhale natural energy from the Earth and will feel it flow through each part of our body and up through our *chakras*. As we exhale we can let go of any tension and negativity while releasing any excess emotions and dense energy that we have absorbed throughout the day. When we open our eyes we may feel calmer and energetically lighter, as we will have cleansed our aura and balanced and grounded ourselves to earth. If not, we can repeat the process, inhaling and exhaling for a little longer while visualizing cleansing our energy and firmly rooting ourselves to the ground.

This method keeps us harmonized using Earth's natural healing energies so that we are stabilized and revitalized. If we practice this next to plants or trees, the benefits will be heightened as the elements naturally absorb waste (carbon dioxide) and replace it with essential, vitalizing, primordial, fresh, and clean energy (oxygen).

Empaths will always be vulnerable to toxic energies, which are capable of penetrating our energy field and causing us harm, so we need to be constantly aware of how energy affects us. The more we integrate these simple methods and repeat them on a daily basis, the more protected we are during times of need. We can repeat the process frequently so that we remain shielded, although within time we will notice we are going through the motions without even being consciously aware. When we are naturally grounding, we won't need to focus as intently on this process; however, time can still be taken to specifically focus on rooting ourselves to the earth. If we become complacent, we put ourselves at risk of harmful toxic energies seeping in.

A very simple way to ground our energy can be achieved by sitting next to a tree as they radiate grounding healing energy. If we cannot get to a location where there is an actual tree, we can visualize one in our mind. We then imagine we are as strong and sturdy as the tree and root ourselves deep into the earth to stabilize and balance our energy as well as keep our physical body upright.

While we are grounding we can use crystals to enhance the process, or we can just keep them beside us as we go about our day. Hematite is one of the best crystals for balancing and grounding as it helps to keep our energetic vibration high along with keeping us grounded to the earth at the same time. It pulls excess energy down through the root *chakra* and into the earth. It also stabilizes any high vibrational energy that may be around us if we have been working with high-energy crystals or if we have not been effectively channeling energy via our *chakras*.

Water is essential for empaths as it is a conductor for emotional energy and it is also naturally grounding, so we can use it in various ways. Water balances, calms, heals, cleanses, grounds, neutralizes, restores, and revitalizes us when we are feeling hypersensitive, overwhelmed, or at odds with the world or ourselves. This is why many empaths are water babies and have a longing to be next to the sea, either watching it, listening to it, or swimming in it, and we often choose to meditate or sit near lakes for soothing, calming, and balancing influences. Human bodies consist of approximately 70 percent water, and as it is a powerful element, a close connection to water works wonders.

Sea salt enhances the natural healing ability of water. When we add a cup of sea salt to our bathwater, we can cleanse the skin along with drawing out any negative entities that have attached to us throughout the day.

Our thoughts and feelings are said to have a profound effect on physical reality, and studies show how our vibrations are capable of affecting the molecular structure of water. Japanese scientist Dr. Masaru Emoto's research found that when water is exposed to words such as "love and gratitude," beautiful crystals are formed with complex and colorful snowflake patterns. Emoto also discovered that both music and the spoken word change the "expression" of water, and that when water is exposed to negative thoughts it develops dull colors and asymmetrical patterns.

We can also use the same concept when drinking water. When we have poured ourselves a glass, we can hold the glass up to our heart center and think and feel positive emotions then consciously radiate the vibrations outward toward the glass. We can then allow our energy to flow so it travels through our body and is channeled through our hands and onto the glass. While drinking the water, we can then think thoughts associated with peace, joy, and love while we express gratitude. We can also infuse a few drops of purified water with positive thoughts and apply the charged droplets of water to the third eye in the middle of the forehead to balance and cleanse the third-eye *chakra*.

Placing bowls of water around the room helps to keep the atmosphere tranquil as water absorbs subtle emotional energy. Small bowls of water balance our emotional states, and tabletop water fountains keep the water continuously flowing and constantly in motion so that our personal energy is constantly clearing and recharging.

One very easy way to ground ourselves is to spend time with nature. When we are away from the hustle of our day-to-day lives, we will notice our senses becoming more alert as we tune in to our surrounding environment. Our awareness of sights, smells, and sounds will instantly heighten and we will feel fully present as we achieve total peace and harmony. If we are not able to spend time outdoors, we can bring the outdoors in. We can surround ourselves with plants, crystals, nature-themed art, and place items around the room that were found on adventures, such as feathers, pinecones, pebbles, stones, or rocks.

Using a full-spectrum light indoors gives the effect that we are outdoors as the radiating light replicates natural light. A full-spectrum light emits a similar intensity and range of colors that natural daylight produces, so it simulates the electromagnetic spectrum that is beneficial to many life forms, including plants, animals, and humans. These lights are used in some therapeutic practices, especially for those with seasonal affective disorder (SAD) as the light emulates natural sunlight. Full-spectrum lights are known to increase energy and enhance our overall wellbeing as bright light elevates serotonin levels, which is the hormone that is associated with mood regulation. The more serotonin released, the happier we will feel.

We can also place a birdfeeder just outside a window so we can watch various species of birds stopping by each day.

Chapter 13

PROTECTION/SHIELDING

An empath's characteristics can be both a blessing and a curse. It is a blessing to have the ability to feel and experience life being highly sensitive, as this means that joy, pleasure, and love are felt as incredibly strong electrical pulses beating through us. However, the curse is that the lows also pulsate at an equally high intensity too. Therefore, it is essential that we learn to protect ourselves by being consciously aware of how external energy influences and affects us. We are then in a position to turn the curses to blessings so that the tormenting and toxic energies are not absorbed and felt within our psyche.

As empaths are able to transmute energy, we may question why we still need to protect ourselves. Remaining conscious to everything that is going on around us, as well as navigating and staying conscious within our own lives, can be extremely exhausting, and this is why many empaths become overwhelmed and debilitated. We are constantly vulnerable to external forces. Therefore, if we put protection in place, we are safeguarded from unexpected or intolerable energy while we process what is going on within our own energetic world. If we have protection in place, we do not need to be on constant guard that something will seep in and affect us without us being aware of it.

Understanding and identifying our emotions so that we can effectively transmute energy is the ultimate way to protect ourselves, although this only happens when our own energy is highly charged. Our energetic frequency can alter moment to moment, so for the times we are vibrating on a low level or unaware of what is around us we need to keep our energy well protected. Otherwise, we will leave ourselves wide open and vulnerable to our energy reserves being drained unexpectedly.

Everyone has a layer of energy that act as a "skin" between the physical body and the outer world. Empaths have a very thin layer of "skin," which means that our surrounding environment and other people's energy can penetrate us far easier. This also helps us to sense other people's energy states and naturally radiate healing energy.

We can protect our energy field by using the visual art of shielding, which involves imagining that there is a magical layer around ourselves that is capable of preventing harmful energy from leaking in and affecting us. By shielding and protecting our aura with simple visualization exercises, we will be far less likely to absorb toxic energy along with unwanted or negative emotions.

Visualizations can sound as though they may not offer a great deal of protection, however, when we believe in our conscious thoughts we then emit powerful vibrations which result in clear and vivid powerful visual images. We also add strength to the protective energy we are radiating when our images are created and infused with feelings. Our thoughts are capable of turning to emotion and our emotions can then affect our overall feeling and ultimately they then alter our belief system. When we change how we think, we can also change how we feel, and thus we change what we attract or repel.

Low vibrational emotions and feelings can have a harmful impact on our emotional and physical health, so when we change our thoughts we are also protecting our overall wellbeing. Our aura is an energy field that changes color depending on the state of our physical body and mind. When creating a visual protective layer, we can choose whatever color we feel is associated with strength. We can then imagine our whole body being cocooned in this thick protective colorful film, filled with the color of our choice. We can visualize the color surrounding the whole of our being and glowing within our aura. As we keep the focus on the color enveloping us, we will feel a barrier building between our physical body and the outside world. When this layer is in place, it reduces the chance of outside energies being able to negatively interact with our own.

We can also try another technique which consists of holding the forefinger and thumb together on each hand and placing both arms above the head and then moving the arms outward to make a diamond shape around the body. Hold the arms above for a few moments, then move the arms out to the side of the body, and then point them to the ground, all the time setting the intention for protection while strongly emanating positive vibrations.

Another option is to wear a piece of clothing that has been charged with high vibrational energy. We can wrap a neck scarf around a crystal that is associated with protection and leave it to marinate in the energy overnight, then when we put the scarf on the next day it will be recharged and infused with the protection elements that the crystal radiated. We can also pop the crystal in a pocket or our bag for added protection.

Although negative energy is capable of penetrating our own energy, we must realize that it is only able to do that if we so allow it to. When we are consciously aware and living in the present moment we will have absolute control over what we absorb and we can then choose to attract or repel energy just by invocation, which is simply asking for help or support to protect us from harmful energies.

Protective shields can be visualized at any time, anywhere. The more often they are used, the stronger the protective layer becomes. A protective layer is quite simply an energetic outline around ourselves; the thicker it is, with no gaps, the better protected we will be from external forces. Therefore, we will not become as overwhelmed when in the vicinity of high or low vibrating energies.

While protective layers can be hugely beneficial, we can try not to rely upon entirely to make us invincible to external emotional harm.

We also have to keep our vibration high and take good care of ourselves so that we do not allow other people to take an advantage over us and deplete our energy. It is vital that we look after our emotional health and consciously separate other people's emotional energy from our own so that we are less likely to be affected by people whose negative energies can have a destructive impact on us.

One way to protect our energy is simply by saying "No" when we are not aligned to something or when it compromises our values or makes us feel uncomfortable. When we refuse to interact with people in a way that allows them to zap our energy, we are in effect protecting our own reserves from being depleted. We do not need to shut them out of our life, we just simply need to disengage whenever a situation is occurring that causes internal discord. It is sometimes difficult to recognize when this is happening, which is why we must remain vigilant of how our energy feels when we are around people to prevent ourselves from becoming drained just so that other people are fed and reenergized (see Energy Vampires).

As we carry out the inner work required to evaluate who and what we are allowing into our lives, we can use methods like protective shields as tools to combat the effects of negative entities. However, the more we process exactly why we are subjecting ourselves to other people's projections and allowing their energy to interfere with our own, we will find that an outer shield is not necessary as we will be building the strength from within.

The energy we hope to protect ourselves from may be in close contact to us or it may be directed towards us from a distance. It doesn't matter how near or far someone is, we can still protect ourselves from negativity attaching to us.

If someone is thinking about us in a way that is detrimental, we will likely sense the energetic attack. We can either turn the negativity to positive thoughts and feelings and send the energy back to them, or visualize a protective layer to deflect the negativity. Doing this from a distance works similarly as someone is in the same room as us and we don't want their energy to interact with our own. We can either deflect the negativity or we can absorb it and transmute it into positive vibrations.

To dispel negative energy or to cleanse, purify, and protect both ourselves and our homes, we can burn sage. Bundled white sage is the easiest to use and is available for purchase from most local herb or health stores.

The smoke from the sage attaches to any negative energy in the air and as the smoke dissipates and clears it carries the energy with and transmutes it from negative to positive. Sage changes the ionic composition in the air, so we will sense the difference in the atmosphere immediately.

Before we burn sage we need to keep in our mind the intention of what we would like to achieve. If there is a particular energy we want to erase from the atmosphere, we can focus our awareness on it so that the cleansing is strengthened and the protection enhanced. When we light sage, a flame might occur. If this happens, we can blow on the flame until only the embers are glowing so that the sage produces a smoky trail. It is common to have to relight sage a few times during the ritual.

Once we have lit the sage, we can first smudge ourselves by slowly waving the sage around us, starting at the floor and then moving it up over our head and around us in circles. We then place the sage with the burning side facing down in a fireproof bowl. Our intuition will then guide us to where the sage needs to travel.

As we walk around each room, we will feel compelled to remain in certain areas longer than others. This is where the energy is at its densest, so there is no hurry just allow the sage to remain burning for as long as is necessary. We can pay extra attention to windows, doors, and any other openings. We can try to ensure we don't inhale the sage while we are moving around.

It is always a good idea to burn sage at the beginning of each new week to clear out the old and make way for the new. We can also burn it at the change of a season or at the start of the winter or summer solstice.

Sage has a masculine energy and incense has a feminine energy, so once we have burned sage we can light an incense stick to balance the energies.

Crystals can also be used as a protection aide. Although there are numerous crystals to choose from, we often instinctively choose ones that vibrate in resonance with our own frequency. Haematite is a recommended crystal as it has a protective energy while also heightening courage and self-esteem. Haematite has a strong mirroring ability, so any negative entities will be deflected away, although it can also encourage us to look at our own issues by turning the mirror effect internally. This is beneficial as it allows us to clear our mind so we can focus with clarity on any issues we need to deal with. Haematite is connected to the root *chakra*, so it keeps us grounded and balances our aura and chakras. Orgonite is another crystal that is essential for protection as it transforms negative energy into positive energy, as well as protecting against harmful electromagnetic frequencies.

Essential oils hold their own energetic frequency and certain oils have a particularly strong and naturally repelling, protective aroma. Peppermint, frankincense, and sage are all recommended for protection.

During meditation we can seal our aura so that we protect ourselves against external negative entities. Visualizing a white light totally surrounding the body with the outer layer of the light a silver color deflects harmful energy.

The solar plexus *chakra* is associated with feelings, emotions, self-esteem, and security. Therefore, for instant protection we can cover this *chakra* with our hands or an object as a temporary barrier to avoid absorbing negativity or leaking emotional energy. The solar plexus is located in the upper abdomen area. Practical exercise, such as yoga or *tai chi*, enhance natural protection, as both practices focus on directing and channeling the breath while moving the body. When the body and mind are connected we will be more grounded, balanced, and mentally and physically stronger.

Sea salt in water can be placed in bowls at the entrance to rooms as it transmutes emotions by absorbing negative energy. Negative energy cannot stick to salt, so wherever there is salt, there will be no negative energy as it neutralises it upon contact. Unrefined or sea salt is excellent for grounding and cleansing as it draws out impurities and negative entities. This is one of the reasons empaths feel naturally pulled toward the sea as salt is one of the purest elements on the earth. Salty tears are also cleansing as they remove stagnant energy away from our bodies and they detoxify our nervous system.

When we shield ourselves, we can try not to make the protection too solid, as energy will struggle to enter or leave. We can visualize a filter surrounding the whole of our energy field that allows energy to trickle through so that it is not overwhelming. If our energy is particularly low, we can set the intention for the energetic filter to prevent low vibrational energy from entering. When our levels have lifted, we can then remove the filter if our energy is high enough to easily transmute negativity.

Our energy field holds and stores memories, so it may quickly reverberate, reform and bounce back to its original state even after balancing and protection exercises have taken place. It is essential to ground, balance, and protect ourselves regularly.

The more often we practice protecting and shielding to create a safe zone, the stronger our energy field becomes. Eventually we will naturally sense a strong guard around us, although we never need to become complacent as internal or external conditions can penetrate and alter our energy at any time.

When we transmute energy, we can still use protection methods to prevent negative energies affecting us, while we focus our attention on transmuting energy. We can also do a very simple "shake off energy" exercise by vigorously moving the body and shaking our limbs to activate and let go of any entities that may be clinging to our physical body or that are lodged in our energetic field.

As we raise our vibration we will find that we are less vulnerable to harmful negative energy, as our high vibration automatically repels the negativity. We also need to remain balanced, centered, and grounded so that we are aware of everything that is surrounding us and so that our feet are firmly rooted and nothing can knock us sideways.

The higher our self-esteem, self-acceptance, self-belief, and self-love, the stronger we are and the more powerful and radiant our aura is, making it far more difficult for external negative energies to penetrate it.

Chapter 14

INNER KNOWING

Empaths have an inner knowing feeling that is far more powerful than intuition, general gut feeling, or psychic ability. We are able to naturally converse with the universe. When we tap into this ability, it delivers information to us in the form of sensations, déjà vu, synchronicities, and subliminal messages through a variety of signs, symbols, and signals. This is the universe's way of guiding us. We may also receive these messages through visions, dreams, and tingling sensations during practice of disciplines such as yoga or meditation or any form of exercise, or when we are living authentically and aligned with our core, out with nature or near water. Our inner knowing is intrinsically connected to the energy radiating from our heart. When our heart is open, the emanating vibrations provide us with clear, strong and trusted inner knowledge.

Rather than using our thinking mind, empaths are generally receptive and use the intensity of all of our sensations to make sense of the world we live in. We observe the electromagnetic vibrations that are sent out and we have the ability to translate the energy so that we clearly understand it. Our inner knowing feeling is basically when we know something without using any of our five basic senses. It is often known as an ESP or extra sensory perception. It is also referred to as a psychic ability. However, with a psychic ability people see images, whereby our knowing is experienced as sensations.

Everything that we have absorbed from our environment and every bit of knowledge we have been taught, along with all the vibrations, sensations, signs, messages, and energy that we come into contact with, mix and blend and absorb and deposit in our psyche. We also experience moments of déjà vu with synchronicities occurring regularly. We usually notice an increased amount of repeated number sequences or unusual, or what seem to be coincidental happenings, whenever we are going through a particularly significant period in our lives.

The word "synchronicity" was coined by Carl Jung and he explained that regular occurrences are more than just "frequent coincidences" and appear specifically to align us to our highest potential by showing us the reality behind the dreamlike world we exist in. They are sharp and sudden unmistakable jolts that are delivered by the universe in the form of subliminal messages. They are sent to gently shake us so that we arise from slumber and no longer walk around in a sleeplike state. Jung went on to explain that synchronicities are essential revelations and they only occur if we are actively participating in them, so if we are experiencing synchronicities it means that we are already involved in the unfolding of our higher purpose.

The reason synchronicities appear is because they are confirmations that we are exactly where we are meant to be or that a person we have met is someone who we are meant to meet at that exact point in our lives. Whenever we place our faith in these occurrences, we will be rewarded by more of the same. Each event, whether minor or major, will direct us closer toward our unique and divine higher purpose and bring with it valuable and essential learning.

Synchronicities also give us a sense of interconnection to all that exists as they allow us to have faith that whatever is in front of us on our journey has been placed there to assure us that we are safe to unravel and evolve. Regardless of whether whatever happens to us is a trial or tribulation, a blessing or a curse, it is all perfectly playing out to propel us to look beyond any illusions and gain clarity and new understanding that is required for our vital spiritual growth. Synchronistic illuminations offer a path to integration and oneness, and when we continue trusting in our inner knowing we will eventually connect with our twin soul. Although many believe the twin soul can only be found through entanglement with another being, we reconnect with our twin soul when we eradicate our ego and peel away all the layers to encounter the vulnerability and humaneness of our soul in all its shades. A twin soul fulfillment can be found within us, when we deter from living as two haves (an ego and our authentic self) and we join in communion with our whole self. We may then go on to meet other souls who we have intense connections with on numerous levels.

"Synchronicity is an ever present reality for those who have eyes to see." ——Carl Jung

Our inner knowledge also generates from lifetimes of data that is stored within our DNA, as well as the knowledge and wisdom held in all universal life force energy. We are not only guided by our individual experiences, we are also guided by everything in the universe. Much of what we perceive is a result of previous lives, ancient teachings, beliefs, and all occurrences. We also have access to everything that has once taken place and that has been passed down throughout history. Our inner knowing communicates with the trillions of cells in our body as our DNA stores cosmic and ancient conscious genetic wisdom passed on from our ancestors as well as all of our own unique individual experiences.

We are also assisted by another term coined by Carl Jung, the "Collective Unconscious." Jung describes the information stored there as the inherited primordial thoughts, instincts, images, and "archaic remnants" that reflect basic patterns common to all beings of the same species. A lot of the data in the collective conscious is separate from what is held in our own unconscious mind, as much of it has never filtered through our conscious mind, so we have not been suppressed it to our unconscious mind. The data in the collective unconscious is accessible, when we are open and receptive, or when we tap into it, and it has been gathered from thousands of years of genetics. A lot of the data will just automatically feed us, though there is so much out there that we can also consciously attune to it so that we receive an unlimited input.

The collective unconscious also adds to the data we internally receive through our inner knowing. It is limitless and it has witnessed everything, absorbed everything, and is able to perceive everything, without denial and without regulation or boundaries. It contains all that is hidden to the naked eye and connects us to our journey by interacting with the signs and feelings that guide our way.

We have a higher force that we are not always consciously aware of and it is collating and storing information constantly on our behalf so that it can feed it back to us when we need it most. Our higher conscious then taps into all the stored data and delivers the information by sending signals via our inner knowing. This data feed keeps us safe in the world. It protects us and sends out signals to alert us when something isn't right or when we are not aligning with something. It is our choice whether we choose to have faith and act on it or whether we override it by listening to our triggers and our conscious mind.

Although our inner knowing comes to us in an instant, we sometimes choose to push it aside and have a preference for logical or seemingly factual knowledge instead. This usually happens when we have lost faith in our ability to sense what is actually taking place. When we return to the initial instinctive feeling that we had, we often see that it was a red flag waving frantically to alert us so to heed its warning and follow its direction.

It is not always easy to have absolute faith in our inner knowledge as it often comes with inner conflict. We don't always want to believe or accept that what we sense is true. However, when we do not pay attention we are often taught harsh lessons and it isn't until we reflect back on the situation that we say, "I should have listened to myself." It is then that we realize that it would have benefited us to trust the original warning signal, which, had we listened, would have offered us a profound insight into what we are getting involved in.

Unfortunately, for a lot of people the only time they trust their inner knowing is when something has gone wrong. Even though by then it is too late to turn back the clock, people seem to have faith in their instinct once the moment has passed. That is when they look back and say that they knew their senses were right all along.

Empaths naturally rely on our inner knowing feeling and it's only if other people try to tell us that we are wrong that we might begin to doubt it. Hindsight is wonderful and we can learn by reflecting, but our inner knowing is far more magnificent and serving. What good can hindsight do for us after the event? This is why it is essential that we learn to distinguish between our inner knowing and our other internal thoughts, emotions, beliefs and feelings so that we know why and when we can trust them. We will then rely upon our inner knowing as a trusty and vital life tool to guide our way.

The main difficulty in trusting ourselves is working out whether how we are feeling is authentic or if the inner sensations are being brought to us because of what our noisy, irrational emotions and thoughts are communicating. We can try to remember that we are consciously in control of our thoughts. When we remain still and focus intently on our sensations, our inner knowing will vibrate powerfully due to the basic knowledge that has been gathered from internally and externally absorbed particles of divine knowledge and data.

When we do not listen to our knowing sensations, they become an inner screeching noise that gets louder and louder as they try to tell us that something isn't quite right. They alert us to pay attention so that we carry out what could be an excruciatingly painful period of introspection. Our inner knowing isn't a sound, it is a sense, and can be energetically felt. It can start off light and then very quickly become an agonizing, debilitating sensation if it is ignored. Until we learn to follow our inner knowing it will resound within us until we are receptive and willing to heighten our awareness and reroute the path we are on.

If time runs out and we are met with whatever our inner knowing was trying to warn us about, we will likely be dealt a painful blow. Not only will we have to deal with the wrong turn we took, but we will also have to cope with accepting we knew about this lesson all along and we could have taken steps to prevent it uncurling with a memorable sting in its tail. The inner knowing feeling is there to protect us from potential destruction and pain.

Whenever we notice an inner discomfort it is because we are not paying attention to ourselves or we do not have a profound understanding of something. The less we trust our inner knowing, the less powerful it becomes. Although it will still exist in the background warning us, it will quickly learn that we don't pay attention and it will be less likely to jump in front of our path when we are about to head in the wrong direction.

We absolutely have to trust in our abilities and embrace them, as the moment we reject our deepest sensations they dissipate and we lose that connection. The more faith we have in our inner knowing, the more we are able to rely on it to assist us when we are unsure and just need a reassuring confirmation. The more we exercise it, the stronger it becomes. It will be an ally protecting and guiding us along whichever path we choose as long as we are prepared to constantly listen to it.

Our inner knowing interacts with our subconscious and unconscious minds. That is where exists unearthed lifetimes of history. Our conscious mind, which can overrule our inner knowing, only has access to a small fraction of this vast amount of knowledge. However, we can attune to the stimuli and information available from many sources simply by allowing our conditioned, conscious thoughts to get out of the way so that we can then focus on and surrender to the sensations that exist. Learning how to trust our inner knowing so that we don't allow our heads to rule this wealth of the knowledge is not always easy. We can only place our trust in the knowledge we have stored when we know that the information we receive is not masked or influenced by irrational thoughts, emotions, false beliefs, fear, or wounded feelings.

When we follow our inner knowing, we accept the invitation to step into a significant phase in our life, one where we are being offered optimum opportunity to break through old habits and charter change. Our movement will be assisted by the electrical waves of magnetic energy that are all around us. They will help us to repel or attract any entities that we want to dispel or draw inward.

We can use our inner knowing to see what's currently happening or slightly ahead so that we can be forewarned or forearmed and empowered to continue. Developed empaths are able to trust their inner knowing entirely. Undeveloped empaths are wary and do not always place their full trust in it, so they may listen but they won't always act on it. It is likely, though, that the reason they may not trust it faithfully is because they first need to understand how to identify and process emotions and feelings and also be confident in what is stored in the subconscious and unconscious minds so that those things do not adversely interfere.

All empaths just *know* things without having any idea of where we have gained the information. It depends whether we are willing to discern, trust, and then have complete faith in the information that makes all the difference. When trying to work out the truth from a lie or a bad decision from a good one, we can see that all the information has been presented to us so that we can use it to make decisions. The information should only be trusted if we are skilled at reading ourselves and others accurately and if we have no ulterior motives or agendas. We can try to ensure that our ego, paranoia or other questionable or disorganized information is not clouding our judgment.

We can support our inner knowing by also paying attention to our five senses when we require added confirmation. As long as our conscious mind or our false beliefs, feelings, or emotions are not interrupting and causing the information we are receiving to be misconstrued in any way, we can directly access a wealth of knowledge.

Empaths will often know what people are going to say before they say it and also know how they are feeling without needing to be told. We instantly pick up on vibrations that others are subconsciously or consciously sending out. When we enter a room we will immediately sense the energy that is present. Without realizing we are doing it, we automatically scan each person to gain the necessary information that helps us to assess whether they are safe to be around or not. We will pick up on whether someone is highly emotional, sensitive, elated, in fear, in pain, troubled, or at peace. This aspect of being an empath is one to be very aware of as other people's energies can easily penetrate and infiltrate our own energy field. This means that we can walk into a room feeling totally calm and harmonized and within moments our energy can flip to take on the chaotic or highly charged energy that emanates from those around us.

When empaths empathize with others, we absorb other people's emotions, beliefs, and feelings, including all the pollution lingering around. We soak up everything as quickly and effectively as a sponge does. Not only do we pick up on the energy from those around us, we are also highly sensitive to negative energy that lingers in rooms or on objects. Empaths will often go somewhere and immediately feel uncomfortable and have a strong desire to return home so we can rebalance and replenish our energy. We will also feel this energy on certain items of clothing or material belongings and we will usually remove them from our homes so the energy associated with them is ejected too.

Energy attaches to clothing, and if a bad experience has taken place when wearing a particular piece of fabric, the energy will cling to it and it may give us an intense edgy feeling. We will then find it uncomfortable to wear certain clothes due to the heavy energetic debris they hold. This also goes the opposite way and certain fabrics hold positive high vibrational energy and we know that if we wear that piece of clothing our energy will be lifted throughout the day. Objects, especially jewelry, hold an array of emotions, and this is why many empaths cannot wear certain items after a relationship has ended. This is the reason many people have sentimental pieces that feel dear to them, knowing that if they were lost identical pieces could never take their place. The loving energy surrounding objects can be felt stronger when we hold a particular item in our hands. This is because the warmth of our hands, along with our own vibration, activates the energy of the item so that it vibrates quicker and more intensely.

Everything that exists is made of energy, and although we perceive the energy to be still, as it appears solid, every item is a collection of atoms in motion. Even if the vibrations are very subtle, they still exist. We can finely tune in to the vibrations radiating from anything.

It sometimes feels as though we are continuously wading through a mass of information. While there are loose and frayed ends scattered everywhere, we are not always able to easily clear our mind so that it functions well. For much of the time we can feel as though we are like Sherlock Holmes, constantly knee deep in processing tiny fragments of information so that we can blend the scraps of data with our inner knowing to make the picture complete.

The inner knowing that empaths are gifted with is a subtle inner voice that awakens us to our instincts. It is something that exists within our genetics and enables us to have access to resources stored within the collective conscience and in past memories. When our knowing sensations arise we are often tempted to suppress and push them back down. It can be quite terrifying to recognize how powerful we are, and when we are alerted to our senses we often initially deny and reject them, fearing the unknown.

Our inner knowing goes beyond our basic intuition (an innate perception of the truth.) It is an instantaneous reaction that arises with no facts, reasoning, or information required to prove or disprove its authenticity. The sensation and feeling that empaths have of just 'knowing something' is a gift that enables us to naturally gain knowledge without needing to process data rationally.

Difficulties arise when we are told that what we know is wrong, as we begin to doubt or mistrust ourselves. If someone is lying to us about something or they are not able to recognize or admit the truth they will not want us to see through the lie either. If we speak out about the discord we sense, the other person may then try to convince us that we are mistaken. Although our senses are alerting us, we also want to place our trust in other people too and this is often one of our downfalls, particularly when we are interacting with someone who is not willing to be open and honest with us. When we have little faith in our inner knowing it weakens.. If someone tells us our inner knowing is wrong when it is actually right, it can bring about immense inner conflict and we will likely rack our minds considering all options and perspectives until we eventually align with what seems to be the truth. When we have eventually pieced all the data together our inner knowing gains a sense of peace, is soothed and settles back down.

Honesty is a frustrating subject for an empath. We do not understand mind games very well or why people try to use trickery or deception to cover their tracks. We can become resentful and impatient when we constantly have to try to figure out a lie from the truth.

Until we have full and absolute faith that we are able to trust and rely on our inner knowing feeling, communication with others can seem like a minefield. It does not matter how long or how many paths we take to unearth the answers, we will keep going until we finally solve the riddle. Part of the reason we do this is for our own peace of mind, as above anything else we need to confirm that our inner knowing can be relied upon.

Psychologist Carl Jung spoke of the voice within, explaining, "Deep down, below the surface of the average man's conscience, he hears a voice whispering, 'There is something not right,' no matter how much his rightness is supported by public opinion or moral code." The feeling Jung describes is that niggling doubt that does not go away despite what other information there is that leads us to believe a point. All people have an inner whisper, but with empaths the voice can become bellowing and will persist, regardless of any reasoning we try to silence it with.

Unfortunately, in the modern world many of us are taught that it is not possible to receive communication through the mind from other sources. We may be questioned as to where we get our information from, or we may be doubted or even wrongly told that the information we have received is not true. All of these things can cause us to lose faith in our intuition and psychic abilities.

Many people are afraid of either being psychic or being perceived as psychic due to some of the ancient myths and tales of witchcraft that surround this ability. Fear will have a profound impact on being able to receive information as it will block the flow and reduce the messages and sensations that are possible when our mind is open and trusting.

To be able to tap into our inner *knowing*, we simply need to sense the vibrations in our energy field. When we understand where our energy ends and another person's begins, we will have a clearer understanding of our own thoughts, emotions, and feelings and also of other people's too. We generally do not intentionally invade another person's energy space. We simply allow information to enter our field if it has been directed toward us. Often people do not realize their thoughts gather energy and are powerful communicators. If someone is thinking or feeling something strongly enough, we are almost guaranteed to pick up on it.

Empaths are able to sense if someone is in danger or pain. We may also know if someone is dying or has died. We may sense when someone is watching us and we will also have a strong sense of what is going on in the environment even if we are thousands of miles from the specific area. Empaths can sense bad feelings prior to events and our instincts scream out to warn us so that we make alternative arrangements. We also receive positive vibrations that tell us how good something is going to be, and we feel the ripples of joy and pleasure run through us before, during, and long after an event as the energetic vibration of it interacts with our own.

We have the ability to communicate with people all over the world without technology and without them realizing that they are signaling messages that come across loud and clear. When we are attuned, we can sense when someone's thoughts are engaging in their mind or even when they are whispering their thoughts and feelings to their friends. People's energy tells us far more than hearing their voices ever could. We can look at a photograph and pick up an array of information just from the visual image. This will include past, current, and present details as the image sends strong currents of energy that we translate easily into emotions and feelings. We can very easily describe someone's personality just by looking at a picture and tapping into the energy. We can also read behind the lines of words in texts and feel the emotion that the person encountered while writing it.

For an empath it is not enough to just trust our inner knowing, we question our intuition and are inquisitive to find out its sole intention. Our inner knowing is an insight into something without having to consciously think about it. It arises within us so that we have the opportunity to consider it and then we contemplate the circumstances or feelings. It is very difficult to just trust our intuition as it can be influenced by fear, love, or other factors. That is why as empaths we revert to the inner knowing that exists within us.

It is vital that in order to thrive we work toward learning to trust our judgment, which comes from our inner knowing, so that we can be at one with and deeply connect to the inherent superpowers we were born with. Our inner knowing feeling is our greatest ally and is there to guide and protect us.

We receive pieces of information that have been "given" to us through energy, and often the details are so precise and clear that even t hough we understand this gift we still sometimes question the magic and mystery of it all.

We are in an age whereby we rely so heavily on technology and are so caught up in making sense of everything we forget that as human beings we have many superpowers that are just waiting to be recognized and tapped into. In ancient times it was perfectly natural to communicate telepathically with tribes all over the world. If there were only two kangaroos in the whole of the country, they will sense one another strongly and are sure to connect. This is the same for many species of animals. However, for some reason many people underestimate the powers human beings have on a mass scale.

When we follow our inner knowing we accept the invitation to step into a significant phase in our life, one where we are being offered optimum opportunity to break through old habits and charter change. Our movement will be assisted with the electrical waves of magnetic energy that are all around us. It will help us repel or attract any entities we want to dispel or draw inward. We can use our inner knowing to see what's currently happening or slightly ahead so that we can be empowered to continue.

We are magical creatures, truly. We just need to believe in ourselves and have faith and it won't take long for the evidence to arrive to prove what we already inherently know, for those that require proof. I trust my senses entirely and no evidence is necessary to confirm or have faith in what I already know that I know, and what is true for me.

Chapter 15

EMOTIONALLY UNAVAILABLE

Due to deeply traumatic encounters we can subconsciously close off our hearts by blocking out painful memories to avoid repeating, reliving, and continuously feeling cycles of the same emotions. When we do this we then put ourselves at risk of not being able to receive new emotions, as our brain will link trauma we previously experienced if it perceives that we are currently in a similar situation. Therefore, if it assesses there is a potential risk of being exposed to those same levels of pain, it will try to block out the associated emotions.

It works similarly if we have experienced physical pain. If we attempt to put our hands on a hot stove, our instincts will kick in to stop us and we will automatically back away from the potential danger. Our emotions are no different, and if we perceive we are going to be hurt, our self-preservation will instinctively cause us to react. This happens because at some level we believe we are preventing ourselves from risking feeling painful emotions again.

When our heart is closed off we become numb to love. We put firm barriers in place to avoid other people getting too close to us. However, we still have that basic human instinct to form close connections with other people physically, mentally, and ironically, even emotionally. What we fail to realize is that when we close off our hearts we put ourselves in danger of experiencing far more pain and destruction than if our hearts remained open. We have to feel the anger, rejection, and pain associated with each experience so that we can look at the history to why we are feeling that way. We can explore the circumstances by keeping ourselves in the moment and then acknowledging the feelings by expressing forgiveness, compassion, and unconditional love. Our emotions can then move on their way as we have isolated, soothed and satisfied the experience so that it is understood and does not affect us again in future similar situations.

We can absorb the lessons we have learned on a logical level while freeing the emotional side so that we are not suppressing or blocking our emotions, which lead to us regurgitating all of the pain. Although we may believe that when we close ourselves off we are preserving and taking care of our emotions, what we are doing has the opposite effect. In order to be able to feel all of our emotions and relate them to each of our encounters, we need to identify and separate the emotions and each situation so that we do not bring them with us when we are faced with new occurrences. We can carry the rational understanding across, without the emotional response.

If we do carry emotions with us, which closes us off, we will end up pushing ourselves and our relationships to extremes so that the emotions are powerful enough to break through the toughened walls that are guarding our hearts. We will unknowingly put ourselves in situations whereby we are guaranteed to fail and so is the other person. Our expectations will be too high and we will test ourselves or the other person continuously just to be able to feel something. We will attract all sorts of wrong; bad relationships, friendships, and situations will magnetize to us, or we will be attracted to them. Our intuition will be out of sync as our hearts will no longer be guiding us, so we will chaotically bounce from one turbulent encounter to the next, or we will avoid interactions completely, which forces us to experience sharp, jagged emotions.

We will eventually find out that just because our hearts are closed off to love it doesn't mean that we are closed off to all other emotions; in fact, quite the opposite. Our vessels become flooded with emotions and we will slowly drown in them. Regardless of how much we try, we will never escape the pain we cause ourselves by desperately trying not to feel. Even though we might think at the time we have control over how much love we are allowing into our lives, we most definitely are not in control over the other countless emotions that life forces us to come face to face with.

When we try to deny love, we will endure wretched loneliness, even if we are in the company of someone. We will receive punishing waves of frustration and anger. We will believe we are unworthy of affection and genuine companionship. We will mistrust others as we will not understand why they would be willing to stay in a one-sided relationship with someone who does not trust themselves enough to feel.

When we block our emotions we may come across to others as cold or uncaring, even though we may not want to feel this way or be perceived this way. Sometimes we trick ourselves into believing that we are open to love and that we are able to feel and experience loving emotions. In the beginning of a relationship we can be immersed in feel-good chemicals that are released when in the throes of excitement and new "love." Basically, we are on a high similar to the feeling one might receive when taking drugs. The serotonin and oxytocin that flush through our system when we spend long periods of time in the infatuating first stages of a relationship can fool us into believing that we are capable of love.

Therefore, when anyone questions whether we are "emotionally unavailable" we will shrug the probe off and think back to the loved up feelings we had at the start of the relationship. However, the love we thought we were feeling was likely an illusion and just chemicals and hormones simulating love, and it is also an illusion, that manages to help us avoid being aware or taking accountability for the fact that our hearts have been closed off.

It isn't until these chemicals and hormones simmer down and we see the relationship in the cold light of day that we start to question and doubt whether what we had been feeling was anything close to genuine love. Despite our frantic desire to silence the doubts, it is possible that what we were feeling did not even come close to love and was more to do with our ego's longings, and our ego has been erected to barricade us from connection and love. Facing our emotions isn't easy and it certainly isn't always pretty, but we have to try to take a hold of ourselves so that we can fully understand our emotions. When we feel unable to connect we may shake ourselves, scream, shout, or cry tears of self-pity. Then, when we have belittled and berated and put ourselves down, we realize we are roaming down the wrong avenue once again.

All of the resentment we are feeling is the very thing that keeps us locked inside the place we are trying to figure out how to escape from. What we could have been doing all along, right from the start, right from the very first moment we felt the first stabs of pain penetrating our hearts, was forgiving, not just ourselves but also other people.

Regardless of anything that anyone does, says, or thinks, we are all mostly just trying our best to get through the complex bewildering labyrinth that we call love. Yet we end up holding on to pain that isn't ours to carry. We take on everyone else's pollution that they pass onto us in a moment of anger or desperation and we take it with us on our journey. Each hurtful word and all the actions that betrayed us are squeezed into a compact space inside our ribcage and suffocates our heart. We have to let it all go. We have to learn to unload. We have to unravel and we have to trust ourselves that we can handle whatever may spill out. After all, we are the ones who accepted each knotted energetic particle, so we can find the courage to witness each piece of it unfolding.

Undoing all the tangles won't happen overnight and it can be quite a distressing process, which is why many people choose to deny the knots even exist. We have to go back slightly before we go forward, right back to the very first memory we have of experiencing emotional pain. Gently we can spend time alone with our thoughts and pick apart the mess that has found home in our heart. We can forgive ourselves and ask others for forgiveness too. We have been hurt, but we have also usually been responsible for hurting others too. Hurt people hurt people. And all of that pain accumulates to form hearts that are too afraid to express themselves.

We may cry cleansing tears as we think about how lost and abandoned we feel as the tormenting memories flood back or we might just receive plenty of "aha" moments as we piece the journey of pain together. We can accept everything that has happened to us and take responsibility for everything we have caused without allowing our experiences to continue hurting us.

Just as we do not set out to purposefully or intentionally hurt anyone else, mostly, those who have hurt us also just got caught up in the chaos of what had been shared and ultimately they had not set out to cause us any harm either. And for those who had meant to cause harm, well, it is time we forgave them too. Our love and forgiveness may be needed in that direction and these things are free and they can never cause harm. If we don't, we are still holding on to the energy of people who did not value us or of those who let us go. Without realizing it, our grudges are keeping that energy alive and we are causing more anguish and suffering.

Sometimes we are afraid to let go if our pain is the only connection to our past. However, that pain will prevent us from ever being able to experience the tremendous feeling of genuine love in the present or future. There is no room in our hearts to hold on to past mistakes or bitterness. We need that space to create and replenish love. We can soothe ourselves with compassion and keep telling ourselves over and over that we are causing ourselves more pain by holding on to it so that we fully understand the need to let it go. Releasing the past also releases the emotional pain associated with it. Many lessons have been learned, so we can release everything else as we don't need an ache in our chest as a reminder.

We don't have to protect ourselves from pain by wearing armor that prevents love from getting through. The protection causes us to feel far more pain than anyone's love could and it is unbearable to carry. It is time to feel love again. And it is time to stop putting ourselves in the line for guaranteed rejection by withdrawing and shying away from anyone who comes close. As we remove the pain, we can slowly begin to allow ourselves to feel again. Love will then easily flow through.

Delving into the heart isn't always pretty. There are demons and monsters that are guarding it and they may have lain dormant since childhood and they need to be acknowledged and released. And for each one we remove, we make a little more room for love to squeeze by and release and enter. All hearts have scars, but loving energy soothes and heals all wounds.

"One man scorned and covered with scars still strove with his last ounce of courage to reach the unreachable stars; and the world was better for this."——Don Quixote

Some empaths find being an empath an extraordinarily painful way to exist. When we are not processing and transmuting emotions regularly, we may find it too difficult to constantly risk feeling high sensations and it might cause us to lock down our emotions. When we put up barriers it can appear to others as though we are unapproachable, reclusive, rude, or even arrogant or ignorant. Being emotionally unavailable causes us to avoid dynamics in which we may have to share or exchange emotions as we prefer to keep to ourselves to avoid having to absorb or process external energy. Other people may not understand this and think we are either playing mind games or that we wish to be left entirely alone. Neither is true; generally, we want to feel but we want our feelings to be manageable and less intrusive and we haven't yet worked out a way to process them without being subjected to an immense amount of pain.

Emotions can become blocked off and guarded to such an extent that we may then become separated from our emotions. At different periods of our lives we can go through stages of feeling disconnected to our emotions depending on how traumatic our encounters are or have been. Sometimes it isn't just our own emotions that are the problem. We can become so used to dealing with the effects of other people's painful and heavy emotions we end up avoiding all kinds of emotion as we don't want to subject ourselves to any more pain.

When we are accustomed to constantly absorbing and processing other people's emotions, we may find that dealing with our own can feel confusing and even unnatural. We are so used to feeling the sensations of other people's energy that our own can feel quite alien. We may then find it tempting to become reclusive so we are able to disconnect from emotions and feelings, not through choice, but through what can feel very much like self-preservation and soul survival.

Empaths are absorbent sponges constantly soaking up emotion. Even if we know how to shield our aura and protect our energy, we can still let our guard down and be vulnerable to powerfully charged emotional waves. Empaths will always feel heightened sensations regardless of how much we try to resist them.

This can subconsciously lead us to making our emotions unavailable as we close ourselves off to prevent and protect ourselves from feeling at a high intensity. Emotions will struggle to enter our energy field and they will also struggle to radiate outwardly.

When we unknowingly suppress the emotions we come into contact with, we may then find it very difficult to express our emotions freely. If we are not aware of this we will build up and store our emotions and compound this by holding on to and absorbing many other emotions that invade us that are not our own. Pretty soon we can be dealing with a situation deep inside us that is just waiting to explode. The weight of all the emotion will drain us physically, emotionally, and mentally, and due to the amount of pressure the emotions will seep out and we will find it difficult to contain the leaks. This can result in depression, anxiety, and a variety of emotional, mental, and physical health problems if we do not find a way to release the pent-up emotions so that we can process them and ultimately allow our energy to flow freely. Our energy levels will drop dramatically low, which will also cause us to feel emotionally low.

The problem occurs because we find it complex to understand why we are in so much pain. We may also find it hard to forgive ourselves for allowing ourselves to suffer, and because we hold on to guilt and shame, we refuse to show ourselves unconditional love, acceptance, and forgiveness. Despite empaths being deeply empathetic to others, we sometimes have little empathy for ourselves and this is often due to long-term mild or serious abuse resulting in low self-worth and self-esteem. We may find it is easier to disconnect our internal emotions so that we don't feel at all and we then believe we are reducing our suffering.

As we are all connected, we must first be empathetic towards ourselves before we can fully have compassion and be empathetic for another. When we cut off this gift, we are unable to function in the way we are meant to. In order to be able to offer healing to anyone else, we must first be willing and able to heal ourselves.

When we are closed off emotionally, we may still desire all the attractions of a casual, romantic, or even fully committed relationship. However, we will not find it natural to connect heart center to heart center. Basically, being emotionally unavailable means that we are not effectively processing loving energy and our exchange of intimate or romantic affection is limited. The physical side of the relationship, along with the intellectual side, may be perfectly aligned but the emotional aspect will be almost nonexistent.

When we are unable to express emotion freely, we will also be unwilling to commit; not just to the emotional side, we will unlikely commit to any other part of the relationship either and we will be very reluctant to move the relationship to the next level. Even admitting or declaring that we are in a relationship may feel like a big step. Simplified, when we are unavailable emotionally we will not be in a position to allow ourselves to fall in love and we will struggle to show up and be accountable in our relationships.

Despite all of the above, we can still have a fun, enjoyable relationship as long as the other person isn't looking for anything too serious or expecting emotional exchanges or commitment. The trouble often occurs when another person sees our inability to be emotional as though it is a challenge. They then think they will be the one who can change our mind and will work to try to charm us into a deeper relationship. All too often the signs are there that we are struggling with our emotions, but the other person may choose to ignore these signs. They might turn a blind eye thinking that we are just playing hard to get and that we will easily be swayed. Also, they may not understand that there are deeper underlying issues that are causing us to feel terrified. Our fear of emotional aches and pains is preventing us from becoming emotionally secure and content within the relationship.

Very often when our emotions aren't available we can be demonized and called childish or a game-player when this isn't the case, although other people may believe this to be true due to us sending out mixed messages. One minute we can appear loving and attentive while the next closed and distant. Even though we are struggling with the emotional side, we may still be interested in developing a relationship but just don't quite know how to. When we try to process our emotions, the one-way valve closes. We find difficulty receiving emotions and it is also a struggle to send them out. When involved in this type of relationship, both partners stand a very high chance of being hurt, bewildered, and confused and left feeling used. Sometimes, the most complex part of this will be the rejection and the effect it has on self-esteem and self-worth on both sides.

The following are some of the signs that we or someone else may be emotionally unavailable:

- A preference for long distance relationships
- Avoiding intimate questions about the relationship
- Being secretive about personal life
- Does not like to be questioned or to have confrontation in any way
- Backs away when the relationship starts to develop, then may bounce back and recoil again
- Rarely commits to future dates or future arrangements
- Not willing to meet their partner's family and friends or makes excuses at the last minute (also a sign of introversion)
- Regularly takes a long time to respond to texts or phone calls (if at all; this can also just be a classic empath trait)
- Does not want to commit to changing the status of the relationship; i.e., boyfriend-girlfriend, steady, engaged, etc.
- Always prefers to text or e-mail rather than communicating by telephone calls
- Unreliable and will often cancel at the last minute (also a sign of introversion)

- The relationship seems to focus more on the physical side than anything else
- Still struggling to move on from and let go of an ex
- May disappear from time to time with no prior warning or explanation
- Using the past as a reason for keeping distance
- No desire to be connected to one another on any social media sites
- Really keen one minute and keeps things at arm's length the next
- Always seems to be a million miles away, struggles to remain focused and in the present moment
- The relationship is one sided and determined by the terms of the one unavailable: when dates are planned, phone calls are answered, and how fast or slow the relationship moves
- The relationship feels more like "friends with benefits"
- Appears complex and difficult to read, constantly keeping the other person partner questioning things
- Backing off if someone appears too keen

If we have very recently gone through a break-up and we haven't yet processed the emotions, or if we are still recovering from a very traumatic past relationship or a bitter divorce, we may not want to become emotionally entangled with anyone else. Sometimes, when we aren't available emotionally it can just mean that we've had emotionally exhausting experiences and we just want to keep things light for a while, at the very least at the beginning of a new relationship. We may be processing our emotions, but just very slowly, and we may move out of this stage quite quickly. Everyone has a unique experience and there are no set times for moving through this. It is possible for the relationship to develop into a committed one even if we are initially emotionally unavailable. However, we will need to take the relationship at our own pace and not want to be pushed. The progression should happen naturally as we process whatever is holding us back. We should never feel manipulated or pressured into committing to a relationship before we are ready as this will very likely have an adverse effect. We may back off completely or remain, but unhappily—and even more emotionally unavailable. The most important thing we will need during this period is space to breathe so that we can go through the stages of trying to reconnect with our emotions.

Ironically, often two emotionally unavailable people attract without even realizing it. It is very likely that while we are emotionally unavailable we will attract a relationship with someone else who has also shut down emotionally. Energetic like attracts like. Sometimes, the biggest sign that we are emotionally unavailable is when we realize that we have attracted this kind of relationship or that we keep attracting similar types and we are repeating the same patterns.

When we discover that we are attracted to people who are not willing to emotionally engage, we can unlock the secrets within our own emotional wellbeing. Sometimes it is quite simply an addictive longing for something that we can't have. If this is the case, we can turn it around and then provide ourselves with whatever we find desirable in other people. We can date, nourish, and complete ourselves so that we fill any voids that we expect other people to fill. Instead of spending so much time and energy trying to please and fulfill other people, we can please and fulfill ourselves. We will then stop looking to other people to see what is missing within ourselves.

Other people can offer a reflection, and by looking at them we can clearly see the parts of ourselves we may not have been willing to acknowledge previously. This does not mean we are the same as them, it just offers us the opportunity to see aspects of ourselves when we observe others. Whether or not we are ready to look depends upon how brave we are. Often it is easier to turn a blind eye than it is to take responsibility and do the difficult work required for change.

Over time, emotionally unavailable relationships can cause discomfort, upset, and trauma, and so we need to look at why we are not open to emotions or capable of accepting or radiating loving vibrations. It is up to us to hold the mirror so that we can self-reflect and clearly see why we have suppressed, stored, and blocked so much emotion and then we can do the work required to heal, soothe, and seal any wounds. We all deserve relationships where we can give and receive in a fair, equal, and constant flow.

We will only become emotionally available when we acknowledge and process whatever has been suppressed that is preventing our heartfelt, loving emotions from feeling safe to open up.

Chapter 16

EMOTIONAL HOARDING

As we are made up mostly of energy it is vital that we allow our energy to flow freely. Our energy is in motion when we are continuously expressing and processing our emotions. Emotions carry an energetic load, and when we repress them we also store the weight of the energy, which causes it to clog up in our energy and physical bodies until it eventually pulls us down. This is known as emotional hoarding.

When we hoard our emotions, we hold on to them rather than processing them. This happens when we push everything that we feel downwards and deny, reject, ignore and refuse to accept our emotions and how we are feeling.

The emotions that we store are shadow ones and they are dense, heavy and have a very low vibration. This means they cause us to feel low and gravitationally held down. Blockages build up due to a gridlock of emotions and it then becomes very difficult to process new ones. Not only will we feel emotionally low, we will also feel physically slow and low. Eventually the mess and chaos of all our emotions manifest and are felt as physical knots and tension that cause aches and pains. We try to alleviate them by switching off to them and we may wish we could climb out of our skin to escape our emotional and physical pain.

Because negative emotions take up so much space and clog up our energetic channels, we find it difficult to open up and allow new pleasurable emotions to enter, such as love, joy, and happiness. We subconsciously turn positivity away as there isn't a clear route for it to flow through. We can imagine this situation as though we are a hoarder of material goods. Instead of hoarding emotions, we sit inside our home packing objects all around us until eventually the number of items becomes overbearing and it feels too overwhelming to sort through them. We will then try to ignore the hoarded items; however, they are not just going to disappear. Without realizing it, we have isolated ourselves. When someone calls at the door, we are not able to answer it as everything that we have hoarded is preventing us from moving and connecting with someone else. We then have to sort through everything that we have stored and either let go or designate an organized place for our hoard so that we have space available to connect with others freely. When we are sorting through our collection, we may find painful or difficult to face memories there. However, we absolutely have to continue processing and clearing. No one else can do it for us.

This scenario is a similar concept to what is happening within. Our energy is trapped due to the amount of emotional energy we have hoarded, and the hoarding prevents us from being able to identify with how we are feeling and it also stops us from being able to easily connect with other people. We won't know which emotions are which, where they have come from, or where they belong. We may then find it simpler to try to ignore it all and feel nothing.

It is tempting to shut off to the amount of emotion we have to deal with; however, every now and then something will happen (a knock at the door) that makes us realize that we are in fact trapped at every angle, so ignoring it all isn't a viable option. We will struggle to make an emotional connection with anyone, not just with those who have hurt us or those who may potentially hurt us in the future. We shut out love at the same time as we shut out pain. Every time we try to process new emotions, we will keep regurgitating the old ones that we have stored. We won't mean to, it's just hard not to when they make up the bulk of what we have contained, therefore it will be difficult to send and receive new emotions.

Our old emotions are highly charged with energy, so they want to move but they are struggling to find a way through. One by one they will recognize something in our day to day life (a trigger) that causes them to rise to the surface, and this usually happens when we are least expecting it. We won't identify with it initially as it is from a previous experience, although it is tormenting and disturbing all the same. It is vital that we become aware of our energetically hoard, so that we can separate everything that is there, understand it, show it love and compassion, and allow our emotions to move freely again.

When empaths come into contact with people who are emotional hoarders, we feel the weight of their load immediately. Often, we may avoid these people or put barriers in place, especially if we haven't cleared out our own storage as we will have no space to work through anyone else's. Other times we may be drawn toward those who are extreme emotional hoarders as we naturally want to support them while they process their load so they can be healed. However, if we do this before we check the state of our own hoarding, we will find ourselves on a rocky road. We won't just be harming ourselves, we will likely cause problems for the other person too. We can try not to blindly jump in to help someone else before we have first helped ourselves, especially if we don't really know how to properly help.

Although it is instinctive for us to reach out to others, it is sensible and wise to know what we are doing before we do so. We wouldn't take our car to a garage where the mechanic wanted to fix cars but didn't actually know how to fix them, especially if we could see that all around the mechanic were fragments of cars that were waiting to be organized and then soldered back together. If we wouldn't put our physical safety in their hands, neither should we put our emotional safety or health in anyone's hands who is already overwhelmed, overloaded, and doesn't know quite what they are doing. It's all well and good to want to support people with their healing, but we first have to know how to help and how to heal ourselves. Otherwise, we will very easily pick up other people's emotional load and try to carry that weight around with us, as well as holding our own. This is one of the contributors to feeling worn down, ungrounded, fatigued and also why we experience extreme debilitation and burn out at times. It is also why we feel like a martyr and as though everyone dumps their stuff on us without a care and just leaves us to sort it all out. We didn't need to take any of it. We chose to! And then we become stuck when we haven't got the strength to work our way through it.

Whether we all like to admit it or not, we are generally drawn to eradicate pain, whether consciously or subconsciously. We heal, we transmute, and we eliminate pain. When we see other people in pain it feels like the most natural thing to heal the pain by doing whatever we can. Quite often that means we put their needs and their pain before our own.

Unfortunately, when we take on other people's emotions we often place their emotional value higher than our own. This can also be known as altruism, adding benefit to someone else's life without a thought for our own, even if it might be detriment to our selves. Altruism can be highly beneficial to society if we are also taking care of our selves, however, it can be unhealthy if we view other people as far more worthy than ourselves and we do not take care of our needs. If we constantly put other people before ourselves, it can be harmful and destructive as we leave ourselves at risk of becoming energetically overloaded and open to be taken advantage of as certain people may also pick up on the vibe that we are sending out and their behavior may reaffirm our false beliefs. Learning to process our own emotions before we begin to navigate the emotions absorbed from other people is a vital and also very difficult lesson for empaths to learn.

Although we can protect our energy, ground and center ourselves, we will find that we are still not exempt from feeling the emotions surrounding us, especially if whoever is struggling to regulate their emotions is someone we know personally or someone we are particularly close to. Other people can very easily and quickly become dependent upon us to heal their pain. They could see us as a "quick fix" and think we can "save them." Or they may hope we will solve their problems by passing them on to us to deal with so that we carry some, if not all, of their load. Although we may seem as though we are helping, as we believe "a problem shared is a problem halved," we are not helping them or ourselves at all as we end up taking their emotional load from them, which doesn't give them a chance to figure out where their emotion originated from. If they continue to pass their emotions on to other people, they will likely go through life going around in circles, repeating similar behaviors without realizing why the same emotions are resurfacing. Plus, our energy has to work around the clock to try to figure out exactly what we have taken hold of, where it has come from, and what we are going to do about it.

When we are aware that we have been carrying other people's hoards, we can take some time to sort through what is going on and probably what has been going on for most of our lives. We can then develop a system similar to a shape sorter in our minds. This allows us to untangle all of the emotional knots and begin to organize and structure them in some kind of order.

When we are taking on the emotions that are around us it is impossible to know what is ours and what belongs to other people unless we become consciously aware of what has been previously happening in our own emotional life. Our subconscious is not rational and will not discern which emotions are ours and which aren't, so it will take on everything that we are feeling and everything that is around us. This accumulative data may then deposit into our subconscious mind and some of it will seep into our unconscious mind. Whatever we have absorbed there, whether the energy is ours or anyone else's, can become our own feelings and eventually it is added to our mixture and becomes our belief system too. Whatever other people believe, we can also end up believing. This includes taking on the pessimistic ways they perceive themselves or others.

Our subconscious mind is similar to an alchemist. It blends together every emotion, feeling, belief, value, thought and opinion that is available to try to create a desired outcome. However, it is actually an irrational alchemist picking up all the containers and not being able to read the labels. Ultimately we want the alchemist in our subconscious to turn this mixture to gold so that we can live happy, fulfilled, harmonized, peaceful, and in love with life, feeling nourished, stable, and emotionally, mentally, and physically secure and healthy. When the alchemist doesn't know if it is adding poison or elixir to the pot, the outcome will be unpredictable and it is highly likely the result will be toxic and do us an incredible amount of harm. Therefore, our conscious mind has to be vigilant and control which ingredients (emotions, feelings, thoughts etc) it delivers to the laboratory. Our subconscious alchemist is a genius and can work miracles for us, but only if it is working in the right conditions and has access to the high-quality potions and carefully selected ingredients.

Unfortunately the alchemist is quite irrational, so it is essential that we work through what belongs to us and what belongs to other people to ensure we are not a mixture infused with other people's energy. Not only that, we must ensure that what does belong to us is serving us well and not hindering our progress or causing us to become intoxicated by emotions that will quickly seep into our subconscious and unconscious minds. Once we have saturated our inner selves with emotion and feeling it becomes very difficult to undo the process. Being vigilant and selective with what we mix in is the only way to ensure we are creating the right environment for a healthy enriching outcome.

If we value other people's emotions before our own and take them on as though they belong to us, they will be the ingredients that are placed next to the irrational alchemist. We need to remove these ones from its reach and ensure the ones we are handing over belong to us and are the ones we want to be included in the tonic we receive. Working through emotions as they come to us is the simplest and quickest way to sort through them. As soon as we absorb something it marinates and becomes stronger. The alchemist doesn't sift through what we deliver, so the full strength will be added to the pot.

When we are consciously aware of what is happening around us and we are fully in the present moment, we will be able to easily decipher which emotions we own and which other people need to claim ownership for. One of the easiest ways to do this is to be aware of external stimuli and pay close attention to what we see, hear, and feel within our surrounding environment. Whenever our mood flips from one end of the scale to the other, it is an instant sign that something around us has altered, so we quickly must figure out what change has taken place.

Often we can be going about our day as normal with nothing seeming significantly different when suddenly we feel like we are carrying the weight of the world on our shoulders. This is a signal that we have just absorbed emotional energy that is not our own. As soon as that happens, we need to sharpen our senses so that we are able to clearly see where this overwhelming burden has come from. Sometimes it may have been picked up from a visual image that has made us uncomfortable or caused internal disturbance. There are images and sights all around us that can cause us to tense and feel anxious due to our high sensitivity to suffering.

When we see something that causes us concern, we need to decide if it is something that we can assist with or if it is a visual that unfortunately we can't do anything about. Often, uncomfortable emotions can come from inaction as they are our gut's reaction to motivate us to create change.

If we can assist in some way, we can do so without taking on the emotional weight that may be accompanying it. We are of no use to anyone if we are taking on external emotions and allowing them to lead the way, as we will not be reacting with a calm, clear and balanced attitude. Whenever we offer assistance we can do so from a rational angle, not an emotional one, as once emotions come into play the overall image is cloudy and hazy and we must be able to see the full picture to see a clear pathway.

This may seem insensitive and as though we are cutting ourselves off by refusing to allow our emotions to take center stage; however, at this stage it is our thoughts and feelings that will allow us to take the required action in these types of situations. We can trust our thoughts and feelings, even though they may not always be correct, far more than we can trust emotions. Emotions are accompanied by such high chemical reactions that they can alter our perception and debilitate rather than enhance our ability to assist.

When we have taken a moment to breathe and let the emotion pass, we can proceed knowing we are doing so with caution, so we are able to support the situation with calm, compassion, and clarity. If we find that we are feeling emotional weight due to something we have heard someone say—for example, if a friend is going through a difficult period and they have talked to us about their struggles—we can try to process how they are feeling without allowing an emotional response to occur.

When we are interacting with someone who is struggling to process their emotions, not only will we likely absorb the overall emotions that is surrounding them, we may also add to our own emotional response based on what they are telling us. Although it may not seem a natural thing for us to do, it is crucial that we mentally put the person at a safe arm's length so we can protect our energy while we are listening. We can still pay full attention and show compassion, understanding, and concern while safeguarding our energy field so that whatever is happening to them does not infiltrate our personal space and seep into our subconscious mind. That way we can protect what we are allowing to blend into our own emotions, feelings, and beliefs, and we can ensure that how someone else feels does not quickly become how we feel too. We will be unable to see anyone else's situation clearly if we are jumping straight into the center of it and dealing with it as though it is our own.

The most significant thing to remember is that we are not here to fix anyone. It is essential that everyone process their emotions, as they are the ones who have access to the information surrounding their situation. Not only that, when we try to take on other people's problems as if they are our own it is hindering the other person, especially if we are doing it regularly, as they will lose the ability to figure out their best options, and to have trust in and rely on their own intuition to help them. Sometimes we think we are making things easier by trying to help, but in the long run we are preventing other people from routing their own way through life. We will then not only be free from carrying their baggage, but we are freeing them so they can be trusted to take responsibility for their own personal decisions. Although this may not seem a loving and caring way to respond, it is actually the most loving and caring thing we can do for someone. It is empowering when we hold space for someone the space to process their emotions and navigate their way without feeling the need to jump straight in and hold their luggage while mapping a route out for them.

It isn't always easy to remain detached, but when we do, we will see that it is possible to guard ourselves from emotional overload while being there to support by listening intently, being understanding, compassionate, offering solidarity, and ultimately showing we have faith that the person has the ability to work through issues and process emotions on their own. When we allow someone to lean on us, from the outside it will appear as though we don't think they are strong enough to stand on their own. When we are in the midst of it, we can see it as support, but eventually this person will weaken as they rely on us rather than searching for the strength within to deal with whatever blows life deals them. Their independence then depends on our excessive interference. They will not be using their vital life skills or learning the consequences of their action or inaction.

We can tweak the dynamic so that we stop shaping people's lives for them and notice how they embrace their individuality and glow as they bask in their newfound responsibilities.

We all have the power to make our own decisions. This may sound a lot like "tough love," although when we are looking from the inside out we don't always have a clear, balanced view. We are not abandoning, we can walk with them every step of the way, even offering a hand to stabilize if necessary, but essentially we are not supporting ourselves or others by carrying other people's emotional baggage. For an empath, this is one of our toughest lessons to learn.

Chapter 17

TRIGGERS

"Everything that irritates us about others can lead us to an understanding of ourselves." ——Carl Gustav Jung

We are all responsible for our own lives and our own thoughts, feelings, emotions, and belief systems. However, certain people trigger us and our responses may cause us to behave in ways that we might not be proud of. This is due to deep-rooted feelings, beliefs, or emotions we hold. When someone provokes them, we may blame them for evoking our feelings, rather than owning and taking responsibility for where they have come from and why they exists.

There is a myriad of reasons that relate to triggers, although the main one is that the people around us are mirrors. This concept may seem confusing as it can lead us to believe that the people around us are the same as us, but that is not the case. Other people aren't just mirrors to us, they are a mirror for anyone who passes, and sometimes when people look at one another they see a small part of themselves projected back. Everyone we meet holds somewhere within them a different aspect of ourselves.

When we see something in the mirror that we recognize, it sparks a reaction. When other people express themselves all that is happening is that we see a glimpse of our own humaneness in the reflection. We may not acknowledge it as belonging to us, as the image looking back may not be a representation of who we are at that very moment. It could be showing a previous memory or occurrence, or a hidden, denied, or even controlled part of ourselves. When we think about the concept of mirrors, it is essential to remember that everything someone else does or says is not a reflection of who we are. For example, if someone speaks words that are hurtful, we can try not to automatically accept those words as a mirror projection of who we are. The image is just showing us something that we will recognize and something we can then separate from ourselves and process. This mirror concept doesn't mean we have the same capabilities, behaviors, thoughts, feelings or desires as the other person, often it is just showing our judgmental instincts rising to the surface, and that in itself is a huge lesson to learn as no one can ever fully judge another person's mental or emotional state. We will know when someone else is mirroring an aspect of ourselves as it will deeply resonate with us and we will feel inner friction that is signaling us to look at why it is causing an internal reaction.

"Your perception of me is a reflection of you; my reaction to you is an awareness of me." ——Unknown

If someone has a specific character trait about them that we really do not like, it means they are showing us something that we refuse to accept in ourselves or that we need to work on opening our mind and accepting people more. If we are allowing someone to treat us in a disrespectful way, it may be a reflection of how we treat ourselves on an inner level.

Seeing other people as mirrors is similar to flicking through old photographs. We may feel triggered when we look at an image that reminds us of someone or we may be reminded of a place that used to haunt us or a bad experience that we would rather forget. We don't have to see our own image to be triggered. Any image that resembles someone or something that is part of our history could cause an emotional response. It is also likely that we will feel indignation or repulse when we are presented with some form of harm or suffering. This does not mean there is a capacity within us that would express these same things, just that we are being made aware of the extremities of human behaviors and capabilities. Rather than adding more dense negativity we can transmute the energies and radiate peaceful healing vibrations to wherever there is pain or suffering.

The photograph album scenario is replicated in everyone we meet and every experience we encounter. Our subconscious and unconscious minds have billions of fragmented pieces of information stored in them and we have absorbed all the data through everything that has happened so far in our lives, or past lives. Our subconscious and unconscious minds hold information about things that we thought we had forgotten, hoped had disappeared, or believed had been wiped out when we became this transformed version of ourselves that is reflected in the mirror today.

Certain people may try to entice a reaction by saying provocative things, behaving in hurtful ways, and purposefully and continuously putting pressure on our weaker buttons. When someone says something, does something, or acts in a way that prods or triggers a particular piece of data, we are immediately brought face to face with the memory associated to it. Even though we may project the blame onto the person who shows it to us, the memory belongs to us and this is a unique and ultimate opportunity for self-growth. The trouble is we often don't remember this memory clearly, so things can begin to get a little complex. We may then react and respond to the person showing us the data as though what they have shown us is solely their issue and not also part of our own. Rather than taking responsibility for the way we feel and using the situation as a chance to own our emotions, feelings, or beliefs and change in some way, instead we project onto the other person by reacting in our conditioned way. It doesn't feel good to associate ourselves with what they have shown us. We believe that what we are shown isn't who we are anymore, or how we have thought or felt, and we want to suppress and deny any link to it. However, when we do that we are suppressing the memory further. Anything that is suppressed will not go away. It lies stagnant and it patiently waits to sneak out, usually when we least expect it. The memory wants to be acknowledged so it can be free and clear itself of any karmic repercussions or any conflict that may arise whenever it is recognized. Our suppressed data wants us to take responsibility for it and claim it as our own so that it can be altered, just like we have.

We can transmute and transform the energy stored deep within us so that it can be associated with positivity. Similar to what happens when we want to change, we don't want to keep being reminded of negativity from the past. When we change consciously, our inner data, our subconscious, wants to change too. Otherwise, the memories will remain blocked inside us and held hostage for a lifetime. When someone holds up something in front of us and silently asks us to recall what we know about it, we have to own it. When we own it, then we can change it.

Blaming someone else for what has sparked a reaction in us just adds more fuel to the raging data that is on fire, burning inside us, causing us pain, discomfort, and leading us to explode whenever something new adds fuel. Whenever we see something we despise in others, we are seeing something we despise in ourselves. If we think back to the last temper tantrum we had, the last sulk, or the last defensive word we mouthed or wrote, we will see that what happened was exactly that: we were defensive. We didn't want to be accountable for our reactions, so instead of taking action we reacted. And these reactions are never pretty.

If we resist something it will persist and it will keep bringing itself to our attention until we finally fully acknowledge it, recognize it, and take ownership for it. Whenever we are shown something that causes an eruption all we have to do is breathe deeply and say, "That's mine. I own it." We can offer it understanding. We can look at it and understand why we are being shown it and the reason that it became part of us in the first place. Not everything that happens to us is our fault—we don't need to take the blame for everything. However, everything that we deny or hold on to becomes stored and we need to understand why before we can create changes. Then we can show forgiveness; it was part of who we were and we can forgive ourselves, or others, whenever we choose to. By forgiving ourselves we release the anger, resentment, and frustration we feel toward ourselves and we are free to heal.

We can also be self-compassionate. We aren't perfect. We never will be and neither will anyone else. We can be tender and caring and send the memory unconditional love and understanding and transform how it feels so it is no longer tense and causing us pain. Then we can let it go so that it is free. We don't need to deny or hold on to it. It triggered us, it got our attention, we now understand it, and it is no longer capable of hurting us or causing us to react. Our lesson has been learned, it was probably learned a long time ago but until we are ready to let it go it will keep repeating itself so that we understand that we also must let go of the attachment to it before we can finally be free of it.

Triggers are simply unhealed scars that are being scratched at, which is why they regularly aggravate us. Other people are showing us where our wounds are located and in doing so they are giving us the opportunity for self-healing. Certain people trigger us, yes. But our reaction to the trigger is all about things that are within us, not other people.

Sometimes we are strongly attracted to energy that feels as though it is vibrating on a similar level, but it can have the opposite intent. We can be just as attracted to the opposite side of the spectrum as our own when it is vibrating as strongly as ours, even though it is coming from a totally different aspect and has an opposing agenda.

A classic example is someone who is vibrating strongly with love may attract someone who is vibrating strongly with fear, aggression, or anger. We may be attracted to the similar strength in energy that is vibrating. The vibrations are on totally different levels but equally as powerful. The loving vibrations are on a high level, the fearful ones on a low level, but they are expressed with the same depth and intensity. These connections will feel like a tornado spinning us around, pulling us in, then catapulting us out with huge force that then disrupts and devastates our inner and outer selves. Intense energy can connect with equally intense energy, regardless of how high or low the vibration. Although we are more able to protect ourselves and disengage from these interactions, often they are vital experiences and can help us become more balanced and evolved, even though it may not always feel that way at the time.

Some people will have no problem at all engaging with people who trigger inner turmoil. We are constantly facing our own demons whenever we are subjected to someone else's behavior. This is why we often attract the same relationships over and over. We will be faced with the same issues until we make a conscious decision to fully deal with them. These dynamics can be essential for soul growth as we are often represented with different aspects of ourselves that we are being called to look at from an alternative perspective.

Triggers are always related to our ego. When we pay attention to whatever friction someone else causes us, we will clearly see that it is our own disorganized and denied emotions, feelings, or beliefs that are highlighted.

Triggers have one purpose: to turn the spotlight so that it focuses inward.

Although this is often a controversial perspective, boundaries for me are a last resort, purely as I prefer not to separate myself and others and also so that I learn more about my triggers and take responsibility for how they make me feel. Where possible I rarely erect them, so when I do, I know it is for very good reason.

The reason for this is that I believe, in most circumstances, are cold and unnecessary barriers that come between myself and other people. When we put them in place they block others from being able to reach us, and us them, on various levels. While I understand that there are those who may think that this is beneficial and essential, what is often not considered is that it also means that people are shut out, denied, forsaken, rejected, blamed, shamed and mostly, that the opportunity will never arise to be able to resolve things.

"Let go of all blame because it only destroys you, and move forward with hope, love, compassion and kindness."—— *Báb*

I try to keep doors open, unless, it is a life threatening, extremely destructive or harmful and physically violent scenario.

My belief is that when we are adults other people's emotional behavior can never emotionally harm us in return unless we take it in and allow it to affect us. Other people can behave in whatever ways they deem necessary and say whatever they choose to and it is always our choice whether we absorb that information and internalize it, or whether we separate ourselves and see the other person's actions as entirely their own and something for which they need to take ownership for.

Although this isn't always as easy to do as it sounds, identifying when other people are projecting on us and by refusing to be influenced by their energetic storm means that we do not need necessarily need to remove anyone, or any situation, permanently from our lives but instead we can allow them a safe place from which they cannot emotionally harm us. We do this by having compassion and remaining at peace within ourselves and reasoning and rationalizing within our minds so that we do not become spun out and affected by how other people behave.

When we cut out people from our lives, we miss the opportunity to learn valuable life lessons that all interactions can offer us. When boundaries are placed between other people and ourselves we effectively deny the opportunity to communicate clearly and for underlying issues to one day be resolved. Sometimes people take a while to realize the error of their ways, and we can hold a place for them without expectation, so they are free to return and make peace if they wish to, or we can reach out to them.

When we have placed a boundary, especially if we have told the other person about it, reconnecting can be more challenging and difficult. In my opinion setting a boundary means that we are placing the fact that we cannot reason with our own mind onto someone else, so we decide to remove ourselves from their presence so that we don't have to control ourselves. We may feel that if that person who triggers us isn't around us, we will not emotionally react. Instead we can recognize that we can control how we feel and take responsibility for our emotional reactions. Therefore, no one else can affect us so boundaries become entirely irrelevant and redundant.

Often we place boundaries around us to prevent people from contacting us due to what we judge are negative behaviors. The unfortunate thing about this though is that negative behaviors are usually a cry out for love and when we reject and deny people, we also add to the feelings of unworthiness and unimportance that they may already hold. All negative acts stem from a fear, so whenever someone behaves towards us in an unpleasant way, rather than shunning them, we can radiate love and compassion their way, and try to understand and hold them in a safe place so that they can express themselves without judgment. This can all be done without us taking it personally and allowing any destruction to occur in our own lives.

We often judge and condemn people based on our own standards, beliefs, integrity, morals and values without fully realizing the extent of the other person's experiences, journey and their subconscious and level of consciousness. We have no idea how anyone else has experienced life and what their subconscious has absorbed. When we do not see other people's journey, struggles, emotional difficulties, trauma or capabilities we then place walls up to prevent other people from getting close to us, and when we aren't compassionate we can assess people as though they are harmful to us, when in fact, they often are this way due to an immense amount of conditioning and genetic determinations. We always have the ability to allow or prevent any harm and when we do not see this we are rendering ourselves powerless. We do not need to engage with anyone that we do not feel comfortable around. It is always our choice. But neither do we need to cause definitive separation that is generated through low vibrational fear based emotions and will always just add more damage leaving further emotional scars.

I have another way of looking at boundaries. Rather than placing limitations on our relationships with others, or having high expectations about other people's behaviors, we can instead allow people to be their natural selves and it is our choice whether we actively engage or disengage with them. I don't believe that it is our responsibility to tell any other adult how they should or shouldn't behave. If we don't want to interact, we can step away from it, but we can do this without judging, and while still being compassionate and understanding so that other people aren't left feeling rejected, shamed or blamed. We cannot control how other people perceive things and how they express themselves, however, we can consciously override our fear based emotions and beliefs and control how we react and respond.

It is not necessary, or our right to say to any other adult "you can't" or "you should" or "you should not." Every adult has the ability to reason and rationalize and also to face the consequences of their behavior. No one else can ever hurt and affect us emotionally, as all of our emotional responses are driven and operated by ourselves, by our own mind. We choose, we can always choose. We can interact, we can remove ourselves at any time—without telling other people how we feel they should act. As soon as we disengage the energetic connection immediately starts to dissipate. If we take our attention away from the interaction and we do not see other people's expressions as a reflection of us, we then are not susceptible to emotional harm.

"Compassion is an action word with no boundaries." ——Prince

Removing boundaries, where we can, and instead controlling our responses towards people allows for connection to develop, equality and acceptance for all beings regardless of the stage in life they are at or of their behavior. It reminds us that we are, mostly, all struggling to navigate this labyrinth of life and that some of the most destructive behavior actually derives from the people who are most in pain. Why add more pain to the mix by rejecting them and denying them further? We don't need to allow anyone a close place in our lives, but neither do we need rock solid boundaries in place to keep people out. How can people approach us in the future if they have identified and changed their ways and this wish to seek resolve if we have bolted and locked the door tightly?

When we do this we will very quickly realize the powerful meaning of cause and effect. We can choose not to be affected by what causes anyone else to display negative behavior and as soon as we do this we will realize that if we don't react emotionally, the behavior more often than not dissipates very quickly.

"You are more strong in your vulnerability than in your walls."
——Jennifer Kass

Remaining open-hearted isn't an easy task and takes a lot of internal strength, humility, empathy, compassion and plenty of practice, but instead of closing down, we can be mindful and allow people to be their unique natural selves, in their darkness, light or whatever shade they show up in, without becoming emotionally affected. Disposing of boundaries does not mean we need to still walk alongside people who behave negatively towards us, throughout our journey through life. It just means not closing off the connection with them. Keeping the door ajar so that people have the opportunity to alter how they engage with us, while we alter how we react and respond. We can constantly alter our emotional responses and learn how not to emotionally react to how other people express themselves. Other people's emotions are not our responsibility and neither are ours theirs. We can all exist in this world with each of us responsible for ourselves. Rather than having firm boundaries that defined are clearly marked out, we can constantly shift our minds to a place of absolute acceptance knowing that no one is responsible for our inner peace, so no one can ever truly affect it.

"If you can't find it in your own heart to be compassionate look in someone else's before giving up altogether." ——*Ashley Young.*

Chapter 18

Energy Attacks

Energy attacks are negative energetic vibrations that are directed toward us via other people's thoughts, feelings, or emotions. We will know if someone has sent negative energy our way as we will feel inner friction compounded by an uncharacteristic unease and our mind will be swirling with repetitive thoughts, likely about the person who is radiating it. To be sure it is a genuine attack and not paranoia or our own projection causing the sensations, we can clear our energy field by meditating and letting all of our own personal thoughts come and go. When we have grounded, calmed, and balanced ourselves thoroughly, we will feel less irritable and hear a strong internal knowing voice that is highlighting the energy that still exists and that it is coming from an external source.

Empaths are at risk of energy attacks, also known as psychic attacks, as our energetic skin is paper thin and we very easily absorb other people's energy. Energy vampires are the most common perpetrators of energy attacks. This is because their energy level is so low that they seek out others whom they can blame or shame for their own dark energy rather than taking responsibility for it. This results in energy vampires sucking their target's energy, but before they do that they often carry out a systematic conscious or unconscious attack to wear their victim down. This ensures the energy that is released by the person they are attacking not only flushes them with a much needed feed, but also that the energy they are receiving has lowered so that it is negative and toxic, which matches the energy in their own system harmoniously.

When we radiate optimistic high vibrational energy, it is a concern to energy vampires and they may target us or other people whose vibrations are high. They may feel resentment towards us as we are a threat because our vibration is not on the same frequency as theirs, so they cannot easily absorb and steal it very easily. If we respond to the energy attack with fear and we engage in the vampire's desired destructive interaction, we are giving them exactly what they set out to gain. Although it is difficult, it is essential that our vibration is continuously high during an energy attack as any weakness we show will ultimately feed the vampire, giving them more strength and power while we will feel depleted.

Empaths are capable of transmuting an energy vampires' negative energy, which means they would not be able to receive a regular feed from us. They would then need to raise their own vibration to survive, resulting in them not feeling the need or desire to suck other people's energy. Energy vampires specifically target people who are emotionally sensitive, so we are usually the main source for the majority of them. They do not feed from other vampires, they feed from people who are willing to give something, be it energy, ego based validation, time, money, or material gifts. If collectively everyone refused to feed vampires in this way, they would soon struggle to exist and instead they would learn to recharge their own energy and ultimately they man then balance their own vibration.

A vampire's existence is born of fear. They are afraid of change and will do anything to hold on to what feels familiar and comfortable, even if it is detrimental to themselves. When our vibration is high, they are not able to attach to us and suck our energy, as we will be well protected and immersed in love and positivity, and these vibrations will likely deter us from being magnetically drawn to energy vampires. However, when we are at conflict with our selves or when we have not protected our energy, they can sneak in, catch us unaware, and latch on for an energizing feed. They are then able to bring our energy down to such a low level that we end up repeatedly engaging with them, resulting in them receiving a regular and nourishing toxic feed.

Many empaths naturally radiate high vibrational love and compassion and ultimately want to carry out a soul purpose to transmute energy, radiate healing energy, and thrive on a vital unlimited supply of universal life energy. However, our reality does not always reflect this scenario. Due to the world we exist in, our energy levels are pulled in every direction and we may find it a challenge to keep our vibration high. Until we learn as much as we can about our own energy, the energy that surrounds us, and how to raise our vibration so that we can transmute energy effectively, we may regularly be pounced on by those who intend to receive an energetic feed.

If an energy vampire can prevent an empath's vibration from reaching or maintaining on a high level, they will have succeeded in securing another outlet from which they can receive a delicious void-filling meal. When an empath's energy is vibrating on a low level, it will not just leak, it will gush out as we are highly sensitive and have a very thin layer of skin protecting our energy field. Empaths who haven't worked hard on keeping their energy safeguarded are the prime victim for an unsuspecting energy attack.

It is crucial to remember not to try to fight back when we are energetically attacked, as when we do we are adding to the negativity, not balancing or diminishing it. We sometimes believe that if we stand our ground and fight like with like we will eventually gain peace and clarity. If we want peace, we must embody peace. We cannot fight for peace. We must be at peace with ourselves before we are able to obtain peace. We may think that if we respond in a similar way to the person attacking they will see firsthand what their behavior looks like, as we will become a mirror for them. Unfortunately, what usually happens is the opposite effect. The person attacking us will be even more powerful as not only have they influenced our behavior to a fighting one and therefore garnered a response, but they also have even more volatile energy to feed off as the drama that has been caused lowers our vibration and causes our energy to flood out. In fact, often our energy is triggered to react so strongly that they are able to feed off our response for days or weeks afterward as we take awhile to come to terms with the toxic interaction and the resulting fallout. Like attracts like. If we take a stance of peace, others will meet us with peace or drop off the radar. If we rise to the bait and fight, we will engage with them on the same level they are at.

When our vibration has lowered, energy vampires will see us as similar to them and become even more magnetized to us and we will be far easier to manipulate and control. Not only that, if we react it gives the vampire ammunition to talk about the drama for days to anyone they come into contact with, which enables them to easily extract more available energy supplies from anyone who offers them sympathy in return for what will likely be a biased and inflated version of the original exchange.

Although we perceive energy vampires as the darker force as they are the ones trying to destroy us, we become equally as dark as them if we try to destroy them in return. We end up becoming the exact energy that we are trying to destroy, however they will always be more controlled as they premeditate the attack and we were caught unaware, plus they often receive pleasure from the fallout while we receive turmoil. Eventually we will become so drained that we are worthless to the vampire. The vampire will move on to someone new who can offer them exactly what we originally gave them, and we will end up feeling used, frustrated, angry, and with low self-worth. Ultimately, we too could become emotionally hungry and may look for feeds from unpleasant, negative-based emotions that are in harmony with our new lowered energy level.

However, empaths are more likely to turn everything internally. Rather than seeking out other people to top up our depleted reserves, we will keep draining our own supply, which is one of the reasons we experience debilitating emotional exhaustion. We can't allow our energy reserves to reach dangerously low levels, so should try not to wait until we hit rock bottom before we decide it is time to change. We have to become aware of the low vibrational thoughts, emotions, and beliefs we are feeding ourselves so that we can make instant changes and automatically renew and replenish our supply. As soon as we change our mindset, our energy supply instantaneously reflects the changes. It is similar to choosing a healthy meal over junk food. We will immediately feel better for it. What we are feeding our mind is equally significant to what we are feeding our bodies, as our emotions eat away at the vital nutrients our body has stored up. Fear-based emotions are the hungriest. They are capable of depleting us within moments. As soon as we become consciously aware of the emotions and beliefs that are debilitating us, we can make the much-needed alterations.

To imagine it another way, we can look at the computer game Pacman. When we visualize ourselves as an "Energy Pacman," we can see that the ghosts and monsters are "Energy Vampires." All of the dots are energy, consisting of positivity, and there is also nourishing food placed around the screen that is essential for our survival. The monsters and ghosts (energy vampires) chase us around the maze and are skillful in trying to prevent us from consuming the energy. Each of the enemies embody a different character and behave differently, so we have to be very careful that we treat them all individually (just as we have to be aware of all levels of behaviors in real life). If we connect with a monster or ghost, our energy withers and subsequently we lose a life. If we connect with the enemies too many times the game is over, we are depleted and the "Energy Vampires" have won.

However, there are four power pellets in the four corners of the screen, and if we connect with them we have the ability to consume and transmute the ghosts or monsters. This changes the color and behavior of the ghosts and monsters and instead of chasing us they run away from us and they are also slower as they have not consumed our energy. In energy terms, consuming this power point is what happens when we change our vibrations to high ones. We think and believe in positivity and are then energized and able to transmute negative entities.

When we consume the monsters or ghosts in the game, we are transmuting the enemy's negative energy to positive energy; therefore, they are no longer a threat. The energy vampires cease to exist in our scope, as we are vibrating on such a high level that they are no longer able to connect with us and destroy us, although we have to be careful as some of our enemies will not give up and will change their color (behavior) and return to try to attack us once more. This is the reason we need to keep our energy elevated by surrounding ourselves with positivity and keeping our bodies and minds nourished and healthy so that our vibration remains high.

Our highest form of protection is a positive, optimistic mindset. If we can sustain this, dark pessimistic forces will find it very difficult to penetrate our energy field. Our energy and their energy will be vibrating on such different frequencies that instead of attracting one another they will automatically repel one another. We will then easily be able to detect when negativity is in our vicinity and we can choose to vibrate higher, consume the energy, and transmute it. We can do this from a distance and without interaction taking place. Our thoughts are a powerful vibration, and as soon as we set the intention for positivity our energy will radiate healing, loving, and compassionate vibes. Our enemies will not be able to harm us with thoughts or actions as whatever they send to us will be caught within our energy field, identified, transmuted, and returned and radiated outward. Just thinking positively about the person energetically attacking us automatically alters the negativity in the energy they have sent us. The person energetically attacking us may not immediately recognize that the energy has changed as the vibration will feel subtle to them due to the low vibrations existing around them. However, if they tune in to their own energy, they will notice that the energy we are sending out is not reaffirming their feelings or beliefs.

If we are not living mindfully and with a heightened awareness strong negative energy can interact with our energy, even if ours is a strong loving vibration on a high frequency. This is why it is essential to remain balanced and grounded as otherwise, if we just vibrate loving, positive high frequency emotions without grounding ourselves, we leave ourselves open to engagements with energy that could dramatically lower our vibration.

Energy attackers believe at some level that the world is a negative place and that people wish to do them some form of harm. This is basically because they look for someone to blame for the pain they are in or for anything that has gone wrong in their life, as it can be too difficult and painful for them to acknowledge, accept and process their experiences. When positive energy that is reflected back to them does not confirm this belief, eventually, even though it may take a long time, change in their vibration will happen.

Change happens immediately, even if it is only very subtle. These negative and positive interactions are sometimes more detectable when they take place directly spoken from person to person and not just through thoughts or feelings. If someone speaks to us in a harsh, critical, or judgmental way, we can choose not to respond and return words that hold love and compassion. The energy attacker will see that they have not affected us in the way that they intended and eventually may change their attitude or behavior toward us. They may dislike our positive radiations as they conflict and cause a discord with their negative radiations; however, they cannot continue to communicate on the level they are used to if we do not give them back what they are hoping to receive. Which, ultimately, is a low vibrational feed of replenishing negative energy.

Again, it is similar to someone looking for junk food and eventually finding that all the fast food stores have closed down. They will still crave the highs of the junk food even though it is not nourishing for them, although they will soon have no choice but to change the way they think about food and eventually seek out healthier options.

Chapter 19

ENERGY VAMPIRES

We all have our own life force energy. And when we are optimistic, healthy, and balanced, our energy flows freely and radiates powerfully. When we are emotionally or physically unhealthy, pessimistic, and out of sync, instead of radiating energy freely we absorb or maybe even steal other people's energy to rebalance and revitalize our own. Energy vampires find it difficult to recharge their energy themselves as they are not standing in and embodying their individual personal power and connected to their own energy source. They are distanced from their sense of self, often due to a preference for a strong association with their fragile, overinflated ego instead and they feed and are nourished by this separate force.. Due to this they are also disconnected from their internal energy centers (*chakras*), so they are not rotating or pulling in a regular dose of abundant universal energy. Their life has superficial meaning because focus and attachments are predominantly external, so materialism, finances, power, and status will all have exceptional high ranking. Energy vampires focus outside of themselves to leave an impression on other people so that it disorientates them and their energy easily leaks out. Any time there is an imbalance, it is easy to extract energy. The refueling of a vampire's energy supply pours in from external sources, when people validate them, praise them, offer flattery, are afraid of them, are controlled by them or consider them to be elite or superior.

As they have minimal connection to their inner core self, they are unable to link to it to nourish, energize and refuel themselves. It is then far easier for energy vampires to turn to other people to top up their energy rather than do the work required to create a life with value and meaning that is directly interconnected to their inner self—a life which ultimately will not rely on anyone else's energy to give them power, inspiration, motivation, or inner strength, as all of these things will be firmly established when their lifestyles directly reflect what matters on a deep internal level.

Basically, they first must discover who they are, acknowledge who they are, and build a life centered around this before they are able to energize themselves adequately. It is not easy, as it requires determination, self-acceptance, authenticity, vulnerability, and an element of risk, so they always need to be prepared for failure and also to be able to deal with it if it occurs. This is why many people will do anything to avoid having to face whoever exists within, including abandoning their core selves. Not living a fulfilling life is a huge part of the reason that people are unable to access the source of universal life force energy and live independently. They find it far easier to absorb energy from other people.

When absorbing energy from someone else, we are similar to a vampire, but instead of sucking blood we suck and drain energy. Energy vampires do not generally just suck the energy from one person, some vampires are advanced enough to exude enough negativity that they can suck the energy out of a whole room. If you've ever experienced the feeling of someone walking into a room and it suddenly feels as though you could cut the atmosphere with a knife, the person is likely a skilled energy vampire who has just zapped all the energy in one go. Rather than recharging their own life energy, energy vampires subconsciously or consciously seek energy from other sources. One particular way they do this is through thinking they are better than others, or hoping to make other people think and feel superior and also through using insults or judgmental behavior to pull other people down.

Although energy vampires suck out the energy from other people, it does not mean they are a "bad" person. Often, people become energy vampires due to emotional pain they are enduring, low self-esteem, low self-belief, and low self-worth. They are behaving in ways that they believe are necessary for their sole/soul survival. It might possibly be learned behavior that they picked up from their caregivers. Energy vampires may be "victims" themselves who were once "bitten" energetically by a vampire. Energy vampires may have had words or actions inflicted upon them as a child that made them feel "not good enough." They may have been the victim of some form of abuse, or just generally went through a very traumatic period that resulted in a lot of negative emotions arising. They might even just believe they are "better" and superior to others and they have discovered that this imbalance makes it easy to overpower and energetically drain other people.

Vampires can become so used to taking other people's energy that it becomes a habit, one that now feels pleasurable and very natural. It can also feel natural to allow people to take our energy if it has been happening consistently throughout our lives. Low vibrational emotions are what cause people to take and absorb other people's energy, and people can be on a negative frequency for many reasons. Although they may not intend to, they then attract relationships that reflect these beliefs and they inadvertently take energy from other people to replace their own draining supply.

Whenever we do not believe we are worthy or we want to prove and exert our worth, we will seek some form of validation in other people, although it can be a dangerous game if our self-esteem is low as in doing so we can also attract those who want to play on our insecurities or vulnerabilities. Either way, we put ourselves in a dynamic whereby someone else becomes the focus of our shortcomings. We project our unworthiness onto other people, and depending on their character, they will either prop us up or they may push us down further. Whenever we are seeking validation, even if it just reaffirms our low self-worth, we will be hoping that we will receive a supply of vital energy from someone else.

Even though we may not effectively manage to suck any energy, we are still a vampire that is hungry and wanting someone to confirm how we feel about ourselves. That is why it is vital that we work on our self-esteem and self-worth so that we are not at risk of becoming an energy vampire. It is also important so that we don't run into someone who can take advantage of our fragility by trying to make us feel worse than we already do. If this happens, our reserves will run dry and we will likely to seek an external source of energy.

Energy vampires are not always easy to recognize as they appear in all forms. They may be romantic partners, friends, family member, colleagues, strangers, religious or spiritual leaders, or teachers. The one thing they all have in common is that they are easily capable of sucking out our energy so they can use it for themselves.

Don't be deceived as vampires aren't always pessimistic on the surface. Often these energy vampires are people who appear on the surface to be optimistic, positive, full of energy, thriving, and upbeat about life. This is usually a superficial front and they are so upbeat because they excel in absorbing other people's energy. They bounce around from one person and situation to the next taking whatever is available along the way.

When we have had the energy sucked from us we will immediately feel weary, lethargic, exhausted, irritated, overwhelmed, frustrated, and anxious, and we will not always understand why we have suddenly been left feeling this way. As soon as we feel any sensations related to these emotions, it is a sign that we may have just been energetically attacked, especially if the emotions come on suddenly and overwhelm us. We often don't think to look outside ourselves and instead we question our own thoughts and feelings, wondering what may have happened to cause us to experience such a significant change. This is why we have to become aware of exactly who and what we are allowing into our lives and take the necessary steps to protect ourselves from them.

The draining of vital energy, known as life force energy (*prana*), needn't be done dramatically. Sometimes it is carried out with no noticeable outward sign whatsoever. Often the person sucking the energy believes they are well meaning and thinks their intentions are harmless. However, they are similar to parasites and the end result is that they need an energy boost and we are their feed.

Vampires may either be highly dramatic or seductive, constantly needing the attention focused on them, or they can be shy, reserved, and needy, looking to others for a boost. They may be moody, with regular temper tantrums, or they could be incessantly looking to blame, humiliate, or shame, trying to make others feel guilty instead of looking at their own behavior. Energy vampires live with the belief that the world revolves around them and that everyone who surrounds them is there as an essential source of nourishment. It is not always that they do it intentionally. It becomes a primal instinct to take energy to ensure they are fed vital energy and therefore survive.

When people suck energy it always comes down to the same thing: at some level they are afraid. Whatever is happening or has happened in their life has left them feeling fear and the fear then drains them of their energy reserve. Sometimes it is a primal instinctual fear and in their desperation to maintain life security they drain other people to get their needs met. This could be for money, a roof over their heads, or for more superficial longings that include comfort and material items to gain a high standard of living. Often they will drain other people, using various methods, to ensure they receive in return whatever it is they feel they need to keep their standard of life,

Rather than looking at the issues for themselves, they will seek out other people's vital energy as a top up to keep them feeling alive. They do not feel capable of creating positivity, as they are not living a life that has inner soul meaning and they have not worked towards their higher purpose, so they feel they have no choice but to steal positive energy from the easiest and quickest sources they can find.

Empaths are often their most targeted victims and the most delicious and fulfilling ones to feed from. This is because we radiate outwardly and often fail to put a stopgap on our source. Empaths literally bleed energy and vampires latch on immediately and don't hesitate to connect to the tube so they can suck our energy dry.

When we imagine the vampire as a pesky parasite and we are its source of nourishment, we can see how we would react if a mosquito or flea was to keep trying to suck our blood. We would gently brush them away and apply ointment to the wound so that it can heal, and we would also protect ourselves by covering ourselves in repelling potions to avoid being bitten again. We can then see how they dynamic works with energy vampires, as although they may not mean harm they are essentially parasites, a drain on our energy. One is sucking our energy and the other is sucking our blood. Both of these things are vital so that we remain healthy emotionally, mentally, and physically.

We can be mindful and compassionate but we can also try to ensure that we keep ourselves grounded and aware so that we don't suffer in these interactions. We can still maintain a connection with energy vampires without giving them so much that we drain and debilitate ourselves. If we are pulled into anything negative, we can choose to disengage until we rebalance our energy. We are no use to anyone if we have not first nourished and taken care of ourselves. When we fully understand that people can only take as much as we are willing to give, we can continue to have positive, healthy interactions with people, without them turning toxic and causing us to spill everything we have outwards. We can still give, but only if we first have enough for ourselves.

As soon as vampires see that we are no longer an unlimited and easy source of energy, they will move on quickly and hungrily to seek out their next victim who will give and give without care for themselves and without awareness. Sometimes we can feel at a loss when this happens as we can become dependent on feeling wanted or needed and we may have grown accustomed to being used as an energy source. We just have to break the bad habit and very quickly we will feel our energy reserves build up again, which will give us the strength to engage with people in an entirely new way. Giving until we have nothing left can be altruistic and can leave us exhausted and wanting to hide away. We are far more beneficial to everyone around us if we take care of our own needs and constantly keep our awareness on how we engage with others and we can then give to others knowing it is a healthy, nourishing exchange.

Allowing someone to be dependent on us is not a healthy way to maintain any relationship. Although it may feel very strange at the start, we will soon appreciate the newfound freedom and vitality that is delivered as we alter how we connect with those who latch on to solely drain us.

Not everyone who is suffering intentionally sets out to absorb other people's energy, but it is almost impossible for them to refuse it if it is on show. They are hungry and depleted, and if they think someone else has a reserve they will naturally feel the need and also feel as though they have the right to take it. Energy vampires will see it similarly to someone putting a plate out for a hungry animal. If it is offered, they believe the person is obviously willing to make a sacrifice, so the exchange swiftly takes place.

Empaths often don't realize that when we enter situations with certain people we are opening ourselves up to being taken advantage of. This is why it is essential that we are aware of how to protect our own energy and also how to guard ourselves against people who can debilitate us.

Empaths are natural healers and soothers and when we see someone struggling we are immediately drawn towards them to ease their pain. We are finely attuned to other people's emotions and instinctively know what to offer to balance and replenish what they are missing. However, we often fail to realize that when we do this we are also at risk of offering ourselves up to a vampire who may see us as their next feed. It is up to us to monitor and control how much energy we give, mainly so that we give in a way that does not make anyone else dependent

Most people who work in healing or are in service roles will be susceptible to having their energy taken as they are constantly sending out energy. They can become vulnerable, as certain people will try to take more than what is offered. Often healers don't realize they are absorbing the pain of their clients or customers when they are working with them to reduce or eliminate suffering. Sometimes, the client knowingly passes on the pain not caring who is absorbing it, ultimately just wanting it gone. They may also prey on the healer's emotions purely to receive an energy top up as they find it difficult to sustain a healthy vital supply. The risk is especially high when we come into close or even physical contact with people who we don't know and we have no idea what exists in their energy field. Although healers essentially want to do their job well and do whatever it takes to assist whoever they are healing, they don't always realize that often they are doing it to their own detriment. This is why it is vital for healers to become aware of the signs and symptoms of energy vampires and what can be done to protect themselves.

People who feel insecure are potent energy vampires. They believe that everyone has sucked the life out of them and caused them to be feeling worthless, so they feel their only option is to rebalance the scales and absorb energy from whoever they come into contact with. Insecure people do not offer a mutual exchange as they are caught in a cycle of feeling insignificant and they believe other people have higher energy reserves. They are not capable of giving anything in return. They just need to take, believing that is the way to refill their tank so they have fuel to keep going.

It isn't just emotionally low people that take energy. When we are physically injured our energy levels also stoop low as so much energy is being used healing the injury. If we imagine how we feel when we are cold, our physical vehicle slows down as our system focuses all the energy on protecting our vital organs. When we are in pain, a similar thing happens. Our energy is directed toward the area that is in physical pain, so we very quickly feel low emotionally as the level of energy required to keep us emotionally stable has fallen and our energy is diverted to where the priority is at the time.

Passive-aggressive people are masters at sucking energy, and although they believe that they are harmless as their outwardly expressions are passive, if we are not grounded and aware, we will find them to be one of the most emotionally harmful and draining types of people to be around.

Vampires and their victims can become caught within a codependent relationship as the vampire offers an exchange in return for energy. The exchange for the energy could be anything from financial benefits to helping the victim feel good about them self. When a vampire needs recharging they will try numerous tactics to elicit energy from someone else. And although it seems like a fair exchange, neither one on the receiving end is gaining something that will ultimately make them feel harmonized or healthily nourished. These exchanges are quick fixes, temporary moments of pleasure for instant gratification. Nothing that takes place in an unequal or unbalanced exchange can ever be wholly good or nutritious for our souls.

It is very easy for both involved in the dynamic to crave and become highly dependent on the quick fix. Instead of looking at themselves to resolve whatever is missing, they are expecting other people to fill the void. When we are able to identify who is zapping our energy and who is offering a mutual positive exchange we will be able to take the necessary steps to change how we engage with those who deplete us to ensure we do not become drained. We will find that the time we spend surrounded by those where the exchange is mutually rejuvenating and revitalizing will leave us feeling highly energized rather than depleted.

Energy is very easily distributed from one person to the next when there is an imbalance between the two people. For example, if one person has a highly paid job and the other person is in poverty, between a teacher and a student, a parent and a child, between people with opposing levels of experience, or between people who consider and believe themselves to be extremely attractive and those who believe they are unattractive or unlovable. The imbalance can be extreme or it can be slight. It all depends on the internally held beliefs of each person in the dynamic.

There are many signs that someone is an energy vampire, and while certain people may only display one or two traits, others will use a variety of tactics depending on the situation. They can become addicted to the high and instant energy intake and will flip from tears to trauma and keep trying different techniques until they eventually find a way that works effectively.

Some people are masters at it, having learned the skill from a parent when they were young. Other people may only temporarily take energy due to going through a particularly difficult time in their lives and not fully aware of what they are doing so. The more aware we are, the better chance we have of detecting a vampire before they find us.

Below are some of the ways people upset the equilibrium to manipulate and suck energy.

- Boasting about material possessions or finances
- Any situation where one person is trying to make the other feel envious or jealous
- Using sexual and predatory behavior to destabilize the other person
- Using hurtful words to make the other person feel inadequate
- Deliberately bringing on tears or dramatic emotional displays to gain a reaction
- Intentionally using intellect or knowledge with the aim of making other people feel stupid
- Using extreme discipline to show control
- Using flattery to overemphasize aspects of a person's character or physical attributes to seduce or derail them
- Extremely revealing outfits that have only been worn to seek out attention
- Saying something that appears nice while body language, intention, energy, or facial expression are sending the opposite signals (passive-aggressive)
- Using silent treatment
- Violence
- Being overcompetitive and then flaunting success to try to prove self-worth
- Complaining and whining constantly about everything and everyone without doing anything to resolve or rectify situations
- Dramatically overreacting in public so that all focus is on them
- Trying to prove that they are right and the other person is wrong
- Dominating and exerting control over someone else
- Using threats to make the other person feel fearful
- Trying to gain sympathy by appearing as a victim
- Displaying insecure or immature behaviors to gain validation or reassurance
- Trying to make other people feel guilty

The traits of an energy vampire: abusive, aggressive, angry, apologetic, charismatic, coercive, controlling, dependent, dominative, envious, jealous, possessive, resentful, seductive..

When we are dealing with someone who is attempting to steal our energy, it is essential to become aware of it as quickly as possible to avoid an onslaught from taking place. Once we know what we are dealing with, we can choose the level of engagement so that we don't become their next victim. We can either allow energy vampires to suck all the life out of us or we can choose to rise above it, alter our vibrations, and be the change we wish to see. Rather than trying to interact, negotiate, or reason with vampires, we can take control of our own behavior and show warmth, compassion, and unconditional love and acceptance, both for ourselves and for those trying to take from us.

As empaths we need to ground ourselves and remain centered at all times so that we are not knocked sideways when vampires come calling. Energy vampires are skilled and can easily derail and sway most people from their paths, and empaths are targeted because they bleed energy. To stay grounded, we must imagine that our feet are firmly planted into the ground, just like the roots of trees. Regardless of who or what we come into contact with, we must have faith that nothing can destabilize us and believe we are strong, and that although we will bend slightly nothing will break us.

When dealing with a vampire, the best thing to do is stay neutral, as whenever we respond negatively we send out a vibration of energy that they will quickly zap to use as their own. Although it isn't easy to remain calm when we are in this situation, any type of reaction is a feed and it will be difficult to disconnect the supply once they have plugged it in and taken hold of it.

We are not responsible for other people's emotions or behaviors, and when we interact and engage with them on a low frequency we are not helping ourselves and we are certainly not helping other people. The best thing we can do is to keep our vibrations healthy and high and our energy will ascend the other person's vibrations too. Unfortunately, some people prefer to remain pessimistic and marinate in drama. There is absolutely nothing we can do about that, as when we try to help them we often get drawn in and descend too.

Sometimes negative situations come into our lives to teach us a sharp but necessary lesson. It is our choice as to whether we open our minds and see everything as a learning curve, whether we react and respond emotionally, or whether we look away and let it flow over us. We all have choices and we can consciously override all of our subconscious triggers when we remain mindful, alert and aware. We sometimes continue along ignoring aspects of our lives that really need to be addressed and it is not until we are experiencing constant friction with someone that our attention is alerted. Certain people can prompt us to take a look at what it is we are allowing and why we are feeling the impulsive need to react and respond. We can still honor, explore and release all of our emotions without irrationally expressing them and aiming them at whoever is in front of us.

We are often tempted to look outside ourselves to see what the problem is first, although it is far more productive and beneficial to first look inside. When we feel a rise of heavy emotion it is due to unresolved issues or trauma that we have suppressed. Energy vampires can draw our attention to this as they make us aware of areas within us that are a cause for concern.

To figure out how energy vampires work, imagine it as though we have an electric cable dangling from our energy field at all times and our energy is leaking from it. At any time someone can come along and detect the cable and easily grip it and plug it into their own energy field. As soon as they have plugged it in the current flows continuously from us to them, but with an energy vampire there is a valve on it that prevents any energy from flowing back to us. There is no exchange, just waves of energy leaving us and flushing into the person on the receiving end. When we are not aware, we quickly become depleted and they are instantly recharged. The longer we allow them to remain connected to our energy, the more ungrounded, debilitated, and exhausted we will become.

When we are healthy and harmonized, energy vampires will not be drawn toward us purely to absorb our energy as they will automatically sense that we have sealed our energy field and closed the valve to prevent a continuous, unfiltered feed. If we engage on a negative frequency, the more negative emotions and feelings we send out and the higher our negative charge is. Vampires will become more revitalized and we will become more depleted. We are in control of to whom, what, and where we send our energy and we can take control of the charge at any time. All we have to do is become consciously aware of what is taking place so that we refuse to allow our emotions to pour out and flood and fed the other person, leaving us depleted.

To protect our energy field, we can shield ourselves by visualizing a brilliant white light cocooning us with our energy field with loving, compassionate, high vibrations. We can also visualize one around the vampire for extra protection. We can infuse it with love and compassion and imagine sealing it with a strong bond for added security. This light becomes a protective force that guards our energy and prevents or deflects negativity so that it does not infiltrate our energy field. We can then engage without reacting in a way that could potentially be harmful to us both.

Some people prefer to envisage a glass wall between themselves and the other person. Any similar visual will work. The most significant thing to note about visuals is that they are mental strengthening techniques, so we must have faith in them so that our energetic field vibrates and responds accordingly.

It is also essential to become aware of how we may be taking energy from others without realizing it. Although empaths are natural givers, we can also become takers when our reserves are low. There is never any need to take from anyone else. We all have the means within ourselves to look at our own issues and discover why they are draining and exhausting us. Any emotions that result from fear are ones that are going to debilitate us.

When we recognize this we can work on why we are allowing these emotions to take precedence and control and overwhelm us and look at the root cause of why we are feeling this way. If we discover where the source of our emotions lies, we can acknowledge them so we can replenish and repair these thought processes and beliefs. We can then eliminate fearful vibrations and replace them with loving, forgiving, positive and high-quality ones.

When we are carrying out healing or showing compassion or empathy, we can choose to send out as much energy as we want to and this should never be a problem so long as we have enough in reserve to keep ourselves balanced before doing so. We are of no use to anyone else if we have not taken care of ourselves first, as the energy we send out may not be nourishing, beneficial, or be carrying with it enough positive vibrations to heal. Ultimately it could then end up influencing other people negatively and causing them harm. It is also important to realize the difference between enabling and disabling people so that they do not become dependent on us, as that prevents them from working through their own issues.

Often people who are vampires are looking for approval, attention, or to increase their self-worth. When we are able to be mindful and offer understanding, compassion, consideration, and forgiveness, we can talk things through with them without providing an emotional response. If we keep the conversation positive and listen carefully to what is being said, we can be a source of comfort to support them without judging or being provoked to react.

The path of an empath is not rolled out so that we can roam along it looking for someone to heal and fix. We are gifted with the ability to feel what it is like to walk in someone else's shoes. That way, we can walk alongside people, not ahead of them believing we know the direction and have all the answers safely hidden away. If someone asks for or seeks our assistance as they require healing, then we can do what we can as we have the ability and means to support them. However, we can try not to step onto their path and interfere with their journey thinking that we are "helping" them.

Everyone is more than capable of connecting to their own source of vital energy. While we are providing people with a constant feed, we are ultimately preventing them from depending on themselves and becoming stronger. If they lost all their external supply of negative energy, they would have no choice but to dig deep and uncover their own abundant energizing source. When we think we can "fix" people by providing them with a never ending supply, all we are doing is giving them temporary meals rather than allowing them the opportunity to provide for themselves. This means they will always be searching for their next intake, and their energy levels will constantly fluctuate.

When vampires see that we are not going to drain ourselves to feed them, they then stand a chance of beginning the journey to seek within themselves. Not all energy vampires will want to engage on a higher frequency and if this is the case, it can be hard cutting their source of energy as we don't want to see anyone struggling or feeling depleted. However, it is not advisable to lower our vibration to feed others, as in the long run we both will suffer. When we change how we engage, we then allow them the opportunity to take responsibility for routing out a channel to uncover their own energy source, which will then provide them with vitality in abundance. Many vampires may just seek out someone else who can meet their needs instead; however, we are not be able to prevent that. We have to all take responsibility for ourselves. And while we try to take accountability for someone else, we weaken them by allowing them to remain dependent on us.

Empaths are healers, soothers, confidants, and consolers, and we are easily able to consider all angles and understand each one. This gives us the insight and clarity to be able to look deep into the soul of other people without any judgment. We can then raise the vibration of those around us through healing thoughts, intentions, actions, and words. However, it is not our role to fix someone by redirecting them to an alternative path just because we believe it is the right one for them. As tempting as it is for us to want to mend everyone else, it is not advisable and we are misguided and naive if we believe we can or should do it. Emotional wounds are internal. They have to be healed internally by the person with direct inner access to them. This is a hard lesson to accept as to see someone in pain causes us to feel pain too. We just need to step back far enough so that we are out of the person's shadow, radiate love and offer enough unconditional love and support so that the one who is struggling may eventually see the light.

We all have our own lessons to learn and our own mistakes to make. We each have to take responsibility for figuring things out for ourselves. As complex as it is, we can try to understand that it is far more beneficial to accept someone exactly as they are without needing to become entwined with their struggles. We can raise our vibrations to offer unconditional love and those vibrations will radiate outward and lift the vibration of all that surrounds us. That is far more productive than trying to map out new roads thinking can change other people's routes.

Just because we accept how someone is does not mean we have to allow their behaviors to negatively impact our lives. There is a big difference between accepting and allowing. We can accept people without choosing to engage with them. When we allow any type of behavior to impact us, we are agreeing to be a pawn in their game. Self-preservation must always come first.

Chapter 20

EMOTIONAL INJURIES

Unfortunately, for many empaths the first time they become aware of their empathetic abilities is due to some form of emotional, psychological, or even physical injury or trauma. When we are in the presence of someone who is causing us harm, we often learn to either consciously or unconsciously tune in to their thoughts, emotions, and behavior so that we can gain insight into their mindset and emotionally and mentally be prepared for any onslaught and respond to their actions. Being highly sensitive to energy and observant to body language allows us to become more empathetic toward the abusive person. We can recognize if there is an ingrained pattern occurring so we can then be more aware of what might trigger the abuse, which gives us precious moments to rationally consider our options.

Although we are honing an aspect of our empathetic ability, it does not mean we will always be expressing empathy and showing compassion and consideration. At this stage we will most likely be tapping into it potentially to keep ourselves safe from harm. Empathy can become a form of self-preservation, and ultimately, in more serious cases, a vital method of survival.

When we are subjected to abuse and tune in to the energy, we feel the level of anger or hatred that is being directed toward us. If an abuser is expressing strong negative feelings, we will also feel the intensity of the dark sensations associated with those emotions. It can be excruciatingly painful for us to see, feel, and experience how someone else views us. When we look into the person's eyes subjecting us to abuse, we can see, feel and sense the volume of their negativity. We not only encounter and experience our own emotions associated with the attack, we also have the added weight of dealing with the abusive person's too. This can make it very difficult for us to see the overall situation with clarity and without emotional involvement so that we can clearly discern what is taking place. We are also at risk of absorbing the abuser's emotions and believing and accepting that whatever is being cast toward us is an authentic reflection of who we are. Although we often say other people are a mirror, this does not mean that however they express themselves mirrors an aspect of our personality or character. People will behave in all kinds of ways and just because we are witness to it does not mean that we deserve it or that it reflects who we are. However, other people's behavior may stir something within us and it is then our responsibility to process and rationalize whatever occurs.

"I am not made or unmade by the things which happen to me but my reaction to them." ——St John of The Cross

When we are willing to clearly identify which of our emotions, feelings, and beliefs are triggered by their behavior and why they are causing us a degree of discomfort, we will be less likely to react and emotionally respond. Just because someone says something or acts in a certain way, it does not make them our mirror and neither should we fool ourselves into believing that other people's expressions are projecting our reflection. When we remember this, we can separate their behavior from ours and realize that how someone behaves is not a direct result of anything we have said or done. Everyone each has responsibility for how they express themselves. We cannot "make" someone feel angry, frustrated, aggressive or any other emotion. We all have the ability to consciously reason with and control our own outbursts and emotions.

Sadly, all too often when we are subjected to abuse we may wrongly believe that everything the abuser is saying about us or how they are treating us is our fault. Therefore, deep-rooted feelings of unworthiness can occur that can develop into severely low self-esteem, poor self-worth, and we may lose confidence. This is often what keeps us caught in the crossfire, as we are not distinguishing between our own and the abusive person's emotions and feelings. We may find it difficult to see that the abuser's words and expressions are not ours to take ownership of. When we are able to separate and clearly divide their energy from our own, we will clearly see that what the abuser is delivering is quite simply abuse. It is a projection of who they are and not in any way connected to who we are.

Although they may try to trigger us by aiming low and pressing our weakest buttons to gain impulsive reactions, there is nothing anyone else can do to hurt us. We only hurt ourselves by choosing to accept the abuse as though it is our truth and then absorbing it and acting on it. They may try their very best to locate our most tender, hidden injuries and they might then scratch and claw at them to cause us to react irrationally. Whether we choose to allow someone to delve into our achingly sore historic wounds is also our choice. Instead, we can stand in our own power and decide that we can be the ones who unearth our vulnerable emotional fractures so that they can receive much needed, long awaited healing. Nothing or no one will then be able to touch or aggravate them or cause them to sting and become unbearable.

Empaths can easily fall into the hands of an emotional abuser as generally we are open hearted, forgiving and we tend to search for the good in people. We also avoid conflict, we are not always assertive, we often find it difficult to stand up for ourselves, and we try to offer unconditional love, compassion, and acceptance. One of the reasons forgiveness is offered so rapidly is that we know that there are many sides to a story and numerous variables that can cause people to behave as they do. This belief can help but also hinder us.

When we offer unconditional love and acceptance, it is always helpful if we don't hold onto resentment, and we can do this by gaining a profound understanding of what has taken place, particularly so that we do not repeat similar negative cycles. If we choose to keep engaging in low vibrational emotions and behavior, we may become a target for other people to aim and offload their issues in our direction. If we don't safeguard ourselves, by disengaging from negativity, our vibration may lower, particularly if we do not remain aware and grounded. Also, our ability to offer forgiveness rapidly, without first clearly understanding what we are forgiving, can sometimes be detrimental. The person we are forgiving could view our quickly delivered forgiveness as a weakness and they may think they can repeat the behavior, especially if we couple it with forgetting just as quickly. However, this doesn't mean forgiveness needn't be administered. It is my own personal belief that where possible we can try to forgive, even if the forgiveness only takes place in our own consciousness, as holding on to emotions always causes us more anguish than it causes the other person. The most injurious thing we can do in this situation is to keep resentment, rejection, and anger alive by holding on to the toxic energy and allowing it to repeatedly hurt us. Our refusal to forgive also means that we are refusing to release the emotions that can set us free.

When we forgive we can try to understand the reasons we are doing it and what exactly has occurred. The forgiveness will then be sincere and we will also have acknowledged that the behavior was unacceptable and that we will not condone it, nor will we allow it to continuously repeat. While offering forgiveness, we can then check in with ourselves to see how we feel internally and if we are willing to keep putting ourselves in a position for someone to repeatedly hurt us. We cannot change anyone else's behavior or actions, however, we can always change our own and we do not need to hang around waiting for repetitive displays. Otherwise, we will be forgiving over and again due to the same set of circumstances, which means that we are repeatedly being mistreated. The most obvious sign that someone has learned from dysfunctional behavior is a willingness to change. It won't matter how many times someone offers us an apology, if it isn't followed up with intentional alterations, the apology will have very little meaning of value.

"Every change in human attitude must come through internal understanding and acceptance. Man is the only known creature who can reshape and remold himself by altering his attitude."——John Maxell

We have a choice as to whether we remain stuck in a situation or whether we learn everything we can to continue stronger, wiser, and with humility and without allowing ourselves to be internally affected by how other people interact. We can move forward with mindfulness as to how we, or others, have been treated and we can make it decide whether we are going to tolerate other people's behavior. We do not need to shut anyone out of our lives, however, neither do we need to accept anything in our lives that compromises us strongly on a soul level. We can listen to what our inner voice is telling us and then decide whether we are placing ourselves in situations that are not mutually respectful and which are causing a constant disruption of peace in our lives.

When we respect the energy exchanges we partake in and we recognize the vibration of lower frequency energy that could cause a dramatic discord with our own, will then be far less likely to attract those who may treat us in a similar way in the future. If nothing else, if we are in these situations again we will spot the signs of abuse far quicker, which gives us the option to refuse to react and respond and we can then make the decision to walk away from it much quicker too, if we choose. We have no control over how anyone else behaves, although, we can control our responses to it. We can intentionally observe what is happening and choose to resist our conditioned response and instead respond with peace, regardless of the situation we are in. Or we can allow our subconscious, which is likely irrational, to predetermine our response and then our emotions will also jump in to affect our peaceful state and pull our vibration down significantly.

If we decide to stay in a dynamic that is energetically disturbing, we can take responsibility for ourselves and question what emotions are erupting and holding us there and we can also then find out what lessons we still need to learn from these exhanges. It could be fear-based emotions that are drawing us into the connection, or it may just be that we are choosing to work on our ability to communicate healthily with anyone who we come into contact with, therefore, we can unconditionally accept people and refuse to allow their energy to cause havoc with our own. We do this by consciously separating our emotions from other people's and remembering that no one else is capable of causing us harm, and that no ones behavior is a reflection of ourselves. Either way, we can accept that we may potentially suffer the consequences of staying in a situation where we are at risk of being emotionally, mentally, or physically injured, but we can benefit from it by being aware of how we react and trying to override unhealthy . We do not know the capacity of other people and the extremes they may go to when their vibration is low and also because we may not yet have mastered our own ability to disengage we may not be skilled in remaining at peace with no internal or expressive response. We can remain mindful and monitor this and engage or disengage depending on what we feel we can handle at the time. We have the option to walk away at any time, or to breathe through our emotions so that we are aware of our triggers and we can discover what causes certain things to cause us inner friction or discord.

Looking inwards allows us to get to know ourselves better, and then we can offer self-compassion so that we forgive ourselves for any rocky, turbulent paths we might chose and also for the ones we wandered along for longer than necessary.

When we acknowledge our own behavior and see our actions clearly and understand them, we can also offer ourselves unconditional love while being consciously aware of anything we may have done that caused our own or someone else's suffering. Who we are now is not a reflection of our past relationship choices or our previous situations, and those things do not define us. We can alter our opinion of ourselves right now, though first we can take responsibility for our past, acknowledge any mistakes, and be accountable for them, accepting that who we were then is not the same person as who we are now. We need to understand where we might have challenged ourselves beyond capacity and caused immense difficulties, to ensure we don't repeatedly do this same thing in the future and so that we do not keep putting ourselves in situations that we can't safely and lovingly deal with.

We are not going to stay this version of ourselves forever, so we may cope with whatever we go through today far better than we would have coped with it previously. Although we may think "I am who I am," this isn't entirely true. We are made up of vibrating, spinning energy, and all of our cells are in constant motion, altering every moment. Our thoughts change, our feelings change, our values change, our body changes, and our external world changes. Every day we are renewed. We cannot hold on to who we were or who someone else was in the past as so many things change in a moment, let alone an hour, day, or a year. Whoever we were yesterday is not who we are today, though we can be willing to change our mindset so we effectively evolve on the inside and expand our capacity to deal with challenging circumstances as they come into our life. How drastically we change depends on how strong our desire is to heal, grow and evolve. If we want to cling to all of our familiar patterns of behavior, our opportunity for growth will be limited. If we remain in the same places and interact with the same people and do the same thing day after day without opening our mind to possibility and without allowing a space for expansion, change will be minimal, if not impossible.

"If you will call your troubles experiences and remember that every experience develops some latent force within you, you will grow vigorous and happy, however adverse your circumstances may seem to be. " ——John R. Miller

We are constantly changing, and as our internal world alters, our external world also alters and vice versa. If we choose to explore the recesses of our minds; encounter new experiences; challenge our emotions, feelings, and beliefs; and be adaptable to the sensations arising within, we will transform incredibly and easily manifest a life aligned with our higher purpose. The people who we are connected with will either change too, or the engagement with them will fade out and diminish and the people we attract and connect with will be those in line with the new higher frequency we are vibrating on.

If we were previously triggered by every slight word or action or we once saw ourselves as victims or if we used to behave in ways that were self-punishing, it doesn't mean that that is who we are now. We have to be gentle toward the parts of ourselves that have kept us locked in unhealthy exchanges so we can acknowledge where we have gone wrong and ensure we do not keep triggering the same behaviors and magnetizing the same situations.

Every second is one that we can choose to create fulfilling and empowering changes. We can make small changes or huge, life-altering ones. We all have the power to create our own reality in every moment that arrives.

"Whatever we plant in our subconscious mind and nourish with repetition and emotion will one day become a reality." ——Earl Nightingale

When we are adults, we are accountable for the relationships and interactions we attract and also for why we react, respond and choose to stay in them. The energy we are radiating is a reflection of how we feel about ourselves and it is in some way it is partly responsible for whatever we magnetize. This does not in any way explain random, unprovoked, or inexcusable attacks or behaviors that we have absolutely no way of preempting, avoiding, or escaping from. It explains the low self-worth and self-love that makes us stay in a situation; for example, a relationship, friendship, career, or any dynamic in which we have the ability to walk away but we choose to stay because we do not value our emotional, mental, or physical health high enough. At any moment we can make the decision to step away from whatever is in front of us and make better choices, which will in turn reinforce a healthier self-esteem and empower us to continue onward on a path that feels true to ourselves.

Often it takes reaching rock bottom before we are able to fully admit that we need to change how we view ourselves. When we see our reflection we can remember that all reflections change depending on how we think about them. Our thoughts interact with what we are focusing on and what is mirrored back at us changes. If we choose to see ourselves in a positive light, we will find ourselves illuminated and that glow will gift us clarity to make decisions and it will also help to guidance.

Even when things seem to go wrong and everything seems lost and impossible to repair, we are resilient beings and we can bounce back from anything if we are willing to try hard enough. We can revolutionize our lives, but first we need to transform how we think about our lives. And more importantly we need to change how we really feel about them. Our feelings powerfully radiate through the energy we emit. There are vital messages in our subtle energy that other people can read. If we are subconsciously feeling inadequate, despite what we are thinking consciously, we are leaving ourselves open to those vibrations being picked up by someone who can manipulate them or use them to their advantage, and they will find it exceptionally easy to do so as when we are vibrating on a low scale we are also vulnerable to harm.

Abusers are like magnets. They lurk around scanning stimuli that they detect as a weak easy to penetrate link. And when they pick up on it, they will draw it in with masterful skill and strength. We have to rewire our internal thoughts, feelings, and values and build up our self-worth so that we are not at risk of being manipulated by their covert tactics. Otherwise, we will continue to repeat the same patterns within relationships over and again, and every time our self-esteem will take a further battering, leaving us more wounded, weaker, and vulnerable. When we are grounded, aware and armed with self-belief and knowledge, we will either not be pulled towards engaging in these dynamics, or we will communicate very differently and we will be able to handle and control how we interact so that they cause us few, or no, difficulties at all. However, when we are vibrating lowly, we are very likely to end up being in a position whereby we are likely to be manipulated and controlled.

When someone then treats up poorly we can end up blaming ourselves, with words like "It cannot be their fault, I must have deserved this." The more we think like this, the more we stand a very high chance of attracting those people whose words and actions reaffirm that we deserve it. Unfortunately, we often choose people that confirm the horrible bedtime stories we have repeated in the darkness each night. We then trust what abusers and manipulators tell us, as it sounds eerily similar to our "truth," and reflects back all the disempowering thoughts we repeatedly tell ourselves.

If we have a belief that we are not worthy or that we do not deserve to be loved, and this belief only exists in our subconscious mind, our subconscious mind is the container that stores and generates a big percentage of our feeling. Our feelings have an extremely powerful far reaching vibration. Those feelings will also seek out and magnetize other low vibrational feelings toward them that are on the same low frequency, so the strength of those feelings soon grows. If we feel as though we have always been a "victim," we will naturally fall into the role of victim as other people will attune to our low self-worth and see an opportunity to exert their egotistical desires and easily place us under their control. We will constantly be validating our belief system by matching what is imprinted internally to what is available externally. If our stored data tells us we are not good enough in any way, we will attract situations and people who affirm these false beliefs..

We can try to keep reminding ourselves that we are not what happened to us previously, so anything in the past that made us feel small does not need to be held on to. We are altered in every moment and we can let go of our past experiences, mistakes, or regrets at any moment. We can empower ourselves rather than incessantly carry out negative, sabotaging repetitions. When we are willing to open our eyes fully, we will see things with clarity rather than through illusions that distort our perception. Sight becomes insight, and we will see what is in front of us on a far deeper level.

Sometimes, it isn't that we can't see what is happening, it is that we don't *want* to see or believe it. Although we may think we don't "deserve" to be treated badly, while this is true, we can also remember that whenever someone someone treats us negatively due to their historic wounds, it is never a reflection of who we are, it is always a reflection of who they are internally. Therefore, rather than taking it personally, we have to remove ourselves from the picture and see their abuse as a targeted act. We have been unfortunate enough to get caught in the crossfire. If it wasn't us in that position, someone else would likely be in our place. We are not the cause of anyone else's destructive words or actions. They have the option and the personal power to resist reacting and to take responsibility for their highly charged low vibrational energy. Blaming others for how they choose to conduct themselves is just an excuse for uncontrollable and inexcusable behavior.

We may also make the mistake of not wanting to see the "bad" in someone. Therefore, we give people second, third, fourth, or even five thousand or more chances. We are desperate to prove that this person can change and that what we are seeing is just a result of a difficult childhood, a previous trauma, or we tell ourselves that maybe they are just going through a rough patch. All of these things and more may be true, but it doesn't ever warrant them using us for target practice. It is essential that we consider our own emotional health and in doing so, we protect ourselves by choosing to disengage in dynamics whereby someone is intentionally trying to disrupt us and affect us emotionally.

Many abusers are people who have once been the victim of abuse themselves. The residues of pain they were left with may be eating away at them and their fear-led emotions prompt them to lash out and drag others down so they have someone to immerse in the pain with them. If we add more hurt, resentment, and anger to the pool, we will not achieve anything other than drowning in an even bigger mass of messy pain. It is not easy, but we have to separate ourselves entirely. We have to see other people's pain as separate to ours. We should not be forced to suffer just to ease it. We are not doing ourselves or the other person any favors by marinating in their low vibration. We absolutely have to pull ourselves away, however hard it may be to do so.

Unfortunately, empaths often make a few potentially dangerous mistakes when dealing with abusers. One vital error is that we might believe that everyone out there thinks and feels the same way as we do as our intention is to love unconditionally, accept and treat people as equals, be compassionate, and try not to cause suffering or harm to others. Therefore, we may naively believe that everyone else must want these things too. Sadly, this is not the case, particularly when we are dealing with sociopaths, psychopaths, or narcissists. If we are not consciously aware these interactions can mean we are lambs offering ourselves up for slaughter. We then become the lion's prey and we will be toyed with, teased, stunned, and eventually our fear can cause us to become paralyzed. This leaves us wide open and entirely vulnerable to be the latest plaything in their manipulative game.

Empaths usually have high levels of compassion and low, if any, boundaries, so we can be seen as the perfect catch for an abuser if we do not remain grounded, aware and alert. They may believe they are be able to stretch us way beyond most other people's limits. And as we often forgive and forget very easily, they might think they can repeat their behavior time and again before we eventually (if ever) reach the end of the line. Unfortunately, sometimes we may not identify emotional abuse quickly and it can often wrongly be perceived as more acceptable than physical abuse we may stay around longer and excuse wounded behavior and pass it off as someone who is in a lot of pain themselves, hoping we can help them heal and that they may change. However, when we are subjected to their painful emotional games, our bodies also suffer as emotional pain eventually results in physiological pain. We then suffer twice.

When it comes to emotional or physical abuse there isn't a "better" or "worse" than the other and they need to be treated as equally harmful. If we have always said we would never stay in a relationship with someone who physically assaults us, we can try to consider this same train of thought about emotional abuse. If someone was coming up to us with a clenched fist ready to swing for us, we would quickly move out of the way and avoid the impact at all costs. This same mentality can be put in place for those who are coming toward us with emotional abuse. We do not need to stand in front of it and allow the harsh vibrations to influence our emotional state. Both emotional and physical abuse can be equally harmful and when we subject ourselves to either they can drag us into an abyss that can be very difficult to escape from.

Emotional pain can stay with us unhealed for a lifetime. It can affect every aspect of our lives, even if we are adamant and try to fool ourselves that it doesn't exist. If we have a physical injury, we can see it, so we are likely to get it treated, but unfortunately, we aren't always as willing to unearth our hidden emotional injuries so that they can receive care and attention too.

Our physical injuries also affect us emotionally. Every experience we have leaves an impression on us somewhere. We have to regularly locate and meet with these imprints, validate, soothe, and heal them and ensure they are not left abandoned and trapped where they can fester and cause us eternal internal unrest. Our pain does not dissipate just because we think it has been forgotten about. We have to consciously focus on it, pay attention to it, and change the emotions and feelings we have been attributing to it.

Although we sometimes want to leave the past where it is, when we are confronted with the same situations again and again it is a signal that there is ignored emotional trauma that hasn't been tended to and dealt with. We can gently delve into it to, acknowledge it, analyze it, accept, and understand it to ensure it doesn't keep repeating itself. The simplest way to know if we have any wounds that are subliminally making their presence known is to pay attention to what irritable sensations occur whenever we are criticized, shunned, insulted, rejected, disrespected, or whenever we feel uncared for or unloved. We can then focus on the emotions arising and try to find where they originated. When we consciously pay attention to our uncomfortable or unpleasant emotions, we will find that we are not just dealing with new emotions that have been generated. Whatever is causing them to be triggered is hidden under the surface and is due to an old experience that once caused us to feel slighted in some way.

When we are fully conscious and aware, we are more likely to think rationally and logically. The things that are capable of hurting us when our subconscious mind is dominating will not have the same effect on us when we are consciously aware. The majority of our stored emotions will have entered unconsciously through conditioning by our parents, friends, teachers, and society as a whole. This means that we may feel emotional pain for something just because we have been led to believe that we should. We are taught which behaviors are "right" and which are "wrong," and when someone displays something that fits in either one we may respond emotionally based on what we have been conditioned to think is the correct response. Therefore, much of our emotional trauma is likely misplaced and irrelevant. What may have been traumatizing for us as a child likely would not have the same effect on us today as our mind is now more open, we are physically and often emotionally and mentally stronger, so we are not as vulnerable, and we can also rationalize and discern better.

Many people grow up remaining caught in a similar mindset as to the one they had throughout their childhood. They struggle to let go of memories and events from many years ago, even though how they think and feel about them now most likely has little relation to what actually occurred. Not only does our memory play tricks on us so we only remember partial details, our mind is also very different from how it was back then. When we locate our emotional injuries, we can tune in to them and fully feel how they feel and try to remember what caused them. We can then rationalize and think about the memory with an open mind and communicate internally to console and reason with the emotions so that they are acknowledged, restructured, and understood. We can then replace any negative vibrations that are emanating from the emotions with loving, considerate, compassionate, and soothing ones.

Sometimes we turn the attention away from our own healing and focus on other people's. If we have not embraced, acknowledged, understood, or bonded our own fractured wounds, we are definitely not in a position to meddle with or try to repair anyone else's. Our unseen injuries are what cause us to attract others who also have open emotional wounds. The silent pain that we are internally suffering from resonates with the other person's on a hidden, soul deep, subconscious level. When we meet people who have also denied or rejected their emotional pain, without realizing we are doing it or without knowing why, we will connect with them in an attempt to possibly not only heal to them, but also, unconsciously, to give ourselves the opportunity to locate our own pain so that we can heal. As soon as we are in the company of someone who emanates a vibration that is in harmony with our own vibrational discord, we unknowingly connect as the resonation gives us a familiar feeling. We then may believe that we have the ability to heal their "broken" parts and "fix" their troubles and struggles, as we know how they feel and have experienced similar trauma. This belief is one that we can try to eradicate, especially if we haven't yet dedicated time to fully healing our own trauma. Even if we have, we are not here to repair, glue, or stitch humans back together or to think we can make someone complete and whole, just as we wouldn't take kindly to someone wanting to think we are broken. Each person is already whole and capable of fixing their own wounds, but only if they so choose to.

While we can still connect and communicate, show unconditional love, understanding, and still send healing, the other person will only respond to our uplifting vibration if they are willing to open to it, embrace it, work with it, and ultimately want to heal themselves. Anything else we do with regards to "fixing" will be similar to knocking on tightly closed and securely locked doors. Not only that, it is patronizing to look at someone and believe they need our "help." Even if we think we are capable of offering assistance as we have been through similar difficulties and healed our own wounds, it is still not our place to decide whether someone wants or needs to be helped. We are all at the same level, we are all equal and we can all heal and grow as soon we make the effort to.

Here are some of the signs that we are in an abusive relationship or that we are dealing with abuse:

- Apologizing - We will constantly be apologizing for doing things wrong even if we have done nothing wrong. Feeling sorry for everything means that the accountability and responsibility for all perceived wrongdoings has been claimed by one person—us. This ensures the perpetrator remains innocent and we are continuously made to feel blamed, ashamed and guilty.
- Cannot make decisions - We will find decision making increasingly complex, as we will feel that whatever we choose will be the wrong choice. Everything we do or say is incorrect, so we feel that we are no longer capable of making rational decisions and so we leave decision making to our

abuser. This gives the abuser even more power and control and disempowers us, prolonging the toxic dance.

- Change - Change is not always easy to notice since mostly it happens little by little, so the process can feel very familiar and natural in some ways. However, if we think back to who we were before the relationship and who we are now, we will probably see major and significant differences.
- Confusion - We will often feel in a prolonged state of bewilderment and confusion. We find it very difficult to trust our own mind, and constantly doubt our thought processes. Our instinct fails to kick in because whenever it does we are quickly told it that it is incorrect, so our intuition becomes a silent and ignored tool, which ensures the abuser remains on top of their game. We will know that there is something seriously wrong, but we may find it extremely difficult to work out what. We will always be wondering if we are overly sensitive as we regularly feel triggered to react and respond to our abuser's behavior.
- Withdrawn - We may become withdrawn or reclusive as we feel so low and beaten down that we have little confidence to socialize with anyone. We will feel safer spending time alone rather than with other people, as when people around us question why we are behaving differently or ask about our relationship we will not have the answers to justify what is going on.

If we go through periods of isolation, depression or severe anxiety, we may find it extremely difficult to function normally within society or even with close friends or family. The abuser at this stage is in a position where they could use this to their advantage to gain complete control, as without anyone to confide in we will find it very difficult to work out that it is the abuser covertly influencing our behavior and manipulatively affecting our self-esteem.

We each have to take responsibility for ourselves as it is disempowering to try to blame other people. However, I am aware that being accountable is not always quite so simple when energetically entangled within an abusive relationship. The abusive person will not want anyone to figure out their game, so they may try incredibly hard to make sure we are alienated from anyone who could offer us support. One of the main reasons for abuse is to create a dynamic whereby the abuser has complete control over their victim so that they are weakened and easy to manipulate. The abuser wants to appear superior, so by making us feel completely helpless, with very low self-esteem, they achieve and retain complete domination. They are then very successful in using manipulative techniques to get whatever it is they want. This can range from simply having their ego stroked and feeling like they are significantly better than us, or at the extreme end they may gain financial, sexual, or material benefits as we feel too emotionally or mentally weak to fight back.

There are many reasons why someone would abuse someone else, but it is always for some kind of personal gain. The abuser has very little interest in us other than using us for their ego's benefit. When we become so low down that we are no longer of any great use, the relationship will die out. The abuser may distance themselves by ignoring us and using silent treatment as an intense form of emotional torture. We then could have no idea what to do to please or satisfy them, and may try to win over our abuser to regain the affection that was shown in the beginning stages. The harder we try to please them, the less satisfied they will seem, which causes us to believe we are not doing enough, so we try harder still. By now, though, it is far too late. Any little amount of respect that the abuser had for us will have been completely depleted and it is very unlikely that the dynamic will change again. The abuser will often walk away, leaving us with a deep sense of frustration, shame, guilt, anger, and often riddled with anxiety and depression. We are left in a vortex that we will struggle to climb out of, which will be compounded by a deep sense of relief that the vicious dance is over. The abuser will walk away with a great feeling of satisfaction, having won each and every battle, and will likely move on to their next innocent victim with even more skill and experience so they can begin this emotional war once again.

After a relationship with someone who has been abusive we may need counseling and a huge amount of support to build ourselves back to a stage where we have confidence and can trust our own mind and intuition. It is imperative that we realize that we have been a pawn in a very callous game. We can then let go of all the blame we have placed upon ourselves and become familiar with the warning signs so that we do not fall victim again.

Anyone who has come through this type of experience might feel debilitated at first, although they are only temporarily weakened. With time we can bounce back stronger than before, having learned painful but valuable lessons along the way. The most important lesson is having complete faith in our inner knowing sensations. As difficult as it is to accept, there are always red flags and warning signs in the initial stages that sometimes we would rather not see as we want to believe the best about people. When these signals show up, this is when we must trust completely in our instincts and never fail to listen to what our energy is telling us. Our fight or flight reactions are there for a reason—to prevent us from entering into dangerous situations. When we feel an urgency to take flight, we must fly.

There is a vast amount of help and support out there. If it is too intrusive to talk to a family member or friend, there are many support groups and organizations that are a lifeline throughout these relationships and also when they end.

Chapter 21

CHEMISTRY

Chemistry in relationships is the chemical process that happens when there is an energetically charged connection between two people that sparks a reaction within their electromagnetic fields. The two people may intensely feel the energy radiating and glowing from one another and any friction that is felt is the energies interlocking. Chemistry causes the pleasure centers within the brain to engage, sending out overwhelming feel-good emotions, and this delivers a craving sensation that can we can rapidly become addicted to.

One thing we can fail to realize about chemistry is that the magnetic pull and attraction that is felt is not always positive or healthy. We attract and repel people based on the electromagnetic vibrations we send out and receive. When our vibrations connect strongly to another person's vibrations, we can then be magnetized to someone and it might be difficult to understand why, especially if our lifestyles or personalities are not compatible in any way. When we find energy that feels soothing, we bask in it and our aura feels warm and has a safe space to glow and grow.

Sometimes we are strongly attracted to energy that feels as though it is vibrating on a similar level but it can have the opposite intent. We can be just as intrigued by energy on the opposite side of the spectrum as our own when it is vibrating as strongly as ours, even if it is fueled by totally different emotions and has an opposing agenda. A classic example is someone who is vibrating strongly with love may attract someone who is vibrating strongly with fear, aggression, or anger. We may be attracted to the similar waves of energy that are vibrating but the vibrations are on totally different levels just equally as strong. The loving vibrations are on a high level, the fearful ones on a low level, but they are expressed with the same depth and intensity. These connections will feel like a tornado spinning us around, pulling us in, then catapulting us out with huge force that then disrupts and devastates our inner and outer selves. Our energy is vibrating wildly, though mostly due to the friction the discord has caused.

When we have chemistry with someone, many things fade that would normally be in place, such as sound judgment, trust, compatibility, and physical attraction. We can find ourselves instantly and deeply entwined on an emotional level with someone whom we might normally have consciously chosen to avoid. Chemistry is what gives us that "love at first sight" or "I want to be with them all the time" feeling. However, it can also have the totally opposite effect, causing us to shy away from someone, leaving us feeling repelled due to the intensity or frequency of the energy waves that are radiating toward us.

Chemistry can bring on feelings of lust, passion, infatuation, bonding, desire, romance, and also all of the opposites, such as dislike, contempt, fear, mistrust, confusion, or annoyance. Or it can cause us to have a complete disinterest in someone. All of these feelings are attached to the ego, our imagined self, and can often provide insightful and profound lessons if we choose to interact further and explore what is causing these emotions to be evoked.

There are so many variations of chemistry and it is related to the energy that is exchanged between the two people. The stronger the energetic interaction, the stronger the chemistry will be. Similar to why the term "spark" is used to explain the connection. The electromagnetic energy will feel as though it is sparking or igniting as the two people are drawn closer emotionally, mentally, or physically.

Generally speaking, there are three types of chemistry: positive, neutral, and negative. When there is a positive connection we will be deeply and powerfully drawn toward someone. A neutral connection is when we may find it hard to connect with someone on any level at all (almost a total disinterest). A negative connection will feel like a forceful push-and-pull sensation as the energies strike against one another, causing an intense reaction and these are the relationships that we may feel compelled to pull toward us yet something is also holding or forcing us backward. This is because one person's energy is vibrating high, the other person's is vibrating low. The negative energy can often be mistaken for positive energy, as the high intensity will have a similar impact on us.

We may often wonder if chemistry can be created. When we imagine chemistry as a constantly changing wave of electricity, it is very possible to see that as our energy changes, so will our reactions to other people's energy too. If we are vibrating at a very low level, we may find it very difficult to have a spark with someone we are interested in if their vibration is on a very different frequency to ours. However, as we raise our vibration, our energy becomes magnetic with others who are also vibrating highly.

It is also possible for a buildup of chemistry to occur. As our emotions toward someone grow, we will also have an increase in the chemical reactions in our systems. These chemical reactions have a direct effect on the strength of the energy that we are sending out, therefore, as our emotions increase, so too will the energy level increase and the energy will impact us as well as those around us far quicker and easier. If the other person is also vibrating highly, the interaction will cause sparks and become more powerful and intense.

It is possible to "fake" chemistry as we alter our mindset to allow either positive or negative energy to flow through us deriving from whatever it is we are thinking about. For example, if we set our thought processes to engage loving feelings, we allow high vibrational loving energy to radiate. We can send out whatever energy we choose; however, how we are really feeling deep inside may not be reflected in the energy that is radiated and people who are highly sensitive to energy will detect this; i.e., if our belief system or inner feelings do not align with our conscious thoughts certain people will figure this out and view us as being inauthentic. We have to really feel our thoughts and believe them to be true before our energy vibrates accordingly.

If we are unsure as to whether someone is "tricking" us with chemistry, we can use our intuition and trust how our energy feels as it absorbs their energy. If there is constant friction, it could be that the motive for their energy flow is not a genuine one. It may be that they consciously want to change how they feel though they have not been able to connect their feelings and emotions with their thoughts. It may just take a little time for their subconscious to catch up with their unconscious mind. It is impossible to be sure unless we use our inner knowing feeling for guidance and trust in what we are sensing. We will be able to work it out if we attune to it and pay fine attention.

Someone who is using trickery to exploit chemistry will also no doubt use trickery with words and actions. If we focus on the bigger picture and take words, actions, and chemistry into account, we will have a far higher chance of figuring out what is true energy and what is inauthentic.

Depending on the other person's agenda, they may use every trick in the book to cast us under a spell; it is our choice how open and willing we are as to whether we fall for it or not. It is essential to keep our mind consciously aware and in the present moment at the beginning of any new friendship, meeting, or relationships so that we are not easily fooled and we are aware of who we are letting into our lives. This is where the saying "love is blind" comes into play. We can be so mesmerized by our energy field dancing with someone else's we become unconscious to the true state of affairs. The chemistry that is fueling and intoxicating our body and mind will alter our perception and make things appear hazy and fuzzy so that we are under an illusion rather than seeing the authentic and far bigger picture. We will ignore warning signs or simply not hear alarm bells ringing as chemistry takes primary place.

Relationships that do not have this high influx of chemicals in the early stages can often work out extremely well and last far longer as both partners have a calm and rational mind to make decisions and judgments as to whether the relationship is compatible. They are then in a position to bond over mutual interests, similarities in lifestyle or they will attract a personality type that is in harmony and balance with theirs. Then, as emotions grow, so too does the chemistry between them, rather than burning and fizzling out when the two people realize there is nothing more than chemistry holding them together.

Very strong chemistry can also hold two people together that may not otherwise survive through the bumps and obstacles that may occur in the early stages of a relationship, though as the chemistry fades the reality of the connection appears. Chemistry can also be responsible for a couple moving through the stages of a relationship extremely quickly as they feel a sense of "knowing one another" due to the strong bonds and attachments they experience. High levels of chemistry can make a relationship feel wild and like nothing on earth as our system pulsates and flushes with chemicals. We not only have that heady and dizzy feeling around someone, we also feel a force pulling or pushing at us. These are the types of relationships we can remain wary of so that we pay attention to what is going on beneath the chemical high.

We may stay in a relationship that we know is unhealthy or one which goes against our ethics and morals while convincing ourselves that it must be "right" due to the thrills, highs, and extreme emotional reactions we feel when we are around a particular person. Our behavior can become irrational, causing us to make decisions that with a clear mind we'd steer far from. Quite simply, the saying "love is a drug" is often true due to the amount of dopamine released when we are around someone with whom our energy strongly interacts with. The feeling we associate with love in the early stages is often chemicals altering our state of mind. We can feel out of control and as though we just want to ride the waves to see where it takes us. An incredible feeling, but if we aren't careful it can also be a dangerous one too.

Chemistry is an opportunity for growth and can be one of our greatest teachers. It exists for a reason and it is entirely our decision as to whether we want to explore the sensations further and pay attention to the rollercoaster journey it can take us on. We are attracted and repelled based on the energy we are sending and receiving and despite feeling magnetized or repelled from someone, we have control over our choices, not the chemicals that try to convince us otherwise. We must pay attention to who we engage with so that we do not allow our hormones and emotions to make our decisions and then take control.

The spark we feel is an electrical connection based on the energy radiating from our thoughts, emotions, feelings, and our belief system. Despite what we may like to think, chemistry is not directly connected to love.

Chapter 22

RELATIONSHIPS

For empaths, all types of relationships—platonic, romantic, familial, or even work relationships—can be highly tricky, and the main reason for this is that we are continuously consciously or subconsciously intuiting their energy and this can cause us to become anxious, overwhelmed and fatigued. Some empaths may not be able to remain in a relationship for long as we need a great deal of freedom and personal space, though ironically when we are in a relationship we can become entangled and deeply entwined as we also adore deep connections. Due to this, we can eventually reach burnout as we have literally given more of ourselves than we have to give and we can end up bolting for the door with a desperate need to completely relax and breathe.

It is essential for an empath that there is respect and a sound understanding of one another's requirement for alone time. Empaths are compassionate, accepting, and forgiving, and although these are all positive traits, if we do not have personal barriers in place they can also leave us vulnerable, leading us to engage in the types of relationships that can adversely affect us emotionally or mentally.

An empath's ideal relationship would be based on accountability, authenticity, truth, care, and acceptance. It would also be one that offers a shared resonance, an intimate connection and respect and space for one another's needs. We love intensely and we form bonds and strong attachments to those we are close to, and we are usually loyal throughout. The mistake we make is that we are often compelled to focus on others without first paying attention to ourselves. We are very quick to love unconditionally and accept other people without judgment, although we are not so great at offering these same things to ourselves.

Relationships with those who have emotional or mental challenges can test us to our limits, and eventually, usually after a long period of time, force us to turn the spotlight inward. One of the reasons we can be drawn to those with tormented souls is that they inadvertently push us toward self-awareness so that we face our own flaws, weaknesses, insecurities, and ultimately our lack of self-worth. Another reason is that we do not like to believe that anyone genuinely intends to cause harm, even though this very thinking is what leads us straight into the thick of so many difficulties. Rather than judging or discarding someone immediately, we prefer to look to their past to discover reasons for their behavior rather than focusing on whatever is happening today. This allows us to sense the energy from their past experiences, which helps us to weave the loose fine threads so that we can clearly see the overall picture. We are then able to see the person in a new light so that we have compassion and consideration rather than contempt and indignation.

We have an innate ability to heal, so we empathize with others as we have often been through our own difficulties. We find resonance with those who also have faced or are facing struggles, as we are aware of how it feels to experience testing times. This is another of the reasons we are magnetized toward those who are in pain emotionally, mentally, or physically.

The concept of someone who helps others by relating directly to their own trauma is known as a "wounded healer." However, we often fail to realize that we cannot "fix" someone else, people aren't broken, and they don't need us to save them or glue them back together. Everyone is on their own journey and they will stumble or run along it as and when they are ready to. Stepping back and allowing this does not come easy for an empath due to our healing, nurturing, and compassionate nature. We see someone in pain and we immediately want to soothe it and take away whatever is causing it. We believe we can stitch up and Band-Aid people we perceive to be falling apart or broken, although in trying to help others we are preventing them from being able to help themselves.

Not only do we try to soothe people, but we also think we can take hold of all their baggage and carry it for them. This just weighs us down further as we become laden with such a heavy load that we then struggle to figure out what is ours and what belongs to other people. Until we protect our own energy, and fully understand our reasons for wanting to reach out and connect, we can try not to delve into anyone else's problems.

We don't always seem to know where the line needs to be drawn, to take care of our own needs versus caring for others, and even if the line is deeply carved out as a warning sign on a step in front of us we will still step over it, believing that we just need to learn how to love harder as love can conquer all. When we take on our partner's difficulties, we can easily enter into a relationship that is codependent. Our partner then becomes dependent on us to validate them or heal their wounds, and we may become dependent on the feeling of worthiness we receive when we are necessary for someone else's survival. This becomes messy very rapidly and we will quickly fall into the same abyss our partner is in. One way to work out how to assess how to maintain healthy

Genuine, authentic love can be a very complex thing for an empath to achieve, although with the right person, someone who is understanding, grounded, free spirited, and trustworthy, love can be an intimate, deeply bonding, healing, fulfilling, empowering, and healthy connection that neither will want to break. A relationship with someone who is deeply troubled is not only troublesome for both concerned, it can also become quite a selfish one. When we are around someone who is in pain, we absorb that pain and we feel it as intensely as though it is our own. A problem shared is a problem halved; however, we don't take on half of the problem. We marinate and torment ourselves in it, absorbing it whole. Empaths want to reduce and remove pain as quickly as possible, so in healing someone else we are essentially also healing ourselves, as we will no longer be experiencing their emotional pain. This is something that empaths often fail to see, as we believe that our intentions are purely outwardly ones and for the greater good of the other person. We think we are selflessly martyring ourselves by focusing our attention toward someone else, yet we also want to eradicate all the unpleasant, uncomfortable sensations we now feel due to absorbing our partner's emotions.

When an empath is awakened to the fact that we have chosen to take on this pain through not protecting our own energy properly, we can look at the situation from an outside perspective rather than being captured at the center of it. We first and foremost need to take care of ourselves and allow those around us the opportunity to do the same.

Empaths have the ability to very easily tap deeply into the energy of those that we are in a relationship with. This means that if we remain aware we are able to see our partner for who they are on a deep inner level, rather than who they appear on the surface. We see all the shades, even the ones they have desperately tried keep hidden. We can also feel it when someone is closed off and has built up walls to protect their emotions. We will notice this blockage when we try and tune in to our partner's emotions and we sense that there is some disconnect between their heart and what they are expressing. To an empath, an area that has been blocked will feel like a dull ache in their energy field. Although we will sense that our partner's emotions are partially unavailable, we will likely persist with the relationship as we are drawn to heal. We desperately want to show care, love, and compassion so that we can help ease securely guarded and closed hearts open. This is often something that causes difficulties as people only open up when they are ready to. Someone trying to pry open their emotions will feel like an unwelcome intrusion. It can be hard for an empath to take a step back, especially as we sense what is happening and feel as though we know what we could do to support them.

An empath who is highly aware and advanced with their abilities and knowledge will fully understand that their partner just needs patience, understanding, and unconditional love, though these things are not always easy to master when we care deeply about someone or are in the full throes of love. The most complex and most confusing part occurs when someone tries to portray that they are someone they aren't. Empaths aren't looking for perfection, we are looking for connection, in whatever shape that connection appears.

Connections that develop rapidly will likely be very intense and can become overbearing. When we find someone whose energy ignites our own, we can almost become obsessive, with the strong desire to retain the electricity that is felt when we are in that person's company. This can cause empaths to appear to fall in "love" extremely quickly. Empaths absorb the energy around them. We can absorb and feel other people's anger and we can also absorb and feel other people's love. Empaths feel the radiation of love emanating from other people simply by consciously or unconsciously tapping into it and absorbing the energy. This means that empaths are capable of feeling the emotions associated with love simply by feeling the resonations of love as they radiate from other people.

Being able to absorb energy easily can cause confusion when it comes to relationships. We are easily able to fall in and out of what appears to be love just by losing ourselves in other people's energy. If we protect our own energy well, remain grounded, and we are very aware of the emotions that belong to us and the emotions that belong to other people, we will not be influenced easily and we won't mistakenly identify our feelings.

Feeling the love that exists in someone else's energy field can also mean that we are able to fall out of "love" as soon as we are have left that person's company. Depending on how strong the connection is between us and the other person, we may instantly lose the bonding feeling the moment we have parted ways. We may even feel as though we are in "love" with someone for just a few hours and walk away and feel no emotions whatsoever. This may seem heartless, although, it is not intentional. However, it is one of the reasons it is essential to do the work on ourselves so that we have high awareness of how powerful and intoxicating energy can be. When there is an open-hearted connection that flows from one empath to the other, it is likely this dynamic will continue even when the two are not connected in any other way. The energy will be felt subtly or even vividly at all times and communication will continue energetically without the need for physical, verbal or written contact.

When someone is radiating love toward us, it can feel exhilarating as we bask in the high vibrations. During the initial stages, both people involved may feel deliriously happy, but empaths cannot usually keep up this level of high intensity for long. It will soon drain us emotionally and physically and eventually we may start looking for an escape route as we start to feel flooded with emotion and as though we are exhausted, drowning, without space and struggling to breathe. The person whom we have shared this brief connection with may feel bewildered and even devastated and the guilt we feel may cause us to prolong a connection with someone who, realistically, we know is not someone with whom we would choose to commit to a long-term relationship with.

From time to time, however, we may meet someone special with whom we share an instant, harmonious, and intense connection that harmoniously vibrates on an emotional, mental, physical and spiritual level. It can feel as though we recognize their soul and feel at home within it. It may be a certain look in their eyes or just their energy that powerfully magnetizes us to them. There may be various things that attract us to a certain someone. It might be the tone of their voice, how they dress, the smell of their skin, or something significant that is said that sparks a flame deep inside that very quickly turns into a raging energetic inferno. All too often these are the first signs we are about to engage in a karmic relationship.

Although I use the term *karma*, I personally don't see karma as a universal punishment or as a price we pay for past errors. I believe that we create our own karma moment to moment, and if we cause suffering to others, we cause it to ourselves as we are all part of the same energy force. As our thoughts change, our perception changes and our energy alters by ascending or descending. Karma, in my belief, is a way to describe the energy that we have generated and this energy can attract or repel people or situations toward our lives depending on how we think, feel, or what we believe about ourselves in the present moment. I don't believe the widely held concept that karma is a predetermined judgment based on our actions in our previous or even current life. I believe that karma is fluid and changes whenever our mindset and feelings change. Karma can be good or bad. It is purely energy. We are in control of it, not the other way around as we can change our thoughts and thus change our feelings and beliefs whenever we choose to. If we feel that we deserve bad things to happen us, we will subconsciously attract those things. In my opinion, karma is basically self-judgment and self-punishment. We can remove the judgment and punishment at any time when we accept our errors, change our feelings, and alter our ways.

When we need a reality check to tell us how much or how little we value ourselves or how high or low our self-worth is, we simply need to take a look at the people and situations that surround us that cause us peace or discord. All around us there are mirrors that provide everything we need to know about our current state of mind. When we meet someone with whom we feel an energetic bond with, we have very likely just attracted a person or situation that reflects an aspect of how we feel on the inside. The connection feels comfortable and we resonate with it well as it is in harmony with how we are truly feeling about ourselves in that very moment, or about a hidden part of ourselves that we are preparing to uncover. The person seems familiar and we will feel as though we have known them before, possibly from a previous life, which can feel very alien, especially if we do not believe in reincarnation. We often get these feelings with certain friendships, but when it happens with a love interest the attraction and emotions are heightened. We may crave their company so we can get to know more about them and also to discover why a piece of their soul seems to slot in straight next to ours.

Although a relationship that feels "karmic" may in some ways seem like the perfect fit and extremely healthy and nourishing, it may also be abusive, either verbally or physically, and it is up to us to look at who we are attracted to and why. If we are choosing partners who disrespect us and intentionally try to cause us harm, we can ask ourselves why we are accepting this behavior, and question why we feel so unworthy that we are allowing someone to treat us in ways that cause us constant disruption. We cannot point the finger at anyone else. We must look at ourselves to discover why we are giving people a place in our lives when they choose to treat us badly and also why we are allowing ourselves to be emotionally affected. What stories are we telling ourselves that lead us to believe we need certain people in our lives and why, when they cause us such difficulties, do we keep repeating them?

How other people treat us is simply a reflection of what we think of ourselves. Therefore, when we let someone into our lives and allow them to treat us badly, we are not caring or loving ourselves enough on the inside. If we were, we would stop allowing their destructive behavior. To change the reflections we see, we only need to change how we think and feel, and immediately other people will appear as new reflections of our inner self. Our thoughts are capable of controlling everything we see. When we change our thoughts, we change how we feel, we change what we attract and then we change what reflects.

Often, negative behaviors can feel comfortable and familiar, as we may have experienced similar treatment at an earlier stage of our lives. When we meet someone who displays traits that remind us of people who have been significant in our lives in the past, we can feel bonded to them even if the relationship is not compatible. Just because we recognize behaviors and they resonate with something inside of us, it does not mean that we need to be allow them to affect us. We do not need to keep learning the same lessons over and over. We can identify why it feels familiar and then refuse to engage emotionally realizing that other people's behaviors are not our responsibility and we certainly do not need to be emotionally harmed by them.

Anger and rage may be very common behaviors in karmic relationships and it may feel as though any small thing rubs us the wrong way and causes an irrational response. Again, this is due to past experiences triggering emotional reactions and responses. It is imperative to learn why we are entangling with others in these ways and then look inside ourselves to find out what we have tucked away that is preventing us from achieving a respectful, peaceful, and loving relationship. We cannot blame others for our reactions. It is entirely up to us to acknowledge our behaviors, heal the hurt, and change our wiring, responses, and perception so that we stop allowing past experiences to affect and influence us now.

Another issue for empaths is dealing with people who enjoy playing mind games. This is confusing mainly because the rules will be so complicated for us to figure out. Being such straight talkers, we are not familiar with those who want to engage in games and we won't join in if someone is trying to coax us into playing them. We may try to gain some control over the relationship by using emotional manipulation or temper tantrums to get our own way. This is very often because we are in fear that we are going to be hurt in some way and we wrongly believe that we can control situations as a way of avoiding pain and trauma. It is the opposite. We cause more pain to ourselves by holding on too tightly to something that realistically we have very little control over. We cannot control someone else's feelings toward us and it is not our place to control someone else's life.

Finding out what it is that we are so afraid of and healing the parts of us that feel insecure is the way to remove control. Often, low self-esteem and self-worth are responsible for controlling behaviors, similarly with jealousy and possessiveness. All of these traits will very likely rear their head in karmic relationships, with each one of them being a result of a lack of inner belief, value or worth.

Rather than allowing relationships to replay all our emotional battles again and again and letting our demons surface, we can take a good look at why these feelings of resentment and bitterness are simmering underneath in the first place. When we do this, we can acknowledge the emotions, give love, care, and attention to them and accept that we are a blend of darkness and light and it is okay to have these feelings as long as we have control over them and not the other way around.

When we are in a karmic relationship we will regularly be questioning our reason for staying. It is as though we know we have profound lessons to learn and patterns to break and we choose our partners as a way of helping us to understand more about ourselves and we role-play with different characters until the answers are unveiled. It may feel that we do not place absolute trust in the relationship and we won't see the other person as a life partner or someone who is going to be a permanent part of our lives. This sounds like a very selfish type of relationship, and in many ways and at various levels it is. The relationship is a stepping stone to reach the next stage and there may be an underlying resentment for one another for showing us both who we truly are, especially if we are not yet ready to see it.

These types of relationships are very common when we have a lot of work to do on ourselves and when we are functioning on a very low frequency. They stretch us and push us through what we previously believed were our limits and they test our extremes so we are compelled to search for our higher purpose and meaning in our lives. It is very often through a karmic relationship that we learn more about what we do want from a future relationship as we learn more about ourselves and as we experience the struggles of working through a relationship with someone who is not right for us.

When we have completed our cycle of karmic connections and stopped attracting repetitive lessons, we will have an awareness and a profound sense of what it is we want and need out of our lives. Some people may work through karmic love relationships very quickly and attract a life long twin soul connection; however, they will possibly still attract karmic friendships or be in karmic battles with family members.

We all have different lessons to learn and each lesson will present to us in its own unique way. Recognizing it and understanding it so that we are fully conscious of the reason for it being in our lives is the most powerful way we can break it down so we understand and resolve it rather than keep playing out the same script, just with a different cast.

The relationships we have around us may not always be healthy and nourishing ones although they may be necessary on a soul-level, and until we are fully aware and awakened as to what it is we have to learn and why we seem to be on repeat, we will remain stuck in the same cycles, playing out the same patterns time and again.

All this being said, it does not mean karmic relationships cannot turn into loving, genuine soul mate connections; it just means that a lot of self-acceptance, awareness, and inner work need to be done before it can move on to this stage. A karmic relationship can be difficult to break free from as they can feel addictive and we may feel compelled to stay to work through the patterns, untangle the mess, and unravel our stories together. However, unless both people are prepared to do the work, it can just mean finding ourselves tied in a tighter knot.

These relationships are not our destiny, they are not our fate, they are simply because we are allowing our past to present itself to us over and again based on how we think and feel, and essentially until we learn what it is that we need to learn and are willing to make the right decisions for a harmonic, healthy, and chaos-free future.

Making changes can be difficult, as our lovers, friends, and family members may want to remain in the character roles that they feel have been set out for them. When we disengage from these dynamics, other people have the choice to either let go so that we can venture on or they can rise to the challenge so that they too can create the changes needed to thrive on a higher frequency. If we are not codependent and are not feeding off past trauma, we will not attract a relationship to figure out our karmic debt. We will be strong, secure, independent, and capable of renewing and relieving ourselves of the debt alone.

All too often we may just be terrified of whatever is unknown and unfamiliar. However, when "unfamiliar" means breaking away from karmic relationships and finding a true and authentic relationship, we will find it to be the least terrifying, most beautiful, peaceful, deliciously nourishing, and overwhelmingly loving thing we will ever do for ourselves.

As empaths we will often take responsibility for how others treat us and for anything that goes wrong in relationships. We have a great amount of compassion and can clearly see other people's emotional wounds, so we make many excuses for why people behave as they do, and this is often to our own detriment. We very often put other people before ourselves as though our partner's pleasure, fulfillment, and happiness are more important than our own. Relationships can often move too fast and can become intense rapidly as we connect on a deep, intimate level instantly due to our ability to absorb other people's energy and emotions. Many empaths are introverted by nature and we can be attracted to extroverts either as friends or in relationships. As with a lot of things, an attraction for the opposite can feel magnetizing. An empath will find the way an extrovert operates extremely intriguing, and when it works, the two can balance and complement each another perfectly. However, empaths can also feel a deep sense of oneness with those who have similar introverted empathic qualities.

The key to a good relationship is one where we feel blessed that someone has come into our lives to offer us an entirely different way of viewing the world. We will appreciate all the tiny things our partners do to offer a safe and loving space, as the world around us can already seem harsh enough. It is important for our partners to let go of everything they thought they knew about relationships and love and relearn it all from the beginning again. It is beneficial to forget society's expectations and judgments, as they hold no importance in an empath's world. We celebrate the differences that are offered within a relationship rather than push the sensitive buttons that trigger uncomfortable reactions. Acceptance is significant. Trying to change us will not be possible. And even if we do change slightly, we will be extremely unhappy on the inside and will be forced to live a life that does not feel natural to us. Change will happen in time and as empaths are always doing the internal work to alter and grow, they appreciate others who are of a similar mindset and with who they can grow separately, but together.

It may be difficult for someone who is not an empath to figure out how our brain ticks. It can seem as though we are wired differently as we see things from many different perspectives. This allows for alternative ideas and thinking and opens up healthy challenges of shared ideologies, lifestyles, and ideas. It keeps an air of mystery and intrigue alive and helps to keep the interest in one another high so that the relationship does not become mundane or routine. We were not brought together to be the same as one another or to merge as "one whole." We are each a whole and require the freedom to express ourselves so that we can be our own person rather than feeling owned and as though we belong to someone else.

Hugging can feel very claustrophobic to an empath, and we can feel as though during a hug our energy is being altered. We will be absorbing all of the other person's energy, especially if we have not protected our energy field. If we want to absorb ourselves in someone else's energy, that is fine, but it is helpful to do so with awareness so that we do not take on all of their emotional angst. For this reason, hugs and cuddles are not always given out and we don't very often appreciate spontaneous ones. It is not that cuddles aren't welcomed at all, it's just that—this may sound insensitive— they have to be given at a time where we feel comfortable and at ease to be able to give or receive them and mainly when our energy is prepared for them. If we are in the frame of mind to snuggle, we may feel as though we never want to let the other person go. If wea are not, it will be very obvious as we will be tense and may back away quickly and nervously. Our energy needs to be in harmony with the other person's before we allow such close and intimate physical contact, otherwise, we need to protect it from being energetically influenced. This is another reason that empaths often prefer their own sleeping space, and if they do share a bed with their partner, they may not wish to sleep all night long with limbs entwined. Our energy fields closely interact and while we are sleeping we also rebalance and recharge our energy levels. We may wake exhausted and feeling a little out of sorts if we sleep too close to someone whose energetic vibration is not aligned with our own.

Empaths often have quite a few little quirks, traits, and characteristics that are worth knowing about and gaining a better understanding of so that any relationship that is formed has a strong survival chance and also so that it thrives.

When we sense something, we are not often wrong. If we think someone is lying or that something is just "not right," you can bet your last dollar that we are not wrong. Therefore, it is beneficial for our partners, friends, and family to meet us with authenticity, as these are the relationships that resonate with us, as although it may not be apparent on a surface level, we are mystical and quite magical creatures.

Love with an empath will be intense as we are energetically sensitive; therefore, we will pick up on everything and anything that is happening around us. Regardless of whether emotions have been outwardly expressed, we will experience our partner's emotions as deeply as we feel our own. It is impossible to try to hide true feelings when romantically involved with empaths, as we will likely have figured them out long before the person feeling them has. We are highly intuitive, although, sometimes we fail to trust this inner voice as too many people have previously tried to wrongly convince us that our gut feelings were wrong. Being a little naive and trusting at times has caused us to doubt ourselves and we may have pushed our intuition aside, meaning we have lost faith in the power we hold within us that alerts us to perceived signs of danger. That being said, the little nagging voice in an empath's head does not subside until the reality and truth have finally been uncovered.

Empaths prefer honesty. However hard it is to handle, we would rather be told things straight than told a lie, even if it is a tiny white one. Although the truth isn't always pretty, it is much nicer than spending days and nights trying to make sense of all the complicated energies and subliminal messaging systems that are going on. If it's one thing that empaths are amazing at it is dealing with a brutally raw and honest relationship. Although we can be rather delicate at some levels, our strength in relationships is found when honesty, trust, and loyalty come before anything else.

"Regarding relationships, I have just one rule: Give me truth, however cold or cruel, or hard it is to hear. I would prefer to have my heart broken if it means I can then move on, than waste a single moment of my time being fooled by a lie intended to preserve my feelings." ——Beau Taplin//Truth

Empaths can be perceived as having hearts that are difficult to penetrate as they have been safely caged in. However, this is only true when we have been deceived so many times that we feel that our only option is strong protection. The true spirit of an empath wants to give and receive love in abundance, though we are only able to do this when we feel secure that we are in a safe place where we can open the door and allow divine love to endlessly flow.

One of the most tragic parts about an empath's character is that all too often our love is cast out in all the wrong places. We feel the pain and sorrow of the whole world and we want to heal and fix the world up to make things better for all of mankind. This can be an incredibly powerful thing and this energy may be exactly what the world needs. However, this can also be an excruciatingly painful way to exist. Not everyone sees the world the way an empath views it, and because of this our hearts will feel fractured constantly and we will bleed endlessly for cruelty, injustice, and inequalities. There will be many who will want to take our love, affection, and kind nature with no care about giving anything in return. While this can teach us a lot about unconditional love and also an immense amount about self-preservation, it is also an achingly painful learning process.

Empaths fail to understand why others do not limitlessly give out care, consideration, and affection, and why other people can so easily turn a blind eye to heartbreak and suffering when healing is what is required. Others may ridicule and belittle an empath's desire to reach out and make a difference, and this can add salt to our open wounds. When we are feeling raw from carrying the weight of tormenting emotions, what we appreciate is compassion, support, and understanding. This comforts and reassures us so that we know we are not alone in wanting to use some of our powerful energy to heal and make changes in the world; if we receive this from a partner, a bond for life will very likely form.

We may fall into the hands of those who want to take advantage of our somewhat naive and caring nature. Again, this is another sharp lesson and one that can cause an empath to develop a sense of mistrust and it is also what leads us to protect our emotions with steel barriers and highly built brick walls. It can also result in us feeling unworthy and enduring low self-esteem, as once we have depleted our energy reserves by giving so much and not knowing how to protect ourselves in the process we can end up with an injured heart and with very little faith in mankind.

It is not generally in an empath's nature to take; we are better at giving. Therefore, to ensure the relationship is one of balance and is harmonious, an empath needs to be shown love in the form of action so that the circle of love flows freely. Words mean little to an empath unless they are followed through with action. Our intuition quickly picks up on something done with opposing intent or when words are false and inauthentic.

To love someone who is an empath means to recognize that we thrive when the flames are turned up, not down. We give off a powerful and energetic fuel of love, light, and radiance, though the fire only fully rages when we exist in a sacred place within which we feel secure enough to glow.

Empaths are soft, delicate, and immensely vulnerable creatures on the inside, although once burnt on the outside we can become incredibly strong. Although we forgive easily, we find it very difficult to forget deep wounds and will struggle to continue a relationship once the foundations have crumbled. The best way for someone to fully connect with us is through working together to create a safe and solid platform to build a relationship upon. If cracks appear through regular mistrust and deceit, it can become immensely difficult to repair them. We thrive on trust, loyalty, and dependability. And when someone expresses these things, the relationship will naturally thrive.

Nothing gets past an empath as we see, feel, and connect with everything at all times. As empaths are sensitive to energy, our worst-case scenarios are confrontations and aggressive situations. Although under normal circumstances we are one of the least violent and aggressive characters, we can very easily lose self-control if we become absorbed in the negative, toxic energy that surrounds us. We are fight or flight characters who more often than not will prefer to take flight and remove themselves from the weight of the energy bearing down on us. If situations like this occur often, it can eventually lead us to become introverted and homebodies, as we may prefer the safety of our own environment where we will not be subjected to the rise and fall of other people's energies. After attending any kind of social situation, we may need downtime to recharge and rebalance our energy field.

Everything that we are passionate about is be given our full attention and we try to live and love fully in the present moment. The past has passed and the future is not yet here. When our minds wander, we are not experiencing life as it is, and we are just temporarily caught up in our mind's illusions. When we in a relationship with others who live similarly, the relationship usually thrives, regardless as to whether we are compatible in all areas.

All in all, it will take a loyal, stable, and grounded person to form a solid, mutually beneficial, enjoyable and rewarding relationship with an empath. Our personality type is a challenging, unique, and enchanting gift. As long as our wings are not clipped and we have the freedom and space to fly, a relationship has the opportunity to be a deeply intimate, incredibly loving, and spiritually awakening coupling for both involved.

A connection with an empath can be one of the greatest offerings from the universe as it offers the opportunity to look at the world through the lens of a vividly colored kaleidoscope. Everything that may have once seemed normal for a relationship will be turned upside down as a new understanding and perspective is learned and the unconscious mind is preened open. At times it may feel like being in the company of a magically gifted being who has special powers that most people have been led to believe do not exist within humans.

When in a relationship, it is helpful to peel back all the layers that society labels as "norms," "standards," and "expectations." We are then free to discover a brand-new way of existing, giving and receiving unconditional love, being fully alive in the moment, connecting deep within the core of our primal being, and reigniting all the superpowers that are inherent within humans.

A relationship with an empath can lead our partner to uncover special gifts of their own such as intuition, energy awareness, deep connection, and a brand-new level of understanding for fellow humans without the need for speech—all the things the modern world has tried for far too long to convince us we should deny.

Love can be given and received in abundance as a free-flowing energy. It is not a limited force—it is limitless, endless. The more that is produced, the higher frequency it will flow at, as the momentum keeps it going.

We don't just have to reserve our love for a chosen "one." Everyone can feel the powerful charge of our emanating love. Love does not choose one. It chooses all.

Many of us have been caught in a paradigm that tells us that love should be guarded, it should only go to those who treat us well, or those who we are romantically or related to, or those who love us in return. No, no, no. Every living, breathing creature on this planet, all life forms, in fact, the whole of the earth can receive our love. It is free. It is renewable. It is not selective. It does not give out and then expect something in return. Love gives and gives and gives. The more it gives, the more it recharges and the more buoyant, joyful and fulfilled we will feel.

We cannot lose by radiating our love.

To be able to give and receive love, we must learn to accept ourselves exactly as we are and not judge, criticize, or feel resentment toward ourselves in any way. Self-love transforms us. When we love ourselves, we are more likely to attract others who will love us too. When we disapprove or dislike ourselves, similarly we will attract others who reflect how we feel. However, we do not need to love ourselves before someone else can love us. This is a myth. People are capable of loving us regardless of how we feel about ourselves, although, when we are generating and radiating limitless love we are much more likely to receive it in abundance externally too.

It is imperative that we give ourselves the very best care so that we are open to the heightened pleasure of loving and being loved, although, even if we don't receive love in return, we will still find peace, as we will feel entirely fulfilled with the love we have feeling for ourselves. We have everything within that is needed to feel complete without the need for anyone or anything else.

We cannot run out of love, regardless of how much of it we give out. We simply cannot become depleted because as soon as we give it, more love has already been renewed in its place. The heart is our most powerful energy center.

The only thing that stunts the growth of love is fear. Fear is the instigator and cause of all of our emotional wounds. Each time we experience a fear-based emotion, our loving energy is constricted and after a period of time, love is unable to fluidly flow through. Fear drains us, but love revitalizes us. Fear causes wounds, but love heals them.

"There are two basic motivating forces: fear and love. When we are afraid, we pull back from life. When we are in love, we open to all that life has to offer with passion, excitement, and acceptance. We need to learn to love ourselves first, in all our glory and our imperfections. If we cannot love ourselves, we cannot fully open to our ability to love others or our potential to create. Evolution and all hopes for a better world rest in the fearlessness and open-hearted vision of people who embrace life." ——John Lennon

To remove our fears we simply need to understand them. We can spend time listening to our emotions and as we do we can remove any tight cords that are binding our hearts. As our emotions are unearthed, we can acknowledge, soothe and then identify the root cause of them. As soon as we empty ourselves of all the hurtful memories we have knowingly or unknowingly been holding on to, and once we have unraveled all the barbed wire that is wrapped tightly around our hearts, we can begin to love without feeling the familiar pangs of pain.

All of our wounds tie us to those who have similar unhealed wounds. It is difficult to have healthy, nourishing relationships when we have so many energetic injuries hidden, denied and forgotten, so this is why we end up in dysfunctional karmic connections. When we are least expecting it, our shadow emotions seep out unexpectedly and project themselves onto those around us. When our emotions are stored up we will feel insecure, resentful, jealous, fearful, angry, frustrated and we will see all of these things mirrored in anyone we interact with. Friends, colleagues, family members and even strangers will take the brunt of our hidden aches and pains.

It is not as complicated as it sounds. We just have to sit with ourselves and listen to the repetitive thoughts that are at the forefront of our minds, and pay attention to the emotions and feelings that arise whenever we connect with someone. What is it all telling us? Trace the sensation. It leads somewhere. Find the root, reason and rationalize with it, soothe and care for it and with tenderness and compassion let the tension and clogged up energy go so that we can allow our inner wounds to heal.

There is nothing at all we need to hold on to. Everything has already affected us, we don't need it to repeat and repeat and cause us lifelong difficulties. We don't need to spin in the same vicious cycles throughout our lives, we can break free from those repetitions and forge a new way through.

The art of loving fully comes with loving all aspects of life, not just ourselves. The planet we live on, those around us, nature, and all creatures add to this mix and they all deserve our unconditional love and respect. Love is a free and constantly renewing energy. However much we give, there is always more in reserve and we will receive an abundance of it in return.

We cannot ever lose something that was not ours to own. We do not own love. Love is an energy that vibrates, and when it is radiated its momentum increases; it is not possible to hold it or place ownership on it. It is a fluid current that is amplified when shared. We have zero control over love. It is inherent within us, and although we can try to block its flow, it is not something we can influence when it is released and existing on a high frequency. Love doesn't hurt, nor does it harm. It is a pure and extremely simple vibration that has no terms, conditions, or expectations.

Self-love is magnetic and has a strong force that attracts those who resonate with its frequency. When we truly love and respect ourselves and live authentically and free from the fear of losing love, we can courageously give and receive love in abundance without hoping for or expecting a return.

What we put out into the world is what we will receive back. When we send out true, genuine love to ourselves, the planet, everyone, and everything around us, it is inevitable it will rotate and we will receive similar in return. How we treat ourselves shows others exactly how we wish to be treated.

Chapter 23

SIGNS OF AN UNHEALTHY RELATIONSHIP

The initial stages of a relationship can be deceiving as we are very often on a high, a chemical high. We feel those dizzy in-love feelings that swim around in our brain, which are essentially just due to a plethora of endorphins that are released when we enter into any type of intimate or affectionate relationship.

Chemicals, such as oxytocin and dopamine, are also released that can drastically affect how we feel and behave. Dopamine is a feel-good hormone that can be very addictive. This is the hormone that makes us crave more of whatever has caused its release. Dopamine is part of the reason we can become obsessive over relationships. Oxytocin is a powerful bonding hormone between lovers that speeds up the attachment we have with a partner and works to create something that looks similar to codependency. Oxytocin is also released during childbirth, so it is also associated with mother-baby relationships as it helps to form a strong and difficult-to-break emotional bond. It is clear to see how these chemicals can have an effect on us in our relationships. They can trick us into thinking we have to be near our partner's side or in close physical contact and cause us to feel a close connection. They can also create something that is not too unlike addiction.

Due to the chemicals pulsating through our systems, we are often blind to behavior that could be a major red flag in the relationship. We may not notice when certain situations are signaling that all is not well. As the chemicals simmer down and the relationship becomes a little less physical and intense, we begin to see a much truer version of the relationship—we basically begin to see what looks a lot more like reality.

Dopamine may also cause a downturn in a relationship, as when the high wears off we can then experience the lows, which can include irritability, fatigue, and possibly depression. When these chemicals have taken effect, if the relationship does not have a firm foundation or any real structure, it becomes apparent that things aren't quite as pretty as they may have first looked.

When signs appear that things are not what they seemed, usually the initial changes are clearer to see in the way *we* are behaving, not the other person. All too often our reactions to other people are a huge indicator that something is not right.

Anxiety is normally the first sign that things are going wrong in our lives. It is a state or inner turmoil and is strongly associated with fear. Even though anxiety is a different emotion to fear, it can be felt when we perceive ourselves to be in some form of danger, whether real or imagined. The "crazy feeling" we get when our head is spinning and we can't catch our thoughts or we don't know whether we are coming or going is often a clue that somewhere something is seriously wrong. If these moments happen regularly within a relationship, it is an indicator that the situation needs to be addressed. Often, it is the clearest sign that the relationship is dysfunctional and spiraling out of control.

Whenever someone is passing the blame on to someone else for things going wrong, it means they are not taking full responsibility for their own actions and behavior. We are all accountable for the role that we play in the dynamic of a relationship, and when we tell someone else they are to blame, we are shifting the responsibility away from ourselves and onto others. We are essentially placing ourselves in the "victim" role. Therefore, if a partner is constantly blaming us for things they aren't happy with, we need to refuse to accept the blame and step away from the situation to look at why they are offloading the responsibility.

Blaming someone is very different to airing grievances. Open, mindful, and constructive communication is essential for a relationship to thrive. Blame lies with power and control, so it is imperative we do not automatically take the full responsibility within a relationship. When we do so, we are immediately weakened, which is the sole purpose of someone handing us the blame.

If we are constantly afraid of how our partner is going to react to everyday aspects of life, it is a clear indicator that the relationship is abusive in some way. The fear can begin with worrying if we miss a call or a text message and can range to being afraid to say the wrong thing or going out with friends. When our partner reacts negatively and aggressively to little things that go on within the relationship, it is then a concern in case something more significant goes wrong. Relationships aren't always plain sailing and we should never have to feel afraid of how other people might respond to things we say or do. Often the person reacting badly will try to blame us for their response or reaction (as above, blame). However, placing blame is a manipulative way to avoid taking responsibility.

When we are in a relationship we need to be able to trust that the person we are with is not going put us at constant risk of emotional, mental, or physical harm. Simple things like feeling scared about missing a call can very quickly lead to walking on eggshells and feeling edgy about how we choose to live our lives. We may also feel nervous about many other parts of our relationship. As soon as we hear ourselves justifying or making excuses for our partner's behavior, we can see this as an alarm bell ringing. It is one thing to explain why someone has behaved a certain way, but there is usually trouble around if we are making up stories that are not a reflection of our reality. We may also begin to believe the excuses we make.

We usually want to see the best in the people we choose to be in a relationship with; therefore, it kind of hurts quite a lot when they behave in ways that are unreasonable. So we make up little excuses here and there to justify their behavior. The worrying thing is these little excuses can quickly develop into a habit that then cause us to turn a blind eye to major red flags.

I'm sure many of us have dated or known someone who believed they were Mr. or Ms. Perfect. The thing is, though, they actually weren't perfect at all; none of us are. Therefore, we all need to take our turn in apologizing. We all make mistakes, we all mess up, and we all need to own up to it, be accountable, and show we are sorry. The problems arise when one or both parties refuse to take any responsibility for making up and accepting the part they played in whatever may have gone wrong. When there is only one person apologizing, a dynamic can rapidly form whereby the "innocent" one will wait until the person who always says sorry gives in and apologizes. This kind of dynamic isn't productive for any relationship. There needs to be give and take as it is never continuously one person's fault if things go wrong within a balanced or healthy relationship.

Unfortunately, wishful thinking can keep us in situations that we know we really shouldn't stay in. We hope, wish, pray, and even firmly believe that people will change. We might wait around, have patience, try our best to love harder and unconditionally, and accept people exactly as they are. However, sooner or later we must be aware of the types of relationships that may cause us harm and those that are stable and nourishing. Although it is always our responsibility for our emotions and in effect, no one else can emotionally harm us, this is easier said than done if we are in a relationship with someone who intends on causing havoc continuously. No relationship is worth sacrificing our emotional, mental or physical health and wellbeing for. As difficult as it sometimes is, we really must figure out who we love more, ourselves or the other person. It is often because we don't value and love ourselves enough that we end up entwined in these types of relationships in the first place.

Many years ago, I would continuously attract people who were not good for me to be around, I mean seriously detrimentally bad for me. I struggled incredibly hard to understand why I was magnetically pulled toward people whose words and actions were intent on causing carnage. The people I chose to keep company with seemed to enjoy pulling me down and apart rather than allowing me to remain together. It wasn't just bad relationships, it was "friendships" too. If I walked into a room and there were fifty people there, I could guarantee I would connect with the one person who would either intentionally or unintentionally subject me to energetic harm. However, saying this, I also learned that no one else is responsible for the negative situations I encountered. I am in control of my own emotional responses and I was a willing party in each and every liaison. I danced the dance and offered myself willingly to each dynamic, therefore I was partially responsible.

I often hear the phrase "we are who we surround ourselves with," or a similar phrase, "like attracts like." This was one of the hardest things to figure. I didn't understand the concept fully. Eventually this attraction to people who I was in energetic discord with became a self-fulfilling prophecy. I began to believe that I was attracting people based on the type of person I was and how I was behaving. I wrongly thought the people whom I became entangled with were an identical reflection of myself. I had been told this theory so many times and I could not find any other explanation, and so I began to believe it.

I found that when I was in the person's company I was triggered to respond to their interactions in a way that was detrimental to myself, and this compounded my low self-esteem and significantly low self-worth. However, it also clarified that at some level I was being guided toward areas that needed serious healing. Whenever I was tempted to retaliate to their insults or put-downs by reacting to them in a mirrored way, I was mirroring back to them what they believed about themselves and I was also suffering for it internally. I eventually worked out that my reactions and responses were due to the weak spots of mine and these relationships brought them to my attention so that I could acknowledge them and heal, grow and change.

I agree, like does attract like. However, it doesn't mean that I had the same character or that I was identical in behavior to the other people. It meant that my vibration was connecting with their vibration as I was spinning on the same frequency as they were due to historic unhealed wounds that had been denied and swept out of sight. Some part of them confirmed some part of me that felt or believed something painful or harmful about myself. My reactions to them were the signals to highlight where each particular emotional injury lay. When I was terrified of being cheated on, I would meet people who betrayed me. I learned that I was unable to control other people's behaviors and that no amount of trying to avoid it would prevent me from being cheated on. If I judged myself harshly, I would come into contact with others who would judge me similarly. In whatever way I abandoned myself, whether emotionally, mentally, or physically, I would energetically interlock with those who showed the same disregard for that same aspect of my wellbeing. The beliefs I had about myself and what I felt I deserved were attracting others whose vibration matched these irrational, immobilizing, perpetuating opinions. Whenever someone scratched one of my unhealed wounds, I would jump to protect it, and in doing so I avoided paying attention to the historic wound. I was too wrapped up in the current one. It took some time and some painful interactions for me to learn that whenever I was triggered, I was also hiding and trying to defend an old, forgotten but unhealed, and infected wound, one that needed my attention.

The people I met also had unhealed emotional wounds, and although they were entirely different battle scars, these injuries magnetized us to one another. If someone else also felt they were no "good" within, our vibrations immediately interlocked. I would then be taught many harsh lessons before I finally discovered the damage my misguided feelings and unwillingness to focus on healing myself had been causing me.

When I got drawn into role-playing and playing out a part that others wanted me to perform, I not only showed my weaknesses, I also gave them what they wanted: my energy, even though I didn't have much to give at the time.

Now, whenever I meet someone and feel that instantly recognizable friction that feels like a familiar fire, I know that at some level, somewhere deep within, I am not acknowledging or valuing my inner self. I can choose my response—to engage and let the flames soar, or to step away and remove myself from danger and work on getting to know myself and loving myself a little bit more.

When I do step into the fire, I know that I am then partly responsible for anything that happens to me. I know that the battle scars and wounds I may receive will be inflicted by my own feelings, beliefs, and actions, not those of anyone surrounding me. I also know that I need to reroute how I would normally emotionally react and respond so that I do not keep repeating the same dysfunctional interactions.

I realized that I needed to figure out what was causing me to repeat these same patterns and also what it was about the people that I was attracting and attracted to that was so appealing. It was a hard lesson, and one that was very difficult and uncomfortable to accept. I felt compelled to be in the company of people whose presence was dangerous to my emotional and mental health, self-esteem, self-worth, and sometimes my physical safety. I didn't feel "good enough" or "worthy enough" to attract good things or good people toward me and I was unbalanced, ungrounded and not aware and alert. My ego was causing me to feel ashamed that my life was not exactly where I thought I wanted it to be. I felt that I wasn't "enough" in so many different ways that I somehow believed that I did not deserve someone who would treat me well. I also foolishly believed I did not have control over things that triggered me or that were causing me to react and behave in ways that I was not proud of. I felt that I deserved much of what I attracted and that I was powerless in preventing my responses. I was almost willing people toward me who helped me to create a self-fulfilling prophecy, as they reflected back at me affirmations that confirmed what my inner-self believed—that I didn't "deserve" any better. Now I see that each interaction was an opportunity to control and alter how I emotionally respond.

I started to realize that my energy was sending out powerful vibrations that some people decoded very easily and they then knew I would be easy to take advantage of. Without realizing it, my energy was repeating the same old story that I had been telling myself every day for years: that one day, in the far off future, I will have gotten myself together, figured it all out, and become someone who was enough and worthy. In the meantime, I believed I was not; therefore, I felt I did not deserve great levels of love, acceptance, or care. I fooled myself that I deserved half-hearted love, as I only loved myself half-heartedly. When I thought about this concept, it occurred to me how ridiculous it sounded. I knew that "far off day" would never arrive. I will never be the person my ego-fed illusionary mind daydreamed of—I didn't need or want to be that person. I didn't need fantasies and fairytales to trick me into thinking that everyone else deserved whatever their heart longed for while I lacked everything I believed I needed in order to be loved. I looked at some of the people who were around me, whatever they achieved or accomplished and whatever their state of mind was I knew one thing—they deserved the highest and truest form of love, especially from themselves. The unique place they were at in their life was ever changing, spiraling through a myriad of experiences and events. Each person was trying their best with the tools they had to maintain their existence and they would often navigate turbulent conditions too. So why was I telling myself that I wasn't worthy and why was I judging myself so harshly?

Whether we are trampling in the mud or soaring through the skies, we are still worthy and still whole people whose bodies and minds ache to love and be loved, regardless of how we behave, how successful we are, or any other circumstance. This overall thinking taught me a few things. One, that there is something exquisitely beautiful when we are willing to love without conditions. To love someone in their natural state, regardless of what position their life is in, is not always easy; it can be full of challenges. However, it is always worth it. *People* are worth it.

We are all worthy. Our emotional, mental, or physical being does not deems us worthy of love. Love is free. It does not cause any distress to give or receive it when we love unconditionally. This, however, is not always easy, and sometimes we have to do it while loving and protecting ourselves first.

The second profound lesson I learned was that I am capable of loving someone and also of accepting and embracing love in return. I do not need to place standards on myself that determine what stage of life I need to be at before I receive love. I just need to open to it and allow the love to flow freely.

I will never reach a state of perfection. I am aware of this. If I wait until I reach my ultimate self, I would very likely not be in a position to receive love in this lifetime. Therefore, I accept myself first and foremost—flaws and all. Not only that, I choose to love myself. Anyone else's love is simply a bonus.

The most important lesson I learned, though, was that although we all deserve love and mostly we all are doing our best, this does not mean that we need to subject ourselves to treatment from others that is harmful, dangerous to our emotional or physical health, or to place ourselves in the company of those who do not have our best interests at heart. We can still love those around us unconditionally. We can accept them fully. We can understand them. However, we do not need to place ourselves within arm's length for them to freely be able to knock us down emotionally, mentally, or physically.

If I met someone whose words or actions I found were harmful, it was my choice to continue dancing with them and risk my own self-worth and wellbeing, or I could choose to love myself a little bit more, be compassionate for both myself and the other person and reason and rationalize so that my inner peace was not affected by whatever was occurring. I could remain consciously aware so that the behavior would not emotionally affect me and I could do this by recognizing that it was up to them to take ownership for their reactions and responses and I did not need to feel guilt, shame or blame for anyone else's emotional or mental state. I also had the option to create a safe space and disengage if I was not feeling centered and rational, so that any interactions didn't emotionally disturb me during those times when I felt most vulnerable. Unconditional love is something I strive for and I do try to live by it, but I also have personal choices and I would not remain in any type of relationship that was intentionally emotionally or physically abusive. Although that may seem a contradiction, it is not a condition it is a *term*, and one that is crucial for emotional, mental, and physical safety.

Unfortunately, and sadly, some people are not healthy to closely entwine with. Some people's agendas, motivations and intentions can do us great harm. However, it is our own self-esteem and self-acceptance that determine whether we remain closely connected to those people so that we are in the line of their fire or whether we choose to decide that we are worthy of more, that we are enough, and that we deserve unconditional love from someone who respects and considers our emotional, mental and physical health.

When we choose to accept, embrace, and love ourselves unconditionally, deeply, and completely, we will soon discover that those around us will not be able to help themselves from accepting and loving us in a similar way too. Plus, when we can accept ourselves fully, we are far better equipped to accept others just as they are too.

We can place on the table as much logic and reason as we think will alter harmful intentions, but, unless the other person's mindset is open and receptive, no aspect of their personality is likely to change. It is quite common for people to refuse to change believing they are perfectly happy exactly the way they are. They may even say, "This is who I am, accept me as I am or not at all." It is then our choice. As the saying goes, when someone shows us who they are, we should believe them. We cannot make anyone change, nor can anyone force us to change. It is personal choice and depends how receptive we are to change.

One of the most difficult aspects of these types of relationships is knowing whether what we are experiencing is genuine love or co-dependency. There has been much written about the belief that some people are not capable of "love" however, I do not believe this is not true. I don't think it is possible to define millions of people with an array of traits and characteristics and then make a generalization of whether they are capable of love or not.

What I do believe though is that these relationships are often based on many illusions and when everything has a veil over it, it is complicated to see whether what is being displayed beneath the veil is love. If interactions are fear based and not love based, it can become very difficult to trace the threads of love and assess whether the relationship was one that was fuelled with love. When we remain consciously aware of exactly what we are dealing with and we have a sound understanding of our own capabilities and we are compassionate, it will be far easier to see that many expressions are a cry for help or a cry out for attention at some level regardless as to whether we perceive that as the right or wrong way to call for it.

I also believe that all expressions are either a desire to show love or a desire to be loved. That being said though, I also know my capabilities and this why I firmly believe it is an entirely personal choice as to whether someone is willing to put themselves through the ordeals that arise when in these relationships or not. What I can deal with and may put up with is always going to be very different to what someone else can or will choose to cope with or may put up with. Each person is different and we cannot compare where the "enough is enough" line is. Some people will draw it out quickly, while other people may never draw it. We cannot ever judge, as many things influence our experiences and we all have personal choice that is based on our subconscious and conscious capabilities and also on the person we are in the dynamic with. There are too many variables to ever judge what someone else should or shouldn't do in these situations.

When we identify what we have to offer in a relationship, we can then make a decision as to whether staying in one where there are difficulties caused by personality disorders is likely to offer us the pleasure we are hoping for or whether it will offer a consistent and insidious feed of harm and pain.

We can drop all expectations that we "deserve" to be loved a certain way, as, other people's actions are not a reflection of who we are or what we deserve, they are a reflection of who they are. Although other people's behavior may highlight aspects of our own character that we can look further into, we are not the same person as the person we are in a dynamic with and it is nonsense to consider that we deserve whatever treatment we receive. When we remember this the hurt and betrayal we experience will immediately and dramatically start to dissipate. We can try to honor, get to know, love, respect and forgive any pain we have caused ourselves and then we can offer this same compassionate sentiment outwards.

I believe it is essential that we stop classifying people who either have a personality disorder or who are struggling to show love as "unlovable" and as though they should be placed in the trash can. Everyone, absolutely everyone, deserves love—it's just that some people can only be loved from a distance. We can remain consciously aware of our limits and of what we can handle before we are pushed and tested by anyone else's.

I believe the most important thing to remember of all is that sadly we cannot just "love" someone better. However hard we try.

Chapter 24

EMPATHS AND NARCISSISTS

We have all been responsible for causing pain and discomfort at some point in our lives. We all have healed and unhealed wounds. We have all behaved in ways that could be perceived as dysfunctional. Some people identify and process their emotional pain, other people deny, reject and project their emotional pain on to others. One isn't "good" and the other isn't "bad." We cannot compare and judge one another's experiences, as we do not know the entire historic content of anyone else's life. I have written this chapter to explain the traits and tendencies of narcissistic behavior and how that plays out in relationships with empaths and how the traits are expressed. Like with everything, knowledge is key to gain a depth of understanding so that it can support a compassionate response. This is my perception of the dynamic between empaths and narcissists, as I believe it is a very common coupling. For further understanding please seek professional advice.

Some key traits of a narcissist:

- Aloof
- Appears tough and strong on the surface

- Arrogant
- Attention seeking
- Boastful
- Cannot deal with receiving criticism
- Center of attention
- Charismatic
- Charming
- Conceited and wants to be more attractive, powerful and successful than others
- Controlling
- Creates drama/overdramatic
- Critical
- Defensive
- Desire for power
- Detached
- Has difficulty understanding other people's emotions/lacks empathy and feels disdain towards others
- Egocentric
- Exaggerates their achievements
- Extremely jealous
- Feels hurt easily
- Grandiosity
- Highly dominant
- Inauthentic
- Has an inflated self-perception
- Likes to be in the spotlight
- Exhibits needy behavior
- Obnoxious
- Patronizing
- Possessive
- Pretentious
- Rude
- Seductive
- Requires constant admiration
- Takes advantage of others
- Tells lies, often without realizing they are doing so
- Vain

Anger: Rages easily and emotions get very quickly out of control over seemingly insignificant issues.

Attention Seeking: Constant desire to be the center of attention.

Blame/Denial: They have no guilt, shame or remorse and project all of their behavior and emotions outwards so that other people take accountability for them. Nothing is ever their fault in their eyes.

Cheating: Not only will they have no qualms about cheating on their own partner, they also have no consideration for whether the person they are involved with already has a partner.

Condescending: Puts other people down and undermines others at any opportunity.

Conditional: They will only remain in a friendship or relationship if the other person consistently meets their needs and their extremely high expectations.

Deceitful: Naturally lies and will often show no remorse for deceiving people and will go to all lengths to deny any wrongdoings.

Demanding: Demands attention, power or control.

Dependent: Dislikes being alone, constantly needs to be in a relationship or around people who pay attention and validate them. Relies on other people to balance their emotional wellbeing and often their financial circumstances too.

Easily Influenced: Talked into anything easily and can be led to do things they wouldn't normally do by people who are also persuasive.

Entitled: They feel as though they deserve special treatment or privileges as they feel "above" everyone around them.

Exaggerate: Makes up stories and exaggerates every experience they have.

Extraverted: Energized when around other people and feel low energy when they are alone.

Fear of Abandonment: They may have issues from childhood or from previous emotional wounds that have caused them to feel afraid they will be left on their own.

Gaslighting: Uses manipulation to make their partner feel as though they are going crazy by getting them to struggle to trust their own intuition and be unable to make decisions.

Grandiose: Believe they are far better than other people with very high self-importance and seek favorable attention.

Hoovers: Uses manipulation or seduction to suck their ex-partner back after a period of separation.

Hysterical:Very theatrical and hysterical behavior and the more attention it gives them, the more they play up to it.

Impulsive: Unpredictable and acts at the spur of the moment without thinking about consequences.

Lack of Compassion/Consideration:Very little humility, compassion, care or concern for other people or their suffering or difficulties.

Manipulative: They use charm, flattery or threats to manipulate people into giving them what they want or into doing something for them.

Mood Swings: Almost bi-polar in their emotions, one minute extremely happy and high and the next screaming, crying or throwing themselves in a heap on the ground in a childish tantrum.

Naïve or Innocent: Very childlike in their speech, words or actions and may genuinely have a very innocent and vulnerable approach to the world.

Over Sensitive: Will be hurt by criticism even if it is very mild and will take offense to anyone saying anything even slightly detrimental to them.

Sabotage: May deliberately hurt or damage relationships with family or friends by saying cruel things or acting in shocking ways and they may even try to sabotage other people's relationships or belongings.

Seductive/Flirtatious/Provocative: Dresses in an inappropriate or deliberately provocative way by flaunting sexuality solely to gain attention. Behavior is highly flirtatious to manipulate or destabilize other people or to impress them so that affection or admiration is given.

Self-Destructive: They may have addictions, or self-harm or behave in ways that turn people against them.

Shallow/Superficial: Everything is focused around image, so they say whatever they think will achieve the best response for themselves and they dress in ways to impress other people, specifically by using brand names to make themselves appear "better" or more superior than others.

Suspicious: Doubts other people's intentions and finds it very difficult to trust.

Tests: They will push people to extremes to test their "love" as they often feel this proves whether someone loves them or not.

Threatening: Regularly makes threats, whether it is to harm themselves or to harm other people's lives. They may swing from threatening to vulnerable behavior within moments.

Like with most things, there is a spectrum. Some people may have mild symptoms, others may align with the above and identify strongly. It is essential that we learn as much as is feasibly possible about this personality disorder so we can identify those who display the traits and then consciously choose how we interact with them. Empaths can be prime candidates for narcissists who are looking for a relationship or any other dynamic whereby they think they have the opportunity of receiving egotistical gains. It is also imperative that we gain awareness about the disorder so that we do not become so internally injured that we take on any of these traits ourselves.

We can all carry some traits of the narcissist, especially when we aren't willing to accept our faults or we aren't accountable for our thoughts, feelings, emotions, or expressions. We may push ourselves too hard, build ourselves up externally, and often the opinions we have of ourselves are unrealistic and don't fully align with our authentic core selves. It can then feel almost natural to take on a false sense of self. We may also align with narcissistic characteristics when we have been emotionally wounded and have not acknowledged or understood the pain. Unfortunately when we spend long periods of time with those who are narcissistic we may also become emotionally injured and we can then take on narcissistic tendencies ourselves. This does not make anyone a narcissist though. The difference being that narcissists have no realization of any harm they may cause and if they do, they often have no care for what difficulties may result from how they behave.

Confusion can arise when identifying narcissism as it is healthy to have self-love; self-worth; to have desires, wants, and needs; and also to value ourselves highly. However, when these things derive from an internally wounded place, one of internal self-loathing, low self-esteem, or deep-rooted insecurities that have not been addressed or when we incessantly need other people's admiration and attention to make ourselves look and feel virtuous, important, and valued, narcissistic traits can develop.

An easy way to recognize narcissism is to ask if we are willing to gain what we need, whether emotionally or otherwise, by doing the necessary work ourselves. Or do we expect other people to lift our moods, comfort us, tend to our needs, resolve our issues, take responsibility for our emotions, make us feel secure emotionally, compliment us on our physical attributes, take care of us financially while feeling as though we are entitled to it and generally maintain our lives with no regard for the person aiding us and no consideration for their suffering, general wellbeing, or their time, care, or effort? If we cause suffering to others without consideration or regret, and if we cannot see or do not care about what other people go through so long as we are okay, then we will very likely have narcissistic tendencies.

Narcissists are selfish; generally empaths are selfless. Sometimes, this can be tricky to comprehend as it may sound as though it is wrong to consider ourselves first as that can be associated with being selfish. It isn't. We can think of ourselves and put ourselves first as much and as often as we want just as long as we don't cause unnecessary harm or compromise ourselves or other people, emotionally or otherwise, while doing so. When we cause others difficulties that constitutes being selfish. It is not wrong to have a healthy sense of self or to prioritize taking care of our needs.

It is important that we see the difference between *selfish* and *selfless* so that we do not neglect ourselves. When we are mindful and consciously aware of our actions and respect ourselves, and others, it is totally possible to put ourselves first without inflicting suffering of any form on anyone else.

Narcissists are often seen as being associated with vanity and self-absorption; however, the full range and extent of the characteristics associated with this disorder are far more complex and extreme. Narcissistic behavior can be detrimental to emotional and physical health, as well as destructive to the self-worth and self-esteem of empaths. Saying this, though, it is more important that as empaths we are accountable for ourselves so that we are not vulnerable in their hands and also so that we do not blame them for any devastation. Blaming someone else for these encounters is the one thing that keeps empaths in the "victim" role.

Although empaths and narcissists often become embittered in a magnetic entanglement, it is vital to be aware that this dynamic is not solely reserved for intimate relationships. Empath and narcissist unions may be between a parent and a child, between friends, co-workers, siblings, or even forged from stranger to stranger. Quite often, something somewhere along the line, usually stemming from childhood trauma, causes a narcissist to internally embed feelings of worthlessness and inadequacy. Due to this they constantly and forcefully seek egotistical external approval, so they connect with people who can compensate for anything they feel they are missing. However, it is possible that the opposite may have happened. Narcissists might have been so ridiculously spoiled and pampered to the point that nothing can match up to their perceived previous precious experiences. Their ego may have been so overfed that they now believe they are "better" and more superior than those around them. They may have been used as a trophy by their caregivers to showcase "perfect" parental abilities. Narcissists care a hell of a lot about what other people think of them, so their children will be brought up to be a reflection of their impeccable parenting. If their children disappoint them in any way, they then face being alienated or ostracized and the children of narcissist parents may then take on their parent's traits and mimic their behaviors until the tendencies feel natural and they then become a way of life.

A narcissist is often the child of a narcissistic parent. One or both parents may have overinflated their child's self-esteem by telling them how special, amazing, and gifted they are and how they would go on to do great things, but then offered no solid foundations or stability from which the child could function. A narcissist's parents may have been so wrapped up in themselves they will only have paid attention to the child when it suited their needs. So the child swings from very little love and attention to the opposite, receiving love and attention in abundance, usually to the parent's benefit and the child's detriment.

A parent who is a narcissist will usually know which of their children they can and cannot manipulate. It is likely only one child in the family will be used as a means to draw energy from as well as exerting power and control on. It may also be that the child subconsciously picked up narcissistic behavior through watching and copying their caregiver. Much of narcissism is learned behavioral patterns, and those who repeat the same behavior over a period of time become accustomed to acting in certain ways that feel familiar. The more they portray these traits, the more the person feels justified that how they think, feel, or express themselves must be acceptable as to them it feels the most natural way to exist.

As it is widely believed that narcissism is a learned behavior, it is also believed that it can then be unlearned. The difficulty here is that before any change takes place, the person displaying the behavior must be the one willing to acknowledge that their narcissist traits exist. Unfortunately, this is not very common, as one of the strongest characteristics of narcissism is that they believe they do not do anything "wrong." They cannot see that their behavior could be harmful to others, so expecting that they will be held accountable or start to peel away the layers and begin the work of unlearning everything they have believed to be true is high unlikely.

To be sure we do not absorb the toxic low vibrational energy that a narcissist radiates, it is imperative to understand how and why they behave as they do and also how the dynamics play out in various types of relationships. The reason for the connection between an empath and narcissist may not be vividly clear in either one's conscious mind. On another dimension, energy is communicating, interlocking, and agreeing on a deal, and it is unlikely that either is aware that it is taking place. A narcissist rejects and denies their emotions or their true feelings. An empath can identify emotions and heal them. The subconscious armies engage and the unwinnable ordeal commences.

The beginning of a relationship with a narcissist can feel like an addictive and intoxicating fairytale, with the narcissist playing the role of the charming prince or princess and their partner being completely swept off their feet. Narcissists will usually fall into (what appears to be) love and want to commit rapidly; however, as time passes and their partner starts to see the truth of what's within, problems can quickly arise as the relationship begins to break down. If we try to address the issues, the narcissists may go into meltdown and complete denial, often attacking with accusations in a poor attempt at defending themselves, or they might go for the vulnerable, sensitive approach. Regardless, they will always be correct, so getting into any kind of debate, argument, or dialogue where faults are concerned will most often prove futile.

When it comes to right or wrong, a narcissist has an impulsive desire to ensure they are right regardless of the cost. If being right costs them friends, family, or relationships, they will most often suffer the consequences of the loss rather than admit to being wrong. However, they will put up a defensive and destructive battle of wills beforehand.

A narcissist will basically role-play and masquerade as whatever manipulative character garners the best response. If they are up against a strong, determined, and independent person they will move into the role of a sensitive, loving, caring, and vulnerable character. If they interact with a codependent type, they will likely move into the role of aggressor. Despite what is external, often deep within a narcissist can experience self-destructive and crippling self-doubt coupled with extremely low self-esteem.

Narcissism is a personality disorder that is defined by an unhealthy sense of entitlement along with a desire for wealth, possessions, prestige, control, or power. Narcissists function from their frail ego and are obsessive about their own personal adequacy. They display vanity, arrogance, pride, righteousness, egocentrism, and grandiosity, and have a desperate need to impress, receive praise, and to be admired for their mental or physical attributes.

Although narcissists are thought of as being "in love with themselves," it is more often the case that they are only in love with the idyllic illusionary image they perceive and wish was the truth. Narcissists see themselves as superior and far better than others. They often have big personalities due to their elevated belief in themselves and they can be very magnetic and alluring. This is so they are capable of captivating others so they can use manipulation to get their needs met. Narcissists are self-centered and other people exist solely to benefit them. They perceive their partner as an extension of themselves and they fail to realize that we have our own emotional requirements, so they will use covert tactics to prevent us from expressing our individual needs. They may view us as an object or possession and will usually build up an extremely close, exclusive, and maybe even obsessive relationship. A narcissist will have complete control and will feel resentful and jealous if we want to break free from their clutches and create an independent life on our own, whether with them or apart.

Narcissists want to feel valuable and significant. Basically, the things empaths have little interest in. Narcissists see other people as a necessary supply to feed whichever egotistical need they have at that current time. Narcissists don't do the necessary work required to feed their fragile and hungry ego. They want other people to stroke and nourish it for them. Their ego grows stronger from external validation and recognition. This is where empaths come in useful. We boost other people, pay attention to them, we show gratitude, validate them, and sometimes allow ourselves to be controlled, and we can easily become powerless. We want people to see how valuable and significant they are. However, what we don't always realize is that all of the superficial attention we pay to narcissists only increases and strengthens their ego. That ego then becomes even more powerful and with the added boosts it tries to berate and eventually defeat us. Generally, empaths are givers while narcissists are takers.

When we look at the attraction from an energetic view, it is not difficult to see why empaths and narcissists connect so strongly, as the vibrations we emanate determine who and what we attract or repel. When empaths are radiating high vibrational emotions such as gratitude, joy, open-heartedness and compassion, we are a bright light that shines and we may then attract those who want to steal our glow and make it their own. We can perceive it similar to the way a moth repeatedly hits a lamp at night and how it won't usually give up very easily, if at all. If we aren't aware that this can happen, we can very easily become entangled in our own glistening web and then a narcissist can swoop in and with ease wrap us into a tight cocoon so that they can regularly feed off the energy we are radiating. If we do not remain alert and aware, we will enter a dynamic whereby we reenergize and refuel the narcissists demanding ego by constantly validating them and putting all of their needs way before our own. In the process we are devitalized and with the help of the narcissist's manipulative and constant emotional or mental attacks, we are energetically pulled down. The narcissist's energy is immediately lifted so it is vibrating a little higher, although still negatively, while the empath's energy is instantly lowered. As the interaction continues we will both then vibrate on a similar negative low frequency and we will likely feel even more magnetized and connected to one another that we did in the beginning. However, this is not because we are experiencing and expressing the same emotions as them or because we have similar personalities or traits in any way. It is because we were not alert and we did not fully protect our energy, so our energy levels will have fallen dramatically and we will be emitting low vibrational emotions such as fear, sadness, guilt, despair and anxiety which puts us on a very similar frequency as them. The most concerning part about this is that we don't often realize that it was the interaction with the narcissist that evoked these emotions, and we continue the destructive dance internalizing everything. Narcissists are also emanating low vibrational emotions, but theirs are likely to be unworthiness, blame, desire, craving, pride, humiliation and possibly jealousy, resentment and aggression. The two low vibrations spark and will ignite a fire, which regularly rages out of control. It is also very possible that empaths and narcissists meet and the two energies entangle when empaths are already vibrating on a low frequency, as many empaths experience high levels of anxiety which means that the energy emanating from a narcissist will feel familiar and harmonious as it is also on a low frequency, however, for very different reasons. Therefore, whether we are feeling on top of the world, positive and glowing or whether we are filled with anxiety and fear, we can still be a magnet for these types of relationships until we take full responsibility for our energy and ground, balance and have full awareness of ourselves and others.

Unfortunately, as empaths we don't always acknowledge our own emotional injuries and we can become so busy concentrating on trying to heal others that we neglect and abandon ourselves. This means that our energy may not be vibrating highly, so if we keep giving to others before we take care of ourselves, we will soon find ourselves depleted, burned out and on a very low frequency. It may also be likely that a narcissist's low vibration may feel very familiar and like "home" to us if we have had a parent or another intense relationship with someone who was also energetically low and emitting similar highly charged emotional energy.

Another reason empaths and narcissists connect is that empaths are exceptionally skilled at reading people. When we come into contact with narcissists, we are often left stumped, as they are so closed off it is almost impossible to penetrate and read their conscious mind and what is currently active in their aura. It is vital to remember that at this stage all of this will likely be happening on a subconscious level. The messages will travel from a narcissist's subconscious to an empath's subconscious and back again. There are many narcissists who will consciously play this out to their advantage from the beginning. However, often they are so unaware of their pain and are so far in denial that they will not consciously admit that they are advanced game players. There are some, though, who will openly admit it almost as though they are proud of this honed skill.

As the majority of the interaction is taking place subconsciously, it could mean that neither the empath or narcissist is consciously aware of the potential devastation that their actions can cause, whether this is damage to themselves or the other person. Empaths communicate easily with other people's subconscious minds; however, many of a narcissist's deep-rooted turbulent emotions are pushed firmly down into their unconscious mind. These shadow emotions will appear regularly, though narcissists will not have them under control as they are the aspects of themselves they have denied, rejected, and suppressed. We therefore mostly relate to them via their subconscious mind and we pick up an abundance of hurt, frustration, sadness, anger, and similar tormenting sensations. In the early days it may seem as though we are dealing with everyday insecurities and turmoil, although it doesn't take long to recognize that there are far greater battles going on that have been hidden deep beneath the narcissist's surface. The weapons and scars will be visible from time to time; however, we still often don't realize exactly how turbulent the situation is until we feel compelled to intervene and become involved in their internal war. We automatically evaluate them and conclude that they are in urgent need of healing energy despite their external arrogant structure. We immediately get to work on all of their past anguish and salve, balm, and Band-Aid all their profusely bleeding wounds. While we are busy focusing all of our attention and energy on what we perceive as essential care, we take our awareness away from everything that is taking place in the current moment.

We are so caught up in doing what we think we do best that we forget the one vital component in all of this: the other person also has to also focus their attention on healing historic trauma. Of course, with a narcissist this is not likely to happen. They have far too much arrogance and pride to accept that they may have injured layers within that are triggering their behavior. They won't even accept that their current behavior is unacceptable and could potentially cause harm, let alone be willing to drill into messy, unorganized, and traumatic emotions from their past.

Narcissists often like to pounce and trap those whom they have become involved with, especially if they think they have a lot to gain from a potential new source. While we are preoccupied scurrying around trying to clean and bandage past injuries, the narcissist will be focusing solely on the future and will already be premeditating a plan to lure us effectively into their lair. Narcissists may try to use brainwashing techniques like love-bombing by showing vast amounts of feigned love and affection early on in the relationship purely to flatter, seduce, and disorientate us so that a bond is formed very quickly. They may even present captivating illusions to keep our attention fixed, switching from caring to ruthless in a flash so that we feel constantly unstable, needy, and frantically clinging to their "love." We may feel scared to rock the boat as at any moment they could unleash a torrent of aggression, and then within moments appear to be the most loving and caring person we could wish for. However, not all narcissists are outwardly aggressive. If our behavior falls in line with what they want, all will go smoothly, so we may try to keep ourselves firmly aligned with them, though it is mainly for fear of losing them rather than love. Sadly, that means we grow confused about what love looks and feels like and we will view it through warped lenses as though it is something that has many conditions.

We feel that to receive a narcissist's love we must act accordingly and please them at all times. If we try to regain some control of our mind and our independence, all hell can seem to break loose and they may try a variety of methods to place us back into a powerless position. We won't want to be involved in conflict, so we might fall into the trap of working hard to keep them stable and happy, meanwhile abandoning and neglecting ourselves. Narcissists are not introspective, so they do not see or accept the damage and destruction that results from their behavior.

Narcissists may be deeply wounded and as they have closed off they find it very difficult, if not impossible, to sense and understand other people's emotions. Therefore, they are unlikely to show sincere compassion or heartfelt empathy when we are hurt or in emotional pain. Although it may seem as though a narcissist's actions are cold, callous, and intentional, they have a distorted image of themselves. Generally, they are not operating from a conscious level and their behavior is often delivered without them being fully aware of the pain and trauma they are causing to others. If they do at some level acknowledge the pain, they are not likely to take any responsibility for their part in it. Instead, as though it comes naturally, they skillfully project and associate the reason for the pain firmly to anyone else within the vicinity.

From a narcissist's perspective, it is always someone else's fault. Refusing to be accountable for their behavior is what keeps them trapped, as they deny any responsibility; thus, they see no reason to change their ways. They have many sides and they choose very carefully which side they prefer to show depending on how it will benefit them and also because they are afraid to unveil their core identity as they are out of touch with their inner self—they are afraid of what lies within and are not willing to spend time getting to know themselves internally. Therefore, when we enter into a relationship with a narcissist it can take some time before their true colors are revealed. For some, this revelation arrives when commitments have already been made, which makes it a little trickier to step away from the dramatics.

They may use forms of gas lighting to blow up situations and make it look as though we are at fault. An example is they may say things and then totally deny ever saying them once we have reacted, or they may be unfaithful or flirt relentlessly but if we bring it up we are told we are paranoid and have trust issues. This wrongly affirms in our minds that we are completely to "blame" and we deserve everything that happens to us. This can also make us feel as though we are going insane as no one around us is able to identify with what we are going through. Narcissists can easily make other people feel as though they are going crazy while they look entirely innocent.

When we engage with narcissists, we are vulnerable to their ability to turn everything around, accusing us of being emotionally insecure or being the perpetrator of deliberate malicious words or actions when usually they are projecting their own behavior on to us, and firmly believing that we deserve the accusations. One of the most bewildering and destabilizing things about being close to a narcissist is that certain people around them fail to see the devastation they cause. This is because they exist behind gleaming armor put in place to distinguish and hide their true self. Narcissists will pick and choose who sees particular sides depending on what it is they wish to gain. If we seek help or support from others, it may seem as though no one else sees what is really going on, or others have seen it and tried to tell us but we hadn't wanted to believe they were right.

Narcissists know exactly who they can weave their web of dysfunction around and who they can't. If they know they have nothing to gain, be it energy, financial or material rewards, or possibly destroying other people's moods, they turn their charm up to the highest degree and dazzle those around them with their happy and joyous "other side." This is simply to make it look as though we are delusional so they can keep up their manipulative behavior without being questioned. This can make it difficult to seek support, as when we turn to someone for advice they may struggle to grasp what we are going through. To us, a narcissist may be controlling, deceptive, and malicious, and life could be upside down, yet in front of other people they may show false jubilation to keep the facade in place. As long as a narcissist is influencing other people's moods, one way or the other their ego is satisfied, regardless of how happy or sad they may appear on the surface.

Narcissists are unpredictable and will swing from high to low like a possessed seesaw, making it impossible to work out what they may do next. We need to remain aware, expecting the unexpected and letting go of unrealistic hopes that the relationship will be a smooth, harmonious, and enchanting ride. However, some narcissists may keep things very calm, appearing cool and collected, though that usually only lasts as long as everything is going their way.

For a narcissist, the notion of peeling away at all the layers and delusions that they have built around themselves is potentially grueling and a painful process they will avoid at all cost, especially when the layers have become protection to prevent them from experiencing similar excruciating emotions to ones connected to their past. Each layer could be marinated in shame, guilt, fear, resentment, bitterness, anger, revenge, and blame. A narcissist will do anything to avoid feeling any unpleasant sensation. It is like handing someone a parcel and asking them to play the game 'pass the parcel.' Pass the parcel is a party game where a surprise gift is wrapped inside many layers of wrapping paper. The parcel is passed around everyone in the room and each person has to unwrap a layer, however, no one knows what might be hidden beneath the layer they are unwrapping. With narcissists if they are asked to peel back their layers to reach their soul, they will feel as though they are playing alone and everyone is watching them as they painfully strip back the parcel one sheet of wrapping paper at a time. They don't know what might be hidden beneath each layer and neither do they want to know as they will likely subconsciously feel as though they don't have the inner strength to deal with whatever they might find. It can all become too much. Therefore, they place the package out of sight and instead focus on ripping at other people's layers instead.

Each layer a narcissist tears off someone else validates them more as they realize they are not alone in their deep-rooted turmoil. Of course they aren't. We all experience a multitude of unpleasant feelings. The difference is that we are usually willing to painstakingly explore our emotions. Narcissists likely won't. Why would they when other people can top up their energy whenever it is low? The games they play with people are distractions that can become a form of entertainment to avoid them having to face their own issues.

If we are not consciously aware of how to protect ourselves and how to transmute energy, we may very easily and very quickly bond with a narcissist in order to try to fix any issues, repair any damage, and attempt to eradicate all their pain. Rather than seeing their pain as belonging to them, we take it from them and try to absorb it as our own. We are the perfect match in a narcissist's eyes—an empath, a healer, someone they hope will carry and deal with all of their pain.

Narcissists want to be more powerful and they need to fill their inner voids with vital energy from external sources. By passing us all their negativity, they are then free to swoop in and take whatever is required to fuel their deficient reserve. If we aren't careful, we are the ones who end up doing all the dirty, tiresome, and unpleasant work, while they look down at us with a side smirk accompanied by pity.

Empaths sense and absorb pain, and if the emotions are heavy and complex we are compelled to remove them from other people so that we can process and transmute them. However, if we are not aware of what emotions are erupting or we don't know how to transmute the energy, we will carry the emotional burden as though it is our own. If we have our own unresolved and unhealed emotional trauma, we will create a set of circumstances that invite us to confront our own injuries so that they can be soothed, healed, processed, understood, and freed. An entanglement with a narcissist is an opportunity to look at ourselves so that we become consciously aware of our own self-abandonment. Unfortunately, it can take some time for us to recognize this. Often, it first takes looking at someone else's wounds and the turbulent effect they have on us before we are ready to turn inward and investigate our own internal pain.

Narcissists are mirrors that reflect a clear image, showing exactly where our wounds are located within our energy field. Sometimes, it feels easier and tempting to blame narcissists for exposing our injuries. We will possibly deny, accuse, blame, and shame narcissists for brazenly standing in front of us and forcing us to look a little closer. Interactions with narcissists are no coincidence. They come to us for a reason, just as we engage with them for a reason. We are both vibrating on a unique frequency that powerfully magnetizes us toward one another. This is an opportunity for immense healing for both involved. The difficulty lies in whether each party is willing to throw down their tools and weapons regardless of whether they are healing or destructive ones so that wound acknowledgment can take place before any type of bonding or conflict begins.

We have received what we need in order to heal. Unfortunately, though, often times rather than looking internally our focus is directed externally, especially if we are not self-aware, taking care of ourselves effectively, able to locate the origin of our wounds, and overall if our energy field is unstable and operating on a low reserve. As empaths are generally selfless, our instinctive response is to heal others before we heal ourselves, especially if we are denying our own emotional needs and experiencing the sensations of other people's at intensely high levels. This is perfect for a narcissist. Here is someone with arms outstretched ready to carry all the energy that they perceive as ugly. What we don't realize is that when we try to embrace a narcissist and take their unpleasant energetic load from them they then view us as "ugly," not on the outside but on the inside. We are now holding everything that they have tried to avoid. Not only is this highly unattractive in a narcissist's eyes, they will also see us as weak.

A narcissist's load is too much for anyone to bear, so eventually we will collapse and crumble. They know this, yet they will keep passing their load to us so that we can sort through it, and ultimately the narcissist is then free. We are weakened; they are stronger and ready to strike. Narcissists can then take from us whatever they choose and we will struggle to find the strength to stop them. Narcissists are energy suckers, emotional vampires. They can draw the life and soul out of anyone they come into contact with so that they can build up their own reserves, and in doing so they use the imbalance to their advantage.

If we do not have a profound understanding of our own or other people's capabilities, this dynamic will confuse and debilitate us. We can try to remember that not everyone is the same, and it helps to put ourselves in other people's shoes and experience their feelings and emotions, however, we can't always naturally tune in to their intentions. We often forget that other people may have an agenda very different from our own and that not everyone is sincere. So when we are consumed by the traumatic emotions narcissists are experiencing at a hidden level, our vision becomes hazy and we do not see with clarity their plans or the manipulative behavior they intend to use on us.

Narcissists have a deep desire to create a relationship with us as we are givers, we are generally not very assertive, and we do not usually have firm boundaries. So we keep on giving without questioning it until our source of energy has run completely dry. This is perfect for narcissists as they are takers. They too have poor boundaries, so they will keep on taking for as long as we have something to offer. As soon as we are totally depleted and feel at breaking point, a narcissist will leave us by the wayside and head off to hunt down the next source willing to offer the same one-sided deal.

When we are in the midst of a relationship or any form of interaction with a narcissist, it can feel as though we are trapped in a cage while trying to decipher a complex enigma. This type of connection is not as complex to decode or understand as we might think. Although we don't realize it, the cage door is open and we can fly out to find all the answers whenever we choose.

Narcissists slip easily into character, so they can sway from generating flattery to sympathy or pity then on to aggression and manipulation depending on whichever situation they encounter. It can be almost impossible to guess what version we will be shown, so it can be difficult to work out if what we are seeing is make-believe or the truth unless we tap into our inner knowing feeling and tune in to the narcissist's energy. We will then immediately sense precisely what is taking place.

If a narcissist views us as "valuable," they will be extremely enigmatic, persuasive, and for as long as we remain "worthy" and for long periods of time they can keep up impressive displays of charm. It all depends on how much they have to gain from the interaction. A narcissist's energy, whether seemingly positive or negative, is extremely intoxicating. Even though everything we see with a narcissist is basically a complete illusion, it is still very easy to be tricked by them as they fully play out their part, often believing their own lies. This means that their emotions appear to an empath as though they are genuine, so we can very easily get caught up in the delusion.

One of the reasons empaths are drawn to narcissists is because narcissists are highly attentive to the words and actions of others. Narcissists, like empaths, are observers and they very quickly decipher other people's body language, tone of voice, and also emotions. To an empath, this can seem as though we have connected with someone else who is empathetic, caring, and compassionate, although this is not the case and is a dangerous assumption to make. Narcissists are generally not going to express empathy or be compassionate. They just easily appear to be empathetic as they hone in on specific details, and at a surface level they will be sympathetic and relate and resonate with what is being said. Although narcissists can read emotions very well, they do not show genuine empathy for the emotions. They are able to turn other people's emotions to their advantage to be used for ammunition so they can debilitate and control as soon as the opportunity arises. We may share our previous encounters with them believing we are being vulnerable and brave by opening up about our fears and painful memories. However, we are actually giving narcissists all the weapons they need so that they can fire cowardly shots toward us to take us down whenever the slightest thing triggers them. They will share a fraction of their past experiences, which will likely be biased and not necessarily based on any truth. They do this with the sole intention of drawing us in to gain attention, compassion, and trust.

As empaths are sensitive to emotions, the highly dramatic ones that spill out from a narcissist can feel magnetic. We want to heal, soothe, and calm people. And when we see someone we perceive to be in lot of pain, we ache to nurture and heal their wounds. As we are absorbing and experiencing all of the raw emotions, we also frantically try to bandage their wounds to eliminate our own suffering. We feel the pain as intensely as if it were our own, so we want to eradicate it immediately. We genuinely and foolishly believe that with unconditional love and tender care we can salve all of the narcissist's emotional and physical pain. This is one of the most fatal mistakes an empath can make. Why would a narcissist need to be healed? In their eyes they do nothing wrong! Everything is everyone else's fault and they are quite happy portioning out the blame rather than feeling and owning the associated shame. Yet we naively believe we have the power to heal someone who not only isn't looking to be healed, but instead wants to inflict wounds on us!

A wounded empath is the perfect bait for a predatory narcissist. As soon as we become exhausted and crippled by the powerful waves of emotion we leak while in the vicinity of a narcissist, we are sitting ducks bleeding valuable energy while waiting in the path of a callous hunter. We are also an enjoyable form of entertainment. Narcissists love watching our reactions to their cruel games and their ego receives immense amounts of nourishment when observing our intense pain. The more we react, the more exciting the game becomes and the more energy we lose and they receive. However, if we are one step ahead and give nothing and offer no emotional response whatsoever, the narcissist wanes and will easily get bored and move on to their next victim.

Narcissists are an empath's nemesis as they are masters at their art and will convince us that our intuition is totally wrong and that we are crazy for doubting or questioning their intentions, words, or actions. If we get into a relationship with a narcissist, we can very easily and rapidly feel as though we are going insane.

Just as narcissists are an empath's nemesis, empaths who stand in their own power can also be trouble for a narcissist. If a narcissist has not succeeded in charming and winning us over, they will quickly want to destabilize or destroy us. This is because when we are grounded and we protect ourselves we are capable of seeing through their superficial exterior. However, we have to be quick. Narcissists are able to easily hypnotize people to ensure they are easily brainwashed and fooled by their meticulous dastardly plans. If we spot a narcissist before they detect us, we pose the risk of stripping off their mask. This means narcissists would be exposed and then be vulnerable as their manipulative tactics will be clearly visible. We may be targeted either by seduction and charm or by a narcissist forcefully condemning us to try to break us down. Either way, if we have not protected our energy well, when faced with a narcissist we will do well to escape the dynamic unscathed.

Like with all situations, when we open our eyes to willingly see what is in front of us we will be far less likely to be caught up in illusions. How great our insight is depends on the color of glasses we choose to wear. Red flags are never invisible when we wear rose-colored tints or any other shade. Clear sight equals insight. When we are prepared to seek and see the truth it all becomes clear.

A game for one has little gain for a narcissist as they need to plug into someone else to receive their emotional "fix." Narcissists are detached from their emotions as there are many blockages preventing energetic movement. The only way they are capable of feeling positive, energizing emotion is when they tap into someone else's energy and take whatever they can find. Narcissists will likely seek out people who have large amounts of excess energy. This is why they try to connect with empaths who are intuitive healers and naturally vibrate loving, healing energy. If we are not taking care of ourselves properly, we will leak out energy at such an intense level that it can be detrimental to our emotional and mental wellbeing. An exchange often takes place as the narcissist is seeking admiration, validation, and has a desire to constantly have their ego stroked. And in return, they will provide whatever it is the other person is lacking. However, what the narcissist offers is only on the surface and comes with conditions that their needs are always met with priority, regardless of the impact this has on anyone else.

This can look like a fair deal, especially to the narcissist, though unfortunately it isn't as the narcissist has a strong need to be in control. We quickly become the prey—the narcissist being the sharp and hungry predator. What may seem like an equal exchange is entirely the opposite. The narcissist will feed to receive validation to such an extent that it leaves us feeling totally drained and worthless. Meanwhile, the narcissist rises above, resting high upon what they see as their well-deserved throne where they fully believe they belong.

A relationship with a narcissist is usually a steady process that has built up over time. Like an insidious drip, we are slowly fed an addictive bittersweet poison so by the time we awake we are intoxicated, dazed, and confused. We have to remember that we choose to drink the elixir. It is never forced upon us. By continuing the toxic interaction, we are slowly but effectively poisoning ourselves.

Narcissists are clever and cunning players of their complex game and they will find little pleasure if an opponent is not eager and willing to partake. If a narcissist comes across someone who is more skilled or significantly emotionally or mentally stronger than they are, the board will be flipped over, tantrums may be displayed, and the game ends before it has even begun. Narcissists may express rage to cause us to rage, and then will move swiftly into victim mode to make us look at fault. When we emit any intense emotions, they will move in for a quick feed. Rather than standing up to narcissists, we often play small and tiptoe around them to ensure everything runs smoothly and they are meticulously tended to.

For those that have not witnessed the timorous chameleon caught in the act of changing colors, narcissists can appear to be the most irresistible, charismatic, thoughtful, caring, passionate, and lovable characters we could ever wish to meet. Initially we are astounded as we think we have met someone who ticks every box and meets all our needs and desires. Narcissists are in their element when we are caught like a rabbit in their headlights, shocked by their magnificence and in awe of their sexual prowess and unfailing charm. Realistically, the narcissist is role-playing. They read us instantly and quickly work out exactly what it is we are hoping to receive from them. If we want someone strong and independent, they will happily show us these traits. If we want a sensitive, deep, introverted type, they have the ability to rapidly put on that mask instead. They are masters at deception and they play a fast-changing manipulative game.

The narcissist is fully in control by this stage and they intend to keep it this way. If they are successful in bewitching us, we are then led directly to their lair. Once we are spellbound and falling head over heels, that is where the real magic takes place (for them). We are basically a prop; however, a willing one.

Now, if we were to suddenly open our eyes, take off our tinted glasses, and remove the narcissist's mask, we would see everything play out just as clearly as though we were sitting in the audience watching people step into their character roles. We are looking to the narcissist to meet our needs. We are projecting on them all the things we want and they are delivering everything we are hoping for. This is a mutually beneficial arrangement in these beginning stages. We ask, the narcissist delivers.

We begin to enter codependency. We place our happiness, hopes, and dreams into the hands of the narcissist and they are then free to put them into a ghastly pot and stir them all up. However, not before they infuse all their own hopes and dreams, which unfortunately do not mirror our own. Narcissists think only of themselves and will work extremely hard behind the scenes to ensure that their lives plays out exactly as they have envisaged in their minds. Empaths do not think only of themselves, they think of both people involved in the relationship. In fact, empaths are far more likely to put the other person way before them.

When empaths and narcissists engage the balance is off and the scales will immediately tip. The spill out is what takes place continuously throughout the relationship. Nothing is ever steady and the scales will always be manically swaying. Every time the scales turn erratic, if we try to jump to safety, the narcissist will steady things once again by feeding us what we want to hear. We stay. Things stabilize, but only temporarily. Soon enough, the narcissist tips the scales once again in their own favor. Repeat, repeat, and repeat, until one day the narcissist has taken all that they need. We are rendered useless, emotionally beaten, and no longer worthy of the superior narcissist's company. They will nonchalantly walk away like a bloodthirsty vampire moving on to bleed their next victim dry.

Or the other more preferable option—we open our eyes. We stop looking to others to provide what we need and feed ourselves large enough doses of love, compassion, consideration, self-worth, independence, forgiveness, and happiness. This means that when we are faced with a narcissist we will not be looking to them to keep us fulfilled and alive, as realistically all they deliver is nothing more than a quick injection of junk food with very little nourishment.

Narcissists are a dazzling light that fireflies cannot stay away from. The fireflies will dance around it to hypnotic music until they have been thoroughly burned. We are the firefly fluttering around and sifting through charred ashes hoping to find codes and clues to figure out what exactly is going on. We find it difficult to believe that what began as a fairytale ended with a far less enchanting story penned exclusively by the Brothers Grimm. When clarity arrives, we are left shell-shocked and bewildered and frantically scrambling to try to understand what drew us toward this raging fire in the first place. We look back puzzled and wonder what type of madness caused us to stand torturing ourselves on scorching coals, refusing to step away so we could take some relief from the pain. Unfortunately, we will find no answers from the narcissist. This is mainly because narcissists will hold all of their cards very close to their chests. They refuse to show anyone their hand due to a fear of being exposed.

Removing their mask would signal the end of their royal and majestic reign. They survive on extreme drama and will want to be on center stage when the show reaches its climax, so they will not want to be seen scurrying through the dark toward the dreary back door of the theatre house. Therefore, we have no option but to work out the dynamics for ourselves and not concern ourselves with the details on the narcissist's agenda. We can try to focus on what attracted us so powerfully in the first place so that we can prevent a repeat performance, and more significantly, be held accountable for our role.

There is not usually "love lost" as there is often no, or very little, genuine or true love. Narcissists are not capable of a heart-felt, loving exchange. It is barely possible to gain love from a narcissist as they have shut their heart down so love struggles to enter or be received. Although we may be sending them love, it will not be absorbed. All our affection and loving actions offer is a stroke to their overinflated ego.

We like to think we can love someone enough so that they will eventually love themselves, but it is not our love that makes this happen. They first have to choose to love themselves before anyone else's love is able to squeeze through.

If we are hoping for love, we can try to wait it out patiently, but we cannot force it, nor can we expect it to be a smooth ride. We have to remember, though, when we are with a narcissist much of what is around us is an illusion. We have fallen for what we perceive to be the truth, what we want or hope to be the truth, a vision that we believe is in there somewhere. We are not falling for the reality. We cling on as we receive glimpses of what we wish existed. However, these glimpses are just carrots to lead the donkey astray.

We are often in love with a projected idea of what we imagine love would look like if the relationship stabilized, although a narcissist is not able to sustain a healthy balance for long. Unless we remove all the attachments to our desired outcome, we will be greatly disappointed and get badly hurt.

We deserve more. We all deserve to be loved. Unconditionally.

Unconditional love is too risky for a narcissist as they think it will leave them vulnerable when they open themselves up and are honest. To do this means stripping away numerous layers so they can discover who they are. Not only that, they only show what may imitate "love" when everything is going their way. Unconditional love means accepting someone exactly as they are. However, that said, we do not have to allow or accept behavior that can harm us emotionally, mentally, or physically.

Narcissists only accept people when they are going to gain something from it. If we do not please them or if they have nothing to gain, they see no need to dish out actions that look like love or affection. Narcissists are superficial. They don't care what lies beneath the surface unless it is benefiting them. And they most definitely won't want anyone else to look beneath their surface, as that is where all their dysfunctional behavior stems from. They keep it locked away and safely guarded and so far out of reach it is even hidden from themselves. They would rather carry on as they always have and take without giving. To them this is a far more preferable, beneficial, and easier option.

So we are deprived of their love and affection. And it is difficult to walk away. Even when we see this dynamic clearly the attraction may still be there. For one, we are emotionally exhausted as we have given so much. We are debilitated and by this stage we are usually at rock bottom. And two, it doesn't feel natural for us to give up. We want to love unconditionally and we may feel as though we have let ourselves and the other person down. We may struggle to understand what has happened to the once loving, attentive, and charismatic person we were once attracted to. We think we could have loved more, forgiven more, understood more, showed more compassion, and we ultimately blame ourselves. Realistically all we had to do was love ourselves more, forgive ourselves more, understand ourselves more, show self-compassion, and stop blaming ourselves. Then we will gain the clarity and strength to see that we are fighting a losing emotional battle.

We will never be responsible for their behavior and believing we are is what keeps us in this dangerous dynamic. We will eventually become immobilized, possibly even living in fear of emotional upsets. We may mistrust ourselves, doubt ourselves. We will lose our ability to think straight, lose our courage, our confidence, we will find it difficult to love, or even like ourselves. We may even be ashamed. We may feel as though we can't talk to anyone as they might judge us harder than we judge ourselves. We will take on all the blame, blame for staying and blame for refusing to see that we would never want anyone we cared about or loved to stay in such a treacherous environment. So why do we allow ourselves to?

"Love is joy. Don't convince yourself that suffering is part of it."
——Paulo Coelho

We think we are the reason. We must be the reason they are angry, the reason they drink too much, the reason they are aggressive, the reason they cheat, the reason they are jealous, the reason they mock us, resent us, the reason they are volatile. The reason they lie. The reason they are permanently wired just waiting to explode. The reason they can't love us. We think we were their reason for everything. We can't see that we aren't. We can't see anything clearly. So we stay. And we stay among the chaos and the trauma.

No one else will do it for us. We have to see for ourselves. We need to put our own loving arms around ourselves tightly and forgive ourselves. No knight on a white horse will be arriving. No one can possibly come to our defense because we cannot bear to tell anyone (a foolish and risky error). We have to take the first step forward and rescue ourselves.

Any attempt to communicate authentically with the narcissist will be futile, as they will certainly not be looking to take responsibility or soothe and heal anyone else. Not only this, they are extremely charismatic and manipulative and have a powerful way of turning everything away from themselves and onto others. If we do try to get them to see the true state of the relationship or the effects of their behavior, they will become very defensive and will lash out in an attempt to deflect any guilt they may be asked to take on and forcefully make us carry the full burden of the reasons for the relationship breakdown. A narcissist will blame our pain on us, plus they will also make sure we feel responsible for any pain they are suffering. They cannot see their flaws, so they will never be accountable for them and they sure as damn won't be willing to repent or offer an apology, at least not one that is meaningful. If *sorry* is offered, it is usually a trap or to catch and hold us once again so they press repeat and reach even higher ground.

When we begin the process of detangling from a narcissist's intricately weaved web, we are so emotionally exhausted it can be difficult to see exactly what has taken place. By this stage we will know we are in a dysfunctional relationship and will feel so insecure, unloved, and unworthy that it can be easy to blame the carnage on the narcissist. Is it them? Is it us? Is it everyone around us? Our circumstances? Bad timing? Where lies the truth? However, we can try not to look to blame anyone else. We have free will to decide to either remain the victim, a pawn in the narcissist's game, or to garner all strength we can muster and find our way out.

To a narcissist it is imperative that they are in a position whereby they can rise above us and be in control. Our agenda is to love, heal, and achieve stability and harmony. There is no balance in an entanglement with a narcissist and it is unlikely there ever will be. The more love and care we offer, the more powerful and in control they will become. The more powerful the narcissist becomes, the more likely we will retreat into victim status. Then, there could an unexpected change of dynamic. We become riddled with pain and are then at risk of taking on narcissistic traits as we too are now wounded, being constantly triggered by the daggers the narcissist has thrown at us.

At this stage, we must realize the situation we are in and wake up to it. It can be a dangerous and hostile phase for an empath as anyone who is deeply in pain and has been hurt badly can behave like a narcissist too. We may turn the focus onto our own pain and look for others to make us feel validated and safe again. We may even begin to take on some of the narcissist's traits ourselves.

If we are not alert and aware, being in the company of a narcissist can causes us so much damage that before long an extremely vicious circle begins. We need energy, validation, and healing, and we have no strength or willpower to offer these things to ourselves. When a narcissist sees that we are wounded, they will play on this and the main intention will be to keep us down. The lower down we are, the higher they feel. We will begin to frantically seek love, confirmation, and acceptance from a narcissist and each cry for help affirms to the narcissist what they are desperate to feel inside—worthy.

The bitter battle continues. As we focus solely on our pain, trauma, and the destruction, we become self-obsessed and fail to see where all the missiles and explosions are coming from. Instead of looking outward and seeing what is causing the chaos, we turn everything inward and blame ourselves.

The most treacherous and testing time of an entanglement with a narcissist is usually when we have been worn down energetically and we are ready to close the door. This is when they will be petrified of taking a damaging dent to their ego that they will go to all lengths to regain control. They often get in touch for seemingly pointless and meaningless reasons or during an occasion such as a birthday or anniversary when they know we will be temporarily weakened and more likely to reply to their "innocent," out-of-the-blue contact. They may also text to ask a simple question about something that is irrelevant, especially considering all that has passed under the bridge prior to this contact. It is possible that they may even use a feigned emergency to capture attention purely to reignite a dying-out fire. It is also common for them to contact our friends, family members, or our work colleagues as a way to sneakily find out personal information. This helps them to work out the most clandestine tactic to sweep us back off our feet and make it look as though the serendipitous meeting was "chance" or "fated." They might also make contact to return belongings even though the items that are returned have little significance and haven't been asked for, or if they were requested at the time of the break-up our pleas were ignored. Strangely, they want to return the items with urgency and might insist on hand delivering them to ensure they arrive "safely." Elaborate gifts may be sent or they may endeavor to charm us with sentimental offerings to make it look as though they have put a lot of thought, time, and attention into them.

Suddenly, it appears as though they have miraculously changed. They want to wipe everything from the past clean so they can begin afresh and with no need to apologize, show remorse, or take responsibility for their previous actions. If they do show these things, they are most probably insincere and fabricated as they go to all lengths to disguise their true intentions.

The reason that this strategy works so well is that they are now declaring all the things we think we needed to hear and mostly the words that make us feel validated. When they left we may have been left in pain and their turnaround fills our aching voids and makes us believe that we were not the ones at fault for their departure. We can be spun into a dizzying whirlwind as all the initial feelings of what we hoped was "love" flush through our veins. Narcissists are very aware of this and will use various romantic or even sexual words and actions to cloud and distort our feelings. They somehow manage to reconvince us that we are the most important person in their world and tell us how foolish they were for leaving. All of a sudden their presence makes all of the loneliness and heartache disappear. They soothe and balm our wounds and we momentarily feel on top of the world once again.

As the "loved up" chemicals flush through our brains, we become intoxicated, everything appears hazy, and we are not able to process it all, so we are unable to think straight and see through their dramatic displays. Narcissists will beg, plead, persuade, charm and use every trick in the book to reestablish the connection. It can be difficult to know whether their actions are genuine or whether we are being used as a substitute to boost their worn-down ego and depleted energy supply.

It usually doesn't take long to see through the facade. If we pay attention to our intuition and trust our instinct, we will know instantly whether their cunning plot is to benefit and enhance their self-worth and esteem or if it is to genuinely make amends due to a spectacular transformation in character. The easiest way to work out sincere from insincere behavior is to focus on ourselves rather than them. How do we feel internally? It is essential that we are truthful when we answer. Have we been secretly hoping for a rendezvous that will prove we meant something to them or did their departure leave us feeling rejected when we were rapidly replaced with someone new? Do we feel resentful toward the partner they exchanged us for and by getting back in touch with them does it now make us feel as though we are evening out the score? Do we feel validated in some way by their return and as though we are valued and worthy?

When we are willing to face up to the reasons that their random return spikes our delight, we are able to look at why we are allowing someone to pick us up, drop us, and then return when they are feeling bored with their current life to trigger old feelings and repeat the pattern. It is likely that they may have had an argument with someone in their current life and are angry, frustrated, or feeling resentful, so they turn to us for a distraction or to spite the person and take their mind away from it; most of all, though, to replenish their draining energy reserves.

Moral code does not come into question when narcissists are seeking a top up. They will shamelessly try to gather up fragmented pieces right where they left off with no regard for the emotional or psychological damage that might have been caused to or will cause anyone who may be involved. Whatever the reasons, they matter not. What is important is what is going on with us that we feel we deserve to be treated this way. If we allow ourselves to get sucked back in once, we can try not to be hard on ourselves, see things with clarity, work on ourselves a little bit more, then let it go. However, if it is happening time and again and the same circumstances are repeating with nothing changing, we have to take a long, hard look at ourselves. We can try asking, "Why are we not taking care of ourselves?" and "What am I missing in myself that I feel they are providing?" We need to immediately stop someone from having a hold over us by exerting charm, power, and control, and do whatever it takes by ourselves to fill any voids or focus on our unhealed wounds.

Although we may feel at the time it is harmless to step back toward them or that we are handling it well and we know what we are doing, this behavior is not acceptable and it can seriously damage our self-worth. Plus, all we are doing is enhancing someone else and allowing manipulation to pull us down again and again. The only option when we are being hooked back in is to disengage - zero contact. Nil. Nothing. Not a return text message, phone call, and definitely no arranging to meet up. If it is an absolute genuine emergency, we will know. Otherwise, before we know it we will be sucked up and back at the start, allowing them the optimum opportunity to tread all over us once more while they ensure their egocentric needs are met on their wretched agenda. Very soon we will once again be discarded when their energy levels are recharged, their confidence boosted, and their life is back in order. Or they may remain for a long period while we suffer and regularly hold ourselves accountable for their shortcomings. Once we have healed ourselves and we are strong enough to engage again without being severely emotionally affected, we can then choose if we want to alter how we engage, but it is imperative that we take care of ourselves until we are in this position. Otherwise, we will very likely just keep getting further and further pulled down.

If they have astonishingly changed, again, we will know about it. There will be no need for trickery as they will be genuine, remorseful, decent, considerate, humble, and they will show integrity, virtue, have good morals, and be true to their word. The only time a narcissist may completely close the door and not look back is when they know that we have seen straight through their manipulative displays and we are no longer willing to be a feed for their hungry ego.

Sadly, people with a personality disorder usually think only of themselves. When interacting with them, it is essential we do the same. We can still show compassion, understanding, forgiveness, and love, but we must also show these things to ourselves. We need to remember that how we allow ourselves to be treated by someone else is a choice, and unfortunately, one that reflects some inner wrongly absorbed story. If we choose to stay in a relationship with a narcissist and refuse to take responsibility for the dynamic, we are choosing at some level something that aligns with what we believe we are worth on the inside.

We cannot let our self-worth be determined by a narcissist. It is imperative we trust and believe in ourselves enough to recognize that we do not deserve the words and actions the narcissist delivers so that they do not affect us. In our eyes, all we searched for was someone to take care of and love, and although we may not like to admit this bit, also so we could be a savior and fix their pain.

That is where the trouble began and that is the most profound part of this that we must realize and take onboard. We want to soothe and balm their wounds and cover all their scars as their pain is essentially our pain. However, we are not here to fix anyone. We cannot fix anyone. Everyone is responsible for and capable of fixing themselves, but only if they so choose to.

"No one is fixed until they make the effort to change." —— Bruce H. Lipton, *The Biology of Belief: Unleashing the Power of Consciousness, Matter and Miracles*

The more empaths learn about the traits of a narcissist, the sooner we will spot one and the less chance we have of developing a relationship with one. If a relationship is already underway, it is never too late to seek help, seek understanding, search for knowledge, and to dig deep into our soul and recognize our own strengths and capabilities. We can then do everything possible to build awareness, courage, and confidence so that we can see it for what it is and so that we are able to walk away if we choose to. We have to take responsibility for the situation we are in. We weren't forced into the relationship. Yes, we will likely have been tricked, deceived, and lied to many times during the early months so we may have struggled to achieve a full understanding of what we were heading into. However, there are usually many warning signals and danger flags frantically swinging in front of us. Unfortunately, we sometimes choose to ignore them as we think that what we have found is true love and we badly want the fairytale.

We may also have to take ownership for the way we have reacted when we were triggered by some of the things that were said or done to us. The levels that narcissists stoop to can be beyond anything we might have believed possible within the realms of "love." At the time, we don't always know how to respond to slurs that are hurled toward us or how to deal with the premeditated and endless emotional, mental, and physical prods, provocations, and pokes. We may not have always been reasonable ourselves, so we have to look at some of our behavior and work out how we can change.

We might have even been tempted to fight back thinking we may regain some power, although all this does is feed narcissists the most nourishing and exhilarating fuel for their soul. It is not recommended to try fighting on the same playing field as a narcissist as they fight callously, cruelly, and without any show of compassion. When we head into battle with them, we then become similar to them. The chance of a narcissist changing is unlikely, although it is possible, and they are also very unlikely to be reasonable during the process, so we can try not to expect that we will be able to negotiate fair terms and neither should we spend our energy wishing for a transformational miracle to magically happen. If a narcissist wants to change, then they will make the changes and we will see them. No one else can open a narcissist's eyes or heart for them; they can only do it themselves.

Change never needs to happen at the expense of anyone else. Narcissists are not always consciously aware of their behavior or the damage it causes, and in their game they will sacrifice anyone and anything for their own gain, regardless of what pretty lies and sweet nothings they try to whisper and trick us into believing.

Empaths are usually authentic and tr to live true to our soul's purpose and we will very likely find the whole relationship a huge lesson, a dodged bullet, and an excruciatingly painful awakening. A narcissist will struggle to have any connection to their authentic self as their ego takes center stage, and they will likely walk away from the relationship very easily once they realize they have lost their ability to control us. The game is no longer pleasurable if they are not having their ego constantly tended to, so they will shake us off to seek out their next victim.

The ability for these two types to bond heart center to heart center is quite almost impossible. The narcissist's heart *chakra* is blocked and therefore closed. An empath's is open. This is nothing short of a recipe for a huge disaster, and not a beautiful one.

When we are intrinsically entwined in a relationship that is emotionally, mentally, or physically draining we are a delicious feed for a narcissist, an energy vampire. When we are drained, we become hungry and weakened. When we are weak, we are willing to accept far less and are easily controlled. As we begin to starve, the narcissist becomes stronger. We are weakened further. We start to become worthless to them. We are eventually debilitated. They freely walk away. This is a painful but simple truth.

The road to recovery is not always an easy one, although once we have recognized and have a good understanding of what we are dealing with it is far easier to offer compassion and forgiveness. Genuine forgiveness prevents resentment, pain, and anger from lingering on and affecting us negatively in future occurrences. It is not easy to accept that this kind of abuse has taken place, but when we remember that narcissism is a personality disorder we can begin to see it as something other than just cruel, nasty, or vicious behavior.

We can try to stand well back from their stage performance and view it for exactly what it is and not allow ourselves to suffer through the experience. Knowledge is key. When we are aware of their behavior and the detrimental effects it has on everyone around them, we can begin to take steps to either protect or remove ourselves from their clawed grasp.

We can try not to allow their illusions of grandeur or power to influence us. It is not reality. We can accept it or step away from it; it is our choice. However impossible it may sometimes seem, we can try not to react emotionally or get too meticulously involved. Narcissists struggle to feel or display their own emotions, so they enjoy watching intense emotions bleed out from other people. Therefore, a public emotional meltdown from anyone around them is their perfect treat, and one they secretly and silently wish for. They may try to goad us to gain some kind of reaction or retaliation to "prove" to others that they are the victim and also to enforce that they are powerful enough to garner an emotional or even physical reaction. Narcissists will only continue their outlandish behavior when all eyes are turned on them, so they may insult us and slender us to our family and friends in an attempt to make it seem as though any wrongdoing is on our end and they are entirely innocent. They may also try to sabotage any other close relationships we have with people and verbally attack our abilities to be a parent, friend, partner, or in our role within our career purely so that we will feel isolated, worthless, and a failure. As hard as it might seem, we have to look away and sometimes slowly back away, at least emotionally.

It is so easy to be triggered as they can play low and use our wounds and fragility to hit us where it hurts most. Maintaining no response, no reaction, or even no contact is not always easy, but they are all significant when we need to keep our self-worth and sanity in check. We never need to allow other people to dictate or control our emotions as this is exactly what keeps us locked in the dynamic. Unconditional love for a narcissist is possible if we remove judgment and stop having expectations that will regularly disappoint us; however, it is essential that we also protect our energy while engaging. This ensures they do not have direct access to the dials on our emotions. If a relationship is going to continue we can try not to see their behavior as a personal insult as it is their issue, their responsibility and a reflection of who they are.

Maintaining our independence ensures that a narcissist will not have the ability to manipulate or control our emotions or ultimately our lives. If we don't reach a sound level of understanding of what is taking place, it is possible that we too will develop traits of a narcissist. Deeply wounded, hurt, and reeling from all the abuse, we may then repeat the cycle of abuse and do unto others as we have had done unto us. Unfortunately, we often attract relationships that feel the most familiar. If all we have known is narcissistic "love," there is a high chance we will attract the illusion of "love" with a narcissist. Narcissists exist surrounded by illusions. Therefore, sadly, a relationship with them is nothing short of an illusion too. We can exist within it if we choose, or we can open our eyes, pick up the pieces, and accept it for what it is.

To heal from the abuse of a narcissist it is essential to realize that we are not the ones who need to carry all the blame. We entered into something with good intentions and we wanted to believe that it was reciprocated. Not everyone has intentions that are mutually considerate, and unfortunately, narcissists are one-sided players. Some people in this world look out purely for themselves. This may take some time for a lot of empaths to fully accept.

After a relationship with a narcissist we must do a tremendous amount of healing work to ensure that we do not either take on some of the wounded traits or attract relationships with narcissists in the future. When we have escaped their clutches, we have survived and we are not a "victim." We are only the victim when we are blaming and shaming the narcissist for how we feel and holding them responsible for our emotions. When we let go of blame and offer forgiveness and compassion instead, we reclaim our personal power and find inner peace.

Although, as adults we are all capable of being consciously aware of how we are behaving, when someone is wounded or their ego is so prevalent it can be very difficult for them to clearly see how their behavior may be harmful. Even if they believe they are consciously aware and in control of their actions they are still under an illusion. What is happening is they are seeing their "truth," although it is very different from the actual representation of the situation. It is not that narcissists aren't comfortable with looking at themselves, they often genuinely don't see they are wrong. And those that do see their behavior as harmful have such a high sense of entitlement and care far more for themselves than anyone around them. They continue on regardless as they believe they deserve whatever they are gaining from any connection, thinking that other people are there to serve many of their needs. (And they think so highly of themselves that they genuinely think that the other person should feel privileged for doing so.) This is the main reason that it is difficult for narcissists to get treatment or to change their behavior, as to change they must first see the original cause and the eventual effect of what they are doing.

It also helps to be mindful of the struggles the narcissist faces currently or ones they may have experienced throughout their lives. As difficult as it is to sometimes acknowledge, narcissists are quite often wounded and in pain themselves and they can't always see how their actions inflict and project that pain on to other people. Hurt people hurt people. Although this is no excuse and I don't think for a moment we need to allow or accept this type of behavior to infect and destroy our lives, I do think that we can try to be open and compassionate to the fact that narcissism is a personality disorder. They do not see things the same way we see them. They don't see their own emotions and feelings with clarity, and neither do they see ours. People behave this way consciously or unconsciously for many reasons, much of which will remain unknown even to the person displaying them. They have unmet needs and clearly require constant validation. They apply negativity and stoop below par to gain satisfaction and what they deem to be fulfillment. As difficult as it may be, we can try not to judge and instead show compassion.

When people are disconnected from their inner selves, everything is turned externally. Although it can often seem as though they just have inflated egos and that they exist on a level far higher than all of those around them, we can still try to understand that it is the detachment from their inner selves that is causing them to feel this way. Whenever someone is focusing on the outer layers, they have no idea about the suffering and trauma that is going on inside, however much they may try to convince everyone differently. When they have no connection to their inner selves, they will find it extremely difficult to connect to any one's inner self too. This is mostly why they do not show regard for any anguish they cause.

In many parts of the world, much of society focuses on external reward and gratification. This can cause people to become conditioned to believe that as long as they are impressing people with their exterior qualities they are "worthy" and succeeding. The more people fixate on how virtuous they look on the outside and how much they impress those around them, the more the cords to their inner selves weaken and the less they feel the need to nourish themselves from the inside out, so they are emotionally wealthy and healthy rather than focusing on these things externally.

Narcissism can be reversed. It is a process, though, it takes some time to unlearn a lot of the egotistical thinking that encourages people to appreciate themselves and other people on the surface rather than for what is underneath. I believe that it is possible for most people to rewire how they think and feel and rationalize and assess core values, morals, and ethics. When we think calmly, considerately, and consciously, we often naturally know what is thoughtful, compassionate, and caring conduct of behavior compared to what is callous, inconsiderate, and cold. Whenever we are mindful, remaining in the present moment, and we are wiling to question ourselves and accept constructive criticism without being defensive or feeling offended, we will start to see that we aren't being personally attacked, and are instead receiving an opportunity for self-growth. Regardless of whether the criticism is right or wrong, we are embracing it rather than rejecting it, and that gives us the opportunity to consider it and think about our expressions.

The key to working on traits that are harmful to either one's self or to others is to remain fully aware and conscious of all actions and the consequences of them.

Although labels can be detrimental, gaining a diagnosis or having a framework that helps us to understand either ourselves or other people on a deeper level can be beneficial for all involved, especially if the person with the personality disorder is willing to work on changing, or if they wish to seek support and guidance.

I personally do not believe that anyone needs to be negatively judged or condemned for displaying these traits, but that compassion and a realistic understanding can be achieved when relating to them. Often people are not even aware that their behavior is harmful to themselves or others and they also may not know how to change.

One of the key traits of people who have personality disorders is that they lack personal insight and are not usually very self-aware, which makes it very difficult for change to occur and is one of the reasons they go through life attracting the same types of relationships and repeatedly stumbling on the same obstacles.

Relationships with people with a personality disorder can work, although, for them to be healthy and long-term both partners need to remove any expectations they may have of what a "normal" relationship should look like, and focus their attention on building firm foundations for the relationship they have. This includes communicating what is acceptable, while still offering unconditional love even if the relationship cannot be continued. For example, for the relationship to work there may be an understanding that compulsive lying, cheating, emotional abuse or violence is not tolerated. The people involved in the relationship can then work out ways to work together on all other issues without negative judgment or resentment creeping in, but if the main outlines are broken, it can be very difficult to maintain a healthy, nourishing relationship. If they are broken, the person who breaks them can help rebuild trust by showing a willingness to change, otherwise, they will very quickly mean very little and it may set up a precedent for them to be regularly flaunted.

It is also possible for the person who does not have a personality disorder to remember that the way their partner is acting is not a personal assault on them. The behaviors they are expressing have often been repeated over and over for so many years that they eventually feel that's the natural way to exist, and it will take time and effort to re-train them to new ways of reacting and responding. It is an unlearning process of everything they have spent their lives learning, so miracles cannot be expected and patience and compassion coming from the non-personality disorder partner will be essential.

There are many support systems in place in a lot of communities and also on the Internet, so I would recommend that advice from a counselor or therapist is sought, whether together or separately. If the person with the personality disorder is willing to take measures to work on the relationship and take accountability for their behavior, this in itself is a major step and as long as it is genuine, and not done just for temporary relief in the relationship, or to gain in any way, there is a chance that the relationship can thrive.

The difficulty with dealing with someone with a personality disorder is that unless we are a mental health professional, it is not our place to diagnose anyone, nor do we need to be judgmental or put someone down who we believe to have a Cluster B (characterized by dramatic, overly emotional or unpredictable thinking or behavior) personality. Neither is it our place to "fix" someone, because unless they want to change, there will be very little we can do.

Perhaps the most unfortunate thing is that most true narcissists will never admit to being narcissistic. They have no idea that their behavior is destructive, so the chance of them contemplating whether they are narcissistic and facing up to themselves is extremely low. After exchanges with narcissists, education and regular affirmations to reinforce how far we have come and our value as individuals is empowering and important. Therapy and support from others who have gone through similar can also help through the recovery process.

Chapter 25

HEALING THE HEART

Falling in love is exhilarating and there is a reason for this. When we fall in love, we also lose control of aspects of our mind. Plus, our body is flooded with chemicals that are produced due to the numerous emotions now swirling around our system. As we fall in love we make a disorientating descent rather than soaring upwards toward a freer elevated version of love.

Falling is associated with physically, emotionally or mentally lowering.

Whenever our body falls and hits the ground hard we injure ourselves physically and experience aches and pains. When we fall ill, it is because our immunity to illness or disease has lowered. Whenever our emotions lower internally we experience anguish and emotional pain. Whenever our hormones or the chemicals in our body fall to low levels or when a dysfunctional situation pulls on us and weighs us down, we suffer psychologically and our mental health levels drop and we struggle mentally.

Yet, we rarely question why we allow ourselves to *fall* in love, especially when we are falling while intoxicated with an elixir of chemicals.

We unconsciously encourage a concoction of emotions to entwine and erupt when we fall in love. Within a relatively short space of time we experience the fear of abandonment if we lose the connection, the excitement of finding someone with whom we share an intense bond, the hope that it is going to last a lifetime and provide us with the fairytale ending that we have been dreaming of. We also go through phases of lust, passion, pleasure, joy, happiness, jealousy and a fair share of heartache and pain. All of these emotions place demands and pressure on love and we are then left in a panic feeling bewildered and shattered when cracks show through and the relationship starts to crumble.

While we fall we associate the drop with love, when really it is lust and attraction that we are experiencing, though we accuse and blame "love" for causing the turbulence. The reason we are suffering is that we are grasping on to threads of love while also clutching at a myriad of other low vibrational entities that, when combined, weigh us down. We put our faith in someone else catching us and providing us with a safe landing. We place an expectation on them to keep us safe from harm and rescue us if we are injured because of the fall, as we think it is partly their fault. We also hope they will protect and save us from being struck and hurt by unexpected obstacles that hit us while we are on the way down.

When we perceive our situation as though we are falling with someone, we may also attach the responsibility for any trauma we endure onto our partner-in-flight. We believe any emotional pain we experience must be their fault as before we fell we were stable—or at least we convince ourselves we were. Basically, when we fall, we become co-dependent as we hope the other person will meet all our needs in the relationship and we also expect exclusivity with the other person. We are essentially more concerned with our own needs than we are with the other persons and yet, we are hoping the other person will satisfy and fill any gaps we feel we are missing. Often, our preconceived idea of love is that it is secure and will deliver us a trusty companion that offers comfort and allows us to escape from loneliness.

We often forget that relationships are unpredictable and there are no guarantees or certainties that whatever we are wishing for will be realized or that the person who we have chosen to fall with will be the one to rescue us if we land awkwardly and need consoling. We forget, that they are also falling and also blinded by the onslaught of emotions flushing through them, so they will not be aware or prepared to take care of all of our requirements as well as their own.

Whenever we fall blindly in love we are not channeling the energy it holds so we end up with high expectations for it, while doing very little work to direct it. We then place a variety of conditions and attachments onto the love and project an imprint as to how we think it should look and feel. The love is then infused with low vibrational emotions such as worry, frustration, anger, disappointment and resentment that pull us down. We enter the fall with the hope of receiving some kind of reward, even if that is just to alleviate loneliness or to fill a void and the illusion of whatever we are hoping for never lives up to the reality. Even if we try to remain positive and revel in the happier moments, the negative emotions will constantly eat away at us and make us feel low and then we fall even lower.

Humans, unfortunately, are not exempt from Takotsubo cardiomyopathy, which is the scientific term for heartbreak. When we subject our minds to emotional pain from stress, heartbreak, or anxiety, a chemical reaction occurs, our blood pressure rises, and our adrenal glands release hormones such as adrenaline and cortisol. If we regularly pump out adrenaline and cortisol, allowing these chemicals to continuously flush through our system, our body will react as though there is a genuine impending threat or some type of danger ahead. This can then lead our brain to spin the situation out of control making us feel constantly alert and wired and can eventually result in paralyzing burnout from emotional or physiological exhaustion. The sooner we ease the pressure of an energetically fractured heart, the better we will feel mind, body, and soul.

Many people have locked down their hearts due to various reasons, but it usually comes back to the same thing: Fear. Love is an addictive feeling. It is highly pleasurable and life takes on new meaning when our heart is full and we feel unstoppable and on top of the world due to love. It is wonderful when we have found someone who we can direct our loving feelings toward. But if they disappoint, reject or leave us, we can be left feeling devastated as we no longer have someone to help us generate this love and to focus our attentions upon. We can also feel as though we wasted our love and time on them and that love is to blame for the withdrawal state we go through when a relationship ends.

The reality is, we do not need another person to be able to generate love. We need no one but ourselves. Even if there was not another human being on this planet, there is still a limitless amount of reasons to feel love. When we are able to see love as a uniquely individual act, and one that needs no other person's involvement, all the fears that are attached to it will dissolve, our hearts will be full, and all of our love will naturally spill out.

Love is not ours to own. When we radiate love, it is just energy that we have narrowly channeled that actually belongs directly to the universe, of which we are part of, but do possess. All we are doing is recycling energy and sharing it around. It really is that simple.

The heart knows nothing of boundaries, separation or judgment. Its sole purpose is to absorb universal energy and generate it into a positive, light but very intense energetic flow. To love in this way can feel painful in some ways, especially when we have a longing to connect our love with another person. The sensation of pure love is like a burning ache in the heart center and it is constantly growing. We can either try to dampen the fire when it rages or we can allow it to rage out of control so that it spreads and touches everyone and everything that we come into contact with.

When relationships break down and fade out it is not because love chooses, quite the opposite. It is fear that decides: irrational, unreasonable, unfounded fear.

Our primal instinct, along with our egotistical driven fears, are afraid of emotional pain and we associate that pain with vulnerability and the feeling of being in love. Mostly, this is because we love the feeling of love and hate the feeling when it ends. However, we don't always realize that it can never end. Even when a relationship ends, we can still continue to send gratitude and love to the person and for the experience, whether it was painful or joyful. We have sole control over our ability to love; it is in no way determined by another person's presence or appearance in our lives.

This can be tricky to understand when we meet other people and feel love bouncing between our hearts, igniting embers of flames that may have been desperately waiting to relight. The intensity of this feeling is intoxicating and we want it to last. We fail to realize that we can experience high vibrational love at any moment of any time, regardless if someone remains in our life, as everything we need to feel love is within. Some people just enter our lives to remind us of the capabilities of our heart and it is then up to us to recognize this and keep that love flowing constantly, regardless of who is around us or what encounters we happen upon.

Even if we meet and marry the first person we date, somewhere throughout the years we will likely be struck by a tragedy that can make our heart feel as though it is crumbling. Sadly, we cannot avoid heartache, nor can we become immune to it. Even if our heartache isn't from a recent crisis, our hearts can hold on to painful nostalgia from previous experiences. Whether we've only known someone a day or a lifetime, the heart wants what the heart wants. When the relationship breaks down, it can leave us with a dull and heavy ache in our chest as we yearn for the lost connection.

Heartache does not only result from relationships, it may be that we have parted ways with a friend, a relative or someone we cared deeply about. If we do not pay attention to what has happened and dedicate time to process the emotions, it can leave us with feelings of remorse, rejection, resentment, and low self-esteem. We then tend to portion the blame to try to make sense of it all. Often we take on the biggest slice of the blame for where things went wrong. We then feel angry and frustrated toward ourselves for the pain we are now experiencing.

Our heartache results from a desperate desire to alter something that cannot be changed. Regardless of whether we resurrected the relationship or connection or not, we cannot possibly recreate the exact experiences that we once had. Nothing remains the same.

We have to remove the need to control every aspect of our own or other people's life. We are all made of constantly changing energy, nothing remains the same, and although this is a difficult concept to accept at times, it is one that teaches us to let go of the attachments we place on people or the situations in our lives. That is why it is important to let go of our grip on the past and put all of our motivation and effort into creating a peaceful present, thus creating a more harmonious future.

Letting go of grief, pain, and any other agonizing emotion is a courageous but very essential process before we are able to fully move on. When we are suffering heartache, one of the most personally destructive things we can do is block out the pain and continuing as though nothing has happened, sweeping it under the carpet, and hoping it will be forgotten. Because, trust me, the pain will sneak back out and force us to come face to face with it when we are least expecting it. It is vital that we remain aware of how we are feeling and allow our emotions to flow through us so that we do not suppress or block them. We can do this without grasping on to them, as that heightens their strength, power, and effect.

Our most powerful enemy when our heart aches is our thoughts. The mind not only plays tricks and holds up illusions, but it also easily falls into a routine of ruminating and obsessing over the same things that keep painful past experiences fresh and raw in our mind. We can learn to take control of our thoughts instead of being controlled *by* them. Our thoughts can become habits that repeat relentlessly in our minds without being questioned or rationalized. We can then easily be tricked as we start to believe our thoughts are our reality, especially when emotions and feelings attach to them, as unfortunately they confirm to our irrational thoughts that what we are thinking must be true, when it is not always the case.

We have to remain conscious, rational, and aware of what we are thinking. If our thoughts are harmful and keeping us trapped in nostalgia, we must change them immediately. Even though it is important to focus our attention on our old, forgotten emotions and feelings, wallowing and repeating them without processing and freeing them are not beneficial in any way.

Thoughts are capable of powerfully lifting or lowering our vibrations as they radiate strong waves of energy. When we ponder happiness or heartbreak, our physical body can lift or lower accordingly. Time is a great healer, although to heal we must look at what caused the injury in the first place so we can discover what beliefs and feelings we are attaching to it and also so that we can try to ensure we don't fall into the habit of repeating the same patterns over and again.

Whenever we are thinking about something that has wounded us, we can then focus our full attention on those thoughts. We will start to notice that emotions are being generated. We can then consciously connect our thoughts and emotions together and *feel* where they originated. There is always a root cause for anything that causes us pain. If we felt abandoned when someone left, it is likely that the abandonment stems from painful forgotten memories from somewhere in our past. If we feel rejected, we were likely rejected previously and we didn't rationalize and let go of that emotion, so when it was presented again the feeling was compounded. The more we experience similar emotions over and again, the more tormenting they become, until we eventually try to switch them off and close our hearts as a misguided form of self-preservation.

Until we organize, rationalize, and heal our past emotional injuries, we will keep attracting and replaying situations until our oldest wounds are acknowledged and healed. Our current traumas are our old trauma's way of demanding attention and declaring that we still have healing work to do. We cannot heal our present inflictions until we have identified our original wounds that are still open, festering and infecting our current moments.

When we see that life is a journey and love is one path that leads us to a greater understanding of ourselves and others, we will find it easier to allow any conflicts to lead us to transformational self-growth. Even though at the time it may all not make sense, when we look back on crises that may have seemed like major emotional obstacles, our mind will clearly see how each encounter slotted into the bigger picture to repair emotional cuts, fractures, and tears. Whenever we feel we are breaking, we can look again. We will then find that we are actually on the verge of a major internal breakthrough.

We know that we are capable of rising in love as when we love our children or a close family member, or for many people, a cherished pet. These are times when we do not fall in love or suffer for the love. Our love is an offering and it inspires joy, harmony, happiness, nurture and growth. Although there may be difficult times, we never look to blame the love or see it as being on a downward spiral or one that we want to separate from. We view any troubles as an aspect of the bond that sits alongside love and we work towards resolving problems so that we build a stronger bond and also so that the dynamic remains secure.

In a romantic relationship, when we fall in love, we often hold the other person responsible for any downward movements and we may relate the drop directly to the love we are sharing with them. If things go wrong we might then shame and blame the other person and try to disentangle ourselves emotionally or physically remove ourselves.

We may automatically think that love is at fault whenever we go through turbulence and we could become infuriated with the other person if they do not live up to our high unrealistic standards and expectations. However, it is usually our own carelessness that has caused us to fall. We jump into what we believe to be "love" without looking where we were going or without first knowing very much about whom we are falling with.

We are the ones responsible if the fantasy we created crumbles away. Love isn't accountable and neither is anyone else. Love will always remain and instead of seeing this we become confused due to the ache in our heart area, which has been caused by our low vibrational emotions such as doubt, jealousy, frustration and resentment and not our high vibrational ones. Rather than falling in love we can rise in love and infuse the dynamic with gratitude, compassion, complete acceptance and freedom. We rise when we are not hoping to receive anything at all from the other person as we are already fulfilled through everything we have offered ourselves. When we are capable of loving ourselves completely, we will not seek others to fill any voids. We will see that no one else is capable of hurting us as any pain that we experience is caused by our own beliefs and mind.

It is then that we rise higher and not only that, our vibration will also lift others around us too. We let go of the expectation of the "perfect love" and offer love unconditionally where it will receive the space it needs to breathe, grow and travel upwards where there are no limitations. We do not offer it hoping it will be returned. We can send out love purely because we love ourselves entirely and the radiation of our love touches everyone around us, not just the one person we have chosen to unite with. The love is then free to fluidly flowing on a high frequency and we will feel as though we are expanding, floating, soaring and carried blissfully along appreciating each moment as it arrives, without looking too far back or forward.

It takes strength to love someone wholly and completely. It takes courage to show up, be vulnerable and to allow our flaws and weaknesses to blaze through so that they receive the opportunity to be held, adored and accepted. It takes a tremendous amount of faith to know that we can love with every cell in our bodies and know that we are going to be okay regardless of whether the love we give is reciprocated or whether someone plays with it or burns it at the stake.

It takes fearlessness to know that we do not need to hold on to love or know what direction it is flowing in. It takes belief in ourselves to know that instead of falling and not knowing whether we will land safely or crash or whether we will face conflict and chaos, there is another option and one that never fails.

It is the simplest thing in the world to love our selves all the way from the inside out and it only takes one moment and happens instantaneously. All we have to do is connect with our heart and feel the sensations of love igniting an inferno in our hearts and warming up on the inside.   Then, instead of falling in love... We can just vibrate highly and *be* love.

All the love we could ever need is ours the moment we focus our attention on it. We never need to look for it in anyone or anything else. Other people's love is a bonus, not a necessity.

When we tap into our own source of love we generate a limitless supply and we naturally rise in it.

"Someday you're gonna look back on this moment of your life as such a sweet time of grieving. You'll see that you were in mourning and your heart was broken, but your life was changing . . ." —— Elizabeth Gilbert

Meditation can be a tool for working through the emotions that heartache conjures up. It won't wipe out all current pain and ancient memories instantly, it encourages us to look at the pain, understand it, feel it, and then process it. Before we begin meditating, we can concentrate on creating waves of love, acceptance, and forgiveness, both for ourselves and the other person. As we are radiating loving energy, we will very quickly feel that similar warm, loving energy rebounding back toward us. Rather than imagining our heart as broken, we can visualize it as being open so that it is able to receive this powerful, loving, healing light.

When we enter meditation, we move to a relaxed state known as alpha. This is the bridge between the subconscious and conscious minds. Meditation takes us away from distractions so that we can slow the mind and calmly and rationally sort through our muddled thoughts. It gives us the opportunity to be still and unravel so we can loosen the tight knots that have been created by overthinking.

This meditation is for balance and will harmonize and dispel blocked emotions. Sit crossed legged or whichever way feels comfortable, with a straight spine. Head slightly lowered. Place the hands in front of the chest, palms lightly together, and thumbs and little fingers touching one another. The middle finger will be in line with the third eye. While deeply inhaling and exhaling, allow all thoughts in the mind to continue for a few moments, floating around. Then notice which thought is repeating continuously. Focus all the attention very briefly on this thought. For just a few moments, acknowledge how the thought makes you feel and then envisage gently blowing it away. Continue this process with all other thoughts that are niggling away at the mind. Allow each of them a few moments, then release them. With deep breathing, the mind will calm and eventually slow down, so the reoccurring thoughts will also settle.

If being beside the sea brings peace, clarity, and calmness, visualize sitting out watching the waves and at the same time repeating, "I feel happy and at peace." Or envisage a huge glowing heart radiating with love and repeat the words "I feel love."

When using affirmations for emotions, try not to use "I am." Instead, use "I feel." We are not one particular emotion, whether good or bad. We are a mixture of emotions at all times. Therefore, when we choose "I feel," instantly our minds associate this with an emotion. We will then feel the sensations that particular emotion evokes.

Meditation is about remaining as much in the present moment as possible. When we are fully present, there is very little suffering felt. Whenever we feel our minds casting back or projecting forward, it is important to gently bring them back to the here and now. As we continue meditating, we will release anxiety and the painful feelings that have been accompanying our thoughts. We can meditate for just a few minutes or for longer depending on how we feel. The more regularly we meditate, the more effective the practice will be.

Once we have completed the meditation, we can transfer this new empowering thinking into our daily lives by remembering our thoughts can become repetitive. The more we think something, the more natural it is for that thought to linger. It is not only the thought that lingers, the emotions that attach to it will also hang around.

When we think good thoughts, we set off our emotions and we can feel good feelings. The opposite is also true. We have the decision to change how we feel simply by remaining aware of our thoughts.

"The emotion that can break your heart is sometimes the very one that heals it." ——Nicholas Sparks

Love dilutes and transmutes our achingly painful sensations. If the heart *chakra* is overactive, we may have no sense of self, feel unworthy, be untrusting, guarded, defensive, and negative toward other people and the world around us. When our heart *chakra* is balanced, we lose attachments to external possessions; we become selfless; we trust ourselves and others; attain peace, wisdom, hopefulness, patience; and we find emotionally stability. Our morals and ethics will be at a high standard. We will be in tune with our conscience and our intentions will be centered, which helps us to stay on track so that our lives head in the right direction. We are also able to make decisions based on our hearts and feelings. By following the heart instead of allowing unfulfilled emotions and irrational desires to intervene, we will attract and accept in our lives whatever aligns with what we truly believe we deserve.

Before we can even begin to offer anyone else profound and absolute love we have to first fully accept and unconditionally love ourselves.

"To love oneself is the beginning of a lifelong romance." —— Oscar Wilde

We can begin to heal the heart simply by forgiving ourselves for all of our flaws, imperfections, and errors. When we let go of the weight that we have been carrying around with us, we are free to live the life that feels right today, rather than being tied to a past that is draining us. We can then begin living aligned to whatever we are passionate about, allowing the heart to lead the way without anxiety or fear intervening.

The heart *chakra* governs how we see ourselves, our relationships, other people, all creatures, and the surrounding world. The heart *chakra* is also where unconditional love is centered. *Chakras* are depicted as colorful circles of energy that highlight the area where their vibrational frequency resides. The fourth *chakra* is the heart *chakra*, also known as the *anahata chakra*, meaning *unstruck*, *unhurt*, or *unbeaten*. It is situated in the middle of the seven *chakras* and is located at the center of the chest and is ruled by the planet Venus, the planet associated with love. The *yang chakra*, which is a positive energy, takes on the role of balancing the lower three *chakras* with the upper three *chakras*.

Unconditional love happens when we love without criticism or placing expectations or judgments on others. We see all darkness and light and we are understanding, thoughtful, grateful and compassionate, which enable us to continue to love regardless.

The heart *chakra* is represented with a lotus and the twelve petals signify elements of humanity: lust, fraud, indecision, hope, anxiety, longing, impartiality, arrogance, incompetence, discrimination, and defiance. The petals are obstacles that we have to acknowledge, understand, and work through so that we can pass them to reach a place of divine and fearless unconditional love.

Wounds that are filled with our deepest insecurities and fears reside around the heart *chakra*. Anything that has caused us emotional pain can get stored in this area, and if we do not clear it, it can become a blockage that prevents love from flowing freely. We will be out of touch with our feelings and struggle to give or receive love. When we are holding on to pain, we are unable to feel emotions fully and we will have a deep fear of being vulnerable. We are afraid that when we open up our feelings they will expose our scars and that will then make us weak or unlovable. We build up walls and protect ourselves from love rather than opening up and letting the pain out and allowing healing energy and love to enter in its place.

Despair, loss, extreme highs and lows, detachment, isolation, panic, fear, and numbness are all psychological stages that are associated with an overactive heart *chakra*. We may be manipulative, irritable, revengeful, pessimistic, controlling, jealous, inconsiderate, unforgiving, and the love we give will be dependent on whether the other person abides by the numerous conditions we set out.

The heart *chakra* is associated with the color green, which is a healing color. The element of the heart *chakra* is air. When we spend time outdoors and with nature we can allow the colors surrounding us to therapeutically stabilize and harmonize our energy while we inhale fresh air. This is why often just by lying down on the grass we feel instantly calmer and more peaceful and we transcend to a natural meditative state. If we are indoors, green lighting or decor can have a soothing effect on the heart, which helps us feel at ease, or we can just close our eyes and visualize the color in our mind.

There are many crystals and gems that can also help to balance the heart *chakra*. Green and pink stones are the two most powerful colors to enhance healing and stimulate the heart *chakra*. We can choose from agate, adventurine (green) alexandrite, beryl (pink), bloodstone (green), calcite (green), celestite, coral (pink), danburite, diamonds, emerald (green), garnet (green), gold, kunzite (pink), malachite, moonstone, quartz (rose pink), tourmaline.

Breathing exercises will also help to clear the heart *chakra*, due to this *chakra* is associated with the element of air. Sitting in an upright position, we inhale deeply through the nose, feeling the belly area expand, and then hold for approximately five seconds. As we inhale, we may feel the chest expanding slightly as this allows the heart *chakra* to open up. While we are pausing, the universal energy stored in our lungs can begin to rejuvenate and recharge our circulatory system. We can then exhale slowly through the mouth before pausing for a few seconds and then repeating. Deep breathing allows the flow of energy (*prana*) to move around the body and helps to relieve any tension surrounding the heart area.

The metta mediation is a Buddhist practice that is often used to assist the opening of the heart *chakra* and allows for unconditional love to occur simply through cultivating the essence of gentle, loving kindness through our thoughts and feelings. Sitting or lying comfortably, we relax the whole body and allow any thoughts to come and go until the mind slows down. Then we can either think of a mantra or phrase to repeat in our mind, such as "May all creatures be at peace," or we can visualize a place where we feel happy and content that invokes a positive feeling. As we stay in this calm setting, we will begin to feel the sensations of good feelings ripple through our bodies and minds. The more positivity we place in our minds, the stronger our bodies will respond to the thoughts. During the mediation we inhale good thoughts and positive feelings with each deep breath and exhale any negative ones.

Once the meditation is complete, we can keep hold of the good thoughts and feelings and express them to those around us through acceptance, forgiveness, oneness, and unconditional love.

"Remember in our inmost being we are all completely lovable because spirit is love. Beyond what anyone can make you think of feel about yourself, your unconditional spirit stands shining with a love that nothing can tarnish." ——Deepak Chopra

Not everyone responds well to high vibrational love, and for some, it can make them feel uncomfortable and they could resist it, and this may result in us feeling ashamed for freely emanating love. Some people may perceive the ability to love freely as a need for a deeper connection. If we tell someone we love them, they may recoil fearing intimacy, believing that what we really meant is that we want to form a lasting mutual connection with them, and they may back away. Free love is not about attachment. It is all about giving without the need to receive, allowing love to expand and re-energize so that there is an abundance of it and so that it can reach far and wide without limits or conditions.

Radiating love, unlike what is often believed, is not a risk. There is no need to fear opening our heart and exposing how intensely we love. Love has no expectations whatsoever, so when we do it without fear we can never lose from sending love.

Heartbreak is a byproduct of fear and not of love. Our fears try to sabotage our ability to love and can cause layer upon layer of worries and excuses so that our heart is locked away tight and unable to function effectively. Suffocating our heart due to our fears is what causes us emotional and also physical pain. We are blocking a very strong and graceful, but powerful energy from being able to radiate outwardly. The heart's energy has nowhere to circulate but within and rather than expanding and travelling outwards, love is contained and frantically trying to look for an escape route.

When we experience love, we also experience the fear of losing it. That is, until we raise our awareness to a height that enables us to recharge love, regardless of whether the love is returned or whether the person who we are directing it toward is even aware that it is being sent. The real key to loving pain-free is to just love, without direction and without control—freely, openly and vastly. When we love in this way, our fears will have no place to reside. They will literally become redundant as we realize there really is nothing to lose or risk through feeling love. We can just love and not worry or care as to whether it is accepted or returned. That is where the real beauty in love is found. Anything else that causes us pain is not love, it is our basic survival instinct and unhealed wounds and it is essential that we stop associating these things with the ability to love.

Many of us find that we block ourselves from radiating love just to make other people feel comfortable. Not everyone will respond well to high vibrational love, and for some, it can make them feel uncomfortable, and this may result in us feeling ashamed for freely emanating love. Some people may perceive the ability to love freely as a need for a deeper connection. If we tell someone we love them, they may recoil fearing intimacy, believing that what we really meant is that we want to form a lasting mutual connection with them, and so they back away. Free love is not about attachment. It is all about giving without the need to receive, allowing love to expand and re-energize so that there is an abundance of it and so that it can reach far and wide without limits or conditions.

Love doesn't cost anything; it is free, and its only need is to feel free. It doesn't matter how much we give out, whether the person we are radiating it to loves us in return, or whether the love we are sending is not even felt when we send it. All that matters is that we don't block the powerful energy center in our heart by having expectations, fears or conditions. We can love someone without them being in our lives. We wildly overcomplicate love, when it really is the simplest thing. Love is infinite. It cannot run out. As long as we breathe, as long as the universe exists, we are capable of continuously generating love.

Love is pleasurable and the intensity of the sensations can feel very similar to pain. Release love back to the universe and notice how the pain immediately dissipates and leaves behind the most incredible and indescribable feeling of joy.

Be love and love freely.

Chapter 26

THE GHOSTS OF ENERGY PASSED

Empaths have the ability to expand awareness so that we are able to view the blueprint of souls. We sense other people's energy and our ability to tap into this energy is not determined by distance or time. Therefore, we can tune in to what has happened in the past, present, or future even if we weren't physically around at the time. This means we are able to pick up on the static stored within repressed or blocked emotions related to the past that are lying dormant in the subconscious and conscious minds.

We can connect with the emotions and thought processes of someone who is in the room at the same time as us, or someone from many years ago thousands of miles away. There are no absolutes with energy. We feel and experience everything in the current moment regardless of when the event took place. Empaths are also able to access hidden memories and repressed emotions that are stored deep within the unconscious mind. When they randomly surface either visibly through words or actions or through the invisible (energy), our observations of these prompt us to conclude the inner emotional and mental state of the person who is emanating them.

This can cause huge difficulties for empaths when in a relationship. We are able to read people's energy as easily as we can read a book. Energy is stored within the cells in our bodies and it vibrates in the atmosphere in our energy field and beyond. Cells in our bodies die off and most take a year to die. Some cells die within a day or four months and others take up to a year, although it is believed that after approximately seven years the majority of the inside of the body has replaced itself. The cells on the outer layer of the brain generally last for a lifetime.

Every minute the average male adult loses approximately 96 million cells and 96 million new ones are replaced. Although it is known that the brain stores all our short and long-term memories, I also believe that all the cells throughout the body hold and store unique information relating to our experiences. Our energy carries its own unique signature and our energy generates and maintains cells and keeps them alive. Therefore, it seems obvious that attached to these cells is also unique data that is capable of being transferred from one person to another as we exchange energy through thoughts, intentions, emotions, and feelings.

Empaths are able to analyze and decode the energy that we are in contact with, so it also means we are able to connect to the emotions someone has felt strongly in their past. This is not always a good thing and it is something most empaths would rather not encounter. It can cause us to go through a great deal of trauma as we consciously, subconsciously, or unconsciously tap into and read the experiences someone else has been through. This becomes particularly more difficult if the person whose energy we are reading is a romantic partner or someone we care deeply about. We are curious souls, so we want to understand what we are picking up on and what has caused any heavy or dense energy to be absorbed in their cells, as it feels natural for us to transmute this energy. We will also sense if the other person has blockages that have been caused by previous heartache or rejection. Sometimes the information we pick up on from previous relationships can hurt us. Generally, we don't want to know the details, as by choice we'd rather that those stored painful emotions weren't there within the other person. However, we cannot ignore it. We want to be in a relationship where the aura is clean and clear so that we can have an intimately close connection and be transparent on all levels. Other people's emotions affect us almost as intensely as they affect the person they are emanating from.

Difficulties usually arise if we ask questions and the truth isn't delivered. Many people believe it is better not to talk about the past, which is understandable; however, the past needs to be processed as suppressing or blocking out experiences is not healthy or beneficial, especially if the energy is impacting current relationships. The emotions will remain stagnant and the obstruction they cause within their own and possibly even our energetic system prevent new emotions from freely flowing so that intimate, romantic, passionate, and overall loving high vibrational emotions can be generated and expressed.

Love is capable of neutralizing and transmuting any negative or painful emotions or experiences, although when someone is guarding and keeping them locked down it will be almost impossible to process and transmute them. So the dense energy will remain.

When we ask a question and the truth is hidden, it generates feelings of mistrust. We know what we sense and our healing instincts want to get to the root of the problem so that we can soothe and eliminate the pain, but when the emotions and feelings are denied we have no choice but to give up. Not everyone wants to open up their soul to us so that we can snip away, cutting cords, releasing pressure, and reenergizing energy. Not everyone believes that our body, mind, and spirit are energetic, and although they may be aware at some deep level that they have lumps of debris stored in their system, they will likely not be forthcoming in offering it to us so that we can clear it, or so they can clear it themselves.

If we ask questions and find out more detail, it can stir these old cells so that they vibrate faster and come back to life. The sensation of this awakening can feel uncomfortable to our partner and it may feel like friction or tension in their system, as they will not know where the irritation is coming from. We will pick up on how they are feeling and this will cause further stress and possibly deeper levels of mistrust. The friction that is felt is caused by confusion and this is because our partner has not fully processed and dealt with their past, and as they are denying the emotions they will not clearly understand why these vibrations are occurring. When we talk about previous encounters with our partner, we reawaken past memories and the sensations feel even more "real" to us as the energy surrounding the experiences becomes much more vivid and intense. We may then become paranoid and believe our partner might still have feelings for another person, when really we are just picking up on cells that are storing old data, which would eventually die out and then be replaced or transmuted. While we may prefer the energy to be cleared sooner rather than later and that our partner is not holding on to past emotional pain, it is not our decision.

Either way, loving memories will eventually replenish, recharge, and replace old tormenting ones. Although it is not easy when someone is not willing to process their emotions, feelings, and beliefs, empaths are capable of neutralizing any negative energy that is stored by transmuting the painful emotions into new ones infused with love. Like with all healing energy, it is always beneficial if the person receiving the high vibrational energy is open to it and willing to also work on clearing blocked emotions. However, we can persist by radiating on a high frequency and within time the other person's repressed lower vibrational energy will lift.

When we "stir" up old emotions we are essentially locating the low vibrational energy by focusing our attention on it, which causes the slowly spinning emotional energy to speed up and spin faster. Whenever something that is lodged spins at a quicker rate, it then has the opportunity to free itself. Healing energy stirs emotions by acknowledging them and in doing so alters their vibrational speed to a much faster one. The emotions can then be processed, transmuted, and we can then let them go.

Basically, if we keep trying to stir up the past with someone who is not willing to confront or acknowledge it or someone who wants to hold on to it, we are fighting a losing healing battle. We cannot force someone to accept healing energy, nor do we need to forcibly direct it where it is unwelcome. All we can do is offer understanding, gentleness, and acceptance and recognize that each person's journey will take its own course for a reason. Not everyone will be willing to evoke memories or deal with their past so that they can clear and flush out the painful energy they harbor. Some people want to hold on to past pain as it feels comfortable to them, and other people are afraid to dig as they don't know what they may unearth. We will not be able to change or avoid this. Old emotions may be attached to their identity and they may also be part of their belief system and unfortunately it will keep them in a self-perpetuating cycle where they will always feel pain whenever something happens that reminds them of it or is associated with it.

If we choose to stay in a relationship with someone who has not dealt with their past, we can try and be patient as the cells will eventually die out. We cannot force someone to confront their past. Even though the energy will be causing blockages, eventually dense energy will dissipate as new high vibrational emotions alter their overall emotions, feelings, and beliefs. The only way this energy lives on eternally is if our partner is holding on to the memories tightly, reliving them and keeping them alive, looking back at them through rose tints without understanding them fully or putting them into context and processing them. This will cause the painful memories to constantly resurface and be a driving force in their life, causing further tension and pain that culminates in emotional or physical aches, pain, or trauma. For an empath, this can cause a lot of unease as we will be constantly picking up this static energy from our partner. It may cause confusion as we will not be able to associate the emotions with our current situation; however, we won't always initially realize that the energy has been stored from the past. It will be difficult to see where it originates from and we will be processing it and clearing it out of our own energy field on a daily basis.

We may go through a similar experience if our own ex-partners are heavily embedded in our cells, and until we make new memories, replenish our cells, or rationalize, process, and transmute the energy, we will also struggle to feel at peace. We will find it difficult to form new relationships as our next partner will pick up on this energy and will become aware that blockages and barriers have built up. If we relive our memories and constantly play them out in our minds, we are adding strength to old cells as when we focus our awareness on something the energy vibrates quicker, giving it more power. We will then be creating new cells based on a false, outdated perception of our previous experiences that will also store similar memories. None of these memories will have a strong correlation to the truth as they will be cloudy and full of illusion, as we do not remember things exactly as they were or see things with clarity when emotions are in play, especially not after the encounter has taken place. This is why it is vital that we regularly flush out stored energy and practice "letting go." Surrendering and allowing everything to pass through sends out a strong message that we are fully in the moment and not gripping on to the past. Frequently letting go is beneficial even if we are in a relationship with someone we care about, so that we do area able to exist without defining the present moment or the future based on everything that has occurred in the past. We can process all our emotions and feelings in the current moment and as our experiences take place rather than holding on to them tightly and allowing them to repeat in unhealthy cycles. As long as we remain consciously aware and alert, we can trust ourselves to absorb what is necessary and release anything that will just cause us numerous difficulties and triggers in the future. When we are mindful and in the moment we can identify and understand our emotions as they arise instead of storing them inside where they will ferment and eventually erupt at some point in the future.

If we are attached to the past, our energy is infused with the energy of people from our past. To live authentically and true to ourselves, it is important that our energy is pure and clear and vibrating on its own frequency, with its own unique signature, and not entangled with the identity of anyone else's. It will be difficult for someone else to freely love us entirely and wholly if we have old stagnant energy or painful emotions that we are holding on to and storing within our cells that are connected to relationships with other people. For someone to know and love us cell-deep, soul-deep, the loving energy that is being exchanged needs to be vibrating freely, pure, and not tainted or being infiltrated by anyone else's dense memories and experiences. When each person is fueled by their own loving energy and they do not have fragments of other people's energy causing discord and distorting their cells, they will be free to harmoniously give and receive love on the highest frequency.

We may also pick up on energy that has attached to certain clothes, jewelry, or even places. Sometimes we may go somewhere and have a heavily loaded feeling and we may find out it was somewhere that holds a significant painful memory from our or our partner's past. Being highly sensitive to energy can be challenging when there is still a lot of emotion and wounded energy tied up.

When empaths love, we love completely and want to experience it authentically and intimately. This means, if possible, we would like to merge energies with our partner and explore their soul without finding the obstruction of ghosts from the past that still linger around and haunt them. If the energy has been processed and cleared from our partner's electromagnetic field, it will likely not affect us. It is usually when there is still an attachment between the person we are with and their previous relationship/s that we sense friction and disharmony within their energy. If we have let our own past go, we will not feel at ease with anyone else's hanging around us either. We have to trust our inner knowing, as it tells us far more than we give it credit for. We have no option as we struggle when trying to ignore it and it doesn't' just disappear. These feelings aren't ones of jealousy but an impulse to eliminate the skeletons that are hanging around in our relationship and causing trapped energy to barricade energies and create distance. It is an uncomfortable feeling to sense that an ex or even exes are still trapped in the energy body of someone we are intimately involved with as these energies prevent deep levels of intimacy and closeness.

The difficulty is, if we ask questions, we then pick up on the energy that comes through with the answers. Therefore, we will know if someone is not being honest or if there is a far more to it than what they are telling us. We can either choose to accept that they still have intricately tangled and knotted energy, or we can disengage if we feel that it will be unlikely that we will get the connection we crave and we can then walk the path alone and see what awaits us along the way. For an empath, it is never going to be easy staying in a relationship where there is an accumulation of energy that tells us that our partner is caught in the past rather than surrendering to the present. We will struggle to turn a blind eye or ignore it. Past partners are never a problem and energy will always exist, and as long as there is peace and understanding without continued illusions, this energy can carry a very high vibration. It is when there is still so much low vibrational debris stored and held within both the physical body and the energy field that difficulties arise.

As empaths we can try to be sure that it is not our thoughts playing tricks on us as; otherwise, we can develop symptoms of paranoia that can be very difficult to deal with. We have to be sure that our intuition, our inner knowing feeling, is picking up on the right information and that it is not just fear, anger,or knowledge we have about the past that is bringing forward the conclusions. When we keep our mind open and our senses aware, we will be able to scrutinize the incoming information so we can see what is coming to us rationally and what is coming through fear. Fear can totally cloud our judgment. And if we are processing our energy with fear, we can try not to automatically trust how we are feeling. Fear is exhausting and crippling and attaches many other emotions to it on its journey; e.g., jealousy, resentment, frustration, anger, and despair. It is vital that before reading energy we clear out any preconceived ideas or misconceptions we may have so that we can absorb and translate the data without emotions interfering.

When we are able to recognize the emotions that occur within us, we can then look at what thoughts or feelings have triggered the sensations. We can allow our emotions to come and go without holding on to them so that they can be released before we consider if the information we are receiving from our partner is based on reality or on how our emotions are causing us to feel. We can easily become susceptible to paranoia if not. Empaths are just as capable of being paranoid as we are capable of reading energy. We can still get caught out when we have not worked through our own past encounters. For example, if we have been hurt in the past we may just be scared that we are going to be hurt again. Although we are excellent at reading energy, we cannot rely on our feelings alone. We can only fully trust that we are reading situations correctly when we are grounded, centered, clear of loaded emotional charge, and have removed any prior beliefs that may influence how we feel. For example, if our partner has been unfaithful previously, we may automatically be drawn to presume they may cheat again. We may then interpret the energy we are feeling and wrongly believe that this is how our partner is also feeling or what they are experiencing when essentially what is happening is we are projecting our own feelings onto them, and then when we read that energy back we believe it to be our partner's (not realizing we are just reading our own thoughts and feelings). Therefore, we are paranoid and projecting and not reading our partner's energy at all.

People who suffer with paranoia are often creative and have vivid imaginations, and it is the imaginative mind that can serve to ignite delusions and paranoia, which cause envisioned scenarios to feel vividly realistic. When low self-esteem is present, it is quite possible that we may become convinced that we do not deserve anything good to happen in our lives, that we are not worthy of being in a relationship with our partner or that our relationship is sure to fail. The fear of losing a relationship can become so great that we may struggle to cope and instead of waiting to see what will happen in due course, we allow other feelings to creep in, such as paranoia.

It is not always possible to differentiate paranoia from genuine fear, so it is important to fully understand our fears, anxieties, and other emotions and address the issues so that we can work out if how we are feeling is a true reflection of our situation. Otherwise, we may find ourselves becoming controlling, obsessive, and feeling like we need to be aware of every movement our partner takes. We may also try to observe changes in their energy, falsely believing that we can avoid any betrayal or future disappointments taking place.

There may be situations where the paranoia has a base of truth; in this case, we need to look at the facts presented with a calm and clear mind and trust our knowledge and also our inner knowing sensations so that we can make a rational judgment, rather than one based on fear and insecurity. Paranoia is a feeling that can creep in to relationships without us realizing it is there. Therefore, what we think is reality and what actually is reality can be two very different things. The more energy we give to negative thoughts, the more our fears begin to feel real. As our mind repeats the negative thoughts and emotions so regularly, they eventually feel realistic and we fully believe that something bad is going to happen.

When we meet someone for the first time, we do not always have the same deep-rooted emotions that exist when we are further down the relationship path and when we are closer and more intimately involved. As relationships progress, our feelings often grow stronger and the fear of losing the relationship can grow more intense, with anxieties, worries, doubts and insecurities kicking in. All of these emotions can bring on bouts of jealousy, which can then lead to feelings of paranoia. Doubts can occur, which make us wonder if our partner is honest, faithful and loyal. If these questions repeat in our minds they can cause us to look for information to warrant, clarify, and confirm what we perceive as our "inner knowing." When this happens the mind is often not rational as it can be flooded with fear, which clouds our thinking. Therefore, any small piece of information we find can compound tremendously our already petrified mind. However, at this stage we might be looking for confirmation, so any evidence that may be found to dispute the fears may be ignored and cast aside in favor of more incriminating evidence. We don't want to be proved wrong, so we convince ourselves with scraps of information pieced together to confirm there must be some truth in how we have been thinking.

When feeling paranoid, we can begin to analyze everything and everyone that crosses our path to further strengthen the debate that is going on in our mind. We can frantically try to find bits of information to prove that the feeling we are experiencing is a gut feeling and that our intuition is not wrong. However, often it is not the gut feeling that is presenting the messages to our mind, it is our irrational and fearful thought processes.

At some level we want to feel perfectly justified in continuing with this damaging behavior, so we set out to prove that our partner cannot be trusted. Paranoia can turn us into emotional wrecks if we allow it to and it also has a negative impact on our self-esteem. It can lead us to search through drawers, pockets, e-mails, check call histories, and spy on our partner. There is no limit to the levels that someone will go to when paranoia has taken a strong hold. It is a tormenting and destructive feeling that can literally eat away at us from the inside out, and instead of getting better over time, if we allow it to fester, it can get worse until it takes over every waking thought.

It is possible to retrain the way we think so that when a negative thought comes along we can notice how it feels for a moment and then learn to let it go. If the thought reoccurs, we can ask if it is justified. Using the knowledge we have, we can make a calm and rational decision without emotions becoming involved so that we can work out if the threat is real or false. If it is false, we can quickly replace the thought with a more positive and loving one and repeat it over and again until we feel calmer and able to let the irrational one go. If the thought is a rational one and needs to be acted upon, we can try to wait until we are not flooded with emotion so that we can decide on the best course of action.

When we work through feelings of paranoia with focused awareness we can raise our self-esteem and gain a greater understanding of the cause and effects of the paranoid feelings that are surfacing. When we look closely at why this has happened, we can begin to get a better understanding of ourselves and also a clearer picture of our relationship. When emotions run deep, we can sometimes act out of character and behave in ways that we don't recognize. However, when we are true to ourselves and confront the feelings, we can begin to take steps to work out what is causing the feelings and discover whether they are genuine or fear led. If we talk about one of our emotions out loud (to ourselves) we will be able to feel the vibration that is held in it. When it is voiced, does it ring true? Or does it sound and feel ridiculous and does not resonate in any way whatsoever? We can probe and question why we feel a certain way, and if our inner knowing sensations are not providing any reasonable answers, it will likely be an irrational, ancient, or wounded emotion that we can choose to let go of. If we cannot make any sense of our emotions, they are probably not holding any value. Our inner knowing has access to such a vast amount of information that if there were any truth to the emotion, it would be able to clarify why we are feeling it.

When we become fully aware of how and why we are thinking and feeling certain ways, we instantly gain some control. When we feel a negative emotion occurring, we can remain still, take a look at it, listen to what it is telling us, and instantly we will feel differently about it. The earlier we catch hold of the emotion, the better chance we have of rationalizing with it, irrespective of how futile or serious the associated feeling may be.

Often, when we are paranoid the situation will get progressively worse due to poor communication and a break down in trust. Therefore, clear communication is vital in resolving any issues. Talking through our greatest fears and insecurities with our partner can assist in bringing the relationship closer rather than tearing it apart. If we have an understanding partner, we can work at resolving any problems together, creating a stronger, deeper, and more supportive relationship. However, it is also imperative to work on our issues alone so that we resolve any inner conflicts that may be ongoing.

If we have a sincere and supportive partner, they will be worth their weight in gold, and the bonds that are created through working out issues together will strengthen the relationship in the long term.

Chapter 27

HONESTY

Empaths will most likely place honesty at the top of the list of qualities we look for in another person. This is partly due to the fact that we usually say whatever we mean. Generally, empaths are loyal and trustworthy, so we look for the same in return. One of the most frustrating things for an empath is that we know when someone is lying to us as the energy that is expressed with the lie causes us friction, although we sometimes can't figure out exactly why. This can cause arguments to flare up, which then lead to accusations and on to resentment. Our senses will tell us more than we want to know and sometimes for the sake of peace and harmony we refuse to believe the messages we receive and turn a blind eye. Our niggling doubts don't go away, though, and this is frustrating as we so badly want to find people whom we can trust without any doubt. We don't want to have to think twice about our partner's motives if we begin to feel sensations that signify that something is wrong. We don't want to consider whether they have an agenda, what they have been up to, or if what they are saying is true. We are hoping for honesty, authenticity, and complete and utter trust. And when we don't receive it, we will just know that everything is not as it seems.

We will all have been lied to on numerous occasions, and no matter what the other person was saying or how they were acting, as empaths we will still know deep down if something isn't right. Sometimes we find that we believe the person at the time and it isn't until we have had time to decipher all the information that the truth sinks in. We will have an uneasy feeling and know that there was far more to what has been said to us than what met the eye. This is usually because of the amount of energy that was circulating around us at the time.

It is not always easy to discern what is true when emotions and feelings are heightened and possibly even conflict is taking place. Although we try to trust our instincts, it isn't always easy when we are told that our suspicions are wrong. With no proof, sometimes we try to accept that what someone is saying is the truth but the friction will constantly linger in the back of our mind.

If and when trust is broken, we may continue with a relationship, and expose ourselves to the possibility of further hurt. However, we will begin to build a protective wall around ourselves. Plus, we will be tempted to subject our partner to a million and one questions to try to establish where the truth lies and also to settle our inner friction that has alerted us that something is not right. If trust diminishes, so too will our relationship as we will drift further apart until one day we may unexpectedly sever the cords. The main contributors to ending a relationship is due to feeling unloved or if the trust has been broken and we have suffered a painful betrayal. If it weren't for these things we would likely stay relentlessly through thick and thin.

Being able to completely trust our partner is the one component that is vital for a solid and healthy relationship. Suspicion and jealousy are two shadow traits commonly associated with an empath, and although we try to master these emotions and we can learn a lot about ourselves when we do, we will not willingly put ourselves in situations where these things are going to consistently bubble to the surface and trigger us through deceit and mistrust. Our ideal relationship is one where both partners are trustworthy so that there is a lot of freedom and plenty of space to breathe on both parts.

Empaths thrive on honesty and integrity. We all make mistakes, tell lies, and trip up many times, even when we have a very strong sense of what is right or wrong. When we do fail to make the right decisions, we will do whatever we can to reroute so that we see our errors and so that we don't fall over the same obstacles time and again. We are usually brutally honest, though we are genuine and sincere with it. We are rarely honest with the intention of hurting someone. Instead, we believe our honesty is what encourages others to share in a way that offers a divine, rare, original, and genuine friendship. We are also aware that there are many versions of the truth, ours is just one shared. There are many levels and dimensions of reality and they are all determined by individual perception. The more aware and awakened we are, the more we are able to witness and perceive all things authentically.

We will most probably say exactly what we think, explain in detail how we feel, and act in ways that are reflections of our authentic selves. We also realize that our willingness to share and speak frankly is one of the reasons we can be misunderstood or ostracized. Not everyone wants to hear or can see the reason for our need to articulate and express how we perceive things. Our words and actions will most likely come from a place of love and with good intention attached to them. One thing empaths do not do very well is fake. Game playing and manipulation are not our strongest points, purely because we don't understand the rules. So if we have something to say, we say it and then can often become confused and entirely bewildered if someone says we have spoken out of line or turn.

Not only are we able to work out whether someone is telling the truth or not, we are also aware if someone is thinking negative thoughts or feeling low frequency emotions. The energy that people send out delivers all the information that we need to decode and work out what is being hidden behind silence, words, or actions. The time this may catch us out is when the person who is hiding the truth is exceptionally good at deception and therefore they believe their own lies. This is why we must keep our energy attuned to theirs so we can instinctively sense the subtle sensations that signify where there is dishonesty. People may hide their innate selves and mask their emotions by portraying themselves on the outside as very different from what they are thinking or feeling on the inside. This is largely due to society's demands that everyone behave in ways that fit in with the silently agreed norm. However, if we keep our senses alert, we have the ability to detect when someone is not being honest with themselves or with us. We also have the natural ability to make these people feel at ease through acceptance and understanding.

It is very common for people to hide their true feelings and display an image that is very different from one that is being felt beneath the outer layers. Since childhood we are taught to behave in certain ways that are considered acceptable and we are also told to control our emotions. By the time we reach adulthood, we are masters at hiding how we really feel and are skilled in the art of emotional deception. Humans often subconsciously alter their outer expression to influence how they are seen rather than show the emotions that are often considered ugly or unpleasant. They regularly hide who they are by adapting how they are seen so that it suits other people's expectations or possibly even to manipulate circumstances. This way of behaving seems to work well for many, as society prefers that we appear well balanced and that we refrain from showing our shadow emotions such as fear, resentment, jealousy, anger, or disappointment. A lot of people can exist within this framework no problem at all until they come across an empath or someone who is highly sensitive to energy.

At first we can be confused by the mixed signals we receive, though when we tune in to the energy radiating we make sense of it by paying finer attention to the friction felt in the vibrations rather than what is being displayed to cover up true intense emotions. We do not generally censor ourselves to suit others and we freely express how we feel.

We are able to sense when someone is hiding their inner pain behind a wide smile or when their laughter is quelling their tears. Through showing compassion, acceptance, offering understanding, and by being nonjudgmental we can help others to feel comfortable enough to allow their inner selves to show through. This allows them to accept themselves enough so that their true character traits and the core of their being radiates to the surface without the need for charades.

We prefer the truth above all else, and when someone opens up and is brutally honest about what exists beneath the shell, all we witness is striking beauty. We will not see any flaws, imperfections, or faults. We find the other person's difficult decision to battle and overcome the fear of being vulnerable, inspiring, empowering, and it leaves us in awe. Exposing a glimpse of our natural selves and continuing regardless of the terrifying risk of being judged is not always easy.

Being deceived is extremely hurtful to an empath, as honesty is something we place in very high regard. When people are not straight to the point with us or when they withhold their true feelings, we can become frustrated as we are able to clearly see what is going on. Empaths are often known for being too honest. We will not understand the reason for hidden agendas or little white lies. We genuinely believe that through honesty comes trust and trust builds a solid foundation for relationships to thrive on. If it were up to empaths, everyone would tell everyone everything and there would be no need whatsoever to withhold anything back. Although this may sound terrifying to many, it would likely be an empath's ideal way to live: delivering the absolute truth with no judgment placed on it.

The ideal situation for an empath is one whereby everyone can lay out their souls and allow them to be transparently viewed with acceptance, love, and without being judged, condemned or criticized. Often, though, people do not want to hear the truth. The truth can be difficult to handle at times and it can also be hurtful. Although the truth can sometimes be painful, for an empath being dishonest is agony in comparison. We are able to handle most things that come our way when delivered with honesty. We are thoughtful, understanding, and forgive easily, so we crave a connection with someone with whom we can express those things with and also with whom we can be our genuine selves.

We do not just listen to the words that are spoken, knowing they only make up approximately 7 percent of communication. We are observant and pay close attention to body language, eye contact, the speed of words, the tone, the pitch, and the volume of the voice, although more than any of this we translate what is being said through absorbing and decoding the energy that is vibrating all around us. When someone is speaking we tune in to the heart center to see if energy is radiating from there and whether someone is heartfelt and authentic in their expression. It also helps to focus on the third eye area so our intuitive abilities are heightened.

Although energy is invisible, it is the most effective form of communication for an empath. Alongside all the sensory clues is the energy that people carry with them. Within that energy is an abundance of information that tells us everything we need to know. When we focus carefully, pay attention to the details, and then allow everything to settle, we can see the line between the truth and a lie. The trouble is, because our thoughts can play tricks on us it may be difficult to be 100 percent sure. We will never know exactly what is going on in the mind of another, their reasons for lying, or what fraction of the truth is being presented. However, there are many ways to spot the most obvious signs that someone is lying without having to look too deeply. When we are aware of the signs, we can couple that with our inner knowing and use all the data we receive to come to a balanced and rational conclusion.

Although many empaths who are in tune with their inner knowing will not need to study visible signs to know if someone is lying, there are many who have been taught to believe that their inner knowing is wrong and that they should not rely on it. We then lose faith in the ability to trust what we know. Therefore, by studying clues we can strengthen our inner knowing by backing it up with the subtle visual alterations that are taking place. Eventually we will not need to focus on the visual at all and we will implicitly trust in our inner knowing. We observe body language and notice that when someone is crossing their arms over their body, crossing their legs, or leaning away from us it may mean that they are keeping something from us. If their body language is open, they are far more likely to be open with their emotions and feelings too. Also, if someone is agreeing with something we are saying, they are more likely to empathize and mirror our body language. The words that are spoken only make up a small percentage of communication. The rest is made up of body language, eye contact, speed of the words, the tone, the pitch, the volume of the voice and their energy. Rather than just trusting the words we are being told, we can allow our senses to alert us to the truth. However, as well as senses, we can also look out for some of the more obvious signs that come into play when all is not as it seems.

- Cheeks - One of the first signs that a lie is being told is when a little color flushes to the fleshy part of the cheeks. A few reasons blood runs to the cheeks are due to anxiety, distress, and mostly embarrassment.
- Voice - Usually the tone will be a slightly higher or lower pitch than how they normally speak. Also, the speed of the words may differ from usual, either rushing or slowing down words, which can signal a lie. They may also speak a lot more than normal or barely speak at all.
- Licking the lips - Telling a lie can put stress on the body. It causes the mouth to dry up, which can result in the person needing to wet their mouth by licking their lips or moving their tongue around their mouth. The mouth may also appear tense and they may clear their throat regularly as saliva is being pumped from the mouth. Also, the breathing may increase as the lungs require more air due to the heart pumping more rapidly and the body being put under intense pressure.
- Body language - Someone lying may move their hands toward their face to cover their mouth slightly when talking. They may also shrug their shoulders as though the body is not agreeing with the words that are being spoken. Basically, the body will be disagreeing with what is being said. If the head shakes or nods in opposition to the words being spoken, that can be another sign that the body and mind are in disagreement. If a person is folding their arms across the body, making fists, or clasping the hands together, these can be signs of wanting to protect something. They may also *cover their body* with something, such as a cushion, a cup, a book, or piece of clothing, as this is another form of seeking protection. However, it may also be because they are trying

to cover their *chakra* to prevent absorbing or leaking energy for a genuine reason. Someone who is lying might also turn their head or even their body in an opposite direction rather than stand face to face.

- Excessive fidgeting is another sign that a lie is being told as when the body is under stress it expels nervous energy, which is expressed through constant movement. They may rub their fingers together, play with their hair, touch, their face or anything else that is within reaching distance far more than they normally would.
- Sweating - When the body is under any kind of stress, often it responds with perspiration.
- Eye contact - Either prolonged eye contact can take place in order to be convincing or no eye contact at all so that they avoid being caught out with obvious eye movements. While these can both be strong signals, too much attention does not need to be paid to this as it will depend on the person's normal eye activity. Some people dislike eye contact in any situation, so eye contact is only a valid form of detection if it is very different from normal.

When a person is lying they often find *the need to overexaggerate details* to make what they are saying sound believable. They may give out far more information than is necessary as a way of trying to prove that what they are saying is true. They may also *respond immediately* to a question before they've even had time to think about what's been said as all too often someone who is lying has already rehearsed a given response. If they repeat the question that they are being asked out loud and add a yes or a no at the beginning or end, this can also be a sign they are lying. For example, a reply to the question "Did you go to the cinema?" can be "Did I go to the cinema? No." Again this needs to be compared with how they would normally speak before assuming that it's an unusual response.

Someone who is lying may also very quickly *try to change the conversation* surrounding the lie, or not wish to discuss it further if the subject is not brought up again. Asking someone to repeat the story might also bring in more clues, as someone who is lying often doesn't remember exactly what they said and therefore may tell things quite differently the second or third time around, adding conflicting information.

Focusing on just one clue when we think a lie is being told is pointless. It is better to look at the energy and behavior as a whole rather than honing in on one or two details. Although it is possible to detect when someone is being dishonest, it is also possible to be mistaken about dishonesty if the person is already experiencing levels of distress, embarrassment, or if they feel under pressure. It is always a good idea to consider the motives for suspecting that a lie is being told. Do we already mistrust this person? Have they lied continuously in the past? Has something happened out of the ordinary that we think doesn't make sense but it is perfectly possible that it has happened? Are we feeling insecure in ourselves and so we turn that outward onto the other person? Are we prejudiced against the other person for whatever reason?

The issue may not be with the person at all, but with our own misplaced judgments, so it is always beneficial to question ourselves before we doubt another. We also must remember not to take lies personally. Even though we may feel hurt about something that is taking place, we also must remember that other people's behavior is a reflection of them and not us. Often lies are being told in order to avoid causing some form of pain or irritation to the other person. Unfortunately, it is often the lie itself that causes far more pain than the initial subject matter would have.

Depending on our perceived reaction to what happens if we tell the truth, it can determine whether we are honest or whether we choose to cover something up. If we think the truth will be taken badly, it can make the possibility of telling a lie increase dramatically in the hope that the lie will be believed and everything will quickly return to normal. Unfortunately, if a lie is not accepted, it can lead to broken trust, resentment, and a loss of respect toward the other person.

When we know the basic signs that someone is lying, we can add them to the sensations rising from our inner knowing so that we have more faith in our instincts. We won't need to ask the other person if we are being led into a delicate web spun with the most intricate lies. We will find that we just know with no more questions needing to be asked. We won't need to debate what we are told. We don't need to feel upset, frustrated, angry, or any other soul-sucking emotion. We won't need to argue, fret, or worry. We can hear the other person out and not get into any kind of argument or suspicious questioning and just listen to what our intuition/inner knowing feeling is telling us and we can allow the information to guide us.

If something doesn't feel right, it is most probably because it isn't.

Chapter 28

CUTTING ENERGETIC ATTACHMENT CORDS

Whenever we lovingly bond with someone, attachment cords (energetic ties) are created that travel from our heart *chakra* to the other person's heart *chakra*. We also connect cords from solar plexus to solar plexus, as this is the *chakra* directly related to our emotions. When these cords have developed for purposes other than a heart or soul connection, the cords could be anywhere in the body. There may be numerous cords and they may be in various shapes, strengths, and sizes.

We also attach cords to other living creatures or even to material objects and places. When cords have been created, we then have direct access to another person's emotional, mental, spiritual, and physical states, and the intentions and capabilities within each one. Overall, we will have a strong link that enables a transfer of energy.

We may decide to cut cords when we have been unable to let go of an attachment. This could be due to obsessively thinking about someone, still feeling remnants of pain due to old memories, repeatedly arguing over the same issues, feeling resentment or bitterness due to a past grievance, feeling tied in or drawn toward someone as though they have a hold over us and overall finding it difficult to move on and start over. There could be thousands of reasons for cords becoming attached and also for wanting to sever them; however, the process for detaching them will still be the same.

The cords can be beneficial, neutral, or detrimental, so it is up to us to tune in to the cords and work out who we are connected to and understand how those connections are affecting our energy. Our *chakras* send out cords continuously as they radiate vibrations toward people. Depending on how healthy and how low or high our vibration is, the cords can represent genuine intentions, positive emotions, and higher love, or they can be infused with manipulation, selfish intentions, and they could be assisting energy vampires in depleting our energy.

When we attune to the vibration of the cords and pay attention to the sensations within our physical body and energetic field, we will easily recognize the difference between healthy and unhealthy connections. Healthy, high vibrational cords are connected to our energy field and are found radiating from our aura. They do not pull in energy but the energy they radiate is extremely powerful and offers unconditional love, humility, care, kindness, compassion, and spiritual growth. Healthy cords have a very light, pure, and clear vibration, and they are also known as "spiritual ties." They are located in our energy field and will not be causing any pain or discomfort.

Unhealthy, low vibrational dense cords are connected to our physical body and are based on dysfunction and are created due to things such as desire, control, fear, anger, abandonment, frustration, rejection, resentment, insecurity, and material or financial benefits. The cords feel thick and heavy and their vibration is dense. They will likely feel tender and the area around them may ache. Even if it is only a subtle sensation, we will notice it when we draw our attention to it. If there has been trauma or heartbreak associated with the cord, the pain will keep repeating on us until we are ready to release it and let go of all the associated memories.

Deciding with our head that we want to move on from previous experiences is not always enough. We need to energetically disconnect emotions and feelings and really believe and feel that we are ready and want to make the break. If we do not sever the ties, we will keep getting caught up in low frequency relationships, which is why we attract similar types of people or the same kinds of relationship over and again. We will still be feeling the same emotions that are associated to past relationships as these cords are keeping us connected to the past. Therefore, we will end up projecting all of our historic emotions and beliefs onto our new relationships, not realizing that we are still being fed from previous occurrences.

We attract what we put out, and if what we are putting out is unhealthy, full of karmic residue, and has a low vibration, we will connect with others who also have a similar vibration and we will become entangled in the same types of relationships that we have been involved in in the past.

Sometimes the cords are mutual and have valves going each way so that energy is relayed and received. Other times they have a one-way valve that gives out energy but receives no return flow. If we are in a relationship and we are sending out waves of energy but not receiving a flow in return, it is likely that we are involved with someone who is emotionally unavailable and if we continue to do this without regularly recharging our own energy we will very quickly become drained.

Often energy vampires connect cords to us without us realizing it. When they do this they are able tap in and take our energy whenever their reserves are running low and they need a top up. This will continue until our awareness has detected it and we consciously make a decision to remove the cord.

When our energy is vibrating highly, our aura will be strong and well protected, so it will be far more difficult for anyone to connect cords to us without our awareness or feed from old cords that may have previously been in place. A high vibration is always the best form of protection as not only does it ensure there are no gaps in our energy field where dense cords can sneak in, it also means our loving, light, high frequency will transmute any negative energies that are associated with any existing unhealthy cords.

Cords can provide us with a detailed insight that enables us to read someone else's energy clearly and also so that we can send out and receive emotions. Cords also enable us to communicate easily and just *know* information about the other person without receiving any words or actions that express how they think or feel. However, they can drain and deplete us if we are radiating too much energy or if the other person is aware that a cord is in place and their impulse is to draw on whatever is available so they can take without giving anything back, especially if it is from someone who has led us to believe they have good intentions for a relationship when really they have no desire to establish anything meaningful.

There are often illusions and misconceptions around the people that we are connected to and cords may have been created without us realizing how detrimental they are. If an energy vampire has connected a cord to us, they may be depleting us without us realizing it. The cord may not be at the heart or anywhere obvious as vampires are skilled at their game, so we have to scan the body meticulously to find where the entrance to the attachment cord is and we also have to scan to see how many they have connected. The cords may resemble fine threads and these ones are more difficult to detect. However, there may just be one very large cord or numerous cords in all sizes with each one being associated with a different person or conflict.

Often, people aren't consciously aware that cords are in place and our energy can be given or taken without us realizing it. When we cut the cords to those we are or were connected to, the other person may notice that they have been severed, so they may be drawn to contact us to see if they can put new ones in place as they are no longer receiving an energetic supply from us. If we don't either consciously or subconsciously disconnect or cut unhealthy cords to our past, we will continue to repeat patterns of behavior and be caught up in the same cycles in our new relationships.

If we have poured a lot of emotion, time, and energy into a relationship the bond could be particularly strong; therefore, the cord will also have resilience and strength. We may not be fully ready to make a cut, as even if we consciously think we are our emotions could be causing conflict by sending out a different message. Therefore, it may be necessary to look at the root cause of the attachment and resolve any open issues that reside there. Often we have underlying feelings that are drawing us toward the person and we may be thinking or wanting to be over them but our repressed or hidden emotions are sending off an entirely different signal.

Sometimes we want to cut a cord with someone so we can detangle ourselves from any negative interactions and emotions but we do not want the person to physically leave our lives. When we remove these low frequency cords, we can still remain connected to the person but the dynamics will change. Instead of subconsciously repeating the past, we can disconnect our energy and allow the opportunity for new cords with a high, loving vibration to attach.

This process can be used in current relationships that have previously had history where difficulties have occurred. We may feel triggered to argue over the same thing continuously, and in these cases we can locate the cord/s that are influencing our emotions and causing us to instinctively react. Our relationship will not suffer when we cut these types of cords, only the negative aspect of the relationship will be eliminated.

We may have to cut the cords that cause unhealthy emotional interactions more than once as the presence of the person may continuously keep pulling particular feelings to the surface. Their presence can strengthen any old cords that we may have missed or possibly even create new ones. Not only do we need to repeatedly cut these cords until this repetitive negative behavior stops, we will also need strong will power so that we do not fall into the trap of responding and reacting in the same way as we may have done in the past. We can also look at the root of the problem to decipher what is causing the negativity to arise in the first place.

Before cutting cords, it is essential that our mind is rational, calm, and clear and that our vibration is high so that we do not negatively influence the process and also so we can radiate loving, compassionate, and healing vibrations. Meditating beforehand will ensure our mind is balanced and we are also grounded during the process. We can then protect our auras to ensure that we are not invaded by dark energy while going through the procedure, particularly from the source of the cord that we are disconnecting from. It is also beneficial to forgive ourselves and the other person for whatever part has been played so that we are not leaving remnants of resentment, retaliation, anger, or bitterness behind, or allowing space for new detrimental seeds to be planted.

We can set the intention to permanently remove the cords for the higher good, for ourselves and also for the other person. To locate the cords, we need to use our intuition to guide us, as the majority of suppressed emotions that are connected to the cord are deep within our unconscious mind. When we have located the exit area of the cord, we can also focus on exploring the reason for its existence. When we raise our awareness and shine a light on the cord, we can gain an in-depth insight into why it is there and what emotion or belief of ours allowed it to attach to us. We can imagine the cords as though they are weeds that need to be pulled out by the roots to prevent them from growing back. We can also ensure the soil is healthy so others can't pop up in their place. Depending on how well we look after and nourish ourselves, the garden will be clear and weed/dense-cord free or there will be weeds/dense cords scattered everywhere. When we gain a profound understanding as to why the cords are in place, we cannot only remove them, but also prevent them from returning.

The main place negative and dysfunctional cords will be felt is in the physical body, although they will run through our energetic field and also be felt in our aura. Cord cutting is done using visualization by focusing on one cord at a time. When we scan the entire body and focus on our sensations, we will notice the dense energy that is associated with the cord so we can easily locate where the most significant and powerful one is attached.

It is quite common when cord cutting to call upon the assistance of Archangel Michael. An angel will only assist if our intentions are pure and for a higher purpose. However, the process can be carried out without using divine intervention, and if need be, we can ask someone we fully trust or someone advanced at cord cutting to sever the energetic cords if the procedure is too emotionally traumatic for us to do alone. If we prefer, the angel or a friend or guide can just be there at our side to offer comfort while we go through the motions, whatever option feels better at the time. If we are comfortable doing it alone, that is absolutely fine. What matters most is how we feel about it, so we can choose whatever feels most natural.

The reason for the divine intervention of Archangel Michael is because he radiates profound love for humanity and he carries with him a blue-flamed powerful sword. The sword carves straight through dense, low vibrational cords, and once the cord is severed Archangel Michael will absorb the negative energy and transmute it to positive energy. He will also place his hooded cloak over us for protection. If the cord is extremely thick and difficult to cut through, Archangel Michael will persist until a clean break has been achieved. Then the root can be dug out where the cord was intact and love and healing light can be poured in its place. If we prefer, we can communicate with Archangel Michael and ask if we can borrow the visual sword and cut the energy cords ourselves. We can then show gratitude and thank him for his assistance.

When we have finishing cutting cords, it is always advisable to pour healing love and light into the area where the cord has been severed. If we leave an open wound, it is highly likely a new cord will quickly be attached as we will be leaking energy and be highly susceptible to anyone who detects this and is hungry for a feed. Once a cord has been cut our energy will change immediately. At first we may feel a little unsettled, anxious, and we may be overly emotional. However, once we meditate and ground ourselves these feelings will dissipate and we will feel lighter, freer, and our mind will be calmer and more balanced. If we feel exactly the same way as we did before the process, it means we have not severed the cord properly and removed it from its root.

When the cords have been cut, all illusions will break away, rendering us free to finally see the situation in a clear light without emotions infiltrating and causing an energetic disturbance.

Chapter 29

Empathic Blending

Empaths are interconnected to everything that exists here on earth. There is no separation. We are connected spiritually, emotionally, mentally, and physically to all other life forms as we are manifestations of the same source of energy. Whenever we are in close contact with someone our energetic fields connect, blend, and resonate together. We are capable of guarding and protecting our energy field so that our energy does not become distorted because of interference from other people's fields. However, when we connect on a heart level, during sex, or when we are carrying out healing, we voluntarily open ourselves up so that we are leaving our energy fields vulnerable so that other people's energies can penetrate and blend with our own.

When our energy fields merge, it can be exquisitely beautiful or deeply painful. We are allowing other people's past, present, and future intentions; memories; and impressions to imprint on our own. We become conduits for energy, and we are exchanging vital information that can be complex to decipher if we are unaware of what is happening or we are not able to read subtle energy forces well.

Empathic blending takes places between anyone who consciously chooses to closely connect with someone else. It doesn't always happen between just two people. Sometimes there may be three or more people involved who are all in very close contact. Blending allows the transfer of energy to freely flow between energy fields. So if one person is feeling depleted and the other is full of vitality, a conscious decision can be made to blend and balance the energy between the two.

Empathic blending consists of giving and receiving in a way that is selfless and where the intention is to connect as one harmoniously, with integrity, no agenda, and no ulterior motive or expected outcome. To blend empathetically, it is vital that all involved are aware that in doing so they are opening themselves up to transferring other energies that may be negative. If anyone involved is not in a healthy, centred, balanced state to begin with, negative influences, bad habits, and even symptoms of depression can be transferred from one to the other.

Chapter 30

LONELINESS VERSUS SOLITUDE

Many people do not realize they are an empath and they carry with them a profound sense of feeling as though they are very different from others surrounding them. I often describe it as feeling as though I was born on the wrong planet. Other people can seem alien to me or I may seem alienlike to them. This can be a problem for us as at our core we see ourselves as connected to everyone and everything, and we recognize that we are all a part of an incredible energy force and we all alter and affect that force continuously. Therefore, the detachment we feel when others don't recognize this can be overwhelming. Due to this, we can often find it very difficult to relate to other people despite a strong desire to connect on an intimate level in both friendships and relationships.

We can find that we compromise ourselves and we may even use empathy to try to tap into how other people feel or how they perceive the world so that we can relate easier, especially if we have been feeling isolated or disconnected. It is possible that we could even take on other people's mannerisms and likes and dislikes in an attempt to be accepted so we can engage in friendships. Of course, this won't be effective, and if it does work, it won't last for long. This search for intimacy can often feel like too much for those who aren't empaths, and when they back off slightly it can make us feel unwelcome, unwanted, and rejected. This can be confusing and frustrating as the one thing we crave is connection, and it is something that seems to elude us.

It isn't often that empaths meet someone with whom we feel we relate to and many empaths often say they rarely meet other empaths, so when we do we meet people that we connect with, we don't want the resonation with the other person to fade out. When we allow relationships to occur naturally and in their own time, we will have a far greater chance of them being healthy and mutually enjoyable ones. We cannot push friendships or relationships to be something they aren't. Neither can we ignore or take for granted the friendships we have and still expect them to blossom. Finding an equilibrium between the two is imperative for nourishing relationships for all involved. When we do connect with people who share our language and a similar perception of the world, we will be fortunate in that they too will understand that while we have a connection we still need to regularly retreat to our cave for much-needed alone time.

For an empath, one of the most troublesome parts of maintaining close connections is the ability to be truly oneself and authentic about how we experience life. Unless our friends are also empaths, there is every chance that people just won't fully "get us." If we are not comfortable in someone's company, we can find it extremely difficult to relax and communicate openly and freely. This may appear to some as though we are rude or ignorant. It won't matter how hard we try. We sometimes just cannot find the words to make a connection. If we try to converse, the words can come out as mumbled and make very little sense.

The more negative and harsh the energy is that surrounds us, the more difficulties we will have with communication. Rolled eyes and false smiles are common when we start talking about our unique mystical world, sensations and universal energy. It sometimes feels as though people try to understand it but they just can't regardless of how hard they try. The subjects that empaths talk about can seem bewildering to other people. If we begin a conversation about seeing auras, reading energy, and tapping into the collective conscious, there will be some people out there who will genuinely think we are losing our minds. That's okay, we can understand that. They don't sense and feel the world exactly as we do. We don't sense and feel it as they do. Differences are acceptable. Although sometimes, even though we rationalize it, it still doesn't feel okay. It can feel incredibly lonely.

Empaths love differences, variations, and alterations between human beings, though not everyone else feels this way. Much of society prefers us to be identical, to all fit in, and to all think the same or at least similarly. It is less threatening to the status quo and less challenging to leaders when we all vibrate on a similar frequency. Empaths just don't make sense to a lot of people. However, if we put two empaths together who have never met one another they will talk in their own language and on such a high frequency that even they will probably find the connection difficult to logically explain.

We aren't always "got" by people. We don't always "get" ourselves. We have mostly got used to that. Empaths are not always naturally reclusive, although we can become withdrawn as a method of self-protection and self-preservation when we find connections too complex to navigate. This can result in us becoming introverted to avoid the emotional and physical pain that can stem from interactions. Other people may see empaths as moody or loners due to the amount of alone or downtime we need. They may struggle to understand that we sometimes choose solitude as part of our coping mechanism. We do like connection, though we need to balance that out by creating a safe space for ourselves to exist alongside it. Alone time is something that we crave. Whether time is spent reading, writing, working, exercising, or watching movies, we like to have a lot of space and prefer to do many of these things on our own.

Whether with friends, a loved one, family members, or colleagues, there will come a period when we either emotionally overwhelmed, exhausted, over stimulated and we will require time out. When solitude calls, it is best not to worry too much about offending other people as our own emotional needs and health needs to be prioritized. Often, a small amount of time alone just to ground and stabilize can be all that is required. However, if a situation becomes too intense to bear we will feel the need to excuse our departure and leave immediately. Finding a peaceful spot with nature, reading a book, meditating, or listening to music can be all that it takes to recharge and harmonize. Something as simple as going to the restroom regularly to be at peace and to experience silence can be enough. At home, we can create a sacred space that is comfortable and calming so that solitude can be honored, energy levels balanced, and emotions and energy levels returned to normal as quickly as possible.

When we explore solitude and are totally alone with ourselves, we have no choice but to get to know our likes, dislikes, emotions, beliefs, intentions, and how we generally feel without any outside influences disturbing us. Many people choose to spend as little time alone as possible as ultimately they are not comfortable or they do not connect with who they are. If they do eventually find themselves alone for long periods, they then have to face the process of understanding why that is and work to resolve any internal conflict.

When we are either forced or choose to be on our own, we come face to face with our core selves. We can turn away from ourselves and use distractions, such as the television, computer games, books, or other means of escapism, or we can tap into the inner parts of our mind so that we can tear off each layer one by one and look at what is trapped within. We can ask ourselves the questions that have been silently haunting our minds. We can make sense of the lies we tell ourselves or other people, or the ones we have frequently been fed either by those around us or by society as a whole.

We often find that when we start to unravel we go into denial. It is not easy to accept some of the grittier parts of our personality and behaviors and we can feel tempted to push those aspects of ourselves away and suppress them further. These things will then become further clogged within our subconscious, so although it isn't pretty, we can purge what rattles to bring it into the light.

When we spend time alone in isolation with ourselves, we cannot avoid the delusions that our mind has created as it foolishly believes it is protecting us. All the illusions that have built up around us will be torn down as we see what has led us to the place we are knee-deep in. We will sift through all of our past experiences and begin to see the patterns that have been repeating. We can see where we have gone wrong, taken risky turns, and can also begin to see which direction we need to be aiming for.

Being alone isn't always easy. This is why it is an option that not everyone chooses. We have no one to blame and no one to project our emotions on to, so there is no option but to begin to process them alone. Or we can reject them, although that will make alone time excruciatingly painful and difficult.

Chapter 31

INTROVERT

Although many empaths are introverts, this does not mean our introversion protects us from external harsh energies. Whether we live internally in our mind or exist internally in the physical world, we are still not able to fully close ourselves off and create a strong enough shield so that nothing penetrates our energy field. We are born as empaths to sense and feel. We cannot escape that.

Energy is not determined by time or distance. Other people's energy can be directed toward us and reach us even if it is thousands of miles away. And other people's thoughts and feelings can interact with our own. We can become entangled and interlocked with energy from all corners of the world and also from planetary activity. Even though we may feel safer within the tranquility of our own four walls or within the familiar surrounds of our own head, we will still not escape the strength and power of energetic frequencies. We are all part of the same energy, and we all flow either with it or we resist it and try to flow against it. Either way, it exists and introversion will not protect us from it.

Many empaths become more introverted as they go through life. This is because we become disillusioned by the external world and we find difficulty in understanding why some humans behave in ways that are destructive, so we turn inward to escape. We feel energy everywhere we go, and even when we have worked hard to protect ourselves it can still pull our frequency down to dangerously low levels in an instant. We are deeply affected by the emotional, psychological, and physical pain that millions of people and animals suffer daily. We literally ache to start a revolution that heals the whole world and we want to take away all forms of harm, yet we know that isn't a possibility. We struggle to watch when people treat one another harmfully, how privilege determines opportunities, and how demands are born from entitlement. We are exhausted by the indifference and disconnect between human and human and between human and all creatures. Introverts see the world with an alternative perception, and due to this we find it extremely difficult to externally slot into how it operates.

Although there are aspects of an introvert's character that would love to venture out into the world and mix freely, when we do we often find ourselves yearning to return to a haven that feels safe and secure as the bombardment of external energy can become too intense. There is constantly an incredible amount of energetic data flushing through our minds, so it is vital that we spend periods alone where we can allow the stimuli the opportunity to simmer down. We are deeply intuitive souls, which means we are ultra-sensitive to other people's energy levels and we are highly tuned to our surrounding environment. While we may adore socializing and creating deep bonds with others, we can also find other people's company intrusive and overbearing. When we are around certain people we often feel as though our personal space is being invaded due to the vast amount of energy that is whirling around and interlocking with our own. Introverts often prefer to exist in absolute silence, whereas extroverts tend to feel more at ease with external visuals, noise, or company for stimulation. Introverts generally do not need any type of outer entity to make us feel as though we are not alone. We are intensely aware of our connection to all things at all times, wherever we are.

Introverts recharge energy internally by going within, whereas extroverts recharge their energy externally through the stimuli in their surroundings. Introverts are hypersensitive to the energy that vibrates outside our personal spaces, which causes us to pick up on frequencies from other people and our environment at a far greater intensity. For this reason, it is imperative to work out which energy is good for us, which is harmful, and how we can deal with all the energy existing around us.

It can be exquisite experiencing life hypersensitive to energy, and it is beneficial to be able to read situations without the need for words. However, it can also be exceptionally draining, traumatic, and can cause emotional and psychological overload and distress. When feeling this way, it is sometimes better to try not to interact with those whose energy feels toxic or those who energy is heavy and weighs us down, as this can result in us feeling even more alone and with a stronger urge to completely close off. It is essential that we take good care of ourselves and protect our energy field so that we do not become emotionally and physically burned out. Rather than becoming affected by energies that pollute and drain us, we can make a conscious effort to raise our vibration so that we attract and absorb positive energies instead.

Many empaths become introverted or reclusive over time as we struggle to find other people who experience life as we do. This can lead us to feeling as though we exist on the outer edge of society and experiencing loneliness, or in more extreme cases, we can become ostracized and isolated. High levels of self-esteem and self-worth can be difficult for introverts to achieve as we do not look to other people to validate our character, neither do we seek ego-boosting compliments or endorsements. We question our identity and scrutinize our core traits. As we spend so much time trying to navigate our inner world and trying to make sense of the enigma of life, we may go through low periods or anxiety or depression while unearthing some of the darker aspects of ourselves and our outer world. We internally suffer as we do not mask the reality of life with distractions. Extroverts may also turn to introversion too, so this is not solely an introverted characteristic.

It can take us a long time to feel comfortable in our skin, though that is mainly due to the fact that we are unlike those around us. When we do eventually find self-acceptance, we are resilient souls who march to the beat of our inner drums and nothing and no one will be able to sway or break us.

By choice, introverted empaths would hibernate winter away, scurry out in the spring to gather and collect necessities for our nest, and then settle back into our haven where we feel loved, understood, and safe. However, we are contradictions, as we also adore exploring new terrain, discovering far-off lands, meeting new people, and marinating in fascinating cultures. We ache to go out, yet we feel strongly compelled to stay in. The main reason for this is that the world largely consists of extroverted people, and social gatherings are mostly structured to suit their desires and preferred lifestyles. For example, restaurants have tables closely knitted together, bars generally allow everyone to freely wander in and out of one another's personal space, and special events contain mass conglomerations of human beings shoulder to shoulder, all inhaling the same oxygen, contributing to piercing noise levels, and emanating varying frequencies of energy. This may sound like social heaven to extroverts, but to introverts it is social hell. To say events are excruciatingly painful is a massive understatement. Introverts do like to venture out, but if it is to the wrong places our energy floods out from us, although we will likely feel energized and at ease at events where there is a common focus (such as concerts, sporting events, and the cinema) as everyone is there for a similar purpose and the energy has accumulated so that everyone is vibrating on a similar frequency. Bars, clubs, and parties do not share this same energetic equilibrium; generally speaking, there is not a shared consensus, as people are there for their own unique purpose. Some may be there to dance the night away, others for one night of lust or romance, or even to find a prospective wife or husband. There will be those wanting to consume copious amounts of alcohol while others may just be out with friends to converse and catch up. There are varying levels of energy in bars, clubs, and parties, as the focus is centered on each individual rather than one central attraction, and this can cause friction and unrest in the atmosphere as each person's energy field radiates depending on their unique intention for the outing. As introverts are highly sensitive to energy, we can very quickly become disorientated and unnerved as the energy levels fluctuate from very high to very low person to person.

Introverts would love to find ambience in large crowds of people at bars, clubs, or parties, though sadly we are more likely to find engulfing and ravaging debilitation. An introvert's ideal social scenario would likely consist of a small collection of friendly but nonintrusive people, a roaring fire glowing while softly warming the room, maybe a guitar or piano being elegantly played in the corner, tables positioned around the edges of the room with barriers around them so that we feel somewhat protected, lights dimmed with candles burning, and gentle but high energy permeating the room—and possibly a mug of hot cocoa. To top it off, there would also likely be a resting room where we could sit back, comforted by pillows and cushions, with very little noise so we could reenergize, ground, and center before reemerging to continue the evening. Oh, and some deep but mind-blowing, thought-provoking conversation. Or our perfect night may just be a cozy night in with good food, something delicious to drink, blankets, and a beautifully written, mind-challenging book or conversation.

To people who may not understand introverts, I can see why they may think we see ourselves as "precious" or "fragile" or maybe too tender for the rawness or harshness of the world. I often used to irritate myself being so totally bewildered and guarded against external entities, so I sometimes berated my personal ways and told myself to "toughen up" and just get out there, breathe, and cope better. In all honesty, this made me feel worse. Instead, we can care for ourselves, show consideration, and accept that humans are not all built the same, so there is no use condemning our introverted natural state.

We are all different. There are some who love peanut butter and jelly, while other people hate it or are even allergic to it. Some people adore being closely connected to strangers, while others abhor it and break out in hives. We can't judge as we don't know the intricate details of why, what, when, or even possibly who caused us to be this way. We aren't even sure if we are born this way, if nurture or nature is the cause, whether it is genetics, evolution, or if it was the blended result of a myriad of reasons.

My words of advice are not to feel forced to carry out grounding practices before going out or to perform rituals to protect our energy field, or to chant mantras, or have a dear friend on standby waiting to pretend-call us with a made-up emergency that no one will believe just so we can escape through the closest exit. My words to introverts are simple: go to the places you choose to go to, where you feel comfortable, where the surrounding energy is soothing to your own, and where you are not constantly on high alert. Travel and soak in the places where the energy aligns with your own. Make connections with people who understand the need for introspection and who reciprocate a similar vibe back to you and one that is overflowing with consideration and acceptance. Seek out the people who understand how it feels to sometimes feel as though you don't belong to this world. Talk with those who remind you that it is okay to be you and it is more than acceptable to not always (or ever) like the same things that everyone else appears to. Don't go anywhere that you desperately don't want to just because "everyone else is going." Set your own route and let quality matter over quantity, and if that leads you to the same places you always go, then go anyway, even if that place is within your own four walls.

We enjoy our lives and find fulfillment and happiness when we answer our own calling and listen to ourselves. We should never have to feel miserable just so to be liked, to fit in, to please other people, or to prove to ourselves or others that we are not weird or reclusive. We have to live with ourselves; therefore, we are the ones who know what makes us content and what satisfies our souls.

There are no rules or regulations that state we must go out to a variety of social events. Where we go is always our decision and ours alone. So choose to be around people who understand this without ever feeling the need to justify it.

For introverts, socializing is exhausting and draining. Introverts thrive in their own company, and we find it invigorating, regenerating, and energizing. Therefore, we have to adapt our lives to complement our own blueprint, not anyone else's or ones that society has mapped out for us.

We can still push ourselves and do things that may not feel as natural, though only if we are not forced or manipulated into doing so. It is believed that when we are just on the outer edge of our comfort zone a physiological energy release causes us to become aroused due to a surge in adrenalin. When our adrenal glands are engaged, we then enter a fight or flight state that causes us to be more alert and engaged so our body and mind are prepared for action and functioning at optimum levels. As we are all unique, our optimum levels vary; therefore, some people will respond well to low levels of anxiety while others are at their best when anxiety levels are higher. If we do not push ourselves at all, we will feel unmotivated, understimulated, distracted, and disinterested. As long as we do not go too far over our own anxiety border, we will not become overwhelmed, hindered, or crippled due to a peak in cortisol. If we maintain a healthy and moderate balance of arousal so that fear and anxiety do not consume us, we will feel pleasantly stimulated and our performance will be enhanced, making us more productive.

****This theory is known as the Yerkes-Dodson Principle, as Robert M. Yerkes and John D. Dodson explained in 1908 how this concept benefits us when we sustain an optimum arousal level.

Anxiety can assist us to be motivated toward achieving better results in anything we put our mind to. When we are secure in who we are and fully accept our introversion, we can then break through our introverted walls if we so choose to without leaving ourselves vulnerable. We can try not to push ourselves to extreme levels of stress to please other people or to meet their expectations of us, as by doing so we neglect our overall wellbeing.

It is believed that introverts naturally perform better in low stimuli, low-pressure environments, whereas extroverts perform better with a higher amount of stimuli and greater pressure. Empaths are not external; we are internal. We feel everything intimately and crave the highs and lows that are found when we adventure, and we ache for close encounters and heartfelt connections. We just require peace, harmony, and tranquility to accompany our introverted hearts, whether the roads we roam lead us indoors or outdoors.

Introverts use alone time as a way to kick back and retreat into our cave for a mini hibernation where we can contemplate in safety and silence. We may regularly take short breaks, either on our own or with someone we are close to, even if it's just for a few days, to escape from our introversion and force ourselves to face the world. We like to slow things down and relax calmly in a place where no one knows us so we can breathe, think things through clearly, and reflect on our recent past. We can focus on serendipities and look at where we are going to make sense of our journey, though when we return we may need a few down days to replenish, rebalance, and recover. We are then able to alter our inner compass and head out of the period of solitude with a great sense of which direction we are going in, where we have been, though significantly where we are right now.

We excel in the stillness of our own mind as it is there that we find our internal voice and also where we explore our creative impulses.

Chapter 32

SOCIALIZING AND FRIENDSHIPS

Socializing can be extremely difficult and possibly even traumatizing for empaths. Many empaths have either mild or extreme social anxiety and we can appear quiet, shy, aloof, unsociable, reserved, unwilling to engage, and maybe even as though we see ourselves as superior to others. However, we generally don't and aren't at all how we may seem on the surface. By choice, we would open our souls and share every aspect of our inner being and would appreciate others doing the same. Unfortunately, it is not quite as simple, as large parts of society confirms that any shadow emotions should be kept locked and hidden inside. This leaves us in a whirlwind of confusion and can cause us to withdraw when in company, as we don't understand why it is deemed so unacceptable to expose who we are without being judged or condemned. Therefore, socializing in large groups or with people we do not know very well can be a minefield. We often struggle to concentrate as we become so preoccupied with observing and analyzing what other people are thinking, feeling, or saying that we end up absorbing too much stimuli, pondering every response, projecting our emotions, and overall becoming overwhelmed, overanxious, and overstimulated.

The mandala artwork was crafted by Krutika Joglekar. To find out more information and view more of Krutika's unique creations please visit www.instagram.com/krutikajoglekar/

As much as we love company and want to have close friendships and form bonds, we may shy away from them as we are aware that they cause our energy levels to dramatically deplete. Therefore, we generally tend to have one or two very close friendships rather than socialize in large groups as we find small kinships are more intimate and less depleting. Our ideal and most rewarding friendships will be with other empaths. Empaths are usually able to identify other empaths the moment they meet. We are kindred spirits and know and understand one another on a dimension that some people will find difficulty comprehending.

When we discover friendships with other empaths, we converse soul to soul with absolute honesty as our souls have an affinity due to having similar blueprints.

It is as though we are fragments of the same cosmic explosion and particles of our energy connects, entangles and interlocks in the air. Energetic ties are instantly formed. Our energy communicates in a unique language that only we can coherently translate. We intuitively know. Although, logically, we "know" nothing at all. We are able to speak our mind and express ourselves frankly without any fear of judgment. We not only "recognize" one another from a distant place in some other realm of time we are also intrigued by the same types of obstacles we have faced and overcome on our journeys so far. We are kindred spirits who often find that our stories read like pages torn out from the same chapter in an old dusty book. The relationships are filled with synchronicities, vital life-lessons, raw and emotional exchanges, shared interests, beliefs and ideologies. They offer an opportunity for our hearts to safely and fearlessly grow. We are crystal clear mirrors for one another as we safely provide each other with insights about our inherent nature that we hadn't yet accepted or acknowledged. This enables us to do the messy work that is required to internally shift stubborn gears. We inspire and empower one another to live truer to what feels important to us and we reach out to deliver assurance, tenderness, care and kindness if a volatile storm tries to temporarily weaken or derail us from our path.

The main element that enhances these soul acquaintances is the ability to unveil, uncurl and fully and safely express ourselves in ways that we haven't felt able, confident or comfortable to around others. This encourages complete self-acceptance as we find that traits, quirks or idiosyncrasies that we may have not fully understood or accepted in ourselves, becomes firmly integrated into our being, as our perception changes and we learn how to celebrate our eccentricities rather than rejecting or denying them.

One of the difficulties we sometimes have with friendships is our requirement for a great deal of alone time. This is an area of contention for us as we want to have close, rich and stimulating connections with others but we find they can be exhausting and draining. Even when we have grounded and protected ourselves, vast amounts of time spent with people we are close to can result in fatigue striking very quickly. Not everyone understands this and it can be extremely off-putting for someone who is in our company as they watch us fizzle out to the point we just need to crawl to a bed to rest and recover. Friends may take this personally and think their company has bored or offended us and they may not see that sometimes the reason we are debilitated is because we were thoroughly enjoying ourselves as the energetic frequency was very high. If we regularly ground, center, protect, and recharge the drain will not be so noticeable. It just means taking frequent periods of time out to a rest room or to find a quiet space to stabilize and rejuvenate so that we can function well.

A lot of people will not be aware of this, and realistically we can't fully expect them to. If they are not empaths they may never have experienced their energy leaking from them until it gets to the stage they are running on vapor from their reserve. We can try to remember that just because we understand and can feel how someone else is feeling it doesn't mean everyone else can understand how we feel. When we energetically deteriorate, our behavior may seem eccentric, odd, or strange to others and they may take it personally or wonder if we are emotionally, physically, or mentally stable or just being plain problematic. This is why it is essential to keep our energy flowing and balanced.

Empaths are often used to being judged, so it won't surprise us if new or even old friends make assumptions about our traits. However, it can still hurt and as we are highly sensitive we will pick up on their feelings and read them before they have had the chance to relay anything. Because we are easily able to tap into other people's emotions and feelings, this could be another reason that people might want to keep their distance. Not everyone enjoys having their insides turned outside, especially if they pick up on the fact that we are able to read them so well or if we say something that totally gives this away.

Other people may wonder how we can just *know* certain pieces of information or details that they have kept hidden and they may question if we have been prying into their personal lives. They will not grasp how we can just *know* what we *know*. This can seem intrusive to some people and they may feel as though their personal space has been invaded and a friendship can break down before it has even begun. We often struggle to know where the line is between what we should and shouldn't share with friends as our natural instinct is to be totally honest and spill everything that is on our mind. However, not everyone else feels this way and that can be a huge barrier in forming or maintaining friendships.

We are loyal and faithful allies and can be depended on when times are at their toughest. We drop everything in our lives so that we are free to assist those in need. Generally, we love close human interactions and forging bonds although, we are only comfortable if the connections are mutually enjoyable, harmonious, and feel at ease. This sounds as though empaths have conditions on their friendships, and although it can seem that way, it is not intentional. We are so sensitive to other people's energy that if we are in the company of someone whose energy is volatile, we will struggle to remain grounded and calm enough to keep the connection steady so that it can be sustained.

Empaths may resort to self-medicating before attending social gatherings with either pharmaceutical or nonpharmaceutical drugs, or we may choose to consume alcohol to ease any chronic social anxiety. My advice is that if a social occasion causes such high levels of anxiety, we can heed what the inner friction is telling us and avoid it altogether.

Empaths can feel like human sponges, soaking up the emotional and psychic static electricity that others send out. Taking on any toxic waste that is cast out to the atmosphere can be destructive and devastating to the inner stability and calm of our sometimes fragile energetic fields. Unless we regularly cleanse our energy fields, just like a sponge, they will become clogged with residual energy from a variety of sources and we will then be unable to think clearly, identify our emotions, or express ourselves well, and we will likely be irritable, agitated, and suffer with chronic fatigue. By keeping certain people and situations at an arm's length, we can use a form of self-preservation to ensure our energy does not become entangled with those who may cause damage by penetrating it with negativity.

Before making any plans or arrangements, it is sometimes advisable to consider what, where, and when they will be to avoid any potential traumatic or uncomfortable situations occurring.

We can often be edgy and nervous in front of people we are not comfortable with, so we may appear awkward, clumsy, bewildered, and shy, and all of these things just heighten our anxiety further. We are very aware of the energy coming from those around us and we will sense if we are being watched, judged, or criticized.

Fair-weather friends and forced interactions are not often easy for empaths to maintain. We have a high desire for authenticity, and if this is not in place, anything else will seem trivial and the interest in the friendship will quickly diminish. Empaths appreciate friendships and we want to socialize, we just need the socializing to be genuine. If it isn't, we will pick up on it immediately and feel as though we are wasting both our own and the other person's time. We just don't do "fake" very well, and if someone we are with has ulterior motives or an agenda in place we will likely pick up on it.

For us to feel comfortable and relaxed, we need to feel at peace within our surroundings. Places with high stimuli, such as bars, cafés, shopping malls, or basically anywhere where there is a large gathering of people can turn into extremely stressful experiences. When out in public we will carefully choose where we sit. Whether it is in restaurants, on public transport, or in a room with family/ friends, we will prefer a place to sit where we feel most at ease and where we have plenty of space. We are not always comfortable eating or drinking in front of people, so we will most likely sit at the edge of the room or on a seat where we are not surrounded by a lot of people. This is also due to the amount of energy that is swirling around in the environment when there are many people in one place. This energy contains all the emotions of the people who are present and we may struggle to guard and protect ourselves enough to prevent from absorbing it.

We tend to avoid places with high stimuli. Places such as the cinema, shopping malls, activities where there are a lot of children, family gatherings, and nightclubs can all lead us to feel overloaded with stimulation. Bright lights, loud noises, and crowded places can all take their toll and our sensory organs can take a battering. Calm, relaxed, quiet, chilled-out places are much preferred to enable inner calm. We will likely find comfort holding a partner or friend's hand or arm during such occasions, finding that their energy forms a soothing welcome blend and helps to create a shield to block some of the surrounding energy.

Empaths have a heightened sensory perception. Artificial lights, volume, temperatures, strong smells, and numerous other variables will have a detrimental and draining effect and will directly impact our moods. Noise and lighting will need to be soft and gentle, as anything harsh may cause us to feel irritable. The cinema, supermarkets, and nightclubs can all feel traumatic to our eyes and ears and may result in tempered frustrations and irritable behaviors.

We will often choose places to visit or live where the energy resonates with our own. Different streets, villages, or even countries hold their own vibration depending on what has taken place there and also due to the energy of the people who reside there. It may be that the energy is calm or on a high frequency. Either way, we will settle easily wherever our energy strikes a chord with a similar frequency.

Aggressive voices, confrontations, and shouting all highly disturb our psyche. We find it difficult to hold a conversation with someone whose tone of voice is very harsh, as our mind will likely go blank and we may feel anxious, zone out, switch off and struggle to pay attention. This is one reason we are not very good at arguing as we often forget what is being said as the turbulent situation feels incredibly stressful. We will usually leave these environments quickly as the stimuli rises to a deafening level too great to bear. It is not that we are being awkward or rude, it is just these engagements can feel extremely volatile and the effects can last for hours or even days following.

After attending social functions, we may feel completely worn out, exhausted and temporarily debilitated, meaning that all we will want to do is sleep or rest, possibly alone, until the sensations from the occasion have worn off. Empaths often have very weak boundaries and this means that we take on and absorb everything that is around us, including the emotional and mental states of other people. Therefore, we can be easily influenced, easily led, vulnerable, and suffer extreme mood swings that shift from feeling low and sulky to exhilarated and elated from one moment to the next. This means we usually avoid interactions to protect ourselves and prevent other energies interlocking with our own. When we learn to shield our energy field, we can guard ourselves better, but shielding is a process that has to be carried out continuously unless our vibration is high. Even empaths who practice shielding regularly can be susceptible to energetic debris that lingers in the air.

At parties or social events, we will usually be found in the calmest place. Often that is in the kitchen, where it is a little quieter, in the rest room chatting to one or two good friends, or navigating to a garden or outdoor space for a little breathing space. Social events can be enjoyable for an empath, though only if they are low stimuli. Stuck in the middle of a brightly lit room, talking to strangers, with lots of chattering, loud music, and a crowded atmosphere can be our worst nightmare. We will feel vulnerable, overwhelmed, and even if we don't notice it at the time, the high stimulation will drain us. We will find it far more enjoyable engaging with one or two friends on the outer edges.

We may often deliberately avoid social situations. If we feel we are not going to be comfortable attending an event, we will find any excuse not to go. Whether it is with family, friends, social or professional gatherings, they can cause us to experience high levels of anxiety. To go to any external event, we need to feel calm and in the right frame of mind. If any arguments or tensions have arisen prior to the event (usually by us causing a little drama to avoid having to attend), it will be almost impossible for us to enjoy, relax, and socialize naturally. If we are in the company of someone who is supportive and understands our social anxiety, it will immediately ease slightly. Just knowing that we have someone keeping a protective and caring eye on us just in case we are struggling is enough to keep us calm at a time when we will be open and vulnerable to overload.

We become very familiar with cancelling plans. If it is someone else that cancels the plans, it can feel like a huge relief as the worry has been taken away from having to attend something that will potentially be exhausting, uncomfortable, and overly stimulating. Often though, we are the ones to cancel. At the time of the invite, an event can seem like a great idea, but as it draws closer the thought of all the stress that might be involved can become too much to bear. Cancelling is simple compared to the worry of how much time, energy, and anxiety is involved if we have to attend. The very thought of doing something we are not comfortable with can cause nervousness that can eat away at our energy reserves, let alone having to actually show up. If we are completely at ease with plans and we are confident about where they are taking place and who will be there, we will likely look forward to them and be far less likely to cancel.

While in a conversation we can find it very difficult to remain focused and hold our concentration so that we can listen fully. This is due to us being very aware that every word we speak is being taken in and judged or assessed on some level by the person we are communicating with. We will notice the subtle changes in the body language and tone of voice of the person we are talking to and we will see how these things alter depending upon the information we are giving out. We are also highly skilled at monitoring eye movements and will notice any changes occurring. These flickers are signals that help us to read into and decode what someone is thinking. Although we are innately able to read energy, we are not able to read thoughts so easily as they occur and change so quickly. That is why we also observe body language intensely so that we have a moment-by-moment commentary of what is taking place.

As a conversation deepens, the signals are much easier to read and we will fluently be able to translate thoughts and feelings. This may cause us to want to end or change a conversation, especially if we feel we are being interpreted wrong or judged unfairly or harshly. This makes it very difficult for us to remain fully present, as we are too busy exploring and observing the aura and physical movements of the other person. This is part of the reason we become cautious and self-conscious around other people. Being able to see through people with x-ray vision can be very difficult if we are aware that the other person is not being honest or direct with how they are feeling. If someone is nodding in agreement yet their energy or body language is saying something very different, we feel the urge to say to the person that we are aware that they aren't communicating what they mean.

Facts, figures, philosophies, theories, poetry, culture, the universe, reality, all of these things and more will capture our attention. Fictional dramas or the latest gossip about other people's private lives will very likely fall on deaf ears.

We aren't always shy; however, our energy comes from within, so we take time out for ourselves to conserve energy, and when in large groups this is not so easy. Downtime after social events is essential, as the energy that has been drained will then need to be recharged.

We usually only have a few but very loyal friendships. We are much happier in the company of a very small crowd, and often, just with one other person. For us to get close to someone, we must be able to feel completely comfortable and to be able to place our absolute trust in them. Because of this, we will place loyalty and trust above all else and will be deeply upset if either of those things break. If we have been hurt in the past when our highly valued trust was misplaced, we may be wary and cautious before trusting again.

We are also aware that our readiness to limitlessly overshare and interact intimately with people results in us appearing naive and vulnerable.

The connections we are crave are the ones that stretch our soul, the ones who challenge us, the ones who see us through to the core for who we are, rather than who they want or expect us to be and the ones who bring more happiness and adventure into our lives. When we find someone who we feel energetically aligned with we will feel instantly comfortable and almost as though we have found a place that feels like "home" in another soul.

One of the most significant things about the connections we keep is that there is space within it, and there will be no attachment to the person so we can have complete acceptance and a sense of freedom within the dynamic, particularly as we need a period of alone time to recharge. When we find a genuine friendship we will not feel as though we need to impress them, feign who we are, or that we need to be a certain way to gain their attention. None of those things will even come into question. We will naturally nestle into a safe space within their energy where we can come and go with ease and our energy will expand to allow them to step in and out of ours.

Even though we may previously have found ourselves feeling as though our personal space has been invaded somewhat when we are around certain people, the connections that we are pulled towards will have entirely different sensations associated with them and they will feel effortless, almost as though the connection grows in strength without requiring any verbal communication or physical presence to prove it exists.

We may often hear that we should be fully whole and complete in ourselves and that feeling that other people "completing" us is either egotistical or it shows that we still have a lot of internal work to do. However, it is my belief that none of this is true. We are human beings having a spiritual experience here on earth and part of our humanness is the enjoyment and peace we gain when we meet others with whom we connect with on a soul deep level and within engagements that just cannot and do not need to be justified or explained.

When two people have a similar vibration is it known as a "sympathetic resonance" or "sympathetic vibration." This is when there is a harmonic likeness that resonates between two people who are vibrating on the same frequency and these can be either negative vibrations or positive vibrations.

We may wonder how we might recognize these people, and to some extent the desire to connect may feel very surreal or even otherworldly. We might instantly feel like we have found a treasured new friend or someone with whom we feel drawn towards on a more passionate, physical level. The reason we are magnetized towards certain people may never be fully known, other than that we feel a strong resonance with either something they say, something they express or quite simply for how the radiation of their heart-centred energy feels. There will be an affinity that is unmistakable and unquestionable and we will just know in our hearts that whoever it is that has appeared, as if from nowhere, is an integral part of the unravelling of our soul journey here on earth.

This person may enter our lives momentarily or they may stay around for the duration, however time and distance with these connections is immeasurable. The only thing we will know for certain is that they showed up to alert us to a part of ourselves that we may have been trying to reject or deny. We will awaken to the realization that despite how much we try to convince ourselves that we are okay all by ourselves and that we don't need others for validation, there is a far bigger picture here that we have possibly not quite yet fully considered.

Humans are not here to explore and adventure all alone. Not only is it essential for the continuation of our species, other people are mirrors who constantly reflect back to us parts of ourselves that are hidden or parts that we are aware are there, but sometimes it takes a resounding "Yes!" from another person before we are willing, or able, to absorb and accept angles of our kaleidoscope inner being.

We are not here to navigate this labyrinth life single-handed. Other people are essential parts of our experience and they often shake us up so that we fully awaken to all that we are.

We can write these connections off as just mere coincidences, but their appearances in our lives are synchronicites and serendipities that we will not so easily or quickly forget. They will cause an internal reaction and we will forever be changed, even if it is just so subtly that it seems like the most natural meeting of two minds or hearts. Or even both.

When we meet them we can try to let go of the doubts, let go of all the "What if's," "How long will this last," or the "Am I good enoughs." Instead we can open up our arms wide and say yes!! Welcome! Without any fearful shadowy doubts or high expectations and love and accept with enthusiasm.

We miss out on so much because we are either afraid to appear "needy," or "bold" or we are just too scared to put ourselves out there and offer our hand to others just in case we get rejected, however, we can connect deeply with others, but with no attachment to the outcome whatsoever. This freedom is what turns all connections from ones that could cause us some level of suffering, to ones of appreciation, bliss and an intensely felt sense of love and joy.

We then start to see other people as butterflies, floating in and out of our lives offering beauty and tranquillity, whenever we are blessed with their presence. We do not need to catch and hold onto a butterfly to appreciate it. Neither do we ever need to do this with any person that we have been gifted the honour to get to know.

Empaths are not always comfortable with talking to friends on the phone, in fact, telephones are often an empath's nemesis and we can find them an intrusive device that zaps our energy. They feel like a violation of our personal space as the ringtone cries out for our attention. We struggle to stay present and concentrate when on the phone. Usually we flat line and our mind goes blank, especially if the conversation consists of small talk or gossip. Everyone has their flaws and this is one of an empath's and one that prevents us from having close interactions with a wide circle of friends. We prefer one-on-one connections and for there to be shared interests so that we can have conversations that exist on an alternative dimension and ones that keep us fully engaged.

We tend to avoid engaging in small talk, social niceties, and chatter about matters that are of no particular concern. We struggle. However, ironically, with a challenging, deep, and meaningful conversation about ideologies, philosophies, or theories we are brought to life and our energy is replenished and refueled. If it is a subject close to our heart, it can be almost impossible to draw the conversation to a close. We become almost obsessive about our special interests and find it difficult to retain our attention when talking about anything other than something that intrigues us. This can appear as a selfish trait, and in a way it is. We do try to remain alert and interested in conversations outside what ignites our mind, and though we manage it temporarily we cannot keep it up and the disinterest will show in our faces and our body language regardless of how hard we try to cover it up.

Generally, it can feel alien to an empath to talk into a phone. We can't seem to grasp the concept that the person we are speaking to is not next to us. We long for real-people conversation, people who are standing or sitting next to us while they are talking. We want to see the people we are talking to so we can read their energy clearly and observe body language. We can't see smiles or eyes light up and we can't feel energy closely interacting with our own while we are on the phone. It all feels so artificial, so strange, and complicated.

We want real talk with real hearts. We want to talk with friends sitting across from us while we are sipping coffee or a glass of wine, or when we're lying by the lake talking nonsense and marveling at the wonders of the world. We want to talk when we're snuggled on sofas with cushions and blankets and we can see smiles, eyes light up, dry tears, and reach out to soothe any sadness. We want to talk in parks, having picnics, or when lying under the stars. We want to talk at 4:00 a.m. or 6:00 p.m. We will happily make the trip, drive or get the train, anything other than talking on the phone. If we aren't feeling great, we are already exhausted, or if we are just having some quiet time to ourselves, we don't want the abrasive interruption of a telephone call to disturb us.

It is difficult for us to switch from one mode to the other, and if we need solitude we may struggle to snap out of it so that we can quickly converse with a friend or family member. If we are feeling a little low or our energy is depleted, we can't pretend to be high-spirited. Our alone time helps us to work through these feelings so we can balance and reenergize. It is nothing to do with who is on the other end of the call and nothing personal. We just find it difficult to communicate when we are not in that mindset.

We may not always respond to texts or calls. We need to feel comfortable before responding, and if our frame of mind isn't right, we will find it a struggle to communicate, so we will delay responding until the moment is right. We are highly unlikely to start calls or conversations unless we feel completely at ease to do so. We also have no clue how to play some of the crazy mind games that are involved when people purposefully hold out with replies to keep us guessing or keen. And we can't work out why some people calculate how long it's taken for us to reply and then double however much time it's taken before calling or texting us back. It's very clearly deliberate behavior and a passive-aggressive response, and we will feel the energy emanating from it and back away further.

We can understand the ones who just hate returning calls (the ones similar to us) and the ones who are genuinely too busy to reply, but the deliberate dynamics people set up to try to antagonize just leave us bewildered and hating phones even more. We long to go back to the old days where people penned handwritten letters with feathers and ink or printed out notes using graceful typewriters, the times we would patiently wait for the mailman to arrive. We want to grow curious about what friends have been up to so the words gush out like volcanoes erupting whenever we connect. We want to be intrigued and excited to meet so we can share our news from yesterday, last week, or last month. Slowly the desire to be side by side and share is being forgotten, and that is what an empath craves most with those we are closest to.

www.VonGArt.com and the name is
Megan Guenthner Clark

Chapter 33

FREE SPIRIT

Empaths are often free-spirited souls who live, or desire to live, outside the mainstream, and we very often have nontraditional lifestyles. Even if our professional life is not in the arts, we may be drawn toward, or daydream of, becoming artists, writers, dancers, actors, or musicians. We are unconventional and have very few attachments or desires for material possessions. Even though we have a great affection for our belongings, it is mainly due to the energetic nostalgic feelings they hold and not because of financial or any superficial value. Music, the arts, philosophy and literary pursuits are at the core of our lifestyle. We are free thinkers who are associated with unorthodox or anti-establishment social and political views, which we express through creativity, free love, acceptance, or even choosing to live in poverty. We have little care for money other than for a basic means of survival.

We generally live by idealism as our minds portray a mental conception of what we believe beauty to be and our beliefs often contrast with the standards set by society or what the fashion industry strongly associates with beauty. Empaths will regularly question and challenge the system and the status quo as our heightened perception offers us an alternative way of thinking and seeing things. We are not always disciplined and find it difficult to follow unwritten rules and regulations. If something goes against our strong personal beliefs, we may be inclined to rebel.

Our high sensitivities mean we care deeply and we may be extremists who push ourselves to all heights to take a stand for what we believe in. We aim to create a fairer, less judgmental, and a more loving and accepting world to live in. We strive to leave the world a better place than we found it, even if the only way we can do this is through our art.

Empaths generally have no care for hierarchies or for bowing down to others who are seen by society to be of a higher standing. We abandon negative judgment and see everyone as equal. There are no airs or graces with empaths. We are who we are and as we see it other people can take us or leave us; we have no expectations or attachments and it will not affect us either way.

We express ourselves through the clothes we wear and our style can change from day to day as it will be chosen purely to suit our moods. The most essential part of clothing is the texture of the fabric we wear. Ethical and soft material and garments that float with the body are often key pieces so we can move naturally and freely and also so that our skin can breathe.

We live for the moment, without regrets. We love wildly and fiercely and would give up all that we owned for whatever it is that we are passionate about. We are deep thinkers and deep feelers who carve our souls open so that the world can glimpse inside.

The lazy Sunday mornings doused in love, music, or art festivals; the picnics in cornfields; the cafés with people and culture; museums, lakes, the midnight walks through forests; and the long and dusty road trips are what make an empath's heart beat like crazy. A relationship where a lover is not only the one we are intimately passionate with, but also who is our best friend is what we ache and crave for. The whole world can seem like a magnificent brightly colored canvas to an empath—one huge adventure playground waiting to be roamed and explored. Our imaginations are wild, and we are impulsive and may set off in pursuit of magic without any planning or packing beforehand.

We quite simply forget to look ahead at what might go wrong. We tend to have a childlike innocence as we are not afraid to be authentic and vulnerable, although this can also cause us to be incredibly naive. We would not intentionally harm others and find it difficult to imagine that others would deliberately wish to do us harm. This can often lead us being wide open to trickery and also to being easily deceived. This is partly because we sometimes leave our guard down as we like to believe that everyone we come into contact with can be trusted. It is a harsh and painful lesson when we discover that things are not always as they seem.

Empaths can come across as vulnerable and fragile on the inside and this can often appear as though we are needy and insecure. While this may be partially true as we can have issues with security, a lot of the thin and fragile outer shell is not all as it seems. We try, fall down, and get back up again a million times or more before giving up and admitting defeat. We are survivors, and with each tough lesson that is sent our way we manage to somehow turn things around to create something positive. And if all else fails, a lesson will have been taken onboard and learned. At least, until we let our guard down again, which usually doesn't take too long!

"You may encounter many defeats, but you must not be defeated. In fact, it may be necessary to encounter the defeats so you can know who you are, what you can rise from, how you can still come out of it." —Maya Angelou

We are free-spirited wanderers who are at our happiest outdoors around nature. We are passionate, intuitive, constantly learning, exploring, and discovering as we have determined and fearless attitudes. We are headstrong, and when we are motivated and put in the effort, we are capable of getting whatever we want and we take on anything we set our imaginative minds to.

Chapter 34

CREATIVITY

"The desire to create is one of the deepest yearnings of the human soul. No matter our talents, education, backgrounds, or abilities, we each have an inherent wish to create something that did not exist before." ——Dieter Friedrich Uchtdorf

The foundations of an empath's artistic creations are built from the energy that lingers within our inner worlds. The first time many empaths tuned in to creativity was during childhood due to an overwhelming cathartic desire to escape to the safety of our imaginative, curious, inquisitive inner minds. The solace of our minds is where mystery and magic live. We are naturally creative and innovative, and we find that art is the ideal platform to express and imprint our complex matrix of emotions upon.

For artistic empaths, our greatest, longest, and most passionate love affair will always be with our art. We often don't recognize the distinction between pleasure and pain when we are submerged within a creative project, and with unwavering focus we relentlessly and resiliently continue until we reach completion. Artists regularly feel inspiration being delivered through sensations, and when we tune in to them we find that we just "know" from whom or where the source of divine energy has originated.

Jung spoke of how our creative expression often comes to us from a force outside our own consciousness. Our creative drive is channeled from our unconscious minds, which has been infiltrated by the realms of information stored within the collective conscious. We intuitively pick up on vibrations that are radiated toward us and we respond to the call by infusing the thoughts, ideas, and feelings into our artwork. We then interpret and analyze the energy and ultimately turn it into original creations. According to Jung, artists are instruments through which social change can occur to restore equilibrium in times of unrest.

"All art intuitively apprehends coming changes in the collective unconsciousness." ———Carl Jung

Our artistic research is focused on our unconscious mind, where our hidden memories, unorganized feelings, and false beliefs reside. When we unearth and bring our unconscious to the surface, we restructure what is stored there and process of it through our creative impulses.

We can become so immersed in our hobbies and passions that innate talents and skills rise to the surface, and this can lead to a high standard of output. We think, feel, and behave in ways quite differently than those around us and our alternative perceptions are visible through our creations. Often, as empaths we can find it difficult to explain ourselves or how the intricacies of our minds work to others, yet through our art we are able to channel our thoughts, ideas, and feelings and put them into context where they begin to make sense.

Although we may share our art, we lose ourselves in it predominantly for our own benefit. This is so that we can weave through and untangle the incredible amount of emotional and psychological data we store.

Although empaths are sometimes the great philosophizers, seers, genius thinkers, inventors, creators, and artists of the world, we are not always the ones who make it to the top of our game due to our desire to live outside the established norm. We aren't usually the ones who happily settle into a career that is not aligned with our higher calling. Empaths may become bored and distracted very quickly if our work does not challenge our mind or nourish our soul. Many of our artistic projects will not last too long. We are known to move quickly from one interest to the next once the initial burning sensation simmers down. However, we leave no stone uncovered in learning everything in record speed as we go along. When we feel we have discovered and explored enough, we swiftly let go and dive straight into the next thing that spikes our interest. We sacrifice all for our art and would choose living true to what resonates with our soul above being surrounded or tempted by material goods or financial wealth.

"The biographies of great artists make it abundantly clear that the creative urge is often so imperious that it battens onto their humanity and yokes everything to the service of the work, even at the cost of ordinary health and human happiness." ——Carl Jung

Even though we express ourselves outwardly, we are quiet achievers and would rather create our art without anyone knowing its source. Although we often choose to share our creations with the world, empaths do not usually do it to seek glory, validation, financial reward, or recognition. Our imagination controls our world and it is there where our art is born and where it thrives. We lead a life of romantic suffering as we become so passionate about our art it feels like a continuous burn in our soul, which leads us on a mission to unravel the purpose and direction of its calling.

Storytelling is one of our skills, and this is often because our imagination can feel more real than reality itself. Everything is felt deeply; therefore, we are able to channel our emotions to create vivid and colorful tales.

We process our emotions and feelings through our art and as this is a deeply personal way to exist, it can be testing for us to open up our soul so it is exposed to anyone who may be observing. Even though we feel compelled to open ourselves up, this is an area of conflict for many empaths as we want to share our art as we feel others may relate and resonate with it, but we also have elements of us that are introverted and private, so we have a strong desire to close the curtains and hibernate where no one can see how we are internally wired..

For an empath, showcasing creativity can rub against our naturally introverted grain. We do not like to be center of attention and this is partly because we are not comfortable with the emotions that can arise when the focus is turned on us. Those around us may become jealous, manipulative, and try various tactics to suppress us. These low vibrational emotions can wreak havoc within our energy field.

Some people are generally more comfortable when everyone is similar and fits into the same tightly bound box to prevent anyone escaping, stepping out of line and into the spotlight. We are not square pegs and when we try to carve out a unique shape that fits who we are. Other people may step in to attempt to reshape and cause us disruption, as they might believe we need to be pulled back down. Other people's insecurities and fears of not succeeding can cause us to be afraid of venturing out to experience what our soul is aching and longing for.

"There is nothing enlightened about shrinking so that other people won't feel insecure around you. We are all meant to shine, as children do." ——Marianne Williamson

As we are highly passionate, we often develop strong connections with our hobbies or interests. Due to our creative side, we may find a resonance with music, dance, writing, art, activism, reading, yoga, meditation, humanitarian causes, or other similar interests. Whatever it is that has captured our mind soon becomes sacred in our hearts. We will become immersed in our hobbies and lose ourselves completely and sometimes this can seem to others as though our interests are the only things that matter to us. Although we will have a deep attachment to our passions, it is far easier to understand that we love all things at high levels of intensity and we need our own interests to survive and feel alive. This can sometimes be difficult for others to understand. Space, plenty of it, and freedom to explore and submerge in our chosen activity is what we need. Asking us to choose between our hobbies and our relationships may not give the desired outcome that might have been hoped for. Our hearts quickly connect to our passionate interests, and once that connection has been made our hearts will be broken if that bond has to be severed. We need plenty of alone time to indulge in our pursuits and we will not want or expect anyone else to dive as deeply into our interests as we do. However, respect and understanding that our interests are significantly important to us can make life a whole lot different.

We often find that our partners, friends, or family may feel ostracized or unwelcome when we are deeply embroiled in things we consider meaningful and pleasurable. This is because there is little chance that we will fully allow other people access to the heart of our hobbies. We find it far more rewarding when we have the time and space to become wrapped up in creative pursuits. This is not selfish or inconsiderate. It is simply how the spirit of art operates.

If we have a connection to something, it is intense and we will very likely prefer to delve into it as deeply as is possible. Passions are a great energy release and we feel as though we zone out while immersed and we will very likely lose the distinction between body and mind as well as all track of time.

The ideal relationship for us is one where we are allowed to take pleasure in our activities, and with the free time this has created, our loved ones take up interests separately rather than allowing any resentment or frustration to build up.

www.VonGArt.com
Megan Guenthner Clark

Chapter 35

ANIMALS EMPATHS

"There is no fundamental difference between man and animals in their ability to feel pleasure and pain, happiness, and misery." ——Charles Darwin

Some empaths have an extraordinarily close connection with animals and are able to tap into their emotions and feelings in the same way as they tap into and read human beings. Empaths who resonate strongly with animals are known as animal empaths. Although some people see a distinction between humans and animals, empaths see no separation at all as we are all part of the same energy. When we look into an animal's eyes we are able to see straight through to their vulnerable souls. Animal empaths often feel high empathy and sympathy for animals due to the suffering caused to the ones who are voiceless and unable to help or defend themselves. Empaths are capable of communicating with animals in a language that needs no words. We translate the vibrations their energy sends so we know if they are emanating love, peace, fear, or if they are in pain.

"How it is that animals understand things I do not know, but it is certain that they do understand. Perhaps there is a

language which is not made of words and everything in the world understands it. Perhaps there is a soul hidden in everything and it can always speak, without even making a sound, to another soul."
——Frances Hodgson Burnett

Many empaths have a strong affinity to the animal kingdom and we identify very easily with the emotional and physical pains that animals go through due to their unique expression or behavior. Unlike humans, most animals do not use manipulation to mask how they feel, so it is far easier to naturally read their energy and body language. If an animal does try to hide its true feelings, it is usually if they are experiencing pain or fear and they do not want to leave themselves vulnerable to a predator. When an animal is in the company of someone who has inner calm and peace, the animal's inherent characteristics will show through.

Animals aren't able to clearly verbally communicate their pain, other than certain animals that may whine or yelp. However, if someone has strong empathy with an animal they are able to relate to animals on a very deep level and can converse with them through touch, tone of voice, and energy. This enables instinctive trust, bonding, and a strong mutual affection to develop.

Animal empaths understand both the emotional and mental state of an animal's mind and through this we are able to connect and interact on an alternative dimension. We are naturally able to perceive how animals experience life and due to this we are able to carry out work that improves the conditions they live in and also their quality of life. This causes a great many of empaths to become advocates for animals by raising awareness so that suffering is reduced or eliminated.

By choice, our days would be spent in the wilderness surrounded by the various animals that roam freely around. Many of us have a special connection to one particular animal, known as a spirit animal. We learn many lessons from spirit animals and also receive guidance, wisdom, and protection.

It is believed that elephants show empathy and concern for other animals, and due to this we are especially drawn toward them or other highly sensitive creatures; for example, dolphins. These sentient creatures are usually acutely aware if a human is trying to help or do them harm, although they are also very trusting, which can be to their detriment. Animals, like empaths, are generally energy aware and they have the ability to sense people's intentions and also what is about to happen in their environment so they can protect and safeguard themselves.

As we are animal lovers, it is very common for us to have a pet and quite often we will have more than one. We don't see pets as creatures that should be on show, dominated, or controlled. Empaths have a unique bond with their pets, which is why they become faithful and loyal companions. The precious bond is treasured, as without pets many empaths would not experience a deep soul connection with another living thing. We usually treat the animals we share our homes with as part of our family and they are shown unconditional love. We nurture, care for them, and together create a pack.

We find being around certain animals calming and soothing, and we are most content when we are watching their curious, gentle, and genuine natures. We will scour rescue centers to find the one that desperately needs a loving home. It won't matter what the animal looks like on the surface, we will fall in love with the heart and soul beneath the floppy ears and tousled, matted fur.

If it was possible, the majority of empaths would, without question, set up a rescue center in our own backyard. We are likely to choose a cruelty-free diet either as a pescatarian, vegetarian, or vegan. And if empaths do eat meat they will be very consciously aware and will likely purchase from local farm shops or farmer's markets. Generally, we ethically source cosmetics and household products to ensure they have not been tested on animals.

Empaths struggle to understand how so many animals are treated so cruelly, whether as a commodity for profit in factory farms, neglected on the streets, or enduring abuse in households. We firmly believe that animals should have the same rights as humans to freely live in their natural habitats devoid of pain and suffering. We also find it difficult to work out why some animal's lives are valued over others. We see all animals as our equal and do not consider a pet's life as any more important than an animal's existence in the wild.

Rather than suffering and feeling pain alongside animals, it is more beneficial for empaths to raise their vibration so that we can send out healing vibrations. A higher vibration is also essential so that we have an excess of energy that enables us to take action by supporting conservation; raising awareness to protect domestic, farmed, and wildlife animals; and also so that we educate ourselves and share the knowledge in order for others to become more aware of the plight and suffering of animals.

It is not easy living in a world where animals suffer emotionally and physically for our consumption. Unfortunately, it is not something that is going to change immediately. We can bless our food and transmute the energy it holds so that whatever we consume does not affect our frequency, and in the meantime, we can try not to judge others and instead be mindful and teach our younger generations alternative produce ethics to the ones we may have been taught.

Industries only exist because of demand. The more people that are aware of the trauma that animals endure at the hands of man, the less likely our future generations will buy into it. We can try to send loving, light vibrations rather than adding to the dark, heavy, dense ones that occur when humans exert unnecessary inflictions to the detriment of another species with no regard or care for their suffering. If we could, we would change the world overnight. Sadly, it isn't possible, though collectively we can absolutely make a difference.

"Animal lovers are a special breed of humans, generous of spirit, full of empathy, perhaps a little prone to sentimentality and with hearts as big as a cloudless sky." ——John Grogan

Chapter 36

FATIGUE

Empaths can experience a sudden onset of chronic fatigue due to a significant crash in energy levels. This can be due to having so many sources connected to our energy supply and also because we profusely leak energy especially when we are not consciously aware, grounded and balanced. We often feel particularly drained when we have spent too much time in the company of other people, and these interactions can cause us to develop emotional exhaustion. Empaths need a great deal of alone time to retreat and recharge our internal batteries.

Our thoughts, emotions, and feelings can all play havoc on our internal system, causing devastating consequences that can debilitate us. If we have regular periods of solitude, we innately process our emotions and feelings during the day. We will then not become as exhausted as we can frequently let go of negatively charged energy that may be weighing us down. When we do not have the space to do this, we may find that our minds are overactive at night when everything is still and quiet and we are not distracted by external stimuli. Our minds can then become overactive rather than slowing down to enable us to relax so that sleep can naturally occur. We might also wake up often throughout the night and be unable to get a restful night's sleep as our minds are constantly trying to alert our attention so that we can process and make sense of anything that is lingering and needs to be dealt with. Our hyperactive minds can then be the cause of fatigue throughout the day as not only are we bombarded with a deafening amount of stimuli continuously, but also our body and mind have not had the opportunity to rest, replenish, and recharge. This can cause us to have erratic sleep patterns, some days needing ten or more hours and other days only one or two, depending on how much energy is attached to our energy field and is pulling us down.

If we are not able to find time during the day to make sense of our internal thoughts, feelings, and emotions, it is essential that we engage in meditation just before we go to sleep so that we can allow our thoughts to lightly come and go without paying too much attention to them or igniting a hormone-induced physiological response. Emotionally charged feelings linked to our memories and experiences can provoke us to feel emotions such as fear, anxiety, resentment, panic, and paranoia, so our brains become convinced that we are under some kind of genuine threat. Therefore, they send signals to the adrenal glands to produce hormones, which then release a surge of energy. When we experience intense or prolonged anxiety or stress, or our lifestyles are unhealthy—for example, too much or too little sleep, substance abuse, overworking, stressful relationships, stressful family situations, or general life crises—we place excessive continuous demands on our adrenal glands.

Our adrenal glands are small kidney-shaped endocrine glands approximately the size of a walnut that are situated in the lower back area just above our kidneys. They are very powerful and beneficial when under stress as they release hormones that help keep us alert, focused, and increase our stamina so that we are able to deal with pressure. However, when we overstimulate our adrenal glands, they will keep producing energy, which causes conflict when we try to rest or sleep as we will feel permanently wired and on high alert. This places excessive stress on our adrenal glands, causing them to eventually burn out and malfunction. The hormones that are continuously being released then stoop to very low levels as they are running on reserve, which can result in adrenal fatigue.

As our energy becomes drained very quickly, we will be tempted to top it back up with quick fixes and may consume food that are high in refined salt or sugar, which burn energy fast so that we receive an instant energy boost. However, this is a vicious cycle as the junk food we crave burns energy very quickly. Our body craves salt and sugar as it inherently knows what it needs. However, we feed it refined salt and refined sugar, which are found in most processed foods or junk foods, instead of feeding it unrefined sugar and unrefined salt, which are nutritious and in healthy doses they can nourish and replenish our adrenal glands. We might also try to raise our energy levels by consuming caffeine-based drinks, such as coffee or energy drinks; however, caffeine just irritates the adrenal glands further. We will then experience regular highs and lows as our energy levels peak and drop throughout the day.

When our adrenal glands are not working effectively, we may feel constantly fatigued, run down, irritable, anxious, dizzy, overwhelmed, we may experience heart palpitations, sugar or salt cravings, low or high blood pressure, and we will also find it very difficult to manage stressful situations. If we are well balanced, not overreacting, thinking positively, our situation is not too critical or extreme, exercising regularly, sleeping well, and have a healthy, nutritious diet, our adrenal glands will not be easily overwhelmed as the rest of our emotional and physical health is well taken care of.

During sleep, our cortisol levels (one of the hormones produced by our adrenal glands) rise naturally, peaking in the few hours before we wake. This happens to give us a good start to the day, and is known as the circadian rhythm, as it elevates our energy levels so that we can function effectively by sleeping when it is dark and waking when it is light. When our adrenal glands are exhausted we will likely wake up still feeling very tired even if we have had a long and seemingly restful sleep. We may feel drowsy most of the day, but then our cortisol levels may peak late in the evening, making it difficult for us to enter deep sleep.

It can take a long time to run our adrenal glands down, so it can take some time to fully repair them, however we can make changes that can have an immediate effect. The most important thing to do is listen to the body and pay attention to how it feels. We can remain aware of how our energy levels rise and fall throughout the day. We will most likely find that certain times of the day are more exhausting than others, so we can make additional alterations as and when we need to.

It is vital that we discover how and why we are placing so much stress on our adrenal glands. When we identify the root cause of our emotions and feelings, we can ensure we don't remain in a heightened state of alert, putting further pressure on these vital glands. Meditation will help us to not only focus on the body so we are aware of any sensations that are taking place, but it will also help us to calm and soothe our mind to prevent us repeating negative thoughts that ultimately cause chemical reactions. Spending time with family and friends or out at social activities can also regulate our cortisol levels as the levels are known to increase after spending long periods of time alone, if we feel lonely, isolated, and separated. If we are content in our own company, we will feel balanced and cortisol levels may not be such an issue.

Our diet and exercise regime can also place added stress on our adrenal glands, as if we push ourselves too much we place regular demands on the glands which causes them to produce too many stress-related hormones. Skipping meals, eating junk food and intense workouts all cause these glands to overwork. If we have food allergies, they will place additional stress on our adrenal glands, so it is vital to pay attention to foods that we have intolerances to.

To keep our adrenal glands nourished, we can try to eat an organic, well-balanced, and nutritional diet with plenty of protein and a healthy dose of vitamin A, B, and C, allowing time for the body to absorb all the nutrients before any physical activity takes place. We can also try to avoid large consumptions of alcohol and reduce or eliminate our refined sugar, refined salt, and caffeine intake.

Creating security, stability, joy, inner peace, being optimistic, and getting a restful night's sleep all contribute to rebalancing our adrenal glands. Just the thought of going to bed can bring on mild anxiety if we think we are going to lie awake for hours, drifting in and out of light sleep, but rarely reaching the highly sought-after delta state. When our adrenals are exhausted, we may wake up during the night alerted, often from high-stimuli dreams that just add to our overanxious state. Sleepless nights are particularly common when we endure a stressful or anxious period, as even if we enter sleep we can wake through the night feeling the adrenalin circulating through our body, but without knowing why. We will then struggle to rebalance our hormone levels so that we can drift back into a sleep.

Disturbances in sleep are most often linked to biochemical reactions due to high levels of stress hormones that flush through our system between approximately 2:00 a.m. to 4:00 a.m. The spike in our hormones dramatically affects our ability to remain calm, which is why our sleep is interrupted. We can rectify this by making up a magical therapeutic little potion consisting simply of honey and unrefined salt. Mix together one teaspoon of pink Himalayan sea salt (unrefined salt), which contains around eighty minerals and elements that aid our bodies in recovery, and five teaspoons of organic raw honey, which supplies the cells in our bodies with energy. Approximately twenty minutes before we want to enter sleep, we can put a small amount of the mixture underneath the tongue and allow it to dissolve naturally. The blend of honey and unrefined salt allows the body and mind to de-stress naturally by regulating our hormones so that by the time we are ready to sleep we are already in a peaceful, harmonious, and restful state. Honey and unrefined salt also both work to sustain the body so that we do not wake up hungry during the night.

Honey provides a stable amount of liver glycogen to the brain, which aids healthy sleeping. If we do not have enough liver glycogen stored, our adrenal glands are triggered to respond by pumping out adrenalin and cortisol, which are both stress hormones. Honey is believed to be a remedy that has been used to promote sleep for thousands of years. The reason honey is so beneficial is that it contains tryptophan, which produces serotonin, which promotes relaxation. When we are in the dark, serotonin converts to melatonin, which enhances restorative sleep. Melatonin assists with our sleep/wake cycle as it works in schedule with darkness and light. When our melatonin levels are balanced, we will fall into sleep easily, stay asleep naturally during the dark, and wake when light gradually enters the room.

Unrefined, 100 percent natural salt has antiexcitatory and antistress elements that keep us calm and stabilized throughout the night so that we get a restful night's sleep. Natural salt also preserves serotonin and melatonin levels in the brain.

Plus, a late-night snack helps us to remain asleep as when we are hungry our brain activates the adrenal stress hormones, which can then put us into fight or flight mode—a high state of alert. We can then sleep straight through the night, waking up refreshed and energized, and we are less likely to have a dip in energy throughout the day.

As an added precaution, we can place a Himalayan salt table lamp by the side of the bed as it removes the positive ions from the environment and replaces them with negative ones, mimicking the ones found in nature. This also removes the electric smog that is caused by electronic devices such as laptops and mobile phones, so the air is clear. Therefore, we will have improved air circulation and healthier and fuller breathing.

Chapter 37

SENSITIVITIES

Empaths are highly sensitive beings, and when we are fatigued our sensitivities become heightened. Many empaths are intolerant of gluten, dairy, wheat, and certain types of food and drinks. Our bodies respond with sensations, aches, pains, or even skin irritations to alert us when we are particularly sensitive to something. If food has been produced in an artificial environment or any suffering has taken place during the process, we will absorb the associated energy that is stored in whatever we consume. Empaths are very often vegetarian or vegan as we are highly empathetic toward animals and cannot bear to think of an animal being in fear or pain just so that we can have a meal when there are so many other options. If meat has been marinated in hormones due to an animal experiencing negative emotions during their life or at the time of death, we ingest those hormones when eating the meat. If an animal has experienced fear or anxiety, we may also feel fearful or anxious if we consume any food or liquid that has been produced from the animal. This is the reason many empaths are particular about the food we purchase, and why, if empaths are meat eaters, we prefer to purchase from ethical sources.

When we are consuming food we may also ingest the energy from our environment, so if there is a particularly heavy, stressful or anxious atmosphere surrounding us, we may experience either subtle or vivid disruptions that may cause irritable conditions associated with our digestive system.

We are also extremely sensitive to additives, preservatives, and chemicals and try to choose products from natural sources. Our skin is highly sensitive as we absorb energy through our skin cell receptors. It may react badly to cleaning products or cosmetics that contain unnatural ingredients. If our skin flares up or feels irritable as soon as we are in close contact with harmful chemicals, it is expressing intolerance, which is also a sign to alert us that the world needs to change to create a healthier existence for future generations.

Empaths often then raise awareness to try to prevent products from being tested on animals or we become activists to eradicate abuse in the fur, leather, meat or dairy industries. Our sensitivities help us to become alert to the cruelty that goes on so that we can help promote much needed change.

We are often specific about the fabric our clothes are made from and will notice any uneven seams, jagged edges, or sharp labels on the inside of garments. We may feel uncomfortable and uneasy wearing particular clothing and this is due to the energy attached to the material. If we buy leather products, we are consciously aware that an animal has suffered and lost its life for our purchase. Even if we do not consciously realize it, we will absorb those energies and they will have a direct impact on our emotions, even if it is only a subtle one.

It is not just the suffering the animals go through that cause us concern, the emissions from bleaching and dying the fabrics also affect our physical body. Choosing organic, ecofriendly, and cruelty-free options not only lessens the unnecessary suffering for both animals and for ourselves, it also reduces the harmful effects on our environment, which in turn affect every one of us. There are many options available, which makes it very easy to purchase garments that have been manufactured without the involvement of animals and with the minimal use of harmful chemicals. Cotton, linen, rayon, denim, and ramie are plant-based fabrics, although they are not always produced sustainably. For a more ethical option, there are organic and sustainable options available. And if we make a conscious effort to choose these options, we will notice a sharp increase in our vitality as they have a direct effect on our vibration.

Empaths are also affected by the stimulants in caffeine, which cause us to feel irritable and tense. These physical changes then have an adverse effect on our thoughts, feelings, and perceptions and can make us feel anxious and aggressive or find difficultly concentrating. Although we have received an energy boost from caffeine, our bodies and minds are intrinsically connected, so our emotions respond to the signals our bodies send out. As our physiology changes, our vibration responds by spiraling downward toward a lower frequency. Everything that is negative impacts our vibration, so when we are attuned to it we will instantly notice any harmful stimuli the very moment we are around it. Our sensitivities are there for a reason, so it is essential we pay attention to them.

Those who are not as sensitive to energy may not notice these subtle changes in their vibration as easily, if at all. They can possibly consume whatever foods they choose and seemingly be unaffected. The higher our awareness and consciousness are, the more intensely we respond to negative energies. As we develop our empath abilities and are able to clearly identify the reactions that are taking place within our bodies, we will find that our sensations become more enhanced.

Our sensitivities can cause us difficulties; however, they are imperative for our individual health and wellbeing, as well as being essential to the overall good of the planet and everything that exists on it. Although it may be tempting to close off our senses, apathy is not the solution for empaths as we will suffer with anguish and anxiety until we understand what is arousing the uncomfortable feelings. Even if we are not consciously thinking about our food choices, we are subconsciously aware of the suffering that animals and our environment endure just so that we can receive meat, dairy, and unethical man-created products. Our digestion is controlled by our autonomic nervous system. Therefore, our digestion and emotions are interconnected.

As soon as we set the intention to alter our consumption of harmful toxins and to surround ourselves with ethical materials, we will notice a dramatic increase in our vibration. Setting the intention to change propels us toward a new frequency, even if the changes don't take place immediately.

Progress is the key to change, as otherwise we will place far too much pressure on the alterations and place unrealistic expectations on ourselves to transform every aspect of our lives immediately. We can make small changes, and soon enough we will feel lighter as the stresses associated with our old lifestyle choices drop away as we replace old habits with new ones that create change that ripples across the earth.

Chapter 38

ANXIETY

Anxiety sucks—literally. It can suck our energy dry, and unfortunately, it is a common ailment in empaths. Anxiety manipulates and tricks us with its many clandestine tactics. We are fooled into feeling afraid when in reality often there is nothing to fear other than fear and anxiety. It can become so chronic that it evaporates every ounce of pleasure from our lives.

Social situations can be a minefield as when we are anxious our brain can automatically revert to fight or flight mode, so we feel as though we are about to be in some kind of impending danger. This releases a surge of a hormone called cortisol into our systems, which prepares us to cope with whatever perceived "danger" we are confronted with. However, when too much cortisol is pumped out on a regular basis we are left feeling wired and fraught with anxiety, as essentially there is no real danger, so we do not use up the adrenalin and other chemicals that are now flushing through our bodies. The buildup of cortisol leaves us on the outlook for a potential threat, and will send our minds into overdrive looking out for any negativity that could be lying in wait. Due to the intake of excess energy, we will feel on constant high alert.

We can also become filled with anxiety due to picking up immeasurable amounts of emotional debris from our environment. Within that debris is an assortment of emotions that cause friction with our energy, often leaving us anxious, debilitated, and worn down. The emotional energy we absorb has to be dealt with. Consequently, not only do we think we are in some kind of danger, we are also bombarded with energy from every angle as we take in everything that is in our surrounding environment.

Empaths don't just pick up on the energy that is in our immediate surroundings. We can also become overwhelmed by anxiety due to consciously or unconsciously tapping into the emotional trauma going on at any time, at any place in the world. This means that we may also absorb other people's anxiety and feel it as our own. So if we are already anxious it can compound it further. When we clearly identify our own emotions from other people's we will be able to separate external anxiety and deal with the root cause of our own anxious feelings while transmuting and redirecting any other energies that are causing us disturbance. It is quite common for empaths to lie awake throughout the night unable to move our body or rid our mind of negativity due to either irrational or rational thoughts and excessive emotional energy resulting in overpowering bouts of anxiety. What we sometimes fail to understand is that the more attention we give our anxiety, the stronger it becomes and the more powerful it grows. Every emotion we then experience will be compounded by anxious sensations. Emotions that we normally might be able to brush off or handle easily become intensified under the crippling weight that anxiety bears down on us.

Anxiety keeps on drawing energy from us until we are unproductive, exhausted, temporarily disabled, and often in emotional and physical pain. We can become afraid to go places, speak to people, make telephone calls, wear certain clothes or eat certain foods, and our creativity is limited. Anxiety can touch us in places we least expect, and quite often we may not even realize that anxiety is making decisions for us. Unfortunately, due to being weakened by it, we allow it to take control.

Anxiety lurks in the darkest corners of our minds, and at the slightest opportunity it will pounce. We need to discover the root cause of anxiety and how to eradicate it, although we first need to understand what exists at the core of our other persistent emotions. When we understand our emotions we can then arm and protect ourselves so that we are prepared to fight the battle with knowledge as an ally.

Figuring out how anxiety works is the most forceful weapon we have. It can take away huge sections of our lives and can totally dominate, control, and consume us if we do not master it. Anxiety can be a warning sign of impending danger that alerts us when something is wrong, and enables the body and mind to prepare for "fight or flight." However, severe or prolonged anxiety can also cripple us so that we are so fraught with emotion and flooded with chemicals that we end up feeling powerless to take any action at all. We then enter a lose/lose situation.

Sometimes it feels easier to give up and to stay under the covers rather than step over the anxious weighted moments that torment us before they pass. But believe me, it isn't easier, and the longer we stay this way, the harder it gets to blow the dense clouds that have gathered out of harm's way. If we do not muster the strength to tackle it, we will succumb to anxiety and have little will power to adequately take care of ourselves. Until we remove ourselves from anxiety's suction, it can be arduous to see things clearly so that we can take whatever steps necessary to eliminate whatever is causing the anxiety in the first place.

The first step to ridding ourselves of anxiety is to comprehend it. Unfortunately, anxiety can become an addiction, a habit, something that feels familiar. Its energy grows until we become overwhelmed, submerged, and frozen with fear. When we are in the midst of anxiety the slightest sound or movement can startle us and propel our fearful state further. Anything within our vicinity that significantly holds a resemblance to an emotionally charged experience from the past could derail and overpower us. Anxiety relates to paralyzing, irrational fear and we need to confront it head-on, face to face. We need to stir the demons within and be willing to listen to what they wish to tell us. There will be an underlying belief somewhere deep inside of us that is signaling to gain our attention. It is important to discover what that belief is, although it is no use paying attention to it when we are in an anxious state. Our minds will never be calm enough to focus effectively and our anxiety will get in the way of seeing it with clarity. When it dissipates we can then turn attention to whatever may be causing it.

If anxiety has been plaguing us, we need to summon it randomly when it is least expecting it—in the same way it takes control over us. First, though, we need to understand anxiety so that it doesn't creep back in when we are trying to eradicate it. Anxiety often begins with a small seed, a very simple thought or feeling that triggers a forgotten past memory or experience. The more energy we give to the thought, the more powerful it becomes. The thought can then turn into an emotion. When the emotion takes hold of us it can turn into a feeling. Soon enough, this feeling can become part of our belief system and nestle deep inside of us. If we are not aware that this has happened, it can then be very difficult to change or remove it.

Anxiety that derives from irrational thinking is no use for anything other than to burden and weigh us down. The benefits of the original thought have mostly all gone and what is left behind is a system overflooded with adrenalin and a brain clouded with emotionally charged chemicals now unable to function effectively. Instead of a clear mind to consider our options in times of difficulties, we have a mind racing at a thousand miles an hour with extreme, ridiculous, and illogical thoughts. The mind becomes overactive, and in order to process anything rationally it is absolutely essential that we discover ways to slow things down so that we stop feeding into the attack.

One of the easiest ways to combat anxiety is to alter the way we think so that we stop instantly trusting every irrational thought that floods in and overloads our mind. Anxiety stems from our subconscious or unconscious mind. When we are fully conscious and existing in the present moment, anxiety cannot exist for long, so as soon as we breathe into the moment, anxious feelings quickly dissipate. Anxiety is fear based. We need to stay still, calm the mind, concentrate on our breathing, and recognize what is causing us to feel anxious so that we can retrain our minds to think alternatively. It is like breaking a bad habit. We become so used to responding in certain ways that it starts to feel natural to continue as we always have done. We need to unlearn what we have been doing and then relearn empowering and beneficial techniques.

Simply telling ourselves to stop worrying, unfortunately, won't work. We need to make ourselves *believe* that there is no need to worry. When we are in an anxious frame of mind, we are prepared for danger. Focusing more on the anxiety will just add to its energy. The quickest way out of an anxiety attack is by changing the image in our minds completely. We need to start by focusing on something positive, something loving and soothing. Then, when things have calmed down, we can tiptoe back to our anxious thoughts and gently probe them to see what was causing the overreaction. We can pay a little loving attention to them and then decide upon whatever action might be needed to deal with the issue. We can then figure out if there are legitimate concerns, and if not, we can make the decision to dump the remaining rubbish and nonsensical thoughts that have been left behind.

We can try not dwell on our thoughts, or to emphasize our anxiety for too long. Instead, we can separate our thoughts and just take the messages that our most prominent ones offer. We can then transmute them by showing them love, understanding, and compassion and then leave, quietly, slowly, and gently.

Endorphins are anxiety and stress busters, which help us to feel good while enhancing our pleasure zones. A smile or laughter that engages the mouth, eyes, and cheeks, along with thinking happy, positive, and loving thoughts, is therapeutic and immediately triggers the release of endorphins such as serotonin and dopamine. Exercise also releases endorphins into the bloodstream. If we are able to exercise with someone we are fond of, we will receive an extra high boost as social activity also increases endorphin production. Like with most things, though, too high a rush of endorphins in our system can also be harmful, as we experience a euphoric high followed by a low as the endorphins drain out. The low can then lead to stress and anxiety, so a healthy dose is essential to avoid becoming addicted to euphoria, leading us to seek manufactured ways to increase the production.

Mediation is probably our greatest assistant so that we defeat anxiety on a long-term basis. Through meditation we can learn to quiet our minds. When the mind is calm, we gain access to a myriad of information that tells us everything we need to know about ourselves. When our minds are still, we can pay attention to what is causing us distress by focusing on one emotion, feeling, or memory at a time. We can then discover what previous encounter is causing us to feel fearful. Often, it is just that we need to rewire our minds so that we understand the difference between real and perceived danger. Many of our past experiences will have convinced us that the world is a "dangerous place," therefore stepping out anywhere new can feel unsafe and even terrifying. This belief is just our conditioned minds' perception of a situation based on past occurrences.

Our DNA has stacked up memories from thousands of years ago, so often it may not even be a current threat that we feel we need to arm ourselves against. What may have felt dangerous in our caveman days is no longer a real danger to us today, so we constantly need to reprogram, recondition, and update our minds. Thoughts will occur that we may recognize to be the cause of our "worry zones." Worrying and fretting never get us anywhere as when we worry we cloud our minds with negativity and the associated emotions that we conjure up makes it very difficult to think straight. When we worry about what has happened or maybe will happen, we are living in the past or the future, and we have no control over either. We can only control the current moment. And while we are conscious in the present moment, we have the very best hope of creating a future that reflects our positive attitude while we let go of the past. We cannot change it, as much as we may want to. All we can do is focus on making each moment worthwhile so that the moments contribute to a far more peaceful future.

"You must be shapeless, formless, like water. When you pour water in a cup, it becomes the cup. When you pour water in a bottle, it becomes the bottle. When you pour water in a teapot, it becomes the teapot. Water can drip and it can crash. Become like water my friend."——Bruce Lee

Instead of battling to swim against the current to reach things that we have already passed, we can calmly be at one with the water's flow. We will only ever pass the same things in the same way once. We can remain in the moment aware, flexible and fluidly moving. We can ride the current, keeping ourselves alert so that we are can see which way the river is flowing. This means we will avoid getting stuck behind rocks or having to unexpectedly maneuver around chaotic conditions that may be looming ahead of us. There is so much going on within the river that we miss it when we are frantically looking too far ahead or too far behind. When we are at one with the water, we can take everything in as it happens and understand that even rivers have parts to them that may seem like they are a hindrance. Though, ultimately, as a whole, it allows for the formation of various natural activities to blossom.

When man interferes and modifies a river to try to control it, it can cause havoc further down the way as the water's energy is increased and becomes more forceful as it navigates a manipulated environment. Such is the same for our own lives. When we try to control our circumstances by not aligning and not being in sync with our inner selves and then trying to alter things that cannot or should not be changed, we can end up causing ourselves debilitation and destruction further down the line. This is why it is essential to stay in the moment, paying attention to everything that is taking place and remaining aware of the numerous entities that surround us that could contribute to or hinder our experience at any time.

When we are harmonious we can conserve our energy for the times we need it most, rather than using up our reserves and depleting them by frantically trying to grasp onto or affect things that are far out of our reach. We can endeavor to soothe and slow the endless chatter and ramblings that hurry through our mind at great speed stirring up trouble along the way.

The more we practice meditation, the easier it is to calm and balance our minds so that we are less likely to experience anxiety, but if we do, we are energized and well prepared for its call.

Mindfulness also helps to eliminate anxiety as it anchors us to the present moment so we are not carried away with what we cannot change from the past or second-guessing what may be awaiting us in the future. Instead, we can allow every moment to exist in its own merit so that we can make conscious decisions based on how we want to feel currently. Simple breathing exercises help to calm heavy, pounding heartbeats and they take the racing mind away from pointless, frantic suffering caused by overthinking. We need to rest the body and mind, slow them down, focus only on how each moment feels rather than ones from the future or past. Our anxiety is signaling that we need time out; we need to rest and recuperate.

Yoga, dietary changes, cutting back on caffeine, breathing practices, and spending time outdoors can all help to take the edge off anxious thoughts. Anxiety is not always just a case of mind over matter. Not only can it be caused by emotional overload and chemical imbalances, it is also believed that anxiety can be passed on genetically. We can try not to give ourselves a hard time when we feel anxiety. We can use loving tactics when dealing with it, and significantly, be considerate and gentle with ourselves.

A small and infrequent amount of anxiety is fine, as it is a coping mechanism that gears us up for when we perceive there is imminent, genuine danger. As long as we retain a healthy balance and we don't become overwhelmed with emotion, it can serve us well to discern the magnitude of perceived threat. It would be great to say that anxiety can be eradicated completely, although it is not always that simple. It can sneak in when we least expect it, hoping to engage in a disorientating toxic dynamic at any time, especially if we also suffer with insomnia. The difference being that when we know how to deal with anxiety we can show it loving kindness so that it becomes less powerful and it is too weak to stay around for long. Anxiety about anxiety makes it worse. We have to treat anxiety with gentleness and soothe our worries, fears, and concerns.

When our anxiety knows we have taken our power back, it may still regularly make an appearance. As soon as we show it understanding and take pressure off ourselves, when we are feeling calmer, we can get to the roots of the reason it exists and retrain our thoughts to be kinder. Slowly, anxiety then sees it has a safe space to back off to and it will remain under our control where we will be prepared for it if and when it does reappear.

Anxiety can visit from time to time, but when it does, we can ensure it arrives with rational concerns so that we can discern the magnitude of perceived threat without all our fear-based emotions popping by to cause a whirlwind and cloud our thinking. We just need to treat chronic anxiety like we would treat a relationship that is going through difficulties: give it a little space; focus on what makes us happy; nourish, love, and take care of ourselves emotionally, mentally, and physically; refrain from fighting with it or trying to blame or shame; think clearly; remove resentment, frustration, and all other negative emotions; forgive and forget; let go; communicate; and most of all, be gentle.

We are all hard on ourselves at times. When we are, we can try to remember the inner child within us all who still feels scared at times and who needs comforted and made to feel secure. It needs a huge hug, tenderness, and to be told that everything is going to be okay. We can instantly change the critical messages we have been repeating to ourselves and think empowering, supportive, positively validating thoughts that are filled with love. When we say them out loud, their vibration is stronger and they become even more powerful. We can then start to really believe in our words and permanently replace a burnt out cable in our internal wiring.

Chapter 39

HEALING OUR INNER CHILD

When we heal our inner child we are able to process our denied, misunderstood, suppressed and unresolved emotions and change patterns of behavior that have been causing us difficulties or hindering us throughout our life. Often, we may not realize that whenever we are emotionally triggered it is due to something that has happened many years ago. It isn't until we route back to where an original emotion stems from that we discover that we regularly react and respond in ways that directly result from our childhood and that actually have very little to do with the present moment. Connecting to our inner child allows us to undo some of the wrongly held historic beliefs originating from our past and it also helps us to let go of old emotional pain.

Initially it can be overwhelming to connect with our inner child as we are delving into history that we have previously tried to deny or forget, especially if we have been through incredible suffering and there is a lot of distress to sift through. Many of the emotions that we feel today exist due to our past experiences and may be the cause for us feeling low self-worth or low self-esteem. However, much of what we feel is just an illusion. Sometimes we are taught and conditioned to believe so much about ourselves that really isn't true and a lot of it stems back to our vulnerable and absorbent days from childhood.

When we are children our minds aren't always rational, and instead of filtering information and absorbing what is healthy and rejecting what is injurious, we take everything in. If someone behaves in a way that is hurtful, we internalize it and take on how they have acted so that we ultimately feel responsible for their treatment. We can then be left feeling worthless, fearful, isolated, neglected, and misunderstood without knowing why we feel this way or knowing how to express these emotions. We don't always recognize that how we are feeling now is associated with what has occurred in the past. Our formative years have a huge influence on who we grow up to become as we move through our teenage years and then into adulthood. At any time we are able to consciously rewind through the years so that we can correct any false beliefs we hold and also so that we can put our experiences and emotions into context.

When we reconnect with our inner child for the first time, we have to be prepared for all our contained emotions to rise to the surface, and often we will experience them as though they are happening in current time rather than belonging to the past. This is okay. Sometimes we have to cry and cleanse to allow these emotions to work their way through. Connecting to our inner child is easier if we take ourselves back to somewhere that feels like a safe haven, whether that is an actual place or a memory we visualize in our minds. We may feel secure at a grandparent's house or a close friend's, or being surrounded by our favorite belongings. Whatever we choose, we can try to recreate a safe and secure scene as best we can whenever we resurrect past feelings.

Rather than going back to a childlike state, we need to remain rational compassionate and with our adult, reasoning mind intact. We basically need to be the adult who is tending to the child. Now that we have learned so much about life, we are in a position where the knowledge and understanding of the world and the people within it can help us to make sense of some of the situations we went through as a child. During childhood we do not properly understand emotions and feelings, so when they arise in us or are expressed by other people they can be confusing and bewildering. Rather than processing them we push them down and mask them, where they remain until we feel ready to acknowledge them. We therefore must be patient and not expect that we are going to be able to heal all of our past wounds in one go. It has taken us a long time to learn everything that we hold inside, so it is going to take us time to let go of it all and relearn more rational information.

The mandala artwork was crafted by Krutika Joglekar. To find out more information and view more of Krutika's unique creations please visit www.instagram.com/krutikajoglekar/

Depending on how painful our past experiences have been, we may want to go within and connect with our inner child in small sessions for possibly only five to ten minutes at a time, or whatever feels comfortable, so that we are not overcome with emotion. When we are dealing with our inner child, we must remember that we are talking to a child, so rather than berate and get angry we create a safe space so that the communication will be light and easy and also ensure we listen carefully and pay full attention. If our inner child is frightened that we are going to be condemning the emotions that he or she has held on to, or if they feel we are not fully interested, they will not communicate freely about whatever it is that is causing the anguish or pain in our lives today. We can pay attention to the tone of voice we are using so that we are not aggressive or too harsh, even if we get frustrated and irritated by what we are purging.

As our emotions emerge, we can remember to pacify and soothe our inner child by being accepting and showing supportive, loving care without expressing any judgment, blame or shame. Every feeling that arises is valid, so we need to respect and trust what comes to the surface rather than feeling afraid and pushing it back down. It is essential that our inner child can trust us to handle whatever he/she shows us, even if some of it appears to be dramatic, irrational, or unreasonable. Our inner child will have felt very differently toward things that happened years ago, compared to how we might feel if they happened now.

We may find that some of the people who are connected to painful past emotions are still in our lives today. Part of the process of healing our inner child is letting go of any anger or resentment. We can try to be compassionate and forgive whoever it was that caused us harm. Holding on to negative emotions does not justify the pain or help us in any way. Letting go of all anger is the only option if we want to move on.

Although we can try not to be judgmental, it is okay to temporarily feel and express all the emotions that are associated to painful childhood memories. We may feel angry, we might want to scream or shout, and feel enraged and furious at how we were previously treated. Our emotions have been kept in captivity and they need to be released. The only way for emotions to go away is by going into them and through them. So that our emotions can process effectively, they must be expressed and sometimes we need to verbally express them; when we use our voice far more energy is added to the emotion. However, it is vital that we do this when we are in a safe space. It is not going to be beneficial to shout or scream at anyone else; all this will do is add more negativity, and we will continuously spiral, repeating the same old emotions.

When we are evoking emotions we can also be aware that we may feel a sense of associated anger or sadness. Certain things that happen to us aren't always fair or right and we may also feel sorrow or deep-set grief. There is no right or wrong when unearthing how our inner child feels. We must remember that this is our childhood mind and it is very different from the adult mind we know today. We can connect to our inner child as often or as little as we want. We can incorporate the communication into our meditations or even just carry the spirit of our inner child with us so that we can channel it into our daily lives.

We have a great deal to learn from our inner child, and by getting to know him/her we can achieve a profound awareness of our sense of self. This connection is the clue that helps us locate the majority of our "missing pieces."

We have grown up with our inner child, yet many of us disconnect from our memories rather than connecting them so that we are stronger and bonded as one. There are billions of fragments of information held within our childhood memories. Some are painful, while others hold a wealth of knowledge. All of them help us to heal and understand ourselves on an intimate level as our inner child is the one person who has been with us every step of the way.

Chapter 40

MOODS

We may periodically experience moodiness if we are not mindful, have not cleansed and protected our energy fields or if we are not vibrating on a high frequency. One of the main reasons for this is that we are at risk of absorbing an excess amount of external energy that causes us to feel frustrated as we try to identify where it has come from and why. If there is toxic energy in the atmosphere, we may potentially attract the energy and react to it as though it were our own. We then quickly fluctuate and flip from one emotion to another, even between emotions that are on opposing sides of the spectrum.

If we are not aware that we are absorbing energy, these mood swings can be confusing and even frightening as it can be a challenge to find any logic to them. We will feel out of control and struggle to take our emotions by their reins, having no clue as to which direction they have come from. This is why it is essential to ground and protect ourselves to avoid shifting from one extreme to another.

Meltdowns, however big or small, can take place when energy is unregulated. The way someone expresses a meltdown differentiates from one person to the next and can either be internalized or externalized. Internally, though, we all suffer similarly. Meltdowns usually appear following a buildup of stimuli, stress, tension, or frustration. They can be purely emotional or they can be in the form of anger-fueled tantrums and perhaps may even be traumatic. Meltdowns can accelerate quickly and appear to come from nowhere. A meltdown may take place when a buildup of energy has accumulated or become blocked in our electromagnetic field. We absorb and take on such high levels of energetic debris that eventually we need to release them, and if we are not aware of how to transmute energy, it can literally explode inside us like an atom bomb. Our words or actions may then carry the negative charge from the outburst and we may act unkindly or cuttingly toward others. Unfortunately, this explosive energy release usually happens with someone we feel "safe" with; for example, a partner, close friend, or family member. It can be extremely destructive for relationships, which is why it is essential that we protect our energy fields and learn how to channel, transmute, and redirect energy.

Sometimes, we may even pick a fight to cause an argument just so that we can jettison the energy that feels loaded, heavy, murky, and toxic. We may unintentionally act excessively jealous or controlling as a way to turn a peaceful situation into one that will result in this simmering energy erupting out. Other times, we may have absorbed one too many bad moods from someone who is in our company, and this final straw breaks the back of the camel and sets off our inner time bomb, causing what can feel like full-scale devastation. Releasing energy in this way can sabotage otherwise healthy relationships and signal the end for friendships. The person on the receiving end will have no clue as to how their slight change in mood transferred onto us and caused our energy system to burst the banks and profusely overflow.

This explanation is not meant to sound as though it is transferring the blame on to "energy" or another person. An energy build-up is purely our responsibility, and ours alone. We have to take ownership of the energy we handle so that we process it effectively and don't allow it to linger until it pushes us to breaking point.

Some females who are extra sensitive or who suffer with bouts of anxiety or stress may also notice that they are more susceptible to many of the symptoms related to premenstrual stress or tension (PMS). At the time of writing this there are no definitive laboratory studies or unique findings that determine the cause of PMS. Studies have shown that hormone levels fluctuate when women are premenstrual, and this results in a chemical imbalance in the brain. However, the changes in hormone levels are currently not believed to be the cause of PMS but are thought to be the result of the changes that are taking place physiologically as we go through our menstrual cycle. Nonetheless, it is my belief that these hormones that require energy input and output are directly related to and are often the main cause of PMS, especially when linked to other emotional and physiological processes we go through. Every process that our body goes through requires energy to function effectively. It is vital that our organs and glands are healthy and energized so that they are productive when we need to rely on them.

During our menstrual cycle both estrogen and progesterone are released from the ovaries. When our hormones are out of balance, the hormone estrogen can increase while the hormone progesterone can decrease. Estrogen is a stimulant. Too much estrogen can cause anxiety, agitation, tension, nervousness, and cell division. It can also cause us to feel shivery and have cold hands or feet, as high estrogen levels limit the blood flow to our extremities. Progesterone, on the other hand, has the opposite effect and is a soothing, rest-promoting hormone, which calms and pacifies; therefore, it balances the stimulating effects of estrogen. We require a healthy supply of both so that we remain calm and harmonic throughout our menstrual cycle and so that the progesterone release neutralizes the effects of high estrogen.

I firmly believe that adrenal fatigue and PMS are directly linked and can become involved in a vicious circle with one another. The reason for this is that they both need progesterone to function healthily and both PMS and our adrenal glands relentlessly take their supply, leaving the other one deficient. When our progesterone is very low, the stimulating estrogen takes over and can cause high anxiety and high stress levels. When we are stressed, our adrenal glands produce cortisol. Progesterone is necessary for the production of cortisol, so we can unknowingly use up the majority of our progesterone quota when we experience long periods of stress. When our progesterone levels are low, our cortisol levels are also affected. So not only do we need progesterone to counteract the effect of high estrogen, the stress we feel from high estrogen is also causing us to produce more progesterone-fueled cortisol.

Although progesterone helps to produce cortisol, these two hormones are opposites. Cortisol is associated with anxiety and puts our system on high alert to prepare for impending threats, progesterone is calming and helps us to relax and rest. Similar to the premenstrual balance with estrogen and progesterone, the two hormones even one another out so that we do not become irritable, agitated, or overanxious. As our progesterone source depletes, our estrogen and progesterone become unbalanced, with our estrogen being high and our progesterone being low. This can then bring on many of the symptoms that are associated with PMS, as there is not enough progesterone to counter-affect the estrogen.

When we are experiencing regular and high levels of anxiety, stress, and we feel constantly on edge, we are placing demands for cortisol to be produced by our adrenal glands. It is therefore essential that we decrease the amount of cortisol that we are releasing on a daily basis so that we do not exhaust our adrenal glands and use up the progesterone needed during the latter stage of our menstrual cycle. When our adrenal glands are healthy and use a balanced amount of progesterone for cortisol, we will then feel calmer and more harmonious when we are premenstrual as our ovaries are able to release an increased amount of calming progesterone. If we don't reduce the amount of anxiety and stress we are under, the amount of estrogen or progesterone that is released will be off balance and this can lead to mood irregularities, irrational fears, restlessness, general fatigue, and many other PMS-associated symptoms.

When we identify and alleviate whatever is causing us anxiety and stress on a regular basis, we can remove the pressure we are putting on our adrenal glands. We are then able to stabilize our progesterone levels so that the hormone can flow freely when we are premenstrual and then it is able to offset the effects of the stimulating, excitatory hormone estrogen.

Estrogen rises in the second half of our menstrual cycle, and this is when our progesterone level should also heighten. During the last two weeks of our cycle, if these hormones do not find a healthy balance, we can also experience the anxious symptoms of high estrogen, as well as the depressive signs of low progesterone. This is known as estrogen dominance (ED). Estrogen can be high due to physiological changes, our environment, lifestyle, and dietary choices. Estrogen dominance can lead to mood swings, pain, irritability, headaches, sweet or salty food cravings, poor concentration, insomnia, sluggish metabolism, weight gain, and lethargy.

Estrogen dominance may also be caused by consuming too many xenoestrogens. Xenoestrogens are growth hormones that are fed to livestock and poultry, and when we consume the associated meat or dairy, we also take in xenoestrogens, which our body can easily mistake for estrogen (adding to high estrogen levels). Xenoestrogens are also found in plastic wrapping and containers; for example, when we microwave food in plastic dishes xenoestrogens will be absorbed into our food.

*** We can also try to reduce our dairy consumption when we are premenstrual as it can also have a volatile effect on our moods due to the varying amounts of progesterone and estrogen that is contained in milk, especially when it is produced by pregnant cows.

High levels of estrogen make us feel anxious, which then triggers the production of cortisol, which then places even further demands on progesterone. This is the dangerous cycle we get caught up in when our lifestyles are not healthy and we put ourselves under too much stress. Our systems take what they need to provide the ingredients required to produce hormones in response to our brains' demands. We are exhausting ourselves by living on high-alert fight or flight survival mode, which ultimately is making our daily survival increasingly difficult.

Taking all of this into consideration, it is evident that an estrogen and progesterone balance is partly determined by healthy adrenal glands, and the health of our adrenal glands is partly determined by a healthy production of estrogen and progesterone. If our adrenal glands are not under too much pressure, we will have enough reserves to secrete enough progesterone to counteract estrogen and therefore we will suffer fewer, if any, of the energy-depleting symptoms associated with PMS.

Our bodies can be demanding, so if we feel we are out of sync, the first step is to get our hormone levels checked out to see how high or low they are.

**Dr. Vitiello, director of the University of Washington in Seattle, carried out research that found low levels of sodium causes blood volume to decrease and the sympathetic nervous system responds by activating to compensate. The sympathetic nervous system activates adrenalin and triggers the fight or flight response that then impairs our ability to get to sleep and also remain asleep.

When our sodium levels are elevated and our blood pressure is high, our adrenals are activated, which put us on a high state of alert due to adrenalin pumping through our system. If we do not use the adrenalin quota as there is no impending threat or we are not highly active, we can become more irritable, impatient, and volatile, and we will be unable to rest properly during sleep, waking up exhausted—classic symptoms related to PMS.

Low sodium levels can also wreak havoc on our adrenal glands. By balancing our salt levels and ensuring we are consuming the correct type of salt, we can reduce the pressure the adrenal system is under, which will also reduce the production of cortisol. Even though many of us believe that we should be consuming a low-sodium diet reduce our salt intake, what is usually happening is that we are not making the distinction between healthy salt and unhealthy salt. We end up consuming the wrong salt, and high levels of the wrong salt can cause us harm, so instead we try to cut all salt out of our diets, which means we are not receiving the benefits of unrefined healthy salt. ********

We are often advised to lower our salt intake when premenstrual, instead of being told to consume a healthy dose of unrefined salt and reduce our refined (table) salt intake, as it is almost pure sodium chloride with not enough magnesium to balance it. Unrefined salt has plenty of magnesium along with other minerals that our body requires, which is why it does not usually negatively affect our blood pressure. Salt has antistress and antiexcitatory qualities; therefore, a healthy supply of unrefined salt when premenstrual helps us remain calm and balanced as it reduces our stress levels.

Unrefined salt also contains lithium, which is used in antidepressant medications, as lithium helps treat emotional and effective disorders. Unrefined salt, and a healthy dose of it, is essential for the function of every cell in our bodies and it provides us with vital nutrients that stabilize our metabolism. Our metabolism needs to be healthy to ensure that it is able to absorb fuel and transform it to energy. We often crave salt without realizing that unrefined salt eases anxiety and enhances our overall wellbeing, though unfortunately we often reach out for processed quick-fix products that contain table salts, which offer little or adverse health benefits.

When we replace refined salts with unrefined salts, such as Himalayan, Celtic, or Real salt, we will notice an increase in energy levels, a reduction in stress levels, and a calmer emotional and mental state, which can be particularly effective in reducing much of the symptoms of PMS. Our cortisol levels will be lower as the adrenal glands are not pumping it out due to feeling as though there is a potential threat, and thus we will have more progesterone available to balance estrogen when we need it.

We can lower our intake of processed food, which contain high levels of refined salt, and instead switch to natural unrefined salt, which can be added to fresh-produce meals after preparation. Most salt carry traces of metals and mercury, so it is advisable to check for salts that are particularly low in these elements. Old salt is preferable as it comes from a salt mine, which is usually millions of years old. It has less mercury and toxic materials as it was made when the earth had lower pollution levels. However, old salt has a few minerals that have lower levels than new salt, so it is always beneficial to research salt carefully and make an individual choice. As long as the salt is natural/unrefined, it will offer an array of health benefits that are not found in refined salt.

***If there are any health concerns, particularly around blood pressure levels, always seek medical advice or carry out further research before making alterations to your diet.

When we do not have a good supply of essential hormones in our reserves, our energy levels drop as our hormones are out of equilibrium. It is vital that we understand how our hormones interact with one another and also how they multifunction. Even minor fluctuations in our hormones can have a devastating and significant effect on our overall wellbeing. If our energy is low and we are vibrating on a low level, we will most likely not be protecting our energy field. This means that other people's energy can easily penetrate our own and we will be more susceptible to absorbing external emotions and feelings.

Women may notice that when we are premenstrual our tolerance levels are lower, so we may get more easily aggravated and triggered by other people and may be more likely to lose our temper. Although we are already irritable due to our own hormones fluctuating and struggling to find a balance, we will also be dealing with the weight of other people's emotions too. Our already thin outer skin that protects our energy field is even thinner due to all of our energy and focus being directed on our hormonal activity and the resulting side effects. We are then extremely vulnerable to outside energies and they can easily seep in and affect our own.

If we are around people who are moody, aggressive, or just generally in a negative frame of mind, when we are premenstrual we will very likely take on their energy without realizing that it isn't our own. We may then instinctively behave in ways that mirror how other people are acting, causing us to be in a terrible mood out of nowhere and not understanding that we are just being easily influenced by whatever is going on around us. This is why protecting our energy field is essential during the latter part of our menstrual cycle. Our hormones are already finding it difficult to create harmony, they are already overworked, they are already surviving on reserves, and other people's energy can be like a match igniting a pressurized dark cloud of toxic, dense energy. Our already low level of energy will drop even further as we then have to request supplies from our exhausted adrenal gland to help us in yet another "fight or flight" situation. This impairs our ability to calm down and pacify situations, and we will burn every ounce of spare energy as we remain in a heightened state of alert, running on adrenalin, pumping out cortisol, and ultimately using up even more progesterone, which disrupts our wellbeing further. We will not just be exhausted, we will become debilitated. We will be difficult to be around. Sleep will not come easily due to feeling wired, and when we do eventually find sleep, we will most likely wake too soon feeling zoned out, fuzzy, and zombielike.

When we are aware that we are absorbing immense amounts of unidentified energy, we will understand how potentially hazardous it is for us to allow it to enter our electromagnetic field, causing us to take on more than we are prepared for or can currently handle. When a great proportion of our energy is being used up to replenish, rebalance, and restore the physiological damage we have done to our internal organs, there is a lesser amount of energy available to stabilize and restore our emotional and mental states. This is another reason why we can become far more easily irritated, worn down, quick tempered, and hypersensitive when we are premenstrual.

We are exhausted as all the hard work has been focused on producing enough hormones to keep us steady due to the emotional fallout these imbalances cause us. This results in us using up excess energy by being emotionally fraught and vibrating on a negative low frequency. Energy should be a continuous flow. As we take it in, we can quickly identify it, transmute it, and let it go. However, when we are premenstrual and already experiencing high levels of anxiety we may fail to do this, putting ourselves and our relationships at jeopardy. The difficulties arise when we vibrate on a low, dense frequency and are therefore far more susceptible to negative energies influencing us and become lodged within our energy field.

Engaging in any kind of argument or confrontation at this time will very likely be volatile and also futile. We will be releasing all of the bottled up energy and emotions that we have gathered, although we can try not to use this as an excuse for behaving in any way deemed harmful. If a relationship is dysfunctional or we are abusive, we can seek professional guidance to regulate our frustration, anger, or aggression so that we can get it under control. As long as our situations are non-abusive and nonviolent, the most loving and effective thing that someone else can do for us is to soothe or calm the situation and allow for some "cooling off" time. Once empaths become aware of how to stabilize emotions daily, and also how to protect ourselves so that we do not absorb and interact with other people's energy, these episodes will very quickly become a thing of the past or be few and far between.

We can balance our lifestyles by taking good care of ourselves emotionally, mentally, and physically and feeding our bodies nutritious foods and alleviating anything that may cause us anxiety or stress. Creating situations where we feel optimistic, secure, joyful, happy, loving, relaxed, and rested will all help to create a healthier mind, thus resulting in a healthier body. Moods may occur if we are not eating a healthy, balanced diet. This is due to our energy level dropping when we eat food that carries a low vibration, or if we are not eating or drinking nourishing amounts proportionate with what our body requires to function effectively. Yoga, massage, meditation, and talking through any anxieties will also help to soothe and stabilize the mind and put any irrational or anxious thoughts into context.

Anything that relates to anxiety or stress draws on our energy. When we are unbalanced in any way, our internal system has to work harder to even things out. This is part of the reason we become exhausted and debilitated. We put far too much pressure on our bodies and the majority of that pressure comes from our minds. When we change how we think and change our lifestyle choices, we will instantly change how we feel physiologically.

Exercising is a great way to dispel negative energy and to recharge our energy supply. We are usually more comfortable where there are no rigid rules or regulations as we will become stifled and overwhelmed when we are told to do things in a certain way that does not conform to how we feel emotionally or physiologically. Empaths prefer more natural methods of exercising; for example, swimming in seas or lakes, dancing to music, hiking, trail running, or basically anything that doesn't require strict membership codes and guidelines for what we must wear or how we should behave.

We generally have far more interest in exercise that works on the mind-body-spirit balance than we do in exercise purely to look physically in shape.

One of the most difficult things for an empath is working out which emotions are ours and which belong to other people. Once we have done that we can begin the process of filtering through our feelings to trace back what may have been transferred from others. Often, the best way to do this is by a process of elimination that requires compassionately holding ourselves accountable and taking responsibility for our own emotions first. When we have dissected how we are feeling, we can look at each sensation and question the reason for its existence.

If we have focused our attention on an emotion and still cannot define the reason for its existence, then it may not belong to us, so we can simply become aware of this and let go of it, transmuting it with the assistance of a deep-breathing exercise if necessary. When we have separated our own emotions from other people's, we can then look at why we are feeling a particular way, what is the root cause of the feeling, and what we can do to resolve it. We will notice that we often subconsciously feel irritated and frustrated about things that are nothing to do with us, and in the scheme of things do not really matter. This method is something that can be done regularly as a way to practice defining what we are holding on to and learning to quickly let go of it. We may be unable to just snap out of moods without first going through this process. Even though do not generally hold on to bad moods for long periods of times, unless we clear our electromagnetic field our ability to feel relaxed, light and free is impaired.

"Emotion can be written all over our face, or the emotion which we feel from others can be secured behind it like a vault door. Sometimes we don't realize this until someone else points out, "You're pulling a face." (Oh, am I?) Or they may ask, "Is everything okay? You had a look…" They may not have felt the subtle energetic changes or emotional surges that occurred in that setting. However, our senses picked up on the vibrations and our natural response may be exposed through our facial expressions. Our smile might tighten. Our eyes might squint. Our teeth might clench. We might stare. We might evade. It can be difficult to maintain composure in some highly charged (positive or negative) situations. Especially in leisurely settings there can be a noticeable lack of discipline in regards to the face. For instance, while watching a show or performance there may be unintentional facial mimicry of the thespians and performers. This is attunement with other's emotional energy, with or without the revelation of it." ——Tina Hudson

Before we attend any social event, it is essential to clear all existing energy, as empaths find it difficult to fake our emotions when we are around people. We cannot easily masquerade the emotions swirling around us. If we do not feel comfortable with someone, communication does not come easily as our energy field will feel particularly heavy as though it is weighing us down. We may even find it an effort to say "hello" to someone or order food in a restaurant if we are overwhelmed with too much emotion. If our energy field is radiating low vibrations, we may unconsciously change the energy of the room we are in, and we will also be more easily influenced by other people's moods.

Without saying a word, we can let other people feel exactly what we are thinking or feeling just by radiating positive or negative energy outward. However, if we are negative, we can remain aware that it could be detrimental to those around us as with a strike of lightning we can bring the energy in the environment crashing down. Energy is powerful and we are fully capable of transmuting and transforming other people's energy or the energy surrounding us; however, we first must be energetically conscious so that we remain vibrating highly so that we set the intention to transmute and transform low vibrations.

The above information is my beliefs and theories that I have explained as an overview, other than where I have quote others. For health related advice please seek professional medical opinion.

Chapter 41

DARK SIDE

In *Star Wars,* "the Force" had many aspects to it. It has been described as an energy field that connects all living things in the galaxy, and those who are ultrasensitive to it are able to tap into it and utilize its power.

The two most recognized energy forces are the light side and the dark side. Although the light side is never actually talked about in *Star Wars,* these two aspects were the moral compass of the Force, and they defined the emotions and conduct held by either side. Although there were effectively two sides, they both emanated from the same energy. Ultimately, *we* choose whether we align with the light or the dark side.

Opting for the light side is governed by our ability to overcome powerful and addictive "dark" emotions. The light side of the Force aligns with love, compassion, empathy, selflessness, self-knowledge, enlightenment, self-sacrifice, healing, peace, honesty, mercy, and benevolence. The dark side of the Force aligns with hatred, greed, covetousness, resentment, anger, aggression, rage, jealousy, and malevolence.

In *Star Wars*, the Sith held the belief that the darker side was the more powerful side of the Force, although this belief is likely held as the dark side is seductive to those with the desire to use it. The dark side can be extremely dangerous, as those who sway to will go to any lengths to achieve status and control. It is a destructive force, with dark emotions that when unleashed can devastate and cause ruin. Those who are consumed by darkness have a desire for power, so they will sabotage anything that prevents them from obtaining it.

In *Star Wars,* both sides are constantly at war, and it is mostly because they deny the other side exists; therefore, they reject each other. The light side tries to dominate using mind control, manipulation, and persuasion, while the dark side uses violence, cruelty, and sadistic acts throughout the battles.

When our dark emotions are dominant, they can very easily intoxicate us and run amok as fear fuels many negative emotions, such as anger, hatred, bitterness, and rage. However, these dense emotions also cause weaknesses, as when we are consumed with emotions our mind is clouded, impaired, and limited. This can leave us open and susceptible to unexpected energy attacks. We are not more powerful or skilled when we are solely on the dark side, neither are we when we are out of touch with the dark side and exist only in the light. We have to acknowledge and understand both sides so that we are prepared for our own or other people's dark energy. Darkness can creep up on us at any time, so we need to remain alert and aware.

Rather than opting to align with one side over the other, we have far more power when we are in touch with all shades of the spectrum—not just dark or light—as we are then able to gain control over all of our emotions, rather than suppressing them or denying they exist. We cannot claim to be "good" when we are rejecting emotions that are part of all humans. We cannot retain balance and harmony when we try to destroy something that is part of ourselves and the whole of humanity.

Although *Star Wars* is based on science fiction, it reflects some of the same principles as Buddhism and Taoism and works on the premise that we are all one, connected through energy. All of the emotions that are expressed in *Star Wars* are drawn from the same energy—*the Force*. The Eastern philosophy of *yin* and *yang* show how opposites—dark and light—provide balance and are complementary when they work together. To be able to coexist means that they need to accept that the other side exists.

The dark side, and the emotions that are connected to it are only powerful when they are evoked through fear and without good intention. Dark emotions hold no destructive power if we understand and know how to work with them so the emotions guide and enlighten us rather than being wallowed in and raging out of control. When we are unaware of how our darker side operates, we are afraid. When we do not understand something, our instinctive reaction is one of fear.

"It is always darkest before the dawn." ——Proverb

From childhood we may have been taught that darkness is scary and that we must remain indoors to keep away from anything that lingers and lurks where there is no light. The same can be said for dark emotions. We may have been conditioned to believe that it is not acceptable to discuss or express our darker thoughts, feelings, beliefs, and actions. We may have been advised to keep them safely contained so that we are not judged, condemned, ostracized, berated, or belittled. Our darker side is also known as our shadow side as it is the part that follows us around yet rarely receives recognition. A shadow only exists where there is a limited amount of light. When we shine a light, darkness dissipates.

We hear stories like "Dr. Jekyll and Mr. Hyde" and we are afraid that if we connect with our darker side we will turn into the ghastly and devilish Mr. Hyde. We conjure up images of the evil monster that was capable of all kinds of insane acts and we want to remain as far from possible from that dark side just in case we are tempted to venture there too. However, there aren't just two paths; it isn't just dark or light. There are thousands of shades in between and we can remain in full control and stabilized as we move from one shade to the other always knowing the light side is just a footstep away. Just because we understand our dark side does not mean we are going to commit monstrosities, quite the opposite. The more understanding we have of our dark side, the more in control of it we are and the brighter our light side shines as we are not only standing in the light, but we are also shining our light on the darkness too. Darkness cannot exist in brilliant light, so there is never any reason to fear it.

When we are out of touch with our darker side, it is very difficult to maintain balance and be at one with ourselves or connect deeply with anyone else, as we have suppressed emotions that are an intrinsic part of all human beings. Our light and dark sides are our *yin* and *yang*. Both need one another to find equilibrium. They accept and complement each other so that we can become stable and find harmony by working together as a whole, not two sides fighting against the other.

We do not ever need to forcibly and externally express our darkest energy. We just need to understand it so that we are aware of our own capabilities and have control over them and also so that it is free to flow through us and out. It can then be transmuted with our loving light energy so that it is not destructive, damaging or harmful. Otherwise, we will live in a permanent state of perpetual fear. When we suddenly step into the dark, we are instantly and naturally afraid. Even if we do not consciously think we are, our subconscious will cause a physical reaction in our bodies as our thoughts turn to ones that fear the unknown when we cannot see clearly, when we do not know what might be lying in wait in our path, ready to pounce and threaten us or cause us harm. This is the same for emotions. When we are unaware of our darker side, we are afraid of what might exist there. When we do not understand something, our instinctive reaction is one of fear.

In the physical, material world, when we step into the dark we can quickly switch on a light so that we can see there was nothing to be afraid of. Our mind just plays tricks on us to keep us remaining in the perceived safety of the light. Even though we cannot turn on a physical light inside ourselves, when we have a strong connection to our inner light, our positivity, we can roam and explore the dark knowing that at any moment we can head back to the security of our lighter thoughts and feelings whenever we choose.

When we connect with our darker emotions, we have to let go of all the words and stories we have allowed ourselves to believe.

These attachments are what make stepping into dark territory so petrifying. We must allow ourselves to clear our minds of all the nonsense we have linked to our emotions so that we can look with clarity and see what exists inside us and why.

Empaths who are secure in who they are and have developed their awareness have a broad perspective and do not only consider our lighter more positive side, we also have consideration for and seek to understand our darker side too. This is mainly because we cannot escape the dark side of souls. The energy is there constantly seeking validation and recognition so that it can be understood, accepted, and freed naturally and without causing harm. Even if empaths are not fully in touch with our own darkness, we are subjected to the layers of the shadow side of others constantly as we come into contact with people from all walks of life and connect intimately with what exists in their subconscious mind. The darker side of humanity is *felt* by an empath even if we do not consciously acknowledge it or see it.

If empaths have not developed their awareness of energy and we remain in denial, we can go through stages or even remain stuck in states of loneliness, separation, depression, and deep sadness. If this is not monitored and understood, we are at risk of turning to addictions or distractions to take us away from the intense emotions we constantly feel, and these things can lead us along dangerous, treacherous roads. When we try to suppress our dark traits and emotions, they manifest within our subconscious mind and transfer to our physical body. The buildup will continue until our body takes on too much, as the emotions that have been generated inside us take a toll on our physical health. This is portrayed in *Star Wars* as those who are aligned with the dark side and have forbidden the light. They noticeably have skin pigmentations, marks on their eyes, and their aging process is accelerated.

Our emotional health also suffers as the stored up emotions lie dormant until something triggers them and causes them to explode or seep out when we are least expecting it.

"Unexpressed emotions will never die. They are buried alive and will come forth later in uglier ways." ——Sigmund Freud

461

It is crucially important to understand our dark side and also the darker side to others. We can then be aware of it and understand it to ensure that we are not at risk of losing touch, even temporarily, with the light. When we only acknowledge and accept one side of ourselves, either the dark or the light, we are attaching to a persona that is unrealistic. We will believe that we are only either "good" or "bad" when neither of these limiting beliefs is true. This is when we become focused on "identity" and we consciously only show the traits that are aligned with a fragile ego and a desire to see ourselves as only one half. We are forcing ourselves to behave in certain ways even if we are not aware of this, as we believe that our actions directly affect who we actually are. This is not true. We are only true to ourselves and exposing our true nature to others when we let go of the need to deny our whole selves and instead naturally allow our core persona to shine through. However, we can only do this when we have an understanding of ourselves from the inside out so that our behavior does not cause harm to ourselves or anyone else. To understand ourselves intimately, we first need to accept the parts we have repressed or tried to black out by hiding them within our shadow.

"Everyone carries a shadow, and the less it is embodied in the individual's conscious life, the blacker and denser it is." ——Carl Jung

We may wonder what good can come from bringing the darker side of who we are to the surface. We may feel safer when it is rejected, as we feel in control and able to behave in ways that we deem positive. However, this is an illusion—it is just our idealistic ego telling us this. The more we look down at our shadow with disapproval and neglect it, the darker, heavier, more negative, and more repulsive it becomes. Only when we remove some of this dense energy, can we then free it so that we are light and liberated, and so that we can grow and transform.

As soon as we recognize that we have a shadow side, we immediately become less judgmental and critical of others. When our shadow side is repressed, we project whatever exists there onto others. We see a reflection of aspects of ourselves in people around us and we give them all the blame and shame for the feelings that arise in us, rather than realizing we feel this way because they remind us of elements of ourselves that we refuse to accept.

Our shadow side is directly related to our unconscious mind. We are often not even aware that we have disowned and deeply buried primitive negative emotions and feelings. Therefore, it can be difficult to even accept that they exist. We have to look at what exists in our unconscious mind objectively and then see that whatever is there does not define us. Every human being has a dark side. It is how we manage our darkness that is key to how it is expressed. The more introverted and withdrawn from society humanity becomes, the easier it is to fall into a vortex of pessimism that collectively can be very difficult to navigate a way out of. This can lead us to feeling insecure, mistrusting, frustrated, angry, resentful, or we may become very self-conscious and develop low self-worth. All of these things can easily cause narcissistic tendencies. It is vital that we create a balance so that we do not cut ourselves off from our emotions just to disconnect from the painful intensity of the emotions we do not wish to address. We can only heal when we purge ourselves of everything that is causing cracks in our psyche. Darkness is heavy and dense. When we push it down, we are actually giving it a place to call home. The home is our unconscious mind. And our unconscious mind is responsible for a large percentage of our instinctive emotions, feelings, and also many of our false beliefs.

We do not need to hold on to darkness. We cannot possibly be light, energetic, and free while we are pushing down and hiding universal intrinsic parts of ourselves. The more we reject parts of our core self, the higher the mound of dirt, mud, and grime builds in our unconscious/dark mind.

"It takes courage . . . to endure the sharp pains of self-discovery rather than choose to take the dull pain of unconsciousness that would last the rest of our lives." ——Marianne Williamson, *A Return to Love: Reflections on the Principles of "A Course in Miracles"*

The unknown and unacknowledged darkness will surely seep out of the cracks of our irrational unconscious mind and connect and interact with our subconscious and conscious minds. There is no light in our unconscious minds, our unenlightened dark side.

We have to consciously shine a light on it so that we can free and release it rather than waiting for the unconscious to trigger the connection when we least expect it. We must also remember that when we shine light on our darkness our shadow moves. It will not be easy to grasp what is hidden beneath as our shadow constantly runs and tries to hide from us, just as our "truth" changes moment by moment. We do not need to cling onto the concept of eradicating our shadow as simply setting the intention to accept it and remove the fearful and judgmental perceptions of it will immediately lessen any power or control it has over us. Rather than fight it, we can accept our dark side and lovingly free it so that the energy is neutralized and transmuted and does not cause any harm.

When we have a strong connection to our inner light—our positivity—we can roam and venture into the darkness knowing that at any moment we can step back to the security of the light. Therefore, we mustn't be afraid to explore our dark side and get to know it so that it is not seen as an enemy but as a comrade helping us balance our inner selves.

When we have no control over something, it then has the option to control us. We can have absolute control over all of our own emotions as we can override them at any time using our conscious and rational minds. Our negative emotions are not our nemesis. Neither do we need to feel ashamed or judge ourselves harshly when they creep up on us. We all have dark emotions, and by denying them we are giving them more strength. When we are secure in who we are and have developed a broad perspective, we will not only be in touch with our lighter more positive side, we will also have humility and acceptance as we seek to understand and accept our darker side too.

We cannot escape the dark side. It exists, constantly seeking validation and recognition. While we are in denial and reject who we are at our core, we also deny anyone else the opportunity to get to know us fully, and we will live in fear of their rejection should they ever witness our darker side. Rather than allowing a full connection, we cause a separation that disconnects us from who we truly are. This means that others will only see the superficial side we portray to the world. We can integrate our dark side so that it weaves into our light and allows us to become more open-minded, harmonized, thoughtful, compassionate, accepting, forgiving, understanding and nonjudgmental, not just toward ourselves but to the whole of humanity.

When we fearlessly open up so that we can view ourselves with clarity and we are willing to take accountability for what we see, we will stop projecting our darkness onto others and accusing, blaming, or shaming them for what essentially is the denial of ourselves.

Chapter 42

Dark Night of the Soul

An empath who has a healed wound that is filled with knowledge gathered from past conflict is known as a "wounded healer." Carl Jung coined the term "wounded healer" to describe how healers are able to analyze their own pain so that they can use the analysis to enhance the healing of their patients. When we have experienced a situation firsthand and we have salved and healed those open wounds, we are then able to use our encounters to empathize and intimately understand other people who are going through a similar crisis. We can use the tools, strength, courage, and wisdom we gained along the way to support others who are in a similar situation, as we have a deeper awareness of the suffering they are enduring.

Often, wounded healers have experienced a *dark night of the soul*, also known as a "psychic death," "rebirth of the soul," or "death of the ego." This happens when we have collapsed under the pressure from various sources, including the pressure we have placed on ourselves. The collective pressure is due to the weight of our denied and repressed emotions and our inability or refusal to connect with our core selves. We have frantically been trying to navigate through a dark labyrinth, and eventually our souls' screams become deafening and we know it is time to escape. At this stage, we have no choice but to admit we are lost. We are then handed a mirror so that we can take a long, hard and difficult look at ourselves while we watch our reflections crumble. It is a war with many battles, as we are confronting our ego and it does not like to back down without an arduous fight.

"The birth of the Self is always a defeat for the ego." ——Carl Jung

Anyone who has experienced a dark night of the soul will likely describe it is a painful catalyst that forces us to catapult in a new direction. We look at the fear, heartache, pain, dysfunction, loneliness, isolation, trauma, obsession, desires, image, abandonment, frustrations, and resentments that our ego has been governing. We come to a moment of pure surrender where a deafening shrill is articulating that it is time to face up to the truth of who we are and what the meaning of our lives is. If we try to suppress the emotions, they will magnify, linger, and haunt us. We have been denying them for far too long and they will continue to simmer on the surface, making their presence known, becoming unbearable until we have no choice but to acknowledge them. Usually, we reach this critical stage when we are burnt out, at rock bottom, or a part of our lives has collapsed and we have no other way to climb but upward. We have found ourselves at the extreme end of darkness and we absolutely have to locate a way out. We look at everything that has brought us to this place and we stand in utter desperation and self-pity.

It can seem like we have everything to lose, although the reality is quite the opposite. Often, we have reached this point after a period of spiritual growth or a phase where everything we thought was once secure has been shattered. We are on the cusp of what is about to be a huge transformation. In order to go forward, we must first let go of everything that has been holding us captive.

We are similar to a caterpillar trapped in a cocoon and we have to beat our wings so frantically in order to escape so that we can make a much-needed transition. It is a time of soul life or death, and this part of our journey isn't always a pretty one. However, it is one that is essential. We have reached a time in our lives where we need to let go of everything that is superficial that has no meaning, that has been weighing us down, and basically everything that is preventing us from reaching a state of mindful awareness that can lead to a profound understanding of life, our souls, and their higher potential.

Similar to an alchemist we have been blending ingredients to create a formula to turn metal into gold. We suddenly find we need to remove certain protons that we once believed were required to create a desirable outcome. Eradicating certain parts of who we are can be grueling as we have grown comfortable with our qualities even if they were doing us harm. We may have felt they were essential elements that are part of our true personalities or we may just be having difficulty accepting that our previous or current lives were not all that they seemed. When we realize that it is time to change dramatically, it can shock us to the core and we can try to grasp on to parts of ourselves that were not serving us well.

We need to let go of who we thought we were so we can become who we are meant to be. During this process it can seem as though everyone we know suddenly misunderstands and deserts us just when we believe we need them most. We are transforming from our old selves toward new selves, reaching for our souls' higher purpose, though many of those around us have grown comfortable and secure being around whoever we once were. Our vibration will be elevating as we let go of our old ways of being and integrate new thoughts and feelings into our belief systems. When our vibration heightens, other people may try to hold us back or pull us down by belittling, condemning, or criticizing these new versions of ourselves so that we remain vibrating on the lower frequency that resonated more harmoniously with them. It can be tempting to allow this to happen as we do not want conflict; however, our personal growth is essential so that we achieve and maintain inner peace, harmony, joy, and a sound wellbeing.

As we change, other people's attitudes toward us change as our vibration unintentionally magnetically attracts or repels people, or their vibration may attract or repel ours. Relationships with family, friends, and loved ones can be tested to the limit. If someone has not been through this life-changing experience, they may have great difficulty accepting and coming to terms with how we are altering and changing. We often find that we lose people we once held dear to us as they no longer recognize us or we no longer recognize them. Through this stage we may feel recklessly abandoned and confined to feeling alone, although it is through our loneliness that we start to see with clarity who we are and where we are journeying.

Our isolation and abandonment is just our refusal to appreciate and accept that we are already intertwined with everyone and everything and that we never need to touch, own, or hold anything to prove the binding exists. Loneliness is a gift that teaches us through aches and pains that we have unnecessarily separated ourselves from others. It yearns for us to find the strength to break through and make genuine heartfelt connections despite what lies we may be repeating that are keeping us feeling isolated, unworthy, or unvalued.

Our previous reality gets broken down along with all the illusions that surrounded it. For the first time, we begin to connect with who we are at our core and we also realize we have never been alone and we never will be. It is not possible, regardless of how our mindset perceives it. Our loneliness transitions and opens toward solitude. However, solitude firmly asks us to be prepared to reconsider what we are viewing as a loss and it casts out all of our unrealistic expectations. The dark night is asking us to let go of our self-damning thoughts and beliefs so that we can allow every aspect of life to naturally flow through us.

Although we are afraid of losing the attachment to who we once thought we were, we know that it is essential so that we can also let go of our attachment to suffering and pain. We see glimmers of our hidden selves shining through and this recognition brings hope and bouts of deep inner peace. Once we glimpse this flicker of light we know we are going to be safe, but it is usually a long and treacherous road home. Although it is dark, it is also an exquisitely beautiful process as we are shedding our old skin and preparing for the new, though it can take awhile to emerge and see it this way.

In journeying back to our inherent natural selves we awaken to the understanding that everything came to our lives for a reason. Every person, place, and situation that we encountered was there for a purpose and for our individual spiritual growth. Ultimately, we uncover more meaning in our lives. And although we feel fragmented at times, we know this path has stepping stones on which we have no choice but to tread.

"There is no coming to consciousness without pain. People will do anything, no matter how absurd, to avoid facing their own soul. One does not become enlightened by imagining figures of light, but by making the darkness conscious." ———Carl Jung

One of the biggest realizations we have when we have escaped the clutches of the dark night of the soul is that the whole thing was just an illusion created by our minds. And also, our ego is an illusion too. This is the biggest lesson we learn about reality. Everything we had been embroiled in up until then was make-believe. Our ego had been created so that we could avoid having to deal with our natural selves. It is far easier to relate to an alter ego that we attach idealistic images to rather than face up to who we actually are at our core. The dark night strips and tears down the pretense that had shrouded us. It removes the delusions that cause us to believe that who we were and what we experienced up until then was all "reality." The truth is, there is no reality when we are presenting a false "ego" self to the world. While we do, no one can possibly truly know who we are and we cannot fully connect or have clarity with anyone or anything else. The ego that we created masked our ability to view the truth about anything internally or externally. We begin to see that our mind had been tricking us all along, and just like the dark night of the soul, everything that existed in our minds was just perception. At any moment we can change and instantly see reality.

Our imagination can feel far more real than reality itself. Therefore, whatever our minds are processing becomes our unique reality. This gives us the power to choose whatever we put into our minds and realize that we have absolute control of how we are thinking, feeling, and what we choose to see and believe. When we accept ourselves as we are and not who our imagined ego tried to tell us we were, we locate the fastest way out of the dark night so we can head toward the light. We can continue believing all the nonsense our ego is feeding us to keep us there, or we can let go of the attachment we have to the bubble surrounding us that prevents us from seeing the truth.

Once we find the courage to burst our ego's bubble, we can connect to everything and everyone on an entirely new level. The bubble doesn't keep us safe. It keeps us separated from reality. Reality isn't something to be afraid of. It is something to embrace. We eventually realize the previous identity that we had strong attachments to was our ego creating narratives to keep itself thriving and existing in our mind. When we accept that we are not these stories, we are not who we have repeatedly told ourselves we are, and we are not who our ego has tried to convince us we are, we can eventually allow ourselves to just "be."

We had been seeing everything through a very narrow lens and the dark night of the soul takes that lens away from us and replaces it with a kaleidoscope. For the first time we begin to see everything from many angles and through a naturally bright light. It can be frightening at first as at an unconscious level we are afraid of what we might find, so it can take our senses some time to build the courage to witness this multi-faceted view. Though when we do, we see we had been willingly holding on to all the dark emotions that had caused us to feel petrified.

Instead of rejecting our shadow emotions we can embrace and accept them as part of our self and also as part of humanity as a whole. This opens us up to acceptance, oneness and unconditional love.

"Knowing your own darkness is the best method for dealing with the darknesses of other people." ——Carl Jung

Once we have reached the light, we will find we are no longer as afraid of the dark. We have witnessed it in its most powerful form, and although we were terrified, we now have the courage face the ordeal again if we had to. That is why we are now able to channel our spiritual wisdom through our personal stories and assist others with their journey. We find the strength to walk alongside other people through their darkness, while reaching out a hand to stabilize if required.

"Who then can so softly bind up the wound of another as he who has felt the same wound himself?" ——Thomas Jefferson

Ultimately, we are aware that everyone needs to face this period of their lives on their own, though we walk closely enough to let them know that they are not alienated or alone and that there is no separation between all living things. If we try to take on someone's load while they are facing their dark night of the soul we could essentially become burnt out and depleted from the amount of dark energy that is circulating. Plus, we are not doing anyone any favors by resolving their difficulties for them. The dark night is a haunting process that everyone has to go through by themselves as it is the place to learn about the true state of oneself. We can be near someone every step of the way, but we do not need to try to walk their road for them or forcibly intervene thinking we know best. When we support someone who is distressed and struggling, we can consciously radiate a loving high vibration toward them to light and guide their way. We can then transmute their fearful, painful vibrations so that they are transformed to ones infused with love, tenderness, consideration, compassion, gentleness, understanding, and forgiveness. Just letting someone know we are there if they need us is often all that is required. Rather than leading someone else on their evolutionary journey, we can align and resonate with them so that our vibrations connect with and raise theirs.

The dark night of the soul awakens us to our true souls' purpose and our highest potential. It is usually a force that directs us along a journey not just toward healing ourselves, but also to enable us to heal others by being of service through sharing the knowledge that was uncovered along the way.

Although the dark night may sound as though it has links to depression, it is not the result of or associated with depression. It is an awakening that happens when we are catapulted to new heights on our individual soul journey.

Although the dark night of the soul can be terrifying while we are experiencing it, it happens for our personal growth and is not the product or byproduct of any medical condition.

Chapter 43

COLLECTIVE CONSCIOUSNESS/ UNIVERSAL KNOWLEDGE

"We are not human beings having a spiritual experience. We are spiritual beings having a human experience." ——Pierre Teilhard de Chardin

The collective conscious is an invisible energy field consisting of shared feelings, ideas, beliefs, moral attitudes, and sentiments that stretch across the whole universe. The collective conscious has always existed and will continue to exist throughout eternity. It is a collective group of minds that share the same inner knowledge and whose thoughts, intentions, and opinions exist on a frequency accessible to everyone.

The belief that we are all one and that everything interconnects and correlates is a notion that has been held throughout the ages by many spiritual traditions. This is partly the reason we often hear the saying, "The answers are within." Everything connects through fractals of energy. Therefore, our minds have access to all the information that exists in the universe without having to seek for meaning or look for the answers externally.

The collective conscious is a higher frequency of consciousness, so we need to raise our own vibration to be able to access the dimension it exists on. We also need to attune to the collective conscious so that we are harmonized with the frequency; this is accessible through meditation when we calm the mind and become consciously aware. All human minds are able to tap into and add to or retrieve this knowledge. The data that is stored includes the conscious thoughts emanating from scientists, artists, philosophers, spiritual leaders, and people from all walks of life. The knowledge that exists contains ideologies, beliefs, values, norms, and moral compasses. It is basically a sharing of similar sentiments that form a consensus in the collective mind. This is the reason that similar thoughts occur between those who are in close contact with one another as well as those who are on opposite sides of the planet. If one individual has an original idea then that idea can transfer into the collective consciousness and it is very likely it will then be picked up on and shared by someone else somewhere else in the world. Every individual thought we have, however small, has an impact on humanity as a whole.

"All truly wise thoughts have been thought already thousands of times; but to make them truly ours, we must think them over again honestly, till they take root in our personal experience." —— Goethe (1749–1832)

It is also why events such as mass meditations take place as the intention and power that is generated from a collection of minds all creating similar waves of energy is felt not just in that specific location but by others that might be thousands of miles away. The people who work together are acting as conductors for energy as they connect not just to one another, but also to the energy in the universe so that they collectively radiate positive high vibrations. Similar gatherings also occur during a stargate, for example during an equinox or solstice, when there is a vortex due to planetary alignment that allows an optimum amount of high vibrational energy to permeate the Earth. During these times, empaths or anyone else who is hypersensitive to energy will be able to connect to this energy and raise their personal vibration, which then in turn benefits and enhances the collective vibration.

Yogi Bhajan introduced Kunalini Yoga, which focuses on expanding sensory awareness, to the Western world in 1969. This was specifically so that we can stimulate and ignite the energy that lies dormant within us. When we are aware and consciously awake we are able to connect to one consciousness and channel, control and guide subtle energy forces. Albert Einstein talked about how we are all connected and how when one thing happens in the universe it affects all other things. The term for this is *quantum entanglement* and the meaning of it is that all energy intertwines, tangles, and interlocks. The friction this causes allows energy to eternally communicate.

Many ancient civilizations and indigenous cultures, including the Mayans, believed in the collective consciousness. They had faith that the shifts that took place were responsible for causing mass awakening. We are all magical beings and capable of so much more than we have been led to believe. During ancient times, supernatural capabilities were considered the norm and were necessary and beneficial tools in every day. When science came into play, it tried to defy and disclaim anything that could not be proved with calculations. This eventually led to the masses losing faith in anything that could not be determined or defined by science. In recent years, there have been major breakthroughs with scientific research that have led many people to once again believe that much of what we see is an illusion and that we have a far greater capacity as human beings than what we may have thought. Now, as science is backing up many spiritual beliefs, on a large scale people are reconnecting to past traditions, beliefs, ideologies, and practices that are assisting us with our personal growth, awakening, and spiritual evolution. This is known as the Age of Aquarius or the Age of Enlightenment and was predicted by the Mayans. It is a pivotal turning point for spirituality, both individually and on a mass scale.

Obi Wan Kanobi described collective energy as, "I felt a great disturbance in the force, as if millions of voices cried out in terror and were suddenly silenced. I fear something terrible has happened." In fact, Star Wars regularly talked of the "Force," and especially its "Dark side."

Obi-Wan Kenobi also explained the force of energy surrounding him as, "Well, the Force is what gives a Jedi his power. It's an energy field created by all living things. It surrounds us, penetrates us; it binds the galaxy together." *Star Wars* is based on the premise that we can all tap into the universal collective energy. When energy is magnified by a large number of people all expressing a similar emotion at the same time, this can be felt as waves within the collective conscious. Multitudes of people all share the same consensus and it spreads like wildfire from one mind to the next. What could start off with just one person thinking or feeling something can then explode across the planet as other minds tune in and detect that something major is happening. Usually this happens at times of great planetary stress or devastation. As the collective consciousness peaks, empaths, being hypersensitive, will feel the effects significantly as we are highly tuned to energy. These shifts of energy suddenly erupt around us, although until we are aware of what is causing the fluctuations of energy we will feel shaken and disturbed and this may manifest in us as fear and anxiety

Empaths can find it tremendously challenging to navigate the pulses of energy that emerge when the universe experiences tidal waves of emotional energy due to a global crisis or even elation. Empaths naturally tap into the collective consciousness and will feel the sensations of the stimuli that have been gathered there. If we exist on a subconscious level and we are not fully present or consciously aware when this happens, it can unground and debilitate us, especially if we have not first protected our energy or prepared ourselves emotionally. It is essential that before we tap into the collective conscious we are aware of our energetic vibration, what information it holds, and ultimately what we could be depositing so that we do not disrupt and negatively alter the energy. This can be especially noticeable if on a mass scale people are tapping in and adding fear-based energy, as it will have a detrimental effect on the overall frequency of what is stored there. This volatile energy may then be felt strongly by anyone who is energy sensitive.

Empaths will feel in pain when the world is suffering and we want to do something to ease this suffering as we are natural born healers. Before we tune in to the collective conscious, we must first clear our energy so that we are not taking with us existing pain or trauma and we are vibrating on a high frequency.

As empaths are problem solvers, having the ability to tune in to the collective consciousness can prove extremely beneficial. If we are struggling to find the answers we are searching for, we can tap into this collective conscious to gain access to the knowledge and wisdom that has been stored there.

The collective consciousness is a buildup of universal data that exists due to an accumulation of energetic frequencies from the past, present, and future occurrences. We can remain aware that the information stored there can heavily influence the choices we make in our individual lives.

Tapping into the collective consciousness is very easy, though it will take a small amount of patience, practice, and trust to gain reliable results. To tap into it, sit cross-legged, spine straight, and hands at the heart center, with middle fingers pointing upward and fingertips touching lightly. Allow thoughts to come and go naturally and inhale and exhale deeply to allow the body and mind to slow and calm down. When persistent existing thoughts have dissipated, focus on what it is you would like to know. We may ask questions relating to our future, but before we do this we can try to remember that the answers we receive will reflect our current mindset and the data held in the energy we are vibrating. We may enter a trancelike state and may begin to notice that we have transcended to a heightened level of awareness. Our senses will be on full alert and smells, sounds, feelings, and an overall sense of who we are will all be elevated. We will have gained greater clarity, illusions will fade, and the true essence of everything around us will become more vivid.

The collective conscious exists to reaffirm what we already know, although it also provides a higher level of awareness that can help humanity evolve for the benefit of the higher good for all. Therefore, we can use this database to confirm details about our soul's journey to guide us toward making significant essential life-changing decisions. We can also access profound and genius ideas, thoughts, perceptions, and wisdom that we can then share with the intention of creating much-needed shifts in society. We also have to be ethical, though, as what we may believe to be change for the greater good may not be the same as other people's ideas or intentions. We have to place our trust in the messages we receive and ensure our ego is not involved in any way so we can be respectful of the data we receive and honor it so that it is used for a higher purpose.

When we have received a response, allow it to remain in the mind for a few moments before looking at it with discernment. When it has settled, observe the emotions that are connected to the response. Has the reply come to us from our own fear or a projection that we made? It is essential to be aware if we are the ones creating clouds filled with negative sensations that are responsible for forcing a particular answer or if the message has been delivered to us from a higher realm void of our own interruption. If we have used fear or desire to override receiving the true answer, begin again, once again clearing the mind of our personal thoughts and feelings. When we have received a response arriving from an external source, we can meditate on it and allow it to consolidate into our psyche. Say thank you for receiving the message, spend a few moments in silence showing gratitude while breathing deeply, then close the meditation to finish.

Alternatively, just before sleep we can ask our unconscious minds to work on a problem to find a solution while we are sleeping. This is a widely used practice and most likely when we awake we will have received the answers to whatever question has been on our minds. Hence the phrase "sleep on a problem." The messages of wisdom we receive can come to us either through either a feeling, a sensation, through words or even through a visual response. Whichever way we receive them will depend upon our own ability to channel and translate information.

This deliverance of wisdom is often known as channeling, or some people say the messages were sent to them through a guide. Although connecting with the collective consciousness is not a commonly known way to access information, thousands of years ago in many cultures it was a perfectly normal thing to do. However, as our DNA discovered how to store memories, many people became reliant on accessing the data stored in our DNA. It is now more common for DNA to assist people with their instinct and decisions rather than accessing our inner knowing feeling and the collective conscious for information. DNA records and stores our cells memories in the same way as a tape recorder does. As people go through life, they search for stored information in their DNA (tape recorder) rather than tapping into their higher selves and the collective conscious. This has caused many people to lose the ability to tap into the collective consciousness and instead means they allow their past to make sense of the situations they are in. It also means they may make subconscious decisions about information they are receiving, which is based on preconceived ideas and feelings that come from their belief system, which will likely be outdated and not be holding a valid representation of the truth. When we tap into this level of consciousness, a part of our DNA alters and strengthens. This then means that the DNA we pass onto our offspring will also store this data and it will form part of our children's blueprint, which allows them to also be able to understand how to access a higher level of consciousness and not rely solely on their DNA to guide them. Their ability will strengthen, and as future generations continue to pass on the DNA it will become much stronger and they will have far easier access to the collective knowledge stored.

Chapter 44

MEDITATION

Empaths absorb an incredible amount of energy throughout the day, so it is highly beneficial, if not essential, that we meditate morning and night, primarily so that we can protect our own energy field and also so that we can still the mind and work through and identify which emotions belong to us and which belong to other people. For empaths, possibly the most significant practice is an early morning one so that we can start the day clear and infused with positive vibrations. Although many of us know that we should pay attention to our energy field regularly, it is something we can forget to do when we get caught up in the throes of the day.

When we set aside a small amount of time each morning, we can balance, ground, protect, and reenergize ourselves all in one practice so that we are ready to face whatever the day might deliver. Many of those who haven't tried meditation or have only tried it once or twice hold the belief that meditation is a difficult thing to learn and master. Meditation is definitely not something that has to be mastered. We just need to focus our attention and then surrender to it.

Meditation really is one of the simplest and most natural things we can do. It is almost as easy as breathing. The focus does not need to be on perfection but on progression. Every moment we spend meditating is a moment that has added value to our minds. The longer we do it and the more we practice, the more rewarding it becomes. There is no pressure or no right or wrong way to meditate. It is a personal practice and one that develops in its own time.

One area that can prove a challenge is trying to keep the mind in the present moment so that we prevent our "monkey" mind from jumping around. When we have a lot going on in our lives, our thoughts can get carried away with themselves and bounce through our minds with no consideration for the fact that we are trying to meditate! The wandering and persistent noise might not give up trying to penetrate and shake the peace, making it extremely difficult to calm the mind enough to concentrate on our practice. This is perfectly normal and it happens to everyone. A lot of people are tempted to give up when they go through this as it may feel too much effort is required to gain inner peace. However, it is just a process that we all go through when we are new to meditation or when we are going through particularly hectic or stressful periods.

Choosing to meditate when our minds are busy is as good for us, if not better for us, than when our minds are calm. When our thoughts are frantic and we have a lot going on in our personal lives that is usually when we need to meditate the most. When our minds seem unwilling to remain calm, rather than going through the traditional steps to meditate, we can benefit from swapping to use alternative methods that achieve similar results. We can try not to focus on the posture or position. Not everyone finds it easy to relax in the lotus position. It isn't always comfortable to sit cross-legged or forming *mudras* with our fingers for a long period of time. It is more beneficial to find what position suits at that current moment than it is to remain in a position that doesn't feel natural.

We can alter our practice depending on what feels right on each particular day. Some days we can sit up straight in a more traditional meditative position, others days we can sink into an armchair or lie on our beds and let the surface totally hold our bodies with plenty of cushions and pillows for support. If preferred, we can cover ourselves with a blanket for extra warmth and coziness. Each practice is different and the position depends largely upon how we feel at the time, what time of the day it is, and also on the location.

More important than how we place our bodies is ensuring we are in a calm, peaceful environment and that we won't be disturbed. Empaths will often prefer the outdoors so that we can be at one with nature. Sitting by a lake, the sea, on grassy fields, or even mountaintops are all places that can bring a great sense of relief and temporary escapism from the hustle of hectic daily lives.

When we are struggling for time or we are somewhere that meditation is not really feasible, or if we are not feeling up to a full meditation, we can just simply inhale and exhale to a set number of breaths. Sometimes going too far inward when we are already overwhelmed or exhausted can feel too intense and intrusive. In these times we can focus on nothing other than the sensation of our ribcage rising and falling as we breathe, to soothe, rebalance, and rejuvenate ourselves when we need these things most.

Empaths often have an appreciation for music and a close connection to it as we resonate with the vibrations produced by certain sounds; therefore, playing a gentle tune in the background while we are meditating can help us relax and take our minds away from current events. The music we listen to doesn't have to specifically be meditation music, it can be anything that has a beat that we naturally harmonize with. We can attune our hearing to become consciously aware of all the instruments in the background so that our mind is solely focused on absorbing the vibration of each note.

When we meditate we are often told to empty the mind, however, that notion isn't entirely true. It is almost impossible to completely empty the mind, so there is no use aiming for something so difficult to reach. Instead of emptying the mind, we can allow our thoughts to drift in and then allow them to leave without causing any disturbance. We can try to pay very little attention to whatever comes to our minds and just gently acknowledge the thoughts, but then just as softly nudge them away again. We can view the thoughts as though we are an observer watching them drift by from a distance without getting too intricately involved with them.

Meditation is a time for deep relaxation so that we have the opportunity to calm irrational fears and soothe painful areas of contention. Often our thoughts can aggravate or cause us distress especially if we wallow on them and they quickly turn to emotions. Even though we can use meditation to access our subconscious and unconscious minds, we can also use it to soothe and neutralize any negativity that has attached to our energetic fields.

We can try guided visualization recordings as an aid. This technique will take us through the steps of a deeply relaxing meditation by using images to give the mind something to focus on. To protect our energy fields, we can meditate while visualizing a brilliant white light or security blanket totally surrounding us. This shield will prevent negativity from entering while we are in a meditative state.

For many, meditating is an enjoyable experience and one that leaves us refreshed and revitalized, not frustrated or feeling inadequate if we haven't achieved unrealistic standards we set out for ourselves. A practice with very little expectation or attachment to the outcome is all that is needed. Regardless of how busy our minds are, even if we only gain a few moments of peace the practice will have been worthwhile. Like with anything, practice and dedication is required to achieve progress. It doesn't matter what time of the day it is, where we are when we meditate, how we are dressed, or how frantic or calm the mind is. Remembering to keep the mind centered in the present moment without wandering to the past or projecting into the future is the only thing we need to focus on. All that matters is that our intention is set for the purpose of releasing thoughts and slowing the mind. Even if we only slow it down for a few seconds, we will still benefit tremendously.

To meditate while the mind is at its busiest is a far greater accomplishment than keeping the mind calm when it is already in a peaceful state. One of the main contributors to insomnia is that our overactive mind is so busy racing with thoughts that we find it difficult to unwind and relax enough to ease into a gentle sleep. When the mind is in this state, even when we do fall asleep we will most likely reawaken many times throughout the night. A peaceful night's sleep has many significant benefits. Not only will we wake feeling refreshed, our immune systems will also receive a boost. While asleep, our bodies set to work repairing any damage that has been done throughout the day. Skin, muscles, brain cells, and blood all use this time for regeneration. Depriving the body of this vital process lowers serotonin, which is thought to be responsible for headaches, depression, anxiety, violence, and various other behavioral related problems. After a full night's sleep we will feel rejuvenated, look better, feel better, and will be more productive in every task throughout the day. Once we learn to fully relax, we can then move into a meditative state and sleep will come naturally.

When we break down the process into stages, from relaxation then on to meditation, then to sleep, it is easier to determine the differences between each one. *Relaxation* is the art of fully loosening the body and mind. When we are relaxed we are still engaged in thought processes. Our minds will still wander and thoughts will constantly come and go. *Meditation* occurs when we let go of persistent thoughts and we are fully present in the moment. Our mind will be calm so that we can achieve a deeper sense of awareness and inner peace. *Sleep* is a period of rest where the body is mostly inactive and the mind is not fully conscious.

There are four main types of brainwave activity. Meditation is frequently used to achieve an alpha brainwave frequency to fully experience the benefits of a heightened euphoric state.

Beta - our regular conscious state.

Alpha - the state between the conscious mind and sleep.

Theta - when we enter a trancelike phase and the mind is at its most creative. We can then experience an altered state of consciousness.

Delta - this is when we reach our deepest level of sleep.

It is believed that theta is most common brainwave frequency reached while meditating. Delta can also be reached but usually it is by more advanced, experienced practitioners and it is used to gain access to the unconscious mind.

Cultivating mindfulness in meditation can assist with eliminating pessimism from the mind and it also helps us to replace negative thoughts with optimistic ones. Mindfulness is, quite simply, being in the present moment, being aware of our thoughts and actions in a nonjudgmental way. By refraining from dwelling on any past or future thoughts, we can bring ourselves back to the here and now. When this happens, we will be concentrating fully on whatever it is that we are doing in the current moment without the mind frantically jumping back and forth.

Mindfulness takes practice, like anything, but the more we engage it, the more natural it becomes. To begin the process of meditation, the most important thing is to feel completely comfortable. If low lighting is preferable, then we can turn the lights down low. Set the room temperature so that it is not too warm or too cold. If the body is cold, it will feel tense and it then becomes far more difficult to fully relax. Gentle music can be played in the background to provide a more serene environment. We can then move into whatever position feels most comfortable to meditate in. For many, when using meditation to promote sleep, lying down on a bed can be the perfect option as it saves moving around when we are relaxed enough to drop to sleep. This is the posture that is covered here. However, feel free to choose the position that suits you. It is a personal experience, and everyone will have their own preference.

The Meditation

Position - Lying on the back, place both arms out by either side with palms of the hands facing upward. Legs are fully stretched out and the feet are hip width apart. Scan the body from top to toe and notice how each area feels. Keep adjusting slightly if needed until feeling fully comfortable. If this position is not comfortable, move to a supported chair and relax into it. Gently squeeze and then release each area of the body, starting with the toes, and then work the way up, eventually focusing on each part of the head. Eyes, mouth and cheeks are all areas that can become tense and may sometimes be forgotten. Relax deep into the surface the body is resting on and let it take the full weight of your torso, head, and limbs.

Mindful Breathing - Begin to pay attention to your breathing pattern. Notice how the body and organs feel while each breath is taken. Focus on the lungs filling up and emptying and the associated sensations. Feel the air move through the nostrils with each deep inhale and exhale. Some people prefer to count each breath as a way of keeping the concentration solely focused on breathing and away from what may be passing through the mind.

Thoughts - One of the biggest myths people have about meditation is that they have to completely release everything spinning through the mind. However, a calm state of mind will come naturally and does not need to be forced. We can allow each thought to enter the mind, pay attention to it for a very short period, and then let it go. Try not to attach any emotions to your thinking; just recognize whatever is floating around and then let it go. Keeping the attention on deep breathing and how the body is feeling will take the focus away from anything trying to enter the mind.

Visualize - Visualizing on a specific scene helps to alleviate unpleasant thoughts. Focusing on a color, a sunset, a favorite object, or any positive image will bring a greater sense of calm. Holding the picture in the mind while breathing deeply allows a gentle flow into a deep meditation.

Lie still, allowing the body and mind to feel all the sensations that are taking place. Try not to rush any part of this process. Just let the meditation naturally progress. Feel the sense of stillness wash over the body as the mind enters a place of calm and tranquility. The entire body will be entering into a deep sense of relaxation and then it will move slowly into a meditative state. While traveling through each stage of consciousness, try to remain as still as possible in both body and mind. Allow the mind to transcend naturally through each change that takes place.

If you reach a feeling of sleepiness and sleep was the intended outcome for the meditation, then we can allow it to happen. Some people like to wake first before drifting back toward sleep. Choose whatever feels best for you. The most important thing is to enjoy how the meditation feels and appreciate the changes occurring within. It is a very personal experience and what is written here is just a guideline. Each person will find their own way and discover what feels right to them.

This process can be repeated at any time during the day or at night, or after a particularly stressful day. If we practice regularly, we will start to notice heightened sensations occurring as soon as we enter into deeper meditative states.

Although this might seem like the most obvious tip, quite often when under duress we forget that a simple breathing exercise can help significantly. Whenever a situation feels like it is too much— or even better, before something starts to feels too much—stop everything, remain still for a moment, and focus attention on the breath arriving and departing. Inhale from the diaphragm and through the nose, then slowly breathe out in a gentle blowing motion. Repeat as often as necessary, aiming to clear the mind of anything other than the sensations found while inhaling and exhaling.

We can also integrate mandalas into our meditation to deepen our practice. Mandala is a Sanskrit word meaning "sacred circle," and they represent the universe, unity, harmony and wholeness. They symbolize infinity and the never-ending quality of life and have been widely used for centuries by Buddhists, Hindus, American Indians and others who find significant meaning in them.

Mandalas were re-introduced to the Western world largely thanks to Carl Jung. Jung considered mandalas as universal expressions of the human psyche. He believed that when we reflect on them we are able to tap into our intuitive nature and bring to light the emotional wounds from our past that we have denied, rejected or buried. Mandalas are often used during meditation; because they are visually stimulating, they help to quiet the mind and reduce repetitive thoughts so that we can achieve a higher state of awareness so that innate knowledge and wisdom can surface. Mandalas can offer us a clearer vision and a profound understanding of ourselves at an intimate, deep, inner soul level.

Mandalas can enhance the awareness of our identity, our relationships, our personal goals, emotions, sensitivities, character, intuition, values, tendencies, and motivations. They can also help us to reflect on the past, understand the present and give us a glimpse into what our future may hold.

To use a mandala while meditating, it is beneficial to set an intention beforehand. There may be many aspects of our life that we would like to gain more insight about, although, there may be one specific part that stands out more than the rest. If we keep our minds still for a few moments, we may notice the same though keeps returning—usually the one most seeking emotional or mental resolve.

While we are considering what we would like to focus our awareness on, we can gaze at the mandala and focus on the colors, shape or pattern.

The purpose of focusing on a mandala is for a deep insightful meditation and for further awakening so that we can gain clarity about hidden parts of ourselves and ultimately receive guidance about a particular area of our lives that we may have been struggling with. We can also look into what exists at the center of our hearts as well as gently unveiling any unhealed, unresolved emotional wounds.

We can meditate for as little as five minutes, or for much longer, depending on how much time we have and on our attention span. As we become more familiar with meditating, we will find that it is effortless to tap into the energy of the mandala. We will naturally feel compelled to meditate for longer and the guidance we receive will be far more vivid. We will receive a constant download of highly beneficial and inspiring information relating to spiritual growth and self-realization.

The meditation is simple to practice. While inhaling and exhaling deeply, just focus on the mandala, softening the gaze and allow the mind to calm so that the shapes become more vivid and enhanced and then gently explore what is lingering in the recesses of the mind.

When reading the mandala, our intuition will guide us toward anything we need to devote more focused attention to. It will also help us to interpret what is happening within our energy field. If we tap into our inner knowing while reading mandalas, we will automatically and instinctively receive the answers to any questions we may want answered.

Each time we meditate we will receive new information and a fresh perspective on an original situation or it can open our mind to something entirely new and from an angle that we likely hadn't yet considered.

The artwork included was crafted by Krutika Joglekar. To find out more information and view more of Krutika's unique creations please visit www.instagram.com/krutikajoglekar/

Chapter 45

READING AURAS

Learning to read auras is an excellent way to determine if someone is communicating or behaving authentically and it is also beneficial for deeper levels of physical, emotional, and psychological healing. Vibrations contain vital information and the data contained in auras is easily translated, so it is beneficial to learn how to read them so we can quickly and easily see the intentions, emotions, feelings, and general health and wellbeing of those whose company we are in, as well as understand our own on a much deeper level. We can use the information we receive to assess or evaluate either for healing or if we are unsure of an agenda.

Each layer of our aura holds information and auras "communicate" with us before any words have been spoken. Our auric layers are in tune with our *chakras*, and whenever we think or feel something, our thoughts, feelings and emotions initially vibrate on an inner level. These vibrations then manifest as energy and radiate outward and exist in our energy field/aura.

We each have seven subtle bodies (energetic layers) known as our aura. The layers form around our physical body to create an electromagnetic field. Our energetic layers transfer universal life force energy so that our physical body is maintained. Although all the levels vibrate on a unique frequency, they also connect with and relate to each of the other levels. Therefore, if one level is out of harmony it can affect other levels too.

Our three lower subtle bodies process energies in the physical plane. The three higher subtle bodies process energies within the spiritual plane. Our middle subtle body is our astral body, which is the bridge that connects the two. Energy passes through the astral body then through the heart *chakra* before communicating with the lower bodies.

Physical Plane

Our first layer is our etheric/spiritual body and it corresponds with the root (base) *chakra*. It is a blue-y/grey color and is composed of vital energy, life energy (*prana*). It extends approximately two inches out from the body and is the closest subtle layer to the physical body. It mirrors exactly what is taking place within the physical body so it is perceived as a template for it. The etheric body transfers universal life energy to the physical body. We gain access to our *chakras* through this layer.

The second layer is our emotional body and it corresponds with the sacral *chakra*. It reflects our emotions and feelings and is associated with the past. It is approximately one to three inches away from the physical body. This subtle layer can be seen in all colors of the rainbow and the colors change in intensity depending on our emotions. Negative emotions appear as dull and darker in color, whereas positive emotions will appear as vivid bright colors. If emotions aren't processed properly, they become stored in the emotional body and can cause blockages. This layer has similarities to a lava lamp. If our emotional health is good and we are processing all of our emotions well, our energy will appear as fluid clouds of energy flowing smoothly. If we suppress or block our emotions the energy will appear as lumpy, slow, and possibly stagnant.

The third layer is our mental body and this corresponds with the solar plexus *chakra*. It is associated with emotions, our conscious mind, our intuition, our thought processes, ideas, and our mental health or illness. It stores knowledge and is responsible for our intelligence and wisdom. It extends from between three and eight inches from the body and emanates a yellowish hue that radiates around the head and shoulders and down toward the body.

Astral Plane

The fourth layer is our astral body and it is connected to the heart *chakra*. It is the bridge to the spiritual plane. It extends from around six to twelve inches from the physical body. The colors are perceived as all seven colors of the rainbow, similar to the emotional body, though the astral body also has pink hues. Through this layer we connect with other people and the energy that stores information is shared and passed from one to the other. As a relationship deepens, rose-colored cords radiate and connect between both heart *chakras*. This is the reason we often say we are seeing someone through "rose-colored glasses." It is also why we often feel as though we need to cut cords or bonds that connect us to someone when a relationship ends.

Spiritual Plane

The fifth layer is our etheric template and it is connected to the throat *chakra*. It mirrors all of our memories and past encounters. When we tap into the etheric body we can connect to our soul's higher purpose. This layer extends from between eighteen to twenty-four inches from the physical body and is visible as cobalt or dark blue.

The sixth layer is our celestial body and is connected to the third eye *chakra*. It is a mirror for the subconscious mind and we connect to it when we raise our vibration and reach a higher level of awareness and consciousness. It glows in opalescent soft pastel shades with silver and gold tones.

The seventh layer is our ketheric template and is connected to the crown *chakra*. It is the outer and last subtle layer. It connects us to our higher selves and is the mental level of the spiritual plane. It extends approximately three and a half feet from the physical body. It contains Kundalini energy that flows up and down the spine. The ketheric template appears as a grid with illuminated gold threads. These threads connect all the subtle layers together.

The colors of an aura relate to the colors of the energy that vibrates in and all around us. We can remain aware of the health and color of our own aura as we view other people's auras through our own. Therefore, if our own aura is not clear and healthy, when we look at other people's auras they will be tinted with whatever hues are emanating from the colors in our own. Before we attempt to tap into and explore auras we need to first protect our own. We can do this simply and quickly by visualizing a brilliant white light around ourselves to protect and also heal. For added protection, we can imagine it has a silver outline that reflects negative energy. We can also transmute any negative energy if our own energy field is vibrating on a high frequency.

When we are vibrating highly we do not need to worry as much about taking care of our aura and protecting it as it will be healthy, strong, and constantly revitalizing itself, taking care of itself. However, we should never become complacent, as our frequency can drop from high to low from moment to moment. If we are particularly low, we can keep our awareness on our aura. When we tune in to our energy field, we will pick up on subtle or intense sensations, which are indications of its overall health and the areas we need to focus on. Auras contract and alter in color and clarity depending on our emotional, psychological, and physical health. Our auras are much brighter in the morning and they fade slightly during the evening. The auric glow is stronger around the face, particularly the mouth, cheeks, and also the neck. They are often seen as an oval shape around our body and a healthy aura has an electromagnetic radiation that spans approximately two to three feet outside the physical body although they can expand up to thirty feet. We can often feel whether our aura is expanding far and wide or if we are keeping it close to try to contain our energy.

When our aura is too far out at the front it means we are looking way ahead into the future. If it is stretching far behind us and not very far in front, we are afraid to move forward and are stuck in the past. The bottom of our aura is associated with balance and grounding and the top of our aura is related to our higher conscious and the ethereal world. Our aura should be in balance with our physical body approximately in the center. The shape of our aura can determine whether we are living in the past, the present, or in the future among many other things.

If we are far too trusting, naive and we are not focused, our aura will literally be spilling out everywhere, taking up a vast amount of space, and could be absorbing all kinds of external negative entities.

The left side of our aura signifies our feminine energy and the right side is associated with our masculine energy.

When reading auras our intuition will guide us toward anything we need to fixate upon. It will also help us to achieve a deeper insight and interpret what is happening within our energy field. If we tap into our inner knowing while reading auras, it will automatically deliver the answers to any questions we may want to ask and it will also provide clues by way of images or words as to the cause for any particular areas of concern.

To see an aura, we use our third eye (the brow *chakra*) and we must also have faith and an open mind. We can practice on ourselves by looking in a mirror, or we can practice on someone who is willing to be patient while we learn the procedure. It is important that the background is neutral, preferably a white or pale color. It is also advisable that the person whose aura we are observing is wearing clothes that are not too distracting. Candles or lamps can be used so the lighting is not too bright or too dark. Natural light is always preferable.

One of the easiest places to start focusing our attention on is the center of the forehead, the third eye. Once we have fixated on a spot, we can remain there, then relax our gaze so everything appears slightly out of focus for approximately thirty to sixty seconds. If we close our eyes for one to two seconds our mind's eye will have taken a picture of the aura., We can open the eyes and keep in a relaxed focus once again and if necessary repeat as many times as needed until we gain a clear picture.

When we hold the focus for long enough a light will appear that is usually seen as a white glow that surrounds the whole body. This is the energy field that is viewed as clear energy. We can try to remain focused long enough for the glow to expand so that we have created a space for colors to appear. As we soften our gaze, the aura will expand outward and color will begin to infiltrate it. If the white glow dissipates, we can then begin again and concentrate on remaining fixated to the white glow.

As the mind is not familiar with viewing energy we may be tempted to look away when colors appear. We must try to resist the temptation to get distracted, as if we look elsewhere the aura we have begun to see will immediately disappear from our view. When first practicing it is quite normal for this to happen. A similar concept is used when we observe "magic" pictures where images appear from a background or we see various perceptions of the same image. When we focus and soften our gaze our eyes will adjust naturally to what is available to be seen.

When we are advanced at seeing auras we will notice how they alter when someone is being honest or dishonest. The colors and shape of the aura will change as they speak. If an aura is very vivid, clear with bright colors, then what we are receiving is the current perceived version of the truth. If the colors are hazy or gray, then the intentions of the person will likely not positive ones. Aura colors help us to understand the emotional, mental, spiritual, and physical health of ourselves and those around us.

The meanings of aura colors are:

- Red: anger, anxiety, determined, energetic, enthusiastic, impatient, impulsive, materialistic, nervous, passionate, powerful, resentment, unforgiving
- Deep red: grounded, inner strength, powerful, sexual, strong-willed
- Bright or light pink: affectionate, disciplined, loving, romantic, self-love, sensitive, sensual, soft, tenderness, innocence, tenderness
- Orange: advanced spiritually, adventurous, control, creative, healthy, honest, kind, leader, outgoing, powerful, stamina, teacher, vitality
- Orange/yellow: creative, extrovert, intelligent, kinship, vibrant
- Yellow: analytical, awakened, content, easy-going, free, good communication, happiness, intelligence, leader, no attachments, optimistic, spiritual
- Gold: affectionate, artistic, inner knowledge, intuitive, strong spiritual energy, wisdom

- Green: animal lover, enjoys the outdoors, balance, healer, healthy, in tune with nature, peace, need for security, nurture
- Dull green: envy, jealous, needs loyalty, possessive, untrusting
- Yellow/green: good communicator
- Turquoise: compassionate, organized, sensitive
- Blue: balanced, calm, caring, free-thinker, generous, good communication, helper, integrity, intelligent, kind, loving, patient, peaceful, sensitive, stability, sympathetic, truthful
- Light blue: intuitive, peaceful, loyalty, moderation, selfless, serenity, truthful
- Royal blue: clairvoyant, strength, elegance, sophistication
- Indigo: depth, intuitive, mystical, self-realization, wisdom
- Violet: artistic, communicator, empathetic, inspirers, intuitive, leader, performer, philosophical, psychic power, philosophical, spiritual growth, visionary
- Lavender: dreamer, imaginative
- White/Silver: Adaptable, etheric, gifted, intuitive, nurturing, psychic, sensitive, spiritual, successful, talented
- Grey: detached, fear, impartial
- Dull grey: fear, frustration, holding on to resentment, pain
- Brown: confusion, low self-esteem, materialistic, negative, selfish
- Black: Anxiety, depression, fear, guarded, grief, guarded, hatred, holding on to pain, illness, protective, guarded, unforgiving
- Cloudy white: difficult to read, lacking consciousness, there may be problems
- Clear white: authentic, cleansing, divine, highly spiritual, pure *prana* energy, awareness, clarity, unity, healing

When reading colors, the shade of the color means more than the color itself. If the colors are very clear and bright, they have positive overtones. When they are dull and cloudy they are negative and often mean the opposite of the words associated with that color. It is also important to look at which layer (subtle body) of the aura the color relates to so we can analyze it in greater detail, as each layer relates to a different aspect of ourselves.

Someone who is advanced spiritually will have a gold glowing aura that vibrates with this color almost continuously. A person who is struggling with negativity, resentment, and fear will have a very dull and dark aura.

Reading our own aura is just as important as reading other people's as we can learn about our own psyche, truth, and what is hidden within us, just as we can learn and understand these things about others.

Empaths are able to sense energy, so we can easily and naturally read auras. However, seeing them as colors offers another dimension. Viewing an aura helps us to achieve a far more in-depth understanding and insight into the body, soul and mind.

Chapter 46

CHAKRAS

Our physical and energetic bodies weave together to form a matrix that interacts to keep us energized and all of our organs and cells functioning effectively. Any disturbance in the energetic body can affect the physical body and vice versa. Our aura and our *chakra* are in constant communication. Our *chakras* regulate all human body processes and correlate with our physiological and neurological systems.

Chakras are visually represented as a vertical row of circles and each one vibrates on its own unique frequency, depicted by a color. The seven *chakras* are each seen as one of the colors of a rainbow and they run up the physical body from the base of the spine to the crown of the head along the Sushumna, which is the central energy channel. This is one of the reasons we may be mesmerized by rainbows and we resonate with them so intensely as they reflect back our human energy system.

The first *chakra* is located at the base of the spine and the seventh one is located at the crown of the head. They each serve as pumps or valves and they regulate our energy flow. The *chakras* of highly sensitive people are usually wide open which means, if we do not have an awareness of energy, we are at risk of leaking or absorbing such high levels of energy that it can leave us exhausted and we may feel highly emotional and overwhelmed. It is essential for empaths to be aware of the roles *chakras* play and it is imperative that we keep them balanced, clean, open, and freely spinning. When our *chakras* are healthy we maintain a sustainable healthy flow of energy and the left and right sides of our bodies, the *yin* (receiving) and *yang* (giving), rotate in harmony with one another.

Chakra is a Sanskrit word that means wheel. *Chakras* are spinning wheels of energy. Our *chakras* draw in the vital universal life force energy (*prana*) the human body needs to exist. Each *chakra* is associated with a color, a specific area of the human body, and also to our vital organs. Our *chakras* provide the organs with the energy they need to function. It is essential that our *chakras* remain open so that energy can flow through them as blockages will cause our energy to slow down, which results in us feeling fatigued and our physical health being adversely affected. When we are grounded and harmonized we are able to regulate the speed of our lower chakras and pull energy from the lower chakras up to the higher ones so that our energy is balanced and harmonized.

Each *chakra* has its own set of spiritual qualities that are enhanced when the *chakra* is aligned and balanced. Quite often many of the qualities within each chakra are unacknowledged and undisturbed and when we focus attention on them and keep them healthy and freely spinning, we are able to gain access to them and utilize them. When Kundalini energy, which lies dormant at the base of our spines, is awakened we become conscious of what is stored in each *chakra* and these qualities enhance the process of self-transformation. Kundalini energy can be awakened and ignited through meditation, yoga, reiki, or Tantric practice.

Our subtle layers and *chakras* correspond with one another to maintain our physical, emotional, intellectual, and spiritual existence. They are our connection to the universe and allow us to understand ourselves on a far deeper and more intimate level. The *chakras* within the subtle layers vibrate at a higher frequency the further away from the physical body they are. The ones closest to the body vibrate on a low frequency and the farthest subtle layers vibrate on a high frequency. This allows our energy to travel through our subtle layers and our physical body so that we can achieve and maintain balance and harmony.

Our *chakras* can become imbalanced when we experience situations in life that are distressing or that induce negative emotions. If we do not transmute and clear blocked energy it can manifest as emotional, mental, or physical pain or illness. To become aware that there is an obstruction we simply need to be aware that our minds and bodies are intrinsically connected and pay attention to how we are processing our emotions. Whenever we feel stress, it manifests itself in our physical bodies. When we have a sound understanding of how our *chakras* operate we can connect with them so that we can heal our *bodies* as well as our minds. We can rebalance and realign our *chakras* by understanding each of their functions and then paying attention to the associated sensations within our physical body.

The first *chakra* is known as the root *chakra* or *Muladhara* and it is associated with the color red. It is located at the base of the spine at the tailbone area. It is our earth element and relates to security, stability, balance, identity, and feeling grounded. It is also connected to survival and generates our fight or flight instinctive and primal response. This is where Kundalini energy is stored and where it lies dormant until it is awakened. If this chakra is blocked due to fear we will develop issues with digestion and food, experience joint pain, constipation, and have lower backache or problems with our legs or feet.

The second *chakra* is known as *Svadhisthana* or sacral/spleen *chakra* and it is associated with the color orange. It is located in the pelvic area just beneath the navel. It is related to emotions, feelings, desire, sexuality, and creativity. If it is blocked due to guilt we may have difficulties surrounding sex; hip, pelvic, or lower back pain; or kidney or bladder problems.

The third *chakra* is known as our solar plexus *chakra* and is associated with the color yellow. It is located in the upper abdomen just above the pubic bone. It is related to our personality, intellect, emotions, willpower, self-esteem, self-expression, and digestion. If it is blocked due to shame we may have stomach or digestive problems, emotional outbursts, feel nervous, fearful, or become angered easily.

The fourth *chakra* is known as our heart *chakra* and it identifies with the color green. It is located at the center of the chest just above the heart. It is related to universal love, compassion, forgiveness, letting go, healing, tranquility, and our general wellbeing. It helps us to understand our relation to everything that exists to assist us to love and accept one another unconditionally. If the heart chakra is blocked due to grief we feel jealous, angry, abandoned, or we may have chest pains and breathing problems or wrist, arm, upper back, or shoulder pain.

The fifth *chakra* is known as our throat *chakra*. It is located in the throat area and is associated with the color blue. It relates to speech, truth, integrity, authenticity, expression, and communication. When we are not communicating well or being deceitful this chakra may become blocked and the throat area will feel pressurized and we may also have neck or shoulder pain, facial problems, or develop ear infections.

The sixth *chakra* is known as our third eye *chakra* and it is associated with the color indigo. It is located at the center of the forehead, between the eyebrows, and is related to perception, foresight, intuition, imagination, insight, discernment, inner knowledge, opening ourselves up, and awakening so that we can connect to our conscious selves. When this chakra is open, we can clearly see both our inner and our outer worlds with clarity. If it is blocked due to illusions, we may experience problems with our eyes or suffer with headaches or loss of hearing.

The seventh *chakra* is known as our crown *chakra* and is associated with the color purple. It is located at the top of the head and is related to awareness, spirituality, wisdom, and consciousness. If the crown *chakra* is blocked due to attachments, we may develop mental health problems, skin problems, physical imbalance, fatigue, and we may be unable to make decisions.

We can check how open *chakras* are by holding a pendulum above each one. If we are checking someone else's chakras we can either stand face to face with them or they can be lying down on their back. We then hold the pendulum still in line with each *chakra*. Starting at the crown *chakra*, we should notice the pendulum moving. It might either sway side to side or rotate in clockwise or anticlockwise circles. When we move the pendulum to the third eye *chakra* it should change direction. From here, as we move the pendulum down through the other *chakras* holding it above each one for a few moments, the pattern should be consistent. If it is not, it is a sign that there are blockages within either one or more of the *chakras*. If one *chakra* is imbalanced, it will have an affect on all the other *chakras*.

We can work with our *chakras* to enhance our own energy system so that we can channel the abundance of energy outward and then on to whomever we intend to offer healing to.

Our *chakras* can become closed due to a build up of tension associated with denied emotions, guilt, abuse, trauma, or anything that has caused us pain or suffering that we have contained instead of processing. The dense energy becomes blocked and stores inside us. One of the most effective ways to clear blockages is by acknowledging our pent-up emotions and working to resolve them. When we heal and forgive ourselves and others the stored emotions will dissipate and the energetic imprints they have left on us will fade and quickly clear. This will remove any blockages that are preventing our chakras from spinning and our energy from flowing freely.

When our chakras are closed, our energy will slow down and this may lead to physical ailments manifesting in the body due to built-up tension. We can regularly open, cleanse, and close our *chakras* to free up any clogged energy. When we open our *chakras* we can work from the root *chakra* up, and when closing them we work from the crown *chakra* down.

Before we begin any cleansing, opening, or closing, it is advisable to do a quick grounding exercise to ensure we are calm and harmonized. We can do a *chakra* opening exercise by focusing on the location of each *chakra* and then visualizing the color associated to it. The colors of the *chakra* are the same as the colors of the rainbow, starting with red at the root *chakra* and moving up to violet at the crown *chakra*.

When opening or closing *chakras* we can imagine something that opens and closes; for example, a flower coming into bloom and then closing its petals is a visual that can work well. When the *chakra* color appears we can look at whether it is bright, clear, vivid, or dull. Then we can clearly see if the *chakra* is freely turning or if it appears clogged and is spinning slowly or with difficulty. As we focus on the color of each *chakra*, we can imagine infuse it with positivity so that it becomes it clean and clear and then place our hands on the area associated with the *chakra* and press slightly to ease any tension that is held there. Our hands hold heat and heat breaks down stored up tension. By rubbing our hands together, we can warm up and stimulate our energy. Then, we can channel energy to flow through our hands, similar to what takes place during a reiki exercise. The energetic vibrations that are radiating will work toward the *chakras* and reignite them so that they spin freely while removing any existing energy blockages. All we need to do is simply communicate with each *chakra* through focusing conscious awareness on it. We then ask for the *chakra* to cleanse and restore itself so that any dense negativity that has attached to it dissipates. We can repeat this process moving upward, focusing on one *chakra* at a time.

While we are working on each one we can also look at the emotions that are connected to each *chakra*. As we focus on the emotions, we can radiate unconditional love, acceptance, compassion, and forgiveness to heal past wounds. When we are experiencing emotional or physical pain, we often believe that our current situations are what have caused the pain. However, it is usually our past, repressed pain that has triggered the emotions we experience today. Our belief system stores data, and when something happens that confirms or conflicts with that data, we are propelled to react and our previous experiences are awoken and rise to the surface. When we clear past tormenting memories, we are also clearing the way for a calmer, peaceful, and less painful present and future.

There are also 144 minor *chakras* throughout the physical body. They each draw energy inward and we can keep these functioning well by focusing our attention on the overall energy matrix and requesting that all of our *chakras* are fuelled with energy and glow bright. We can do a simple visualization exercise at the same time and imagine rays of brilliant light cascading toward our physical body.

To clear the *chakra* channel, which is a cord that links all the *chakras*, we can visualize a cord from the earth going up to the base *chakra*. As we clear energy via this cord we can flush it down from the crown *chakra* toward the root *chakra*. Focusing on one *chakra* at a time we can clear any blockages in the connecting cord and then visualize any negative energy flowing freely down to the earth, where it is neutralized and transmuted into positive energy.

When our *chakras* are clear and our energy is flowing well, we will experience vitality along with optimum physical, emotional, mental, and spiritual health.

Our chakras communicate with other people's chakras through invisible energetic cords and we relay messages to one another without the need for words. The root chakra communicates nurturing, the sacral chakra communicates physical desire to touch, the solar plexus chakra communicates guidance, the heart chakra communicates loving feelings, the throat chakra communicates talking and understanding one another, the third eye communicates seeing one another clearly the crown chakra communicates knowing one another at a higher level and without illusion.

Cords instantly develop between a mother and her new baby, the main one being from the root chakra, which is the chakra associated with security and stability and it allows the mother to know if her baby could be in any kind of danger whenever she is not within close vicinity.

Chakra cords connect either for some form of communication to take place, for energetic healing and when these etheric cords are in place the energy can pass from one to the other without us having a consciously awareness that anything is occurring.

Chapter 47

HEALING

Generally speaking, many of us have become so disconnected to Earth that we have lost our natural ability to connect with nature and make use of our inherent healing abilities. Empaths are drawn toward natural environments—for example, mountains, rivers, or forests—that help reenergize and replenish depleting energy levels and also so that we can be at one with nature. Empaths tend to respect all areas of life and understand that healing takes place through a variety of channels, such as food, mantras, music, dancing, singing, meditation, yoga, touch, communication, movement, and essentially through the energy we radiate.

One of the first signs that tell us that we are an empath is the incredibly painful sensation that we feel when we are around someone who is suffering either emotionally, mentally, or physically. Often, though, when we feel compelled to heal it can also be a sign that we have aspects of ourselves that have not yet healed.

Before we radiate healing energy, we can try to ensure that we have cleared our own energy field so that the energy we send is pure and high vibrational and not infiltrated with any current difficulty or emotional struggle we may be going through. We will always be on a path of self-discovery, and this will include unearthing old wounds and processing the associated emotions and feelings. Therefore, when we carry out healing work we can try to take extra care of any of our significant soul injuries before we offer out healing energy to ensure we do not pass our emotional distress on to anyone else.

Our hands' are transmitters and are incredible tools to soothe and heal as our touch connects our energy directly with other people's. Empaths have the innate ability to know the area that the pain is coming from and often what is causing it. We can then channel our energy to flow through to our fingertips and the energetic waves transfer through our hands to balance and harmonize the energy of the person we are offering healing to. When healing, we do not need to physically touch anyone else. We can simply hold our hands above the area and radiate the healing energy. We can also do this through a visualization imagining the scenario in our mind as though we are radiating high frequency energy in person.

It isn't just humans that empaths are drawn to offer healing energy to, we also use our gift to soothe the suffering of animals, Mother Earth, and the universe. While we can offer healing energy to others, for the healing to be effective each person must ultimately take responsibility for healing themselves by dealing with the pain at the root and also by being receptive to incoming high vibrational energy. Empaths are able to detect the traumatic deep-seated emotions that other people hold on to and it is this energy that causes blockages within their system. When we are grounded and balanced we have the capacity to be highly empathetic and are the nurturers, caregivers, and healers. Many empaths serve humanity through finding work in holistic therapies, spiritual arts, energy work, psychic fields, nutrition, counseling, psychology, social work, teaching, and the medical and veterinary fields. The empaths who are not professional healers will most likely still be radiating healing energy whether they are doing it consciously or subconsciously. The most important thing that all empaths need to remember is that because they absorb and store such a high amount of debris from other people's energy, it is vital that they cleanse their auras fully before offering soothing, balancing, healing vibrations.

The reason we feel other people's pain so intensely, whether emotionally or physically, is because we have the divine ability to radiate healing energy through sending powerful energetic waves of universal energy and transmuting negativity. Everyone, whether an empath or not, can radiate healing energy. We sense repressed or ignored pain and we are able to unearth the root causes and offer compassion and unconditionally loving, pure, light energy. However, the difficulty here is that not everyone wants this pain to be uprooted. Unraveling past and painful experiences and memories is not easy and not everyone wants to delve into and pick at old wounds. What many people fail to realize is that the pain they are carrying around with them ferments. It will lie there stagnating until it seeps out and erupts when least expected. It will not just disappear so it is essential that it is recognized, unearthed and transmuted.

We can very easily absorb other people's emotions during healing as our energy expands to incorporate the aura of the person we are healing. Therefore, it is essential that we protect our energy fields well. We also need to be aware that we can become inflicted with pain from our own past memories when we tap into our previous experiences to access knowledge and gain resonance so that we can relate deeply during healing. Therefore, it is crucial that we do not offer healing energy that is infused with our own emotions, feelings, beliefs, values, intentions and memories, as this information will be transferred from us to the person we are offering healing energy to.

While we can tap into our own history to relate, we should not use that energy as healing energy. We must put all that aside so that we are providing healing from the limitless amount of pure energy provided by the universe and not from our own experiences and reserves. Before we offer healing energy to anyone else we must first clear and protect our own energy fields and deal with the lingering emotions that exist there. Then, we can ensure we are not only shielded from absorbing painful emotions, but also that we are not unintentionally reawakening our own closed wounds and transferring them to the person we are intending to heal. To effectively assist anyone else with their internal conflict we must first acknowledge, understand and if possible, clear, and process our own. When we are aware that we have our own emotional injuries, we can make a conscious effort not to evoke that energy so that we can still send healing energy to others.

Whenever we see someone physically or emotionally wounded, our gut instinct that rises from our sacral *chakra* is to reach out with our hands. When we offer healing energy, we also engage the heart chakra, as healing is a process of showing compassion while transcending and radiating love. Rose quartz is one particular crystal that is used for healing as it strengthens empathy and opens up the heart chakra to allow a path for love and compassion to enter. It carries a strong vibration of unconditional love, so it is capable of transferring painful emotions into loving ones. Pink is a naturally loving and compassionate color, and while healing, rather than envisaging a white light surrounding and protecting our bodies, we can envisage a soft pink light as this enhances our healing power and it infuses it with unconditional love. We can also use the healing power of sound to cleanse and purify the body and psyche. Mantras can be spoken, hummed, or sung to generate powerful energetic vibrations.

Reiki is a magical universal spiritual life force energy that is deep within us all. As we are all made of the same energy, we are all connected therefore when generate and radiate high vibrational energy, it automatically connects and interacts with all external energy. To connect to Reiki for the purpose of healing is very simple and natural. We can easily channel this universal energy to balance, heal, and harmonize the body and mind and raise our own vibrations and the vibrations that surround us. The word *Reiki* derives from two Japanese words. *Rei* translates to wisdom or higher power, and *Ki* translates to life force energy. Reiki can be used as a therapy to alleviate physical, mental, or emotional pain, though it is also a way of life if we align to the principles and practice them regularly.

We all have the capacity to heal ourselves and to send healing vibrations out to others. When we are still, we are able to scan the body and mind to find exactly where the root of conflict or pain lies. As Hermann Hesse explains in his book *Siddhartha* and Paulo

Coelho in his bestseller *The Alchemist*, everything we need to know can be found when we are still and listen to our inner selves. We can listen to our inner selves when we practice meditation.

For centuries, Reiki has been protected, with the teaching practice being passed down through strict lineages. Often, high fees are charged in order to learn the skills and qualifications needed to practice and pass on the principles. However, like with most things, we can pay for an experienced and qualified person to give us a quality treatment or we can learn the basics so that we can treat ourselves when we need instant healing.

Empaths often find that after a particularly stressful day or if we awake during the night full of anxieties our bodies are tense and holding on to an overwhelming amount of painful emotions. Reiki is a tool that can instantly calm, heal, and soothe, and once we have practiced it on ourselves we can then send any excess healing energy out into the universe so that it can be absorbed wherever it is needed.

Reiki is a practice that anyone can tap into at any time. The philosophies of Reiki are similar to those of Buddhism, yoga, and many other spiritual practices.

"The secret art of inviting happiness

The miraculous medicine of all diseases

Just for today, do not anger;

Do not worry and be filled with gratitude

Devote yourself to your work

Be kind to people

Every morning and evening, join your hands in prayer

Pray these words to your heart and chant these words with your mouth." ——*Usui Reiki treatment for the improvement of body and mind*, Usui Mikao, the founder

The basics of Reiki are mindful living, conscious thoughts and actions, alleviating negativity, being grateful, and a profound appreciation for life. When we have a headache, we instinctively place our hands on our heads. If we allow the mind to calm so we are focusing on the feeling of the energy flowing from our hands to our heads, within moments the pain subsides and any stress that has built up will be alleviated. The same process can be practiced with aches and pains anywhere else in the body and also with emotional pain. Emotional trauma that lingers eventually manifests in the body as physical pain, so we can scan the body to locate the area and allow our energetic vibrations to soothe and heal.

We can also uncover issues that we are holding on to that we may not have realized existed. When we are able to acknowledge and heal emotional pain, we are able to rid the body of the physical pain that is connected to the emotional injury.

When we practice Reiki regularly we will find that as soon as we think about Reiki healing our hands will instinctively begin to tingle with sensations and warm as the energy is channeled in preparation for the practice. As soon as the connection from the mind to the hands is made, both the healing energy and the heat will naturally build.

To benefit fully from the energy that Reiki creates, it is necessary to calm our minds so that we can relax and surrender to the treatment.

A basic Reiki healing treatment: either sit or lie down somewhere comfortable and totally relax the body. To connect with the body, scan it from top to toe and pay attention to the sensations and signals it is sending out. This will indicate if there are any tension, aches, or pains. Focusing on the mind, let go of any thoughts. Slow the breathing and inhale and exhale deeply. Consider if there is anything that may be causing emotional or physical distress. If so, trace the sensations to find the root cause. Allow the energy from the surrounding energetic field to be directed toward the hands and channel the vibrations so that they filter through them. Visualize a surrounding brilliant white light and pull the energy inward toward the hands. The hands may begin to feel hot or tingly. Move the hands, sweeping them over the body, moving slowly over the *chakra* areas, and allow them to rest when it instinctively feels right to do so. As we move our hands over the body, it also helps to harmonize the energy field. Place the hands on or above the area that needs attention. The area that we are drawn to will likely feel tense, be aching slightly, or have subtle sensations. When we focus on this area, our awareness increases and we can tune in to what is happening within the body. We can then visualize the area of concern as a shape with color. The shape may be tiny in structure or it could be huge, expanding out of the body. As we visualize the colorful shape, we can channel and direct warm, loving, healing energy toward this area and remain focused on it until the shape reduces in size. As it reduces, we may also notice the physical sensations dissipate.

We can either put the hands physically on the body or hold them just above the area when we are healing ourselves. If we are healing someone else it will depend on their personal preference, though if we prefer to hold the hands above the body that is our ultimately our own decision.

Remain in this position, allowing the energy from the body to flow through to your hands. Keep the mind calm, relaxing as much as possible, letting go of any negative energy that may be emanating from the shape or anything else we may be unconsciously holding on to. When the tension has released and the area has reenergized, the hands will begin to move again. We can then scan the body again and focus on any other areas that cause the hands to slow down. Again we repeat the process, holding the hands in place until the energy has cleared. Pay fine attention to how the body and mind are feeling.

When we have finished, we can rebalance and cleanse the aura from top to toe, starting at the head and moving the hands toward the toes in a sweeping motion to clear out any negative energy. When ready, slowly awake and rise gently. After a Reiki treatment it is natural to feel a glowing radiance through and around the mind, body, and spirit. Although we have focused on a specific blocked area, the energy that we have channeled will radiate so that both the body and mind have received a full healing treatment. As we clear blockages, our universal life energy is free to flow through us, and not only do we heal ourselves, we are also in a position to channel our energy so that we can also heal others.

A Reiki healing session can feel similar to how it might feel being wrapped tightly and secure in a spider's cocoon, completely safe and protected. The experience is one of being entirely immersed in a loving divine light. The body, mind, and spirit are connected as one while a safe, warm glow surrounds us.

Reiki is not something that is explained easily, it is something that is felt and experienced. Many people may not consider Reiki as they think it is a complex practice that takes a lot of training. However, Reiki is a simple and loving exercise that we can do for ourselves anywhere at any time. It is a blend of mindfulness, understanding ourselves clearly, and soothing and reenergizing areas that have become blocked due to build ups of energy that result in feeling physiological pain.

Once we know how to give Reiki to ourselves, we can also send healing vibrations to animals, to other people, to the Earth, and out to the universe as energy crosses through space and time. Radiating excess energy is the perfect way to keep energy fluidly flowing through us. To do this all we need to do is set an intention firm in our mind for the reason we are radiating our energy and then we can visualize where we want our energy be sent. We can either look at a picture, which works particularly well if it is someone we know who we want our healing energy to go to, or we can imagine the person, cause or place in our mind or we can repeat their name a few times so that the energy is directed effectively. We then just breathe deeply and enter a calm, relaxed meditative state and as we feel our hands start to warm up and tingle, we will also sense the energy around our body vibrating and as it rises to a higher frequency and we feel a glow surrounding us. We can then start to consciously direct the energy outwards and we will sense it flowing with good intention towards wherever we have chosen to send it, while holding the thought that the energy is for the greatest good for whoever, or wherever, receives it.

If there is no one particular we intend the healing energy to go to, we can then radiate any excess high vibrational energy out into the world, where it will be sensed and received by whoever is open to absorbing it, and it will still affect all, even if only subtly. After channeling universal energy during a Reiki healing session, we will not usually drained, if anything we will feel energized as we always heal ourselves at the same time as we heal outwardly.

At the end of a Reiki session it may take a few minutes to reground and awaken fully, so it is essential to take as long as needed to arouse. Drinking water or eating a piece of fresh fruit after any energy works helps to ground and rebalance energies as our energy has entered a new frequency, so it is important that we remain aware of this so that when the Reiki session is over we blend our physical and energetic bodies and center ourselves. This prevents us feeling too 'high' after this outer body experience, so focusing on our breathing and then gently awakening allows us to come back to "earth" slowly and gently.

There is an abundance of universal life energy. It is limitless. The more we connect to it, the more energized we are and the more enhanced our healing powers will be, so the energy will continuously recharge and radiate out from us and on to wherever else it may be needed.

Chapter 48

CRYSTALS

"In a crystal we have the clear evidence of the existence of a formative life-principle, and though we cannot understand the life of a crystal, it is none the less a living being." ——Nikola Tesla

Crystals appear solid and still, but they are a collection of highly vibrating atoms. They started out as liquid or gas situated under the Earth's surface. When either the liquid or gas rose to the surface and cooled it bonded and formed to be what we now perceive as a solid state, with each atom organized in an orderly, repetitive pattern. These atoms vibrate at a very high speed and both temperature and sound can influence their frequency. Many empaths have a strong connection to crystals as they not only recharge our energy levels, they also offer energetic protection, help strengthen intuition, clear emotional blockages, absorb negative entities, and emanate high vibrational waves that assist when we are transmuting and carrying out healing.

"Crystals are living beings at the beginning of creation." ——Nikola Tesla

Empaths are drawn to crystals as each one has its own unique vibration. When we use our intuition, we are able to connect with the crystal or stone that has a vibration that resonates with our own. When we are around crystals or gemstones our energy levels balance, harmonize, and heighten as they alter and raise our vibration. Crystals awaken the cells within our bodies that are vibrating on a low frequency. They engage with them to lift our vibration so that our cells are vibrating on a similar frequency.

Just as crystals are capable of influencing our frequency, we are also able to influence the frequency of a crystal. Temperature is one indicator that causes change. As soon as we hold a crystal in our hands, we activate it and its vibration will automatically alter. This is why when choosing a new crystal, we place it in the palm of our hand until it warms to body temperature, and when the vibration stabilizes we are able to feel how it strikes chords and attunes to and resonates with our own vibration. Placing a crystal near a candle will also warm and activate it so that we feel its powerful vibration while meditating.

When we receive a crystal and we are ready to connect with it, we can sit in the lotus position, if comfortable, and cup the crystal in our more dominant hand, with our least dominant hand underneath. Inhaling and exhaling deeply we can focus on the vibrations emanating from the crystal. The vibrations from the crystal will radiate through us and interact with our own energy. We can then reprogram the crystal by imagining we are immersed within it. We can then attune to the crystal and voice a clear and pure intention for it. We will begin to feel a resonance with the crystal, which may consist of either subtle or more noticeable sensations. We can then swap the crystal to our least dominant hand with our more dominant hand underneath to balance the energy throughout our body. The crystal will then be programmed to our set intention and each time we hold it we will reconnect and realign with it. As the crystal's vibration and our own vibration merge, we will harmonize on the same frequency so that we have absolute resonance with the crystal. We are then able to heighten our awareness as our vibration is raised and we will be able to reach a higher level of consciousness.

It is imperative that we take good care of the crystal so that harmful energies cannot interfere with it. We need to be careful where we store it and also be aware of who else may be handling it. After anyone else has touched it, we need to cleanse and reprogram it. It is common for people not to allow anyone else to handle crystals they are specifically working closely with. It is also essential to reaffirm the intention regularly, even if the crystals have been stored safely.

Although empaths are drawn to various crystals, the one we often have the greatest connection to is rose quartz. Rose quartz gets its name from its beautiful rose-pink color. It is a transparent pink crystal that has a soothing and calming essence that offers empaths the perfect healing tool when our hearts are feeling empty, heavy, and distressed. It communicates directly with the heart *chakra* and its peaceful energy circulates a loving vibration. This helps us let go of anger, resentment, fear, and as it recharges the heat *chakra* it also enhances our ability to show love and compassion and accept ourselves and others unconditionally. The soft and gentle feminine energy that emanates from rose quartz helps to tenderly soothe aching hearts and heal old wounds. It assists us with releasing ourselves from the past so that we can refrain from repeating old patterns of behavior that keep us caught in a rotating cycle of pain. Rose quartz helps us to connect with the inner knowledge we have and also helps to strengthen it.

We can keep a small piece of rose quartz close to our hearts by popping it into a piece of clothing or wearing it on a chain with a small piece as a pendant. Keeping rose quartz near to us heightens general feelings of wellbeing, self-worth, self-love, and unconditional love for others. The gentle but powerful energy radiates and vibrates in our aura. Rose quartz can also be placed around the home to harmonize each room as its presence emanates soft, warm, sensual, and romantic sensations.

Yellow Jasper is another highly recommended crystal for empaths as it replenishes and rejuvenates energy, so it is worth carrying a piece along to any social events or places that we think may drain our energy.

Clear quartz is one crystal that is very easy to program as long as our intentions are for our own or an external higher good. It has excellent communication qualities, helps to gain clarity, and it clears emotional blockages.

Amber is not a stone or a crystal, it is fossilized resin, although it works in a similar way. It is an essential one for empaths to consider as it helps us to remain grounded and it also absorbs negative energy easily, so it is particularly valuable when we are subjected to vast amounts of external volatile energy or when we are out anywhere where there are large numbers of people. It also clears the mind, brings stability, offers psychic protection from energy attacks, and encourages peacefulness.

Another crystal that is highly beneficial and a favorite of many empaths is amethyst. One of the main reasons for this is because amethyst helps us when we are transmuting energies as it clears and calms the mind to allow for greater clarity and a clearer insight so that we can identify our own and other people's emotions easily. It also protects us if someone is sending out negative harmful vibrations and it neutralizes these vibrations so that we are not adversely affected. Amethyst also reduces stress and eases any tension-related aches and pains such as headaches and migraines.

Crystals can be used in various ways. We can place them under or in our pillows, wrap our clothing around them and leave them to charge the fabric overnight, carry them loose in pockets or purses, we can use them while meditating, or we can place them around rooms as a visual aid. I often meditate or sleep with a large piece of rose quartz in my hand, especially if I have had a particularly emotional day as it soothes and calms my energy field instantly, and I always ensure there are crystals on the bedside table. I also place a large crystal in front of any device that has electrical smog, such as televisions, computers, so that it blocks and neutralizes any harmful radiation.

Certain crystals complement and interact with our *chakras* and are beneficial when we are doing any opening or alignment work with our *chakras*. When lying down, we can place the crystals on our body in line with our *chakras*. We can match the color of a crystal to the color of our *chakra* to balance and remove blockages.

Here are a few crystals and gemstones that have been specifically chosen as the colors match.

- root *chakra* - red crystal
red jasper - reduces stress, stabilizes, balances energy throughout all the *chakras*
ruby - healing, improves overall health

- sacral *chakra* - orange crystal
carnelian - balances and awakens energy, helps release blockages, promotes confidence, boosts energy
orange calcite - creativity, enhances sexuality, happiness, eliminates negativity

- solar plexus *chakra* - yellow crystal
citrine - cleanses, dispels negativity, alleviates depression, shields and protects the aura from absorbing negative emotions; citrine doesn't need to be cleaned as it repels all negative energy
yellow jasper - cleansing, protective, balances, stabilizes, removes negativity

- heart *chakra* - pink or green crystal
rose quartz - heightens empathy, transmutes pain and fear into love, unconditional love, heals emotional wounds
pink tourmaline - calms, cleanses, energizes, infuses love
green avenutine - enhances empathy, alleviates anxiety
green calcite - helps with forgiveness, balances emotions, promotes compassion

- throat *chakra* - blue crystal
blue lace agate - peace, harmony, improves communication
blue calcite - healing, calming, soothing

- third eye chakra - indigo crystal

sodalite - calms the mind, enhances rational thought, promotes clarity
lapis lazuli - spiritual love, inspiration, connection to higher self

- crown *chakra* - violet crystal
  amethyst - balances emotions, opens and purifies the *chakra*, protects, enhances awareness, relieves physical and emotional pain
  ametrine - strengthens immune system, reduces fatigue, brings clarity and focus

When we are around crystals and gemstones we will feel energized, balanced, grounded, calm, and centered. We will also find that we will not need to carry out protection visualizations or grounding techniques quite as often as the vibrations from the crystals and gemstones naturally protect our energy.

It is essential to cleanse and clear crystals regularly as all kinds of entities can accumulate, as they do not discern between harmful or beneficial properties. They can easily become contaminated with either our own or external negative energies. Crystals that are highly absorbent and used essentially to absorb negativity should be cleansed more frequently.

Setting the intention with the power of thought is the most powerful and direct way to communicate with a crystal and clear it. We can channel whatever thoughts we want to towards the crystal, so if we want it to hold the foundation of the program we were already working on, so that it retains some of the memory of the work that we have already done with it, we just need to set the intention for this to happen.

Whatever we want from the crystal, we can achieve through directing our thoughts and radiating them towards the crystal while thinking about what we want. We can ask the crystal to reprogram completely, or we can ask for all negative entities to detach from the crystal while allowing the ones associated with our original intention to remain. We can do this after meditation so that our mind is calm and focused.

Once the energies have cleared, recharged, and restructured we can then set a new intention for the crystal or continue to work with the original one. We can transmute and neutralize any negative energy that has attached to the crystal simply by holding it in our hands and radiating high-frequency waves infused with love, light, warmth, and respect. Whenever we clear any excess unwanted energy from a crystal, we recharge it at the same time as we are taking it back to its vibrant natural energetic state and the vibrations of the crystal will be able to spin freely once any dense, low-vibrational energy has dissipated. If we feel that the crystal has a lower charge than it should, we can visualize rays of brilliant white light penetrating and reenergizing the crystal.

There are various ways to cleanse and clear a crystal, though we can always complement any physical cleansing we do by maintaining a clear and high vibrational intention for its purpose before, during, and after the cleansing. Sea salt is a natural cleaning agent, so we can leave crystals in a bowl of water with a tablespoon of sea salt. Not all crystals should be cleansed with water; generally, ones that end in "ite" should not be left in water. It is always better to check if water cleansing is suitable. Often our intuition will guide us.

Breathing exercises can also cleanse and clear the crystal. We can relax into a light meditation. Once our mind has balanced, we can inhale deeply and then gently blow the exhaled air over the crystal while maintaining a positive mindset. This will dust away any harmful or unassociated debris or discordant entities that have attached to the crystal.

We can run crystals under flowing water, either a tap or a waterfall, to remove any residual energy along with dirt and grime. Alternatively, sound vibration harmonizes them or we can choose to smudge crystals. We can also bury them under the earth so that they can reconnect to their natural environment and Earth's energy can realign and recharge them.

Once crystals have been cleansed, we can leave them out under the sun, although not on days that are too hot. We can also place them out beneath the moon and stars so the natural energy that is transmitted can reenergize and recharge them. If we are leaving stones outside that cannot be cleansed with water, we can first check the weather to ensure they do not get soaked during rainfall. A new or full moon is an opportune time for cleansing and recharging as they are periods of releasing and letting go of negative entities.

Chapter 49

FLOTATION TANKS

Whenever we feel low on energy and need external assistance to instantly and powerfully reenergize us or even if we just want to indulge in some deeply relaxing time for ourselves, we can opt for a flotation tank experience, which recharges and revitalizes the physical and energetic bodies both at the same time. Flotation tanks isolate us from all external stimulation by blocking out sound, light, and touch. When all outer distractions are removed our senses are disabled, so the only thing that is being stimulated is our conscious mind. There is nothing to hear, see, or feel, so our mind is free to explore the areas that are usually suppressed or forgotten.

Flotation tanks were originally called *sensory deprivation tanks*, and were developed in 1954 by neuroscientist Dr. John C. Lilly, who also studied dolphin communication. Lilly's purpose for creating them was to find out what kept the brain stimulated when all external stimuli had been disconnected. These enclosures are built to contain an adult, with plenty of space to move and stretch the limbs. They are highly recommended for anyone who is highly sensitive to their environment as all external stimuli is removed so that the body and mind can fully balance, relax, heal aches and pains, and we can also achieve absolute peace and serenity.

With the only thing to focus on being our breathing, our brainwave pattern shifts from our natural waking state, beta, then onto alpha, and can then progress to theta waves. Theta is the brainwave that is usually associated with advanced levels of meditation and this state is achievable within the very first flotation session. Although we reach a deep stage of relaxation, the brain remains alert, offering reflection while also improving mental clarity. We can then enter a dreamlike state similar to one that is achieved just before we go to sleep. It is believed that two hours in a flotation tank gives the same benefits we receive from an eight-hour sleep. Epsom salt is added to the water to simulate zero gravity, which increases the buoyancy and allows the body to rise to the surface to replicate the feeling of floating in midair. We achieve a comfortable sensation of weightlessness, and this helps the brain to close down as we use a large amount of our brain to cope with gravity. The water is set to skin temperature so that it is difficult to distinguish between the water and our physical being. There is no dependence on the outer environment as all external energy sources are disconnected. Therefore, the stimulus to our brain is isolated, so the brain has the opportunity to decelerate. The effect that is created deprives us of our vital senses so that our brain does not have to work hard to process information. This enables the logical side of our brain to relax and slow down so it can harmonize with our creative side. We can fully relax and enable our mind to drift into a state of "nothingness" or we can remain alert and consciously infuse our subconscious with inspirational thoughts, creativity, introspection, insight or positive affirmations. When we are at our most relaxed state, the subconscious is better able to absorb data. Our imagination and visualization abilities are also heightened. Studies have shown that heart rate and blood pressure are lowered, which dramatically reduces the release of anxiety and stress-related chemicals.

While we are cocooned in the tank, "feel-good" endorphins are released, which encourage general overall wellbeing and they also provide natural pain relief. Flotation tanks offer an original and profound experience where we can be alone with our mind and quickly cross the path from the conscious to the subconscious and then down into the unconscious mind. They evoke a myriad of sensations, visualizations, thoughts, and inner and outer explorations that depend entirely on how we are feeling at each present moment during the experience. During any period where there may be higher than normal levels of anxiety or stress, a flotation experience can be the perfect antidote to calm, soothe, and relax the body and mind. Flotation tanks not only alleviate aches and pains, they also reduce anxiety, stress, tension, and fatigue as our heart rate settles into a gentle, natural rhythm, enabling us to receive a tranquil and pleasurable emotional, mental, and physical therapeutic experience.

Chapter 50

Five-Minute Energizing Hand Exercise: Jin Shin Jyutsu

Jin Shin Jyutsu is an ancient Japanese art, philosophy, and a powerful alternative health practice. It harmonizes the vital life force energy in the body, which promotes physical, spiritual, mental and emotional health. According to this tradition, each part of the hand is connected to different emotions or organs

thumb - emotional pain, worry, sadness, grief, depression, anxiety, stress, tension, stomach issues, skin conditions, headaches

index finger - fear, terror, mental confusion, frustration, backache, gum issues, digestive problems, kidney, bladder

middle finger - anger, rage, resentment, irritability, indecisiveness, relationships, headaches, fatigue, cramps, circulation

ring finger - anxiety, preoccupation, worry, fear of rejection, negativity, skin conditions, digestion, respiratory problems, lungs intestine

little finger - low self-esteem, family, insecurity, nervousness, judgmental, blood pressure, sore throat, bloating, heart, intestine

palm - fatigue, depression, despondency, diaphragm

This hand exercise takes just five minutes and helps us to release our emotions while also delivering the following benefits:

- promotes pain relief
- induces relaxation
- reduces the effects of stress
- enhances sleep
- decreases anxiety
- increases circulation
- improves concentration
- reduces fatigue
- enhances the immune system
- improves the condition of skin
- promotes regeneration
- improves circulation and breathing
- detoxifies

While concentrating on the emotion or ailment in need of attention, hold the first finger with the opposite hand, wrapping all the fingers and thumb around the specific finger being worked on. Inhale and exhale deeply and feel a flow of healing energy flowing into it. Hold each finger for approximately one to two minutes, and within a short time a pulsating sensation will be felt. This is perfectly natural.

When working on the palm of the hand for mental calmness, press down with the thumb of the opposite hand, angling toward the middle finger, and again hold for one to two minutes. When pressed, the palm of the hand can offer nourishment for the entire body. Inhale calm, peaceful, serene thoughts and feelings and then exhale, letting go of any emotional attachments or physical blockages or discomforts that you wish to clear. While letting go of emotional or physical tension, imagine the energy draining out of the fingers and down into the earth, where it will be neutralized.

As energy channels run through the fingers and correlate with specific emotions or organs, the negative energy disperses and is replaced with recharged rejuvenating positive, high frequency energy.

For a full body balance and harmonization repeat the exercise on every finger and hold the pressure for a little longer.

www.VonGArt.com and the name
is Megan Guenthner Clark

Chapter 51

LETTING GO

"Letting go gives us freedom and freedom is the only condition for happiness." ——Thich Nhat Hanh

We often look for happiness outside ourselves. We create busy lives and fill them full of pretty, expensive, and sentimental items believing that they will add a layer of depth to our self-worth and provide us with much sought-after happiness. Something that escapes many of us is that happiness does not depend on anything that surrounds us. Regardless of whose company we are in, how much money we have, what car we drive, or the value or beauty of our material possessions, none of these things will bring us true everlasting inner peace or happiness.

Having attachments to people or material things pins us down emotionally and physically. The trouble with attachments is that they exist alongside the fear of loss. Buddhism teaches that attachment is at the root of all our suffering. Often we believe that we need certain entities to gain inner happiness and to maintain it. While having certain physical or emotional connections around us can lift our spirits and bring temporary joy and pleasure to our lives, they are not responsible for providing us with eternal happiness or a deep sense of internal peace. Instead, the attachments we place are a direct link to our suffering, not a link to happiness.

We hold on to things that feel familiar, whether it is relationships or material possessions, and we search for comfort in them. To create happiness, we shine the focus on things outside of ourselves instead of taking responsibility for creating happiness within. We then depend on relationships, friends, or family members to create our happiness. We put a great deal of pressure on people so that they are responsible for how we feel.

We do not need to depend on anyone or anything else to feel okay. We have all the power within ourselves to create our own happiness, we just need to know how to tap into it and release whatever is preventing us from experiencing the full pleasure in each and every moment.

Letting go is the most effective way to jettison attachments that aren't necessary so that we have an abundance of space for happiness to thrive.

We can let go of:

- Negative thinking - Every thought can directly spark our emotions. The more we idly dwell on things, the greater our emotional response becomes. As our emotions develop, they then create chemical reactions, which turn into feelings. Therefore, our negative thoughts can very quickly result in a negative physical reaction within our bodies. It is extremely unhealthy for the body and mind to think negatively as they accumulate to send out a powerful toxic wave of energy that vibrates within and all around us.
- The past - The past has passed. We have absolutely no control over it. It doesn't matter how much we stress, overthink, or ruminate over it, we cannot change anything. All we can do is make amends and accept it. We can try to forgive ourselves for everything, forgive others, and then allow all the worries and cares to be carried along with the wind.
- Bad memories - Without thinking about it, we can repeat past memories over and again in our minds. However,

they have no place in our lives today. We have already suffered and lived through the crisis; we do not need to keep replaying the guilt, trauma, errors, or sadness that remind us of troubles and difficulties that no longer exist. When we relive old memories, we also relive the emotions that were connected to them, so we constantly drag up old feelings that cause us distress every time we reignite certain thoughts. We can choose at any time to change the channel in our minds so we have space for new memories to be made.

- People who are unhealthy for us to be around - It can be difficult to disengage from certain people, especially if it is someone who has been a long-term friend or if they are a relation. What we can do, though, is let go of the effect these people have on us. We can place people at a safe emotional distance and loosen our connection so that we can still have people around us but at an arm's length so that their negative influence does not have a direct impact on our energy. We can still love, accept and engage with those who are insincere, resentful, pessimistic, or those who do not have our best interests at heart, as we eliminate any negativity that these connections cause us when we do so with compassion and acceptance for how they express themselves and also without any expectations at all so that these interactions do not emotionally affecting us.

- Putting ourselves down - Self-criticism and self-doubt can cripple us and become a very bad habit that is limiting and debilitating. When we have low self-worth, we attract situations that reflect how we feel on the inside. Other people become affirmations of our innermost thoughts. If we feel bad about who we are, we will connect with those who also tell us we are bad or who subliminally send messages that confirm our poor self-esteem. It is imperative to our wellbeing and happiness that we accept ourselves exactly as we are, which includes our darkness and light.

- Taking things personally - We often wrongly believe we are at the center of our social universe, workplace, or family and that how other people behave must be a direct reflection of who we are or what we are putting out. We forget that everyone has their own life going on. However similar they may seem to us, every person is a unique make-up of culture, education, nurture, nature, experience, and teachings. Sometimes we think the way someone else is behaving is a projection of who we are instead of being a projection of who they are or what they are going through. We take so many things personally when instead we can remove ourselves from the equation so that when someone lashes out at us intending to ruffle or destabilize us it doesn't have a detrimental effect.

How someone behaves always says far more about who they are than it will ever say about us. Their thoughts and belief systems conjure up stories to try to make sense of the world around them. And due to this distorted conditioning, not all of their beliefs will be true, in the same way as not all of our beliefs are true. We cannot possibly expect anyone else to see us in the same way that we perceive ourselves, regardless of how hard we try to make them open their eyes. It just isn't possible, and we have to immediately try to stop reacting to other people's behavior and also stop trying to gain their validation, approval, or appreciation. Neither can we take things personally if someone treats us disrespectfully or callously.

We can try not to be paranoid or overthink situations as we may convince ourselves that other people's words or actions are connected to us when often they have nothing to do with us and are all about the other person. When we cling to things that we believe make us happy, we build mental walls and barriers and block our energy flow, which cause unnecessary grief and discomfort. Ironically, sometimes the very things we believe make us temporarily happy are the very things that have caused us prolonged suffering. We hold notions about happiness that don't make sense. We place the responsibility for happiness on other people's shoulders. We expect others to make us happy and we also expect to feel happy all the time. No wonder we struggle to find happiness with so many demands, expectations, and conditions.

We can't just let go of the expectations *we* have for ourselves, we have to stop expecting so much from others too. We also have to let go of what other people think or expect of us. We aren't perfect, and neither is anyone else. If other people aren't happy with us exactly as we are, then why should we make ourselves unhappy just to make other people happy? There is only one way out: we have to drop all of the nonsensical expectations and remove the ridiculously high pedestal we place others or ourselves upon.

When we let go of expectations, we can then question where they all came from in the first place. We often find that none of them belong to us. They usually don't align with how we feel on the inside or what we want on the outside either. The expectations derive from subliminal messages we have received from every corner of our lives. We live our lives with ideals that we come to believe must be adhered to, and yet we have no idea who made up all the unwritten rules. It is utter madness. We often exist in a miserable and self-destructive environment trying to conform to an unrealistic expectation of what is perceived to be the "perfect," "happy" person. We then settle into a lifestyle that most definitely does not make us either perfect or happy. The only thing that realistically stops us from achieving happiness, peace, and everything we dream of is our inner self, using other people's expectations of us as resistance. So the only thing to do is to work out how to drop the weight we have shouldered for far too many years. And truthfully, it is the simplest thing we can do. We have to just let it go.

We have to let go of the crazy thoughts that rotate in our minds, of the commitments that have no meaning and are against what we believe in, of the unnecessary fretting and worrying over things that hold no importance whatsoever. We have to jump off the hamster wheel and remove every obstacle that prevents us from running freely. It is okay to just be okay. It is okay to mess up, it is okay to be imperfect. It is okay not to be everything to everyone and not to excel at everything. It is okay not to excel at anything all.

We have to stop attaching self-worth or validation to success or achievements. We are all incredibly vital to the world exactly as we are. Just living, breathing, inhaling, and exhaling is enough. Smiling is enough. We don't need to be more or better or equal to or greater than anything or anyone else. We just have to be ourselves and find comfort there.

It is okay. It is more than okay. It is perfect. Self-acceptance in itself is perfect. We don't need to compete. We are unique. We are enough already. We are absolutely and abundantly worthy exactly as we are. It doesn't matter if we achieve a million formal certificates or we gain not one single one. Those things don't define or validate us, no matter what anyone says. Our properties, our cars, our clothes, our bank balances are not who we are. They are attachments that surround us, they aren't a reflection of what's underneath. What's inside us is the only thing that defines us, and as not one of us have the exact same blueprint, we are all essential for the diversity of the world. Each one of us makes a difference, just as a butterfly's fluttering wings powerfully alters conditions. We have to feel this, not just think it. We have to believe in our worth. One by one we can strip away all the labels, layers, and definitions that we have painted over ourselves. We can begin a journey of unlearning everything we once thought to be true and relearning a whole new way of being: existing authentically. We no longer need to live to ideals, icons, or unreachable expectations. We can live to our own truth and our own simple guidelines—that's where we find ourselves.

As we let go of the many things that do us harm, we will find space and energy for things that revitalize, nourish, and reenergize us. Nonattachment and letting go do not necessarily mean detachment. They just mean not placing demands or emotional attachment on anything that could be taken away or that could change at any moment. We can still love with full hearts and cherish everything around us. It is about learning to find the equilibrium between not clinging and grasping on to things and allowing everything to exist without any expectation.

Life is a precious gift and so is everyone around us. We can celebrate each and every thing that happens to us and allow it to exist in its own right without placing ownership or conditions on it. We can simply allow everything and everyone to exist separately in their own entirety. Everything should be a bonus in our lives, not an additive that is required to create a formula for perceived happiness. Happiness is not something that is "found" and then continuously remains with us. It is something that we need to be consciously aware of moment to moment. It comes to us and it can quickly go again, all depending on perception and our state of mind. We just very simply need to live in the present moment, not dwell on the past or cast our minds to the future. We need to appreciate the pure joy, pleasure, and happiness that is found just by existing and inhaling and exhaling life, the good and the bad.

Life does not need expectations; it will deliver to us a series of experiences and we have the complete power to choose to alter our perception of them in each moment that arrives. Every moment will softly pass. When we allow moments to naturally come and then calmly go, they become a gentle memory rather than tensely filled moments that we have anxiously squeezed the joy out of.

We do not need to cling to any emotion or to harbor or hold tight to the feelings that are presented to us. We can simply let our thoughts, emotions, and feelings come, acknowledge them briefly, and then peacefully allow them to move on.

Nothing stays the same. Everything constantly changes. When we continuously practice letting go, we can alter and adapt to accept the beauty, magic, and excitement offered in each new moment. We can let go of all the tension, the worries, the fear, frustrations, anger, resentments, and anything else that we harbor in our minds, bodies, and all of our cells. It does no good. It all existed in the past.

Everything that has happened along the way we can let go of. We can let go of the first love that broke our heart, and we can let go of the last break too. We can let go of the time a friend we thought was best turned on us, or the residues of spite and fury that resounds in our minds. We can let go of the trauma that injured our flesh or bones so we can allow deep wounds to heal. We can forget the rejection we felt when others failed to recognize our worth. We can let go of the tears that cleanse our soul, let go of the mistakes that everyone makes, and let go of the times we gave with no return. We can let go of mistrust, resentment, and jealousy, let go of lies, betrayal, and deceit. We can let go of the one who got away—they were not meant and it is a myth that there is only "one."

We can let go of the time someone tripped and caused our fall, and forget the times we gambled but forgot we could lose. We can let go of the whispers, gossips, and stories—they are all make-believe, an illusion. The truth only lives in ourselves.

We can let the mind sit still and forget about irrational fear, it paralyzes. It is useless. We can let go of perfection—it is unobtainable. We can let go of time and allow our heartbeats to decide. We can then let go of letting go and allow the release to naturally occur.

Everything is already a part of us, the lessons have been learned, the memories etched, and the effects have sunk in. There is no need to hold on. It all already exists, so allow it. Let it be, without grasping, without pressing repeat. It all had a purpose once, long ago. Even if it was yesterday or a minute ago, it has now passed.

So breathe . . . breathe again. Deeply. Right here, right now. We are alive. We survived. In this very moment, this one . . .

We can choose: choose to live, run, fly, wildly—begin again and begin to feel alive. To *feel*. Everything and nothing and all in between, feel it all. Flushing through your veins and every fiber of your being, let it in, let it sit, and then let it go. Exist in this very moment. Feel the release and notice the weight falling from our shoulders. Breathe and breathe again. Each time the mind strays to negative waters, nudge it back gently, and breathe again.

Slowly, but surely, we can replace all of the old with new. Add to it, infuse, and blend whoever we were and who we are now with who we are about to become. Alchemy: we can turn to gold. We can stir storms with rainbows, pleasure with pain, and create. Let go of the old. Sprinkle in new. Stardust. Magic. Wanderlust. Mystery. Moonlit skies. Forests. Deserts. Sparkle. Dance. Faith. We don't have to look far. It is here. It always has been. Right now, in this very moment.

Let everything go. Surrender. Be free.

Chapter 52

LOVING KINDNESS

Right now, let go of everything, step outside, take a full breath of fresh air, look up to the sky, and feel your feet firmly placed on the ground. Breathe and feel the beat of Mother Earth's inner drum.

You are grounded to Earth. You are part of something special. You are spinning in a universe. You exist on a shared planet, a place where over seven billion people and billions upon billions of creatures exist, and you are unique, one of a kind. There is no one else out there quite like you. Always remember that. Celebrate, honor and respect it.

You are exquisitely imperfectly perfect. You are part of nature. You are alive, live fully.

Breathe out breathe in. Pay attention to the breeze and feel the sensations on your skin caused by the sun, the rain, the warmth, or the cold. It is magnificent. The air that you breathe is essential for keeping you alive. Each breath you take is vital.

Be grateful for everyone. Take a pen and a piece of paper. Write to someone you love or care about or anyone at all. Handwrite a few words or a few paragraphs. Post the letter. Pick up the phone. Dial the number of someone you've been meaning to contact. Hear how their voice sounds on the end of the line.

Communicate and listen. Feel gratitude for the opportunity to connect this way. Tell someone what you've been meaning to say or let them know what they mean to you, or just absorb in how it feels to talk. Appreciate the amazement that the world provided all that we need to create technology that allows us to talk to those who are too far away to communicate in person. It is miraculous.

Visit. Take a little time away from your schedule and go and see that one person you've been meaning to see. Or pop in next door or down the road, take some home-baked cookies and share them with someone who is alone. Let them know your number and tell them they can visit or call you any time they need to hear someone's voice.

Take a walk. Before you go, take a bag of leftover food or nourishment that is in the kitchen. Scatter it in the forest or next to trees or along the riverside or anywhere that hungry animals may find it. They are on this planet trying to survive just like us and they will be grateful to feed themselves and possibly their babies for another day.

Smile. At whoever passes by, find the courage not just to smile but to say, "Hi, how's your day?" If they don't respond, let it go. You may never see them again, or if you do they might remember what you said and find the courage to say "Hi" back the next time. It doesn't mean they were rude or ignorant for not responding, they probably just aren't used to someone friendly reaching out. So just continue to smile. It's contagious, it spreads like wildfire.

Share. Pack up clothes or blankets or household items that are no longer required and share with those who may need them. Donate to a charity, a local dog shelter, put an advert on a local site "free to collector." Someone somewhere will silently thank the universe for answering their call. Pack a pair of new socks in your bag next time you go out shopping, or even add new underwear, a thermal t-shirt, or whatever you can afford. The next time you see someone who is homeless, ask if they would welcome them. While a coffee or lunch is important, simple things like fresh clothes can be a luxury too. Stop for a moment and ask them how their day is going.

Eat outside. Pack a basket, take a blanket, something delicious to drink, and choose a serene spot to relax. Go into the garden, to the beach, to a grassy park and sit under the trees in the forest, or by the river. Absorb everything while you slowly nourish your body as well as your mind.

Read. Take a paperback book, one that you've been meaning to read and settle down somewhere cozy. Go outdoors, snuggle in bed, or sink into your favorite armchair, anywhere where you are fully at peace. Savor each word. Lose yourself temporarily within the chapters. Don't think about anything other than each sentence that is delivered. Reading is magic.

Have no expectations for any of the above. Don't expect a call to be answered, a letter in return, anyone to be thankful, or for any reward from anything you do. Do it because you can, for the simple fact that you are reading these words right now means that you are privileged more than most.

Give just a little or a lot, or a medium amount, anything at all. It doesn't matter how great or how small, and give with no conditions. There is abundance, enough for everyone. Give a little time, a smile, a connection, compassion, or a material gift.

Don't expect to feel "better" or "greater" because of the actions. Expect to feel connected to yourself and to all other living things. Connection is the greatest gift you will receive in return. Even if there is no response, the connection has still been made. Connect with yourself, then reach out and connect with others. Do it quite simply, because you can. It might not be easy, but it will absolutely be worth it.

Chapter 53

LOVE YOURSELF

Until we are in love with ourselves and totally accept who we are, it will be almost impossible to connect with anyone else who values us in this same way. This does not mean that we do not deserve to be loved. We all deserve the most magnificent, unconditional love that is possible. What this means is that if we do not feel and believe we are worthy, we will emanate vibrations that may attract those who reflect that untrue perception back towards us. The most important, vital thing we must do for our wellbeing is to ignite an inferno of love inside our own hearts. Self-love is the ultimate gift we can give ourselves.

For years, I battled to understand this. I went down so many wrong paths searching for something or someone who could validate who I was. Relationships, religions, spiritual paths, and friendships all too often led me through murky waters. All they did was confirm the ridiculous theories inside my own head that I wasn't good enough. I felt I deserved the horrible experiences and sometimes very dangerous situations I put myself through, all because I didn't know how to accept or love myself.

"Your task is not to seek for love, but merely to seek and find all the barriers within yourself that you have built against it."
——Rumi

I vividly remember the moment it all changed. It seemed so obvious and easy, I had no idea how I had not known that all along it was right there with me, inside me, all I had to do was learn how to connect with it. The answer was simple: understanding how to radiate my energy so that it vibrates strongly, starting from within. My own inner awareness was already there, I just had to focus attention on it, feel the sensations arise, and then radiate the energy outward. The very second I did this I felt my whole existence change. I felt true love for myself finally. And not just any love, warm, comforting, unconditional love.

To connect with the love within is similar to meditation. It can take seconds or we can spend hours deeply meditating, depending on how we feel at the time. All we need to do is close our eyes, calm the mind of any thoughts we are having, and go deep inside ourselves, and then connect with our inner being. Imagine there is a warm glow or even a fire of love burning brilliantly. Allow the feeling inside to overcome any negative thought processes that are eating away at the mind. Notice the vibrations on the inside growing stronger until we feel that our hearts are overflowing with love.

As soon as this radiation of love breaks out, others will feel it too. We instantly appear different, more loving and more accepting of others, and people may comment on it as they will be sensing, feeling and perceiving our aura to be radiating strongly even if they aren't visibly seeing it. Our eyes sparkle, our smiles will be broader, and the energy surrounding our bodies will alter, and this will vibrate vividly on the outside instantly. Things that may have irritated us moments before will suddenly be viewed with love and compassion, which will help us to deal with everything differently. The love we radiate will be transmuting all negative energy.

We can think, feel, believe and radiate positivity the moment we choose to. We are truly magnificent beings on this earth, regardless of anything that we may have said or done in the past. We are all human and we all make mistakes. We must accept them, learn from them, and not allow them to become who we are today. Our errors have taught us things that we needed to know and they helped us to get to know ourselves better.

Each one of us deserves love, regardless of any nonsense we tell ourselves. We deserve an abundance of unconditional love and it absolutely has to begin within. We will naturally draw others close to us whose energy aligns with ours. When we feel such intense waves of love for ourselves, it will be much more difficult for others to penetrate this and cause us the same suffering. Instead, we will be raising the vibration of those around us as our higher frequency of energy will engage, interlock, and lift theirs.

Patterns and behaviors will change. We will stop repeating the same destructive cycles. Our interactions with others will change and we will also stop allowing people to treat us in ways that are unacceptable. The way we communicate will be more genuine and sincere, and this will have a positive effect on others. Once we change, it is fascinating to notice the difference in other people's actions and behavior towards us.

Tell everyone, "My happiness depends on me, so you're off the hook," and then demonstrate it. Be happy no matter what anyone else is doing. Practice feeling good, and before we know it, we will not pass the responsibility to anyone else for how we feel. The only reason we aren't able to love others fully is because we use other people as our excuse to feel bad about ourselves.

It takes practice and also patience. We will trip up often and feel ourselves going down the same critical paths that used to lead to destruction. However, we will be much quicker in picking ourselves back up and showing love instead of frustration, blame, and anger. Learning to love ourselves can happen in an instant. However, we will continuously need reminders, as in the heat of the moment it is too easy to be triggered and get caught up in our old patterns and routines.

Take a breath, take a moment, close your eyes, and feel your heart.

Chapter 54

An Ending Note

When you look at yourself, do you see what I see?

Your eyes. They encapsulate a wild storm. They have have witnessed things they would really rather not remember. Blink it all out. It is over now. Let the toxic rainfall wash down your cheeks and be gone. Notice the burn pulsating. Feel the lightning charging through your bones.

I think you forget that you are magic, and I know sometimes you don't see your unique multidimensional significance. You may have received a few cracks, however, you will never be broken. Even when the world can seem dark at times, there is far more light shining out there. You have to be willing to open your soul and let it all in.

You might have entangled with ones who twisted your love or foolishly mistook your courageous vulnerability for weakness, but they aren't dragging you down. You are doing it to yourself. So stop. You are more than that loss, that rejection, or the aggression and resentment that someone may have once showed. You are more than your grief or your insecurities or your fear of being abandoned again. You are more than every minuscule or outrageous experience that has ever happened to you; you are limitless and you haven't even tapped into your full potential yet.

So do not let whatever has happened so far define you, as every new encounter is a catalyst. Instead, let it catapult you ahead so that you may be carried with the waves and the wind. You will always rise wiser and stronger no matter how weakened you might feel at the time.

Parts of your journey may be irreparable, but you are resilient. And although you sway and bend, you will never break. Even when people do things that hurt every fiber of your being and you bruise and ache due to the excruciating avalanches of ice-cold cruelty that freeze you to the bone, as soon as your passion for life rages inside, you will quickly thaw out.

You are windswept and fragile at times. I know. Curled in a ball to keep your self safely tucked out of cruel harm's way. Old friend, please take my hand. I will stay here with you. While you uncoil a little, just enough to let the sunlight reach in and soothe your deepest, darkest wounds. Existing on this planet can be harsh at times, but the burning bright flame inside you that originated from magnificent exploding stars will never die out. It just temporarily fades when protective layers of armor guard it.

Your fire is safe. It has been glowing for billions of years, so it's not going to quit on you now. You have to keep moving however rough and turbulent the road gets. Through. You have to move through. Shake up and awaken every cell. Put up the fight of your life and search for any missing pieces. Don't look too far as you are not lost, just roaming a little off track.

Gaze into the eye of the storm and recognize the reflection at the center. That's where you are. In the safest, most secure place. The spinning, vibrating hurricane is twirling on the outside, taking care of you.

Do not glance forward or back right now. Remain calm, harmonious, and at one as the bewildering force of the universe that is chaotic at times is now holding you tight. It will always come when you call, although it will also unexpectedly arrive to test you, usually through encounters with people who are not aware how valuable and cherished and essential you are. But you will always emerge, essentially altered, so you have to surrender to yourself and never doubt your worth. Make sure you disregard that noise that frantically tries to destabilize you.

I'm here to tell you not to whisper softly. It is time. Now gather your luggage, toss it aside and let out your loudest roar. You don't need that weight. Or its old tangled tales. It mysteriously tells of a life that you don't even really know anymore. Its memories are tainted. Its charm all but gone. Its nostalgic pull tugs at your heart and never fails in pinning your tender shoulder down. You may stumble and falter, but you must keep moving. You may even fall apart. However, you are a warrior my friend. And courageous, wise warriors fall often too. But each shattered piece knows where it belongs and will find its way back. The volcanoes erupting in your veins will slowly simmer back down.

You can break through and conquer this. It's only your repeating, menacing thoughts and beliefs that are keeping you trapped in a cycle by telling you that you can't. Bend and twist them and turn them around or throw them right out. They are keeping you stuck where it feels familiar.

The incessant ramblings that are holding you are challenging you to stand straight and question them, to regain the reins and fix your crown. You are in control. Those triggered thoughts and old beliefs are not the truth, they are just an option and one you can choose to forget. It's time to stop allowing them to drain your energy. You have the power to create and decide.

You've barricaded yourself in so that no one sees how damaged that delicate but fiercely pounding heart of yours is and you've hidden that contagious curve in your smile for far too long. That's okay. You needed some space and time. But those people out there now need your laughter. And they need your tears. They need you, however you show up. There is someone specifically out there who needs you more than you know. More importantly, *you* need you. There are magnificent moments waiting beneath those downy wings. And they are yours, pausing, so very patiently, until you open and uncoil from this tight spring.

You may not realize this right now, but I promise you, you are a vital gift to the earth. I'm just here to remind you to feel *everything* deeply. Feel it all, let it run over you. Scream if you want to and let it all out, but don't ever be afraid of love. The stirring in your soul is necessary. Allow it to move through you and out so it touches everything that exists, regardless of proximity. Find some thread, stitch up your wounds with colorful thread and create a beautiful tapestry all over your skin. Piece yourself together like a beloved patchwork blanket and watch how the battle scars that adorned your mind miraculously heal.

"There is a crack in everything. That's how the light gets in." ——Leonard Cohen

You are not broken. You are just breaking through.

From here onwards, please, no more doubting yourself. No more second-guessing or failing to trust your inner knowing, your heart, your primordial, instinctive feelings. No more being afraid to be exactly who you are at your core. No more failing to recognize how enchanting and mesmerizing your presence is. No more comparing your self to others or placing unrealistic expectations on yourself. Believe me when I say the only place that takes you is down the rolling road to low self-esteem. I have been there.

No more aching because you can't make someone love you. No more trying desperately hard to win over someone's affections. No more frantically trying to entangle your heart with someone else's. No more chasing. Love or happiness should never be chased. You will never ever catch them. Not ever. True love is like a firefly and is magnetized to the light. All you need to do is glow. It will arrive.

You are magical. Don't let anyone tell you otherwise. It is okay to believe in unicorns or dragons, and to know that you are made of stardust and are an absolute miracle whose existence is essential on earth. You just need to open your eyes wide enough to see that anything is possible and that you are not bound down, you are limitless. Fairytales and happy-ever-afters exist, but here is the thing—you have to create these things for yourself. No other man or woman is going to do it for you. Not your papa or your soul mate or anyone else out there knows how to build the life you dream of. Only you can do that. And you are entirely capable.

Nothing is ever going to matter as much to that exquisite heart of yours as that which you achieve with your ingenious mind, your incredible imagination, and your restless, creative hands.

Also, let me let you in on a little secret. No one has it all figured out. No one. I've written this, but believe me when I say I've written it as much for myself as anyone else. And if I read it a hundred times over, parts of it still won't fully sink in. A niggling doubt will still try to enter my mind. That's why we have to keep repeating these words over and over, even if it takes a million times before they ring true.

We've spent years being conditioned into believing that we cannot be the fullest versions of ourselves. We are afraid to stand in our own brilliant radiance and shine, as every time we try someone is hiding in the wings ready to knock us straight back down. There will always be those who are watching from the stalls in the arena, praying and hoping we fall. Allow them the role of spectator if they really must, but make sure you shock them to the core when you show them how fast you are willing to rebound again and again.

Goddammit, even if you stumble, you've got to at least give it one hell of a shot.

You are a work of art. All artwork is a process. All masterpieces take time, and the most important thing is progression, not perfection. We must witness the beauty in ourselves; it doesn't matter what anyone else thinks—we are the only ones that need to feel our self-worth.

Just like with art, those who are willing to do the hard work will also recognize the beauty in others who have done the same. If we are not willing to do any work and we remain stagnant, we will attract those who aren't willing either and they may try to pull us down.

Just because you may be a little different from others doesn't mean you are weird, strange, crazy, or odd. You are not a square peg, or a round one for that matter. Your shape will change every moment of every single day. You are you, and of all the seven billion people on this planet, not one other person shares your blueprint. Every single person is rare and unique. It is essential that you learn to appreciate and adore your differences. Until you do, no one else stands a chance of getting to know all the bits and pieces that make up your puzzle, and they won't work out how to love them all either.

"Comparison will strip you of power of grace and influence. Each person is unique. How then can you possibly compare unique to unique? You can't. And when you try, you annihilate your brilliance." ——Amy Larson

It's time to stop searching for approval. It is time to stop asking or hoping to be liked. It's time to stop looking for love in the wrong places. You are never going to find the truth when you are seeking too hard. It will always elude you. You will only see the illusion of what you hope to find. We are never going to gain the approval of all others. It is impossible to be accepted and liked by everyone. We will never find the true essence in love when we do not sit back and allow it to delicately touch us to let us know it has arrived.

There will always be those who judge through fear, speak harshly, or find pleasure in criticizing or putting us down. Negativity stems from fear and jealousy. People are afraid of what they do not understand. Take care of your heart, but love people all the same, then love them harder. When you shine, your brightness hurts their eyes. It dazzles and bewilders them. Your light touches the edges of their shadow. It highlights parts of them that they are afraid to look at. It is easier for some people to tear others down rather than build themselves up.

When others look down at you, or even straight through you: Don't you worry one bit, as they have no idea of your strength. They've never carried your pain. They just don't know how much you've held. They don't know what it takes for a back to break or how strong you need to be to stumble along with this load for so long. They may never know. You're not the weak one though. You have courage, conviction and fierceness, unlike anyone I've seen.

No one knows your road. No one knows the battles and wars you've lived through.

But, I'm here to tell you not to whisper softly today. It is time. Now gather your luggage, toss it aside and let out your loudest roar. You don't need that weight. Or its old tangled tales. It mysteriously tells of a life that you don't even really know. Its memories are tainted. Its charm all but gone. Its nostalgic pull just tugs at your heart and never fails in pinning your tender shoulder down.

I ask of you gently: Give yourself permission to be whoever you are meant to be. Torn, ripped apart and fragmented is just as beautiful as all together and whole. Ask the stars. They understand. They have split into billions of pieces and no one thinks anything less of them. And when they fall, we gasp in awe and then make a wish. We don't know what those stars have been through, we can't even guess. But we know they burned. Fearlessly. Blazing brightly.

Do not waver. Do not pause. And don't consider waiting until tomorrow arrives. Now. It is time to rise. Listen to me and let my words reverberate all the way through your mixed up mind.

This is your time. Rise up, make your wish, ignite and alight and roar.

Not everyone will want to see you soar. And that is okay. When you are flying high, you won't even notice or care what others think. You will see that those who are flying by your side with grace are the ones who will pause to be the wind blowing beneath your wings if you weaken. They are the ones who will help you climb higher, not be the cause of your fall.

If someone is happy with themselves, they will never ever feel the need to pull another person down. Don't get drawn in or pulled under; open your heart, do not judge through fear, and above all, show compassion. Always remember, hurt people hurt people.

"Darkness cannot drive out darkness; only light can do that." ——Martin Luther King Jr.

You'll make mistakes, plenty of them. You always will. It's okay to be afraid. And it's okay not to know. In fact, it's okay to make these same mistakes over and over and over, again and again. Here's the thing. It's not the mistakes that we make that matter in the end. What really counts is how we rectify them. We can't take an eraser to the past, although we can turn the past around. We can turn every negative into a positive. There's more to be learned from mistakes than anything else life shows us.

You're just on a life adventure. Surrender to it. Make yourself a promise: let go of perfection. It doesn't exist. Believe in magic. It exists. Above all else, if it is the only thing you believe in, believe in yourself. Be yourself. Do not change for anyone. You should never have to say sorry for being you. If other people don't like it, it is their problem to work through, not yours.

It's not always easy. I can't promise you it will be. But it is possible. Be who you are, don't falter. You only need to answer to yourself. Don't think too much, too hard, or too deep. Feel.

No one is watching and no one is caring. Just remember this one thing. Please, never forget: *you are not here for others, you are here for you.*

Don't make excuses. Don't think you can't soar. You have your whole life ahead to do whatever you choose. Spread your wings. Fly fast, glide, and do not be afraid. You will discover secrets in the clouds, in dirt, and bird tracks, in leaves on the ground, under toadstools, and in fireflies dancing when day reaches dusk. But most of the magic unearthed on the road will derive from your mystical spirit, embedded with long-forgotten power, which once awakened cannot be forsaken or cast aside.

Your gifts may feel like a blessing and sometimes a curse. To deny them means to search for an antidote that will never be found. The only option is to surrender, be charmed, enchanted, and mystified. See each one as a challenge that unravels another layer of your personal truth.

The sunset looks different each time you look, depending not only on the land you rest on, but also where you choose to place your mind. Wherever you roam, you will find a piece that reminds you of home. At the end of every day, take a little memory of the world along with you while leaving a small memory of yourself behind in exchange. Everything connects. Everyone entangles.

We all shine, we all radiate, and we can all see our image somewhere in each other's multifaceted reflections. We are all one magnificent, glorious sum of energy. Although there are many similarities, we are all divinely unique, and we are each a universe in entirety.

"Your heart and my heart are very, very old friends." ——Haviz

REFERENCES

** Decety. J, Chenyi. C, Harenski. C, and Kiehl. K, A. *Frontiers in Human Neuroscience*, 2013.

A Brain Scientist's Personal Journey by Jill Bolte Taylor

The Eye of Revelation: The Original Five Tibetan Rites of Rejuvenation by Peter Kelder

**http://www.nytimes.com/1989/07/04/science/science-watch-salt-and-sleep.html

*** http://news.harvard.edu/gazette/2006/12.07/11-dairy.html

****Yerkes, R. M. & Dodson, J. D. (1908). "The Relation of Strength of Stimulus to Rapidity of Habit-Formation." *Journal of Comparative Neurology and Psychology,* 18, 459–482.

***** Jill Bolte Taylor, *A Brain Scientist's Personal Journey.*

****** Bruce H. Lipton, *The Biology of Belief: Unleashing the Power of Consciousness, Matter and Miracles*

******* Dr. W. Ludwig, *Informative Medizin*

******** Dr. David Brownstein, *Salt Your Way to Health*

47320444R00361

Made in the USA
San Bernardino, CA
27 March 2017